Dollars and Sense

Dollars and Sense

An Introduction to Economics

SIXTH EDITION

Marilu Hurt McCarty
Georgia Institute of Technology

HarperCollins*Publishers*

Sponsoring Editor: Bruce Kaplan
Project Editor: Robert Cooper
Art Direction: Jaye Zimet
Text design Adaptation: North 7 Atelier, LTD
Cover Design: Jaye Zimet
Cover Photo: © Jay Brousseau/The Image Bank
Photo Research: Carol Parden
Production Manager: Kewal Sharma/Jeffrey Taub
Compositor: Better Graphics, Inc.
Printer and Binder: R. R. Donnelly & Sons, Inc.
Cover Printer: Lehigh Press

Dollars and Sense, Sixth Edition

Photo Credits:
Chapter 1: Doug Wilson/Black Star; Chapter 2: Ton Chee/Stock, Boston; Chapter 3: Barbara Filet/TSW/Click Chicago; Chapter 4: Mike Mazzaschi/Stock, Boston; Chapter 5: Darry Krist/Uniphoto; Chapter 6: Lionel Delevinge/Stock, Boston; Chapter 7: Henley & Savage/Uniphoto; Chapter 8: Brent Jones/Marilyn Gartman Agency; Chapter 9: Scott, Foresman; Chapter 10: Bob Daemmrich/TSW/Click Chicago; Chapter 11: Photri/Marilyn Gartman Agency; Chapter 12: Michael Hayman/Stock, Boston; Chapter 13: Hazel Hankin/Stock, Boston; Chapter 14: TSW/Click Chicago; Chapter 15: Cary Wolinsky/Stock, Boston.

Library of Congress Cataloging-in-Publication Data

McCarty, Marilu Hurt.
    Dollars and sense : an introduction to economics / Marilu Hurt
McCarty. — 6th ed.
       p.   cm.
    Includes bibliographical references and index.
    ISBN 0-673-46323-0
    1. Economics.   I. Title.
HB171.5.M46   1991
330—dc20   90-46515
                                                         CIP

91 92 93   9 8 7 6 5 4 3 2

In Memory of John Ottley McCarty

Contents

Chapter 6
Labor Markets and the Labor Movement 114

Chapter 7
Measuring Economic Activity 142

Chapter 8
Cycles In Economic Activity   166

Chapter 9
Government Finance and Fiscal Policy   190

Chapter 11
Inflation   252

Chapter 12
Unemployment   272

Chapter 13
Poverty and Income Distribution   290

Chapter 14
Economic Growth   310

Preface

The fundamental goal of *Dollars and Sense* is to help students develop the ability to use economic reasoning to analyze the issues and evaluate the policy proposals they will encounter in a rapidly changing world. To this end, the text emphasizes a set of basic economic tools and shows how these tools can be applied to topics of current interest such as minimum-wage legislation, environmental pollution, inflation and unemployment, poverty and public assistance, fiscal policy and taxation, the trade deficit, international competitiveness, and the ferment in Eastern Europe and the Soviet Union. The continuing goal of this Sixth Edition is to make the subject matter and methods of economics more comprehensible to today's college students.

Dollars and Sense is written for use in one-term economics courses for students with little or no background in the subject. The text's emphasis on current issues should help students from other disciplines acquire habits of systematic thought that they can carry with them to their own fields of study. At the same time, the text provides the kind of analytical foundation that will enable interested students to proceed to more advanced study in economics, with greater understanding of its scope and methods.

ORGANIZATION AND COVERAGE

Each chapter is divided into two parts. The first, *Tools for Study*, presents both verbal and graphical examples of the theoretical foundations of economics. Economic behavior is described and analyzed and the results of behavior appraised within the context of existing social, political, technical, and environmental conditions. The second part of each chapter, *Theory in Practice*, includes practical applications of the analytical tools discussed in the first part, examining recent events, debates over current policy, and business practices.

Chapter 1 introduces the student to the economic problem and the importance of an economic system for allocating resources efficiently. The concepts of scarcity, opportunity costs, and marginal analysis are discussed and applied. Problem solving through marginal analysis is introduced at the level of the family unit and local government.

Chapters 2 through 5 provide the core of microeconomics: How price and output decisions respond to supply and demand in free markets, and how imperfect competition prevents markets from responding efficiently to supply and demand. Chapter 6 deals with supply and demand in markets for productive resources, with emphasis on labor resources and the labor movement. Chapters 7 through 10 provide the core of macroeconomics: The definition and measurement of gross national product, the equilibrium level of GNP, and the use of fiscal and monetary policy to affect equilibrium.

Chapters 11 through 13 present current domestic problems and issues: Inflation, unemployment, and poverty. Recent policy applications include wage and price controls, collective bargaining procedures, and poverty in the cities. Chapters 14 and 15 consider the broader long-range problems of economic growth and international economic relations.

Current applications include population growth, Malthus, exchange instability, and multinational firms.

CHANGES IN THE SIXTH EDITION

The Sixth Edition of *Dollars and Sense* incorporates changes suggested by users of earlier editions. Chapters 2 and 3 of the previous edition have been expanded to three chapters including one general chapter on markets and separate chapters on demand and supply, with separate treatments of price elasticity of demand and supply. The discussions of fiscal policy in Chapter 9 and monetary policy in Chapter 10 have been revised and updated to include an expanded discussion of Gramm-Rudman-Hollings and the savings and loan crisis.

New articles in the series *Contemporary Thinking about Economic Issues* include Robert Heilbroner and Paul Bernstein on the federal deficit, Victor Fuchs on day care costs, Marshall Goldman on perestroika, Alan Blinder on the peace dividend, Joseph Pechman on the progressivity of the income tax, and T. H. Tietenberg on economic incentives for environmental improvements. Other commentaries include population growth and the economic impact of oil shale mining in Colorado. Other additions include a section on organizing and financing a new firm and an updated economic forecast. It is hoped that these articles will spark students' interest in objective research into current economic problems.

A new series has been added to the Sixth Edition to bring home to students the real impact of economic change. The items are called *How Things Have Changed,* and they include such things as changes in prices of familiar goods, spending patterns, union activity, effective rates of taxation, merger activity, and manufacturing processes.

Finally, new discussion questions have been added to most chapters, referring students to recent developments in familiar markets.

SPECIAL FEATURES

This text incorporates a number of special features to make it attractive and useful to instructors and students alike:

Level and method of presentation. A determined effort has been made to use familiar language and to enliven explanations with humor, personal experiences and observations, and invitations for the student to relate topics to his or her own life. Simple equations and graphs are used judiciously to reinforce verbal descriptions and for further development of basic principles in applied situations.

Tools for independent study. Three features of the text encourage independent, self-paced instruction by the student. *Learning Objectives* at the start of each chapter give the student a set of goals to accomplish, and *Current Issues for Discussion* provide thoughtful questions to answer (or analyze intelligently) while reading. *Test Yourself* questions throughout the chapters require students to apply immediately concepts they have just learned. The *Self-Check,* a set of multiple-choice questions separating the two parts of each chapter, allows students to test their mastery of the concepts presented in *Tools for Study.* Answers and explanations for the self-checks are found at the end of the book.

Terms to remember. Important terms and concepts in each chapter are set off in bold-face type and are formally defined at the end of the chapter.

Problem-solving tools. The *Theory in Practice* section of Chapter 1 presents a six-step model for analyzing and solving economic problems that can be used throughout the book as well as independently outside the course.

Viewpoints. Short *Viewpoint* essays throughout the text discuss topics of special interest and show how economics operates within a historical, social, and political framework.

Topics for Discussion. Discussion questions at the end of each chapter include review questions requiring definitions or factual information as well as "brain teasers" that require students to apply the tools they have recently learned to current issues.

Supplementary materials. Although the text itself includes many features of a workbook, a **Study Guide** for students is available to reinforce and expand the material covered in each chapter. An **Instructor's Manual** is also available.

Reading lists. The **Instructor's Manual** includes a list of recent articles in news magazines and professional journals, selected for their clear, straightforward language and relevance to fundamental economic principles.

ACKNOWLEDGEMENTS

I am especially indebted to my good friends and colleagues who reviewed portions of the original manuscript and offered worthwhile suggestions and comments: Carl Biven, Jack Blicksilver, Sherman Dallas, Eva Galambos, Virlyn Moore, Beverly Schaffer, and my father A. Raymond Hurt. I also appreciate the help and advice of Robert Ebert, Baldwin-Wallace College, and Jerry Johnson, University of Wisconsin, Eau Claire, who provided an extensive review of the previous edition, and who offered many good suggestions that I have tried to incorporate in the Sixth Edition.

Marilu Hurt McCarty

Dollars and Sense

Chapter

Scarcity and Choice

or Nothin' Ain't Worth Nothin'— But It's Free

We Americans love a challenge. Our ancestors readily took up the challenge of settling a wild and remote continent. They cleared the land, suffered the winters, and raised the cities. They fought for the right of self-government, and they took up the responsibility of using the nation's resources to satisfy national goals.

The tradition of pursuing noble goals has continued with each new generation of Americans, and our efforts have succeeded beyond our forefathers' grandest dreams. We have prospered greatly, and we have extended our prosperity to more and more segments of our own population, as well as to populations abroad. Our material prosperity has brought improved health and living conditions, better education and job opportunities, and—most important—the potential for fullest personal development to us all.

Challenges did not end with the pioneer era. In fact, the problems faced by today's generation have more frightening possibilities than any we have faced before. More of the world's people want more things. At the same time, more of the world's resources are becoming depleted or are concentrated in the hands of people whose preferences regarding resource use are different from ours. There are more conflicts over access to the "good life," both in our own nation and in the world as a whole. Regrettably, our capacity to inflict harm on each other has increased faster than our capacity to do good.

Today's Americans are being forced to make difficult choices and to decide complex issues that impose costs now for the sake of benefits far in the future.

Many of our choices involve economics. Economics is both the basis for our prosperity and the reason for our struggle. Through understanding economics, we—as individuals and as a nation—can make the decisions, shoulder the responsibilities, and find the solutions to the problems that confront us.

That is our challenge!

ECONOMICS AS A SCIENCE

The study of economics evolved along with mankind's everlasting drive to make sense of our environment. As human beings, we do not like to think of ourselves as mere combinations of cells with specialized functions enabling us to consume food, grow hair, and so forth. We become uneasy at the thought that we are, after all, only engaged in some collective "milling around" during our stay here on planet Earth. We want to understand the order in our surroundings and to find a place for ourselves in our universe.

The drive to understand and explain our environment began in the period of European history known as the Renaissance, during the fourteenth century. More plentiful food supplies and a gradual improvement in living standards made it possible for some people to use their time for tasks other than for producing the necessary food and shelter. Instead, they could devote their energies to investigating the mysteries of the world environment.

In the beginning, the emphasis was on understanding the physical environment. Astronomers made the rather comforting discovery that heavenly bodies are subject to physical laws governing their orderly movement through space. Biologists discovered the circulation of the blood and the fact that we are ourselves orderly systems controlled by understandable biological laws. Through investigations like these, scientists developed a body of natural laws to explain the order in our physical world.

In due course, scholars turned to the *social* world in search of the natural laws that explain people's relationships with one another. 1776 was an important year for two new social sciences—political science and economics. That was the year the American nation began its experiment in political democracy. And it was the year Adam Smith published the first complete explanation of how an economic system works.

The name of Adam Smith's book was *An Inquiry Into the Nature and Causes of the Wealth of Nations*. The book is often spoken of as simply *The Wealth of Nations*; but the full title is important because it describes the author's investigations into the creation of wealth. The ability to create wealth depends on a nation's economic system.

What is an economic system? Why is an economic system necessary? Answering those questions is an important goal of your study of economics.

THE PROBLEM OF SCARCE RESOURCES

Throughout the history of life on this planet, human beings have faced the problem of scarce resources: limited supplies of materials, labor, and equipment to produce the goods and services we want. With scarce resources and unlimited wants, we are forced to *choose* the things we want most. We find that to obtain some of the things we want requires us to give up other things we might have had.

If all resources were free—that is, if all of us could have as much as we wanted of everything—we wouldn't need an economic system. There are, in fact, some resources that we might consider free. Fresh air and sunshine are free on a tropical island. Each person can have as much as he or she wants, and there will still be enough for everyone else. In a crowded city, on the other hand, fresh air may be very much a scarce resource. We must pay

Viewpoint

ECONOMICS AND THE HISTORY OF IDEAS

The social science of economics developed along with the natural and physical sciences; but social sciences suffer from a distinct disadvantage relative to the other sciences. Investigations of the social world cannot be as systematic nor as unbiased as investigations of the world of nature. Social scientists bring to their explorations their own prejudices and political self-interests, with the result that their conclusions might be biased.

Another difficulty is that the social world itself is constantly changing, giving social scientists new information and forcing them to change their explanations. Much of our world has changed since the Industrial Revolution, when modern economic theory began. In those times, competition was vigorous, and competition prevented the growth of market power. The advantages of competition produced an economic theory known as "laissez-faire," from the French expression for "let alone." According to laissez-faire theory, an economic system functions best if individuals are completely free to pursue their own self-interest, without government intervention.

The worldwide depression of the 1930s brought a change in economic theory. Without government intervention, production in our nation's economy fell by almost half. John Maynard Keynes, a British economist, proposed that government help put farms and factories back to work. After World War II, the Employment Act of 1946 required a more active role for government in the economic system.

In recent years critics of government's role have complained that government has grown too powerful. Some economists favor a switch to total laissez-faire; others recommend still greater government intervention. (A few even suggest that we start all over from scratch!)

Economic issues change. Economic analysis and policy evolve in response to changing social, political, and economic conditions. (Then there's the story of the old economics professor who asks the same exam questions year after year but keeps changing the answers.) Economics is a developing course of study. Students of economics must always question the theories and policies of the past and look to the changing needs and opportunities of the future.

TEST YOURSELF
What economic issue currently dominates the nation's agenda? What political interest groups favor alternative policies? How do the economic problems of other nations affect our own economic prosperity?

a price in order to obtain it. The price of pollution control (or of an airline ticket to a tropical island) is an example of the price we might pay. Unfortunately, as we soon discover, most resources are scarce.

Because resources are scarce, they must be used wisely. Every community, whether of cave dwellers or high-rise apartment dwellers, must establish a system for allocating its scarce resources. Resources must be channeled into production of the goods and services the people want most. How much of the scarce land should be used to produce wheat and how much to produce strawberries? How much of the scarce metal resources should be used for autos and how much for airplanes? How much of the scarce labor power should be used to build dams and how much to teach college students?

We can't have all we want of everything. So we must choose the things we want most. That is why we have an **economic system**. An economic system provides a way of choosing.

The Economic Problem

The problem of scarce resources and unlimited wants is called the **economic problem**. We have said that every society faces limits on its ability to satisfy its ever-increasing wants. With scarce resources and available technology there are limits to the quantities of goods and services we can produce. The economic problem requires that a society use its scarce resources efficiently so as to produce the goods and services most appropriate for filling the needs and desires of its people.

The Four Kinds of Resources

Productive resources are classified in four groups: land, labor, capital, and management or entrepreneurial ability.

Land may be thought of as "natural resources." Land includes all the original and nonreproducible gifts of nature: fertile soil, mineral deposits, fossil fuels, and water. All are fixed in amount but, when combined with human ingenuity, may be made to produce wanted goods and services.

In years past the vastness of the earth's natural resources tempted us to regard them as inexhaustible and, therefore, free. Threats of future shortages, however, remind us that we still must avoid wasteful exploitation of our land resources.

Labor may be thought of as "human resources." Labor is the productive activity of human beings: teachers, psychiatrists, lathe operators, roustabouts, statisticians. Failure to use productively a single willing hour of labor resources results in a permanent sacrifice of the good or service that resource might have produced.

Capital may be thought of as "manufactured resources." Capital includes the tools and equipment that strengthen, extend, or replace human hands in the production of goods and services: hammers, sewing machines, turbines, bookkeeping machines, components of finished goods, specialized skills. Capital resources permit "roundabout" production: Thus, through capital resources, goods are produced indirectly by a kind of tool rather than directly by physical labor.

To construct a capital resource requires that we postpone the production of other goods and services today so that we can produce more in the future. To postpone production of needed goods and services is difficult, particularly when a nation is poor and in desperate need of goods and services for use today.

Economists do not think of money as capital, because money by itself cannot produce anything at all. However, money is a convenient means of "storing" resources for use in future production. We will have more to say about the process of "storing" resources for future production later.

Management or entrepreneurial ability may be thought of as the "creative resource." It is the human initiative that combines other resources to produce a certain good or service. Entrepreneurial ability is provided by the owner or developer, creator, or administrator of a productive enterprise.

The entrepreneur plays another important role in our economic system. Because the future is not known, the developer or creator of an enterprise must take risks. Entrepreneurs will undertake the risks of loss only if they believe there is also the possibility of gain. It takes a certain kind of person to be a risk-taker, and the entrepreneur is that type of person.

The first three resources are certainly necessary. However, the fourth may be even more critical for producing the largest possible quantity and quality of desired goods and services.

THE THREE QUESTIONS: WHAT? HOW? FOR WHOM?

A society's stock of resources can be combined in a variety of ways to produce goods and services. To decide how to allocate its resources, a society must answer three basic questions.

The society must first decide **What?** to produce. "How much military equipment?" and "How many consumer goods?" might be the choice facing a nation preparing for war. "How many new houses?" and "How many machines?" may be the critical choice for a developing nation. "How many agricultural products?" and "How many manufactured goods?" may be the choice for a nation dependent on international trade.

Whatever goods and services the society decides to produce, it must at the same time sacrifice other goods and services it might have chosen.

Second, a society must decide **How?** resources should be combined to produce the desired goods and services. If the society is rich in land, it may decide to emphasize the use of land in production. This was true in our own country in the nineteenth century and is true in Argentina and Australia today. If workers are plentiful, the society may emphasize the use of labor, as in populous China. If the society is rich in capital resources, it may emphasize the use of machinery, as in today's Japan. A country without fertile land and with few human resources may choose to develop and encourage entrepreneurial ability through training in business management.

Whatever resources the society decides to use in production, it must at the same time sacrifice other goods and services those resources might have produced.

Finally, any society must decide **For Whom?** output is to be produced. Who is to be rewarded at the time goods and services are distributed? Brain surgeons or ballet dancers? Poets or industrial designers? Teachers or soldiers? Often, a worker's reward reflects the value the society places on the good or service that worker produces. A generous reward will encourage greater production of a good or service the society wants most.

Needless to say, whatever workers the society decides to reward generously, it must at the same time reward other workers less well.

ORGANIZING PRODUCTION

An economic system is the way a society organizes itself to answer the three basic questions. Economic systems differ according to their supplies of resources and according to the value systems of their people, value systems that have evolved over years and years

Contemporary Thinking about Economic Issues

THE FAILURE OF AN ECONOMIC SYSTEM

After the Communist Revolution of 1917, the USSR set up a system of central planning to allocate resources and determine output. Central planning worked well for establishing heavy industry, for recovering from two world wars, and for maintaining a large military capability. However, central planning worked poorly in such areas as agriculture, light industry, and technological innovation.

Under central planning, farmers were forced to deliver agricultural products to the state for distribution at low prices to urban factory workers. Without price incentives, farm workers were not encouraged to increase output. By the 1980s the Soviet people were expressing dissatisfaction with the limited availability of food and other consumer goods and services.

Even worse than these shortages were problems of technological backwardness, in which the USSR seemed to be falling farther and farther behind other nations. In 1985 Soviet Communist Party leader Mikhail Gorbachev proposed to restructure the nation's economy to include some of the incentives that drive production in market economies. The Russian word for restructuring is "perestroika."

Perestroika is proving to be very difficult. One problem is that incentives in agriculture depend on increasing food prices. Rising food prices will increase food production and farm incomes, making it possible for prosperous farmers to buy the products of light industry. Increased production and incomes in light industry will ultimately increase the wages of urban factory workers.

Such developments don't happen overnight, however. Before prosperity can

---

of history. There are three basic kinds of economic systems, although many variations and combinations of the three have evolved in particular times and places. As you read the descriptions that follow, think about the nations with which you are familiar and compare their systems for organizing production. What resource supplies and what value systems have influenced their choice of economic system?

The Traditional Economic System

Very primitive societies generally answer the three basic questions through traditional means—repeating within the family, generation after generation, old, familiar patterns of production. Farming families continue to till the land. Farmers, carpenters, and tailors pass on their skills within their families, who continue to produce in the same old ways.

Traditional economic systems exist where resources are few and the margin between life and death is narrow. The community may barely be able to feed itself, with little surplus left over for trying new ways. As a result, there is little room for experimenting and few opportunities for economic growth or development.

Traditional economies continue to exist today in remote parts of Africa, Asia, and Latin America. You may know of particular

spread from farm to factory, many urban workers will suffer rising food prices and lower living standards. Their complaints reflect increasing opposition to perestroika and increasing political problems for Gorbachev.

Another problem involves the many interconnections within a modern economy. Price incentives in one sector of the economy are ineffective unless similar incentives apply in such areas as delivery of raw materials, maintenance of transportation facilities, improvements in machinery and equipment, and a whole host of related activities. Turning around an entire network of relationships is more difficult than turning around an ocean liner. In fact, it has been compared to turning around a dock that has been firmly anchored to the shore.

Many observers of the USSR hope the Soviet people will have the patience to work for a better standard of living in the future rather than revert to the backwardness of central planning.

Can you suggest measures that might help Soviet leadership accomplish the change to a market economy while reducing the short-range problems faced by the population? What additional problems must the Soviet people overcome if they are to make their economy more efficient?

Marshall I. Goldman, *The USSR in Crisis: The Failure of an Economic System,* Norton, New York, 1983.

Marshall I. Goldman, *Gorbachev's Challenge: Economic Reform in the Age of High Technology,* Norton, New York, 1987.

communities or groups in the United States that organize production in the same ways as their ancestors did many years ago.

The Command Economic System

In some societies new resources may be discovered and better production techniques developed, so that it becomes possible to produce more goods than the minimum necessary for life. When the society can produce a surplus, it must decide what additional goods and services to produce. Such a society might answer the three questions through a system of command.

In a command economic system a central authority decides the priority of needs, makes plans accordingly, and then sees that the plans are carried out. Often the plan focuses on some national goal, such as military power or economic growth. A central authority can make sure that the necessary sacrifices are made for producing military equipment or building capital resources. The Soviet Union used a command economic system to build its industrial capacity after the Communist revolution. Even the United States uses some forms of command, such as when it collects taxes and uses tax revenues to finance public projects.

You can imagine how difficult a command

Contemporary Thinking about Economic Issues

BUILDING A HEALTHY ECONOMIC SYSTEM

Many economists include in their study of economics concern about the other institutions that make up the society. Mancur Olson is one who combines thinking about economics with thinking about political science, sociology, and history. The result of his research is an interesting theory about what makes some economic systems healthy and what may weaken others.

The focal point of Olson's theory is the organizations or groups that make up the society and influence its practices and policies. Organizations are difficult to construct, because the benefits gained by members of many organizations can be enjoyed by large numbers of people, whether or not they belong to the organization. Forming organizations requires a long period of social stability, during which incentives and disincentives build up to strengthen organizational tendencies. When a society has been stable for a long time, there is greater likelihood that there will be many organized groups representing many special interests within the society.

Some examples of organized interest groups in the United States are associations of businesses, workers, and the professions: trade associations like the American Dairy Association, labor unions like the International Ladies Garment Workers Association, and legal and medical organizations like the American Bar Association and the American Medical Association. The important point about such organizations is their incentives with respect to production and distribution in the economy as a whole. Because each organization represents only a small fraction of the economy as a whole, the gain each would enjoy from increasing the nation's total production is relatively small. Similarly, the loss each would suffer from decreasing total production is relatively small. For both these reasons, small organized groups have little incentive to increase the nation's total production—

economic system is in a modern, complex economy. It is particularly difficult without computers for deciding production and without rapid communication and transportation facilities for carrying out the production plan.

The Market Economic System

In Adam Smith's *The Wealth of Nations*, the great economist described a third kind of system for organizing scarce resources. It was the market system, which he saw developing in the newly industrializing nations of Western Europe. The market system differs from either the traditional or command system in that, under the market system, decisions about production are made by the people of the society themselves.

The market system represents a kind of economic democracy. Just as people vote in political democracy for the candidates they prefer, the market system allows people to

and, even worse, few disincentives to decrease production.

Without incentives to contribute to greater production, small organized groups concentrate instead on gaining a larger share of existing production for themselves. Conflicts over shares consume energy that could better be used to increase output, and they tend to reduce total production. If the economy is to grow and prosper, it must reduce the power of organized groups and concentrate on developing policies that will enhance the prosperity of the greater whole.

There are a number of ways to do this, some more pleasant than others. A particularly unpleasant way—but one that was ultimately successful in Germany and Japan—is war, which destroys many existing organizations and requires a united effort to rebuild basic productive capacity. A more pleasant way is free trade, which opens the nation to competition from other nations and forces organized groups to compete with highly motivated groups from abroad. Another way is to strengthen the nation's political parties. According to Mancur Olson, political parties are large enough to absorb small organized groups and improve their incentive systems. Because each of the two major political parties in the United States represents almost half the nation, increases in production that are achieved by one party or the other do indeed benefit their members. Thus, there is greater incentive to cooperate toward increasing production.

Understanding economics is important. Along with your study of economics, however, you should try to understand the institutions that underlie the economic system and affect its performance. Consider also your own participation in organizations and their contributions to total production.

Mancur Olson, *The Rise and Decline of Nations,* Yale University Press, New Haven, Conn., 1982.

vote—with their dollars!—for the goods and services they want most. Business firms try to satisfy people's wants and receive profit as their reward. Profits give profitable firms the funds they need to invest in new capital resources—machinery, factories, and transportation facilities—and for research to develop new products and new kinds of production. According to Adam Smith, when a society organizes production through the market system, the people live better and enjoy ever increasing material wealth.

ECONOMIC EFFICIENCY

We began this text with a description of the challenges our nation has faced. The fundamental challenge of our past, present, and future is this—to use our scarce resources to produce the goods and services we want most.

The United States has chosen the market system as the basis for making economic decisions (although we have elements of tradition and command, as well). We believe the market system is the most efficient system for answering the questions **What? How?** and **For whom?** Efficiency is an important concept in economics. It refers to the quantity of output obtained from a single unit of input, or, stated differently, output/input. An economic system is efficient if it produces the maximum possible quantity of wanted goods and services with its limited resources; thus, the greatest output/input.

In fact, there are two kinds of efficiency: technical efficiency and allocative efficiency. **Technical efficiency** refers to the total quantities of goods and services that are produced with available resources and technology. Our free market system provides the incentives that encourage business firms to produce the largest possible quantity of goods and services with the smallest quantity of scarce land, labor, capital, and entrepreneurial resources. Technical efficiency helps us enjoy rising material standards of living and improved quality of life.

Allocative efficiency refers to production of the particular goods and services the people want. Our free society guarantees each of us the right to choose the way we want to live, including how we work and how we spend what we earn. The right to choose enables us to allocate our nation's resources toward producing the particular goods and services we want.

We can sum up our study of economics this way: Because resources are scarce, production is limited. Deciding to use resources in one way requires the sacrifice of other things we might have had. We want our economic system to be efficient: to produce the most of what we want with the least sacrifice of what we might have had. Understanding economics helps us make these choices efficiently.

OPPORTUNITY COSTS

Economics is the study of choosing. The sad fact is that every time we make a choice we pay a cost. The cost to use a resource to produce one good or service is the next most desired good or service we might have produced instead. Economists refer to the alternative uses of a resource as the resource's **opportunity costs.**

The cost to an athlete of a tennis match is the golf game he or she might have played (or the nap in the shade). The cost of homemade bread is the picture the homemaker might have painted instead (in addition to the flour, eggs, and other ingredients in the bread). The cost to a college student of intensive study for one subject is the ''A'' he or she might have earned in another.

As consumers, we all make choices based on opportunity costs. With limited financial resources, a decision to spend a dollar for one good means the sacrifice of another good we might have bought instead. The purchase of a new sweater may require the sacrifice of a pair of concert tickets.

Producers consider opportunity costs, too, when employing limited productive resources. When a business firm employs an hour of labor, a piece of machinery, or an acre of land, its managers must consider the alternative uses of these resources. Labor and materials can be used to build schools or bridges, ice rinks or pizza parlors, airplanes or trains. The cost of each is the other good or service not produced. An acre of land used for tennis courts is not available for use as a parking lot!

If a society allocates its resources to produce the most wanted goods and services with the least sacrifice of other goods and services, we say the society is efficient. By choosing efficiently, we reduce opportunity costs and enjoy the largest possible quantities of wanted goods and services.

MAKING CHOICES

We have said that the subject matter of economics is choosing. The study of economics develops habits of thought that help us choose better—to compare the benefits of every choice against the opportunity cost and to make efficient decisions.

The economic way of thinking is important to every one of us in our roles as consumers and as producers. As consumers we compare the benefits of every spending decision against the cost. We compare the benefits of a new car with a family trip to the beach, a night on the town with a new sport jacket, or a motorcycle with a year's membership in a health club. We want to get the most benefit out of every dollar of our limited budgets.

As producers we compare the benefits of every production decision against the costs of resources for producing it. We know that our resources are scarce. So we produce the goods we want most with the resources we have in greatest abundance: boats from plentiful fiberglass, wheat from vast western plains, and clothing from abundant cotton.

CHOOSING AT THE MARGIN

Our most important economic decisions depend on comparisons at the margin. The margin is the edge or border where we must decide whether to take one more step, whether to purchase one more unit of a particular good, or whether to use one more unit of a particular resource.

Most of us use marginal analysis unconsciously every day. We use marginal analysis when we allocate our time, continuing one activity until the benefits gained from spending one more minute are less than the benefits from spending that minute doing something else. Marginal analysis helps a student allocate study time or a worker allocate work time among a number of tasks. (Even a fun-seeker allocates pleasure time by comparing the benefits gained from spending one more minute playing with the benefits of spending that minute resting!)

We also use marginal analysis when we allocate our money. We spend for one item until the benefits gained from spending one more dollar are less than the benefits from spending that dollar for something else. A sports fan attends football games only up to the point where he or she believes a bowling match would be more fun.

Business firms use marginal analysis to decide the level of production. An auto manufacturer produces autos until production of one more auto brings in less revenue than it costs to produce. A barber keeps his shop open until one more hour brings in less revenue than the cost of staying open.

Business firms also use marginal analysis to decide how many resources to use in production. They hire salespeople until hiring one more worker adds less to sales revenue than the worker's wage. They buy land for shopping centers until one more acre of space adds less to revenue than it costs.

In effect, our entire economic system makes decisions at the margin. We increase production until one more unit is worth less than the resources required to produce it. In this way we help ensure that our scarce resources are used efficiently.

Economics is the study of choices in the market system. In the second part of this chapter you will learn how economic decisions are made by a hypothetical family and by a government, both of which have to choose among several alternatives. In the chapters that follow you will learn how markets work in theory and how they often work in the "real world."

Self-Check

1. **The economic problem is concerned primarily with:**
   a. Relieving poverty.
   b. Redistributing wealth.
   c. Motivating people to work harder.
   d. Choosing how to use society's scarce resources.
   e. Gathering data for economic analysis.

2. **Whenever society chooses to produce one type of output:**
   a. It must sacrifice some other type of output.
   b. Resources will be fully employed.
   c. It avoids opportunity costs.
   d. It may also increase all other types of output.
   e. It avoids the problem of decision making.

3. **The philosophy of laissez-faire:**
   a. Favors the free pursuit of self-interest.
   b. Recommends government involvement in the economy.
   c. Was born in the Great Depression of the 1930s.
   d. Was developed by John Maynard Keynes.
   e. All of the above.

4. **Which of the following is *not* a true description of a capital resource?**
   a. Construction of capital allows us to produce more goods in the future.
   b. Capital is money.
   c. Capital allows roundabout production.
   d. Production of autos requires more capital than production of hamburgers.
   e. Nations differ in the quantities of capital owned.

5. **Which of the following correctly describes a free market economy?**
   a. It is not necessary to make sacrifices in a free market economy.
   b. Under the market system a central authority plans economic growth.
   c. A market economy provides little opportunity for technological advance and growth.
   d. A market economy responds to dollar "votes" of consumers.
   e. The market system is based on preserving past methods of production.

6. **Which of the following statements is false?**
   a. Even simple day-to-day decisions involve opportunity costs.
   b. If there were no scarcity, there would be no opportunity costs.
   c. Opportunity costs are foregone alternatives.
   d. Opportunity costs are always measured in dollars.
   e. Consumers often compare opportunities at the margin.

Theory in Practice

PRACTICE IN CONSTRUCTING AND INTERPRETING GRAPHS

Economists use graphs to illustrate important relationships. Graphs are like symbols. They express ideas quickly with few words of explanation. There are many symbols we recognize instantly without explanation. Do you recognize these symbols?

With a little practice you can learn to construct and interpret graphs. You will find them useful in your study of economics and in your work after you leave school. In this course in economics you will use graphs to measure such things as production, costs, prices, incomes, and employment.

Figure 1.1 is a graph of the quantity of production associated with various quantities of labor resources. The graph is drawn on two axes or perpendicular lines. The horizontal axis shows hours of labor employed per day at Country Kitchen Bakery; the vertical axis shows daily production of bread. If 10 hours of labor are employed, 25 loaves can be produced. Follow the dotted line from 10 hours

Figure 1.1   Daily Bread Production at Country Kitchen Bakery.

The graph illustrates a direct relationship between the two values. As hours of labor increase, bread production also increases.

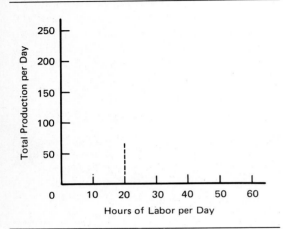

up to 25 loaves. If 20 hours are employed (two workers for 10 hours each), 75 loaves can be produced. Again follow the dotted line from 20 hours to 75 loaves.

Points for every combination of labor hours and bread production were plotted on the graph. Then a line was drawn connecting all the points. Because some quantity of bread can be produced if, say, 5, 23.75, or 51.33 hours of labor are employed, the line was drawn as a continuous curve. The zero point (0) on the graph is called the **origin**. The graph of bread production begins at the origin because when zero hours of labor are employed, zero bread can be produced.

Over the range of employment shown in Figure 1.1, there is a direct relationship between hours of labor and bread production; that means that as labor increases, bread production also increases. Likewise, as labor decreases, bread production decreases. On other graphs the relationship between the two val-

ues might be inverse: as one value increases, the other decreases.

The data in the table above Figure 1.2 describe grain production from one acre of land when various quantities of fertilizer are applied. Use the information in the table to construct a graph on the figure. Label the horizontal axis "pounds of fertilizer applied during the growing season." Label the vertical axis "bushels of grain harvested per growing season." On the horizontal axis mark off spaces representing 10, 20, 30, 40, and 50 pounds of fertilizer. On the vertical axis mark off spaces representing 50, 100, 150, 200, 250, and 300 bushels of grain. Plot the points shown in the table.

Even if no fertilizer is used, the field produces 100 bushels of grain during the growing

Figure 1.2   Constructing a Graph.

Pounds of Fertilizer	0	10	20	30	40	50
Bushels of Grain	100	150	175	200	200	175

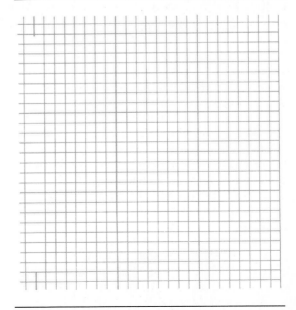

season. Therefore, your first point should lie on the vertical axis at 100 bushels. Follow a line up from 10 pounds of fertilizer to 150 bushels for your second point. Plot all the remaining points and connect them with a continuous line.

What can you learn from your graph? Describe its shape. Why do you think it has this shape? Based on your graph, what would you estimate total production to be if 25 pounds of fertilizer is applied during the growing season? Is there a direct relationship between the use of fertilizer and grain production? Over what range? A portion of your graph illustrates an inverse relationship between the use of fertilizer and total production. Can you explain this result?

PRACTICE USING THE MODEL OF PRODUCTION POSSIBILITIES

Now we will use a graph to illustrate the most fundamental concept of economics. Remember that we described economics as the science of choosing. A graph that illustrates the problem of choosing is called an **economic model**. A model is a simplified view of reality. It includes certain fundamental features of the economic environment but omits unnecessary details. Models make it possible to focus on the problem as a whole and to project the likely results of alternative choices.

The model for choosing production is called the **model of production possibilities**. To illustrate, let us suppose that a society has a particular quantity of natural, human, manufactured, and creative resources and that it enjoys a particular level of technical knowledge. With its resources and level of technology, the society can produce a range of combinations of particular goods and services. It can choose to allocate all resources toward one product—food, for example, or industrial machinery or military equipment. Or the soci-

ety may own such a wealth of resources that it can choose to produce more frivolous products—sports cars, sonic mouse traps, and whirlpool baths.

Figure 1.3 is a graph of the model of production possibilities. The society in Figure 1.3 can produce two kinds of goods: coal and wheat. The two axes on Figure 1.3 represent quantities of the two goods. Thus, the horizontal axis represents quantities of coal, mea-

Figure 1.3 Production Possibilities Curve.

Given its limited resources and state of technology, a society can produce any combination of goods up to its production possibilities frontier. Point E is beyond this society's present capabilities; point F underutilizes the society's resources.

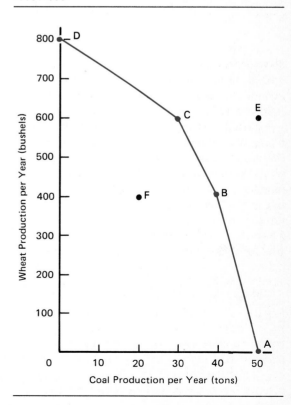

sured in tons on a scale from 0 to 50. The vertical axis represents wheat, measured in bushels on a scale from 0 to 800. Table 1.1 shows some of the possible combinations of wheat and coal that can be produced.

If all resources are devoted to coal production, the maximum output per year is 50 tons. Follow the horizontal axis in Figure 1.3 to 50 tons and notice the point *A*, which represents the maximum quantity of coal this society can produce. If 50 tons of coal are produced, the economy will produce no wheat. Thus, the opportunity cost of 50 tons of coal is the amount of wheat that could have been produced instead. (Can you look at Table 1.1 and determine the precise opportunity cost of 50 tons of coal? What is the opportunity cost of each ton?)

If all resources are devoted instead to the production of wheat, the maximum output is 800 bushels. Follow the vertical axis to 800 bushels and notice the point *D*, which represents the maximum production of wheat. If 800 bushels of wheat are produced, the economy will produce no coal. The opportunity cost of 800 bushels of wheat is 50 tons of coal. (What is the opportunity cost of each bushel?)

Now let us suppose that the society wants to produce some combination of both goods. (Without coal for heat, it's difficult to use wheat for making bread.) The maximum combinations of coal and wheat are: (*A*) zero wheat and 50 tons of coal, (*B*) 400 bushels of wheat and 40 tons of coal, (*C*) 600 bushels and 30 tons, and (*D*) 800 bushels and zero tons. Locate these points on Figure 1.3 by moving

along the horizontal scale the appropriate distance and then moving up the vertical scale.

A line connecting the points of production possibilities has been called just that—**the production possibilities curve**—the frontier beyond which this society cannot produce. Point *E* on Figure 1.3, for example, represents quantities of coal and wheat (50 tons and 600 bushels) that are impossible to produce with the society's limited resources and existing technology. Point *F* is a combination of products that underutilizes the society's scarce resources. At point *F*, some coal miners and wheat farmers are unemployed, causing a permanent loss of the output they might have produced.

TEST YOURSELF
How much coal and how much wheat would be produced at F? How much more coal could be produced? How much more wheat? (Answers to Test Yourself are at the end of the chapter.)

UNEMPLOYMENT AND INFLATION

When the United States entered World War II, observers in this country and abroad were amazed at how fast we were able to begin producing tanks, planes, guns, and ammunition. The reason we were able to move so quickly into war production was because many of our resources were unemployed. This was the period of the Great Depression of the 1930s. In the depths of the Depression, 12 million workers or one-quarter of the labor force were unemployed, and many others were underemployed (working at jobs beneath their full capacity). The U.S. economy had been operating at a point inside our production possibilities curve until the wartime emergency shifted unemployed workers, idle machines, and empty factories into useful work.

Table 1.1   Production Possibilities Curve.

Wheat (bushels per year)	0	400	600	750	800
Coal (tons per year)	50	40	30	10	0

Conditions were quite different in the 1960s when the United States entered the war in Vietnam. Except for a relatively small number of workers who would normally be changing jobs, the U.S. economy was operating at full employment. To increase production of military equipment required a sacrifice of the civilian goods and services that were currently being produced. The war was unpopular, however, and President Lyndon Johnson hoped that more military goods could be produced for the war without forcing civilians to pay the opportunity costs.

Economists reminded the president of the model of production possibilities. They pointed out that increasing production of one good or service would require that other kinds of production be cut back. The U.S. economy could move along its production possibilities curve but not beyond it!

If the United States had a command economic system, it would be easy to cut back civilian production by changing the central plan. Then the required resources could be moved into military production. Even our free market system has ways to force consumers to reduce their purchases of civilian goods so that resources can be moved into purposes decided by government. In fact, a tax increase was proposed to do just that.

It was several years before the tax increase was finally passed, however. In the meantime, consumers continued to buy civilian goods and services while government increased its spending for military goods. The nation was spending beyond its production possibilities at point E.

When total spending is greater than the supply of goods and services, the ultimate result is rising prices. Consumers and government agencies bid against each other for the limited supplies of goods, and prices are forced up. A general increase in prices is called **price inflation**.

Price inflation prevented consumers from buying all the civilian goods and services they wanted, so the U.S. economy did remain on its production possibilities curve after all. In fact, price inflation acted as a kind of tax. Because each dollar of consumer spending bought fewer goods and services, the quantities of civilian goods fell, and scarce resources did move into military production for use by government.

RESOURCE SPECIALIZATION

Have you noticed that the production possibilities curve is bowed out in the middle? The largest combinations of total output are near the middle where some resources are used to produce wheat and some to produce coal. Why is this? The reason is the character of particular resources. All resources are not equally suited to the production of coal or wheat. When workers can choose among two or more types of jobs, they will generally choose to work where they are more productive, and they will become more skillful as they work. Furthermore, if too much labor is employed in one type of production, each worker will have less of other resources—land and capital equipment—with which to work. Total production may not grow very much as more workers are added. To use all resources in one type of production or the other pulls the production possibilities curve down at the edges and causes a bulge in the middle.

It is not practical to draw a model of production possibilities with more than two axes, but we might imagine a multidimensional figure in which the possible combinations of all goods and services are shown. Then the society must choose the appropriate combination for which its resources will be used. Producing a combination on the production possibilities curve achieves technical efficiency. Producing the precise combination that the people want achieves allocative efficiency.

CHANGES IN PRODUCTION POSSIBILITIES

In Figure 1.3 we used the model of production possibilities to illustrate a nation's maximum possible production of goods and services. The model of production possibilities is useful also for illustrating the effects of changes in economic conditions over time.

First, suppose the nation discovers new resources: new mineral deposits or, perhaps, untapped labor skills. New supplies of productive resources increase production possibilities and cause the production possibilities curve to shift to the right. Advances in technology have the same effect, changing the shape of the production possibilities curve to show increased capacity for producing the good favored by the new technology. The production possibilities curve in Figure 1.4a

shows a nation with relatively greater technical progress in the production of wheat. Figure 1.4b shows relatively greater technical capacity for producing coal.

Now consider the effect of a decrease in available resources or a failure to develop new technologies. The result is lower production possibilities and a backward shift of the production possibilities curve. Figure 1.4c shows a backward shift of production possibilities, with reduced capacity for producing both goods.

Changes in the shape of the production possibilities curve reflect changes in the costs of production of the two goods, measured in terms of opportunity costs. Look again at Figure 1.4a. Technological progress favoring wheat production has reduced its cost, such that fewer units of coal must be sacrificed for each additional unit of wheat. Indeed, America's growth as an industrial power is largely a result of advances in the technology of agriculture. As fewer workers and machines are needed to produce food, more of our nation's

Figure 1.4   Changes in Production Possibilities.

Increased capacity for producing wheat (*a*), or coal (*b*), is shown by a shift of the production possibilities curve to the right. Reduced capacity for producing both goods (*c*) is shown by a shift of the curve to the left.

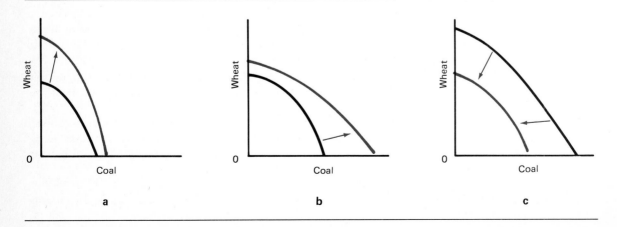

a   b   c

resources can be shifted into construction of factories and other kinds of capital equipment.

America has prospered also because of our large, integrated national market. Our rich and varied resources allow regions to specialize in particular types of production. There are no barriers to free trade among regions: no customs duties, no currency exchanges, no restrictions that might slow the free movement of goods in trade. When regions specialize and sell to a wider consumer market, it is easier to develop advanced technology for improving efficiency. The result for our nation has been a continued shift to the right of production possibilities, with rising standards of living for our people.

TEST YOURSELF
How will each of the following affect the position and shape of a nation's production possibilities curve:

1. A war that devastates much of the farm-land and kills many young workers?
2. The "green revolution," which increases the use of chemical fertilizers, disease-resistant seeds, pesticides, and herbicides in agriculture?
3. State-supported vocational schools to provide low-cost training to disadvantaged groups?
4. Widespread emphasis on "doing one's own thing," rejecting society's standards, and refusing to conform to accepted behavior? (A number of answers is possible here.)
5. The "Puritan ethic" with its disapproval of conspicuous wealth and its emphasis on hard work and thrift?
6. The formation of a "common market" of nations, within which barriers to free trade are gradually removed?
7. Legislation forbidding certain uses of a region's air, water, and landscape?
8. A trade embargo that reduces imports of a commodity necessary in all kinds of production?

PRACTICE IN PROBLEM SOLVING

You make choices every day that involve economics. Should you buy a second pair of shoes or a pair of slacks or, perhaps, save your money? Should you buy a car or rely on public transportation? Should you take a new job that offers a higher salary or stay at your old job within walking distance of your home? Should you do your own repairs around the house or hire a professional?

These simple examples illustrate a number of economic concepts you have already learned: scarcity, opportunity cost, production possibilities, marginal analysis. Making such decisions is not always easy, but a knowledge of economics can help you make decisions efficiently.

How can you learn to think "economically"? You may learn to use economic reasoning automatically only after you are well acquainted with economics. (It is hard to think in a foreign language until you have mastered the language!) Following the six steps to problem solving below can help you learn to apply economic concepts and principles to your daily life:*

1. Define the problem.
2. State your goals or objectives.
3. Identify the economic concepts involved in the problem.
4. List the alternative choices available to you.
5. Evaluate each alternative.
6. Decide which alternative is best in light of your evaluation and goals.

Now let us use the six problem-solving steps to solve some common economic problems. (This section is optional. You may want

* For more on problem-solving methods, see Rendigs Fels and Robert Uhler, *Casebook of Economic Problems and Policies* (West Publishing Co., St. Paul, MN, 1974).

to substitute an economic problem from your own experience. Apply the six problem-solving steps to suggest a solution to your own problem.)

A Problem in Family Budgeting

The Wilcoxes live in a one-bedroom apartment for which they pay $670 a month, including utilities. Both the Wilcoxes work, and together they earn a yearly income of $30,000 after taxes. Lately they have been complaining of not knowing where their money is going. For the past year, it seems, they have been unable to save any of their income, even though they believe that a certain portion should be saved for emergencies or for future needs.

The Wilcoxes know that certain regular expenditures are necessary and cannot be cut back to allow them to save. Their necessary expenditures include housing costs (rent and utilities), food and other household needs, and transportation to and from work (they do not own a car and must use public transportation). According to their calculations, the minimum they can spend on these necessities is as follows: $8000 a year for housing, $4000 a year for food, and $2000 a year for transportation.

Other purchases the Wilcoxes want to make include additional units of housing (in the form of new home furnishings, electrical appliances, etc.), food (an occasional dinner out), and transportation (a day at the seashore). They also want to use some of their income for recreation, health care (including health insurance), and clothing. However, the necessary expenditures for housing, food, and transportation must come first—that is, they must allocate a total of $14,000 a year to cover their necessary expenses before deciding on other uses of their income.

The Wilcoxes need a plan for using their income more efficiently: to achieve the maximum possible benefits from their limited in-come. Let us see how the six problem-solving steps can help.

1. *Define the problem.* The problem, as the Wilcoxes put it, is that they do not know "where the money is going." There are too many unnecessary or improper expenditures and too little (actually zero) saving.

2. *State the goals or objectives.* The Wilcoxes' goal is similar to that of our economic system as a whole: to use their limited resources efficiently to achieve the largest possible quantities of the things they want.

3. *Identify the economic concepts involved in the problem.* The concepts include: living with scarcity (the Wilcoxes must decide how to allocate their limited income), opportunity cost (money spent is not available for saving, and money spent on one good is not available for spending on another), and marginal analysis (the family must decide how to make use of each additional dollar of income).

4. *List the alternative choices.* Once the Wilcoxes have allocated a total of $14,000 for necessary expenditures, there are a number of ways they might use the remaining $16,000: purchase additional units of housing, food, or transportation; purchase other things such as health, recreation, and clothing; save the money; or a combination of these.

5. *Evaluate each alternative.* To simplify the decision, the Wilcoxes break down their income into units of $2000. They now have 15 units of income each year for allocating among the choices available to them.

    In order to evaluate their choices, the Wilcoxes must have some way of measuring the benefits from each. After some thought, they come up with a measure they decide to call utility points, or utils. They assign a value of 100 utils to each essential purchase of housing, food, and transportation. Then they assign fewer than 100 utils to less essential purchases, depending on the urgency of their need for each.

Table 1.2 shows the benefits in utils the Wilcoxes expect to enjoy from each single purchase. The first four $2000 purchases of housing provide benefits worth 100 utils each, for a total of 400 utils; the first two $2000 purchases of food provide a total of 200 utils; the first $2000 purchase of transportation provides 100 utils. Other purchases yield the benefits shown in the table.

The Wilcoxes' necessary purchases of housing, food, and transportation yield total benefits of 700 utils. How should they use their next $2000 units of income? As shown in Table 1.2, an additional $2000 spent for housing or food is not an efficient choice. The next purchase of housing yields only 85 utils, and the next purchase of food yields 70 utils. However, a purchase of health care yields 95 utils, the largest amount available among the remaining choices. Thus, the Wilcoxes obtain the maximum total benefits by using their next $2000 to purchase one unit of health care.

The Wilcoxes should save the next $2000 unit of income, because the first "purchase" of saving yields benefits worth 90 utils. (The high value reflects the importance of saving to the Wilcox family.) The next choice could be a first purchase of clothing or a fifth purchase of housing, because both yield 85 utils. The following choice is the 85-util item they did not choose.

6. *Decide which alternative is best in light of the evaluation and goals.* The Wilcoxes repeat step 5 until they have allocated all 15 units of income. For each successive $2000 they spend, they consider all the alternatives and choose the one alternative that yields the greatest benefits. Their final budget is shown in Table 1.3. Total benefits from the final decision are 1370 utility points, the maximum total benefits possible with their income of $30,000.

Most families do not (consciously!) go through such a detailed process when planning a budget. The usual practice is quite similar in principle, however, to the Wilcoxes' plan. A family planning a budget considers alternative uses of family income and allocates each dollar according to the benefits they expect to receive from its use. They do not choose, for example, to use $2000 for recreation if they need that money to pay the rent!

Table 1.2 Utility Points from Spending Each $2000 of Money Income (measured in utils).

	Housing	Food	Transportation	Recreation	Health Care	Clothing	Saving
1st unit	100	100	100	80	95	85	90
2nd unit	100	100	80	75	60	70	80
3rd unit	100	70	40	60	25	55	70
4th unit	100	50	0	60	0	30	40
5th unit	85	25		45		0	0
6th unit	70	0		35			
7th unit	40			20			
8th unit	20			0			
9th unit	0						

Table 1.3   Wilcox Family Budget.

Good or Service	No. of Units Purchased	Income Spent for Each Good or Service	Utility Points from Each Purchase
Housing	5	$10,000	485
Food	2	4,000	200
Transportation	2	4,000	180
Recreation	2	4,000	155
Health care	1	2,000	95
Clothing	1	2,000	85
Saving	2	4,000	170
Total income		$30,000	
Total utility points			1,370

TEST YOURSELF

Explain how the Wilcox budget demonstrates decision-making at the margin. What are the opportunity costs of each alternative choice? How would the Wilcoxes use $8000 of additional income?

A Problem in Planning Government Expenditures

Governments, like families, allocate their budgets among public projects according to priorities, comparing the benefits and costs of expenditures at the margin. Unlike families, however, a government's primary concern is social benefits rather than private benefits. Governments select projects that provide the greatest benefits per dollar for the community as a whole.

Another difference is that many public projects are not divisible into small units. Public projects involve large lump sums. A road must go from somewhere to somewhere. A baseball field must be of a certain size. You can't build three-fourths of a gymnasium! For this reason, government spending decisions are not typical marginal decisions.

Moreover, the benefits of public projects are difficult to measure. The value of a public service is the amount its users would pay for it if it were provided by private business. How much would you pay for the use of public roads or public education, for community protection against smallpox, or for a swimming pool in the city park? Your willingness to pay depends on your own expected benefits, which you may not be able to measure.

Total costs are also difficult to measure. The cost of land, labor, and materials is easy to calculate. (Remember that these costs measure the opportunity cost of using these resources in certain ways.) However, there are other broader costs that should also be considered. The disruption and dislocation of homes and businesses during construction imposes costs on the community that may be impossible to measure precisely.

Table 1.4 gives hypothetical benefit and cost data for three groups of public projects. Estimated benefits and costs are expressed in thousands of dollars. For example, a new school costs $6.5 million to build but will yield benefits to the community estimated at $19.5 million.

TEST YOURSELF

See if you can go through the six problem-solving steps to choose the allocation of resources that yields the maximum social

Table 1.4   Benefit and Cost Data for Public Projects.
(Figures are in thousands of dollars.)

	Benefits	*Costs*	$\dfrac{Benefits}{Costs}$ = *Benefit-Cost Ratio*
Education			
New school	$19,500	$6,500	_____
Gymnasium	1,000	800	_____
Driver-training course	750	500	_____
Transportation			
Highway	$ 4,000	$2,000	_____
Rapid-transit service	6,000	8,000	_____
Bus service	1,750	500	_____
Recreation			
Stadium	$ 1,200	$ 900	_____
Golf course	1,000	2,000	_____
Pool	1,200	500	_____

benefit for each dollar spent. First, calculate the expected benefits per dollar of cost for each project. (Divide benefits by costs.) Assume the government's budget for the year is limited to $10 million. What projects should be undertaken? What is the total cost of this year's public projects?

A ratio of expected benefits to dollar cost is called a **benefit/cost ratio**. A benefit/cost ratio greater than one means that benefits outweigh costs; a ratio less than one means that costs outweigh benefits. What would a ratio of exactly one mean? What projects in Table 1.4 have benefit/cost ratios less than one? What projects are economically efficient, even though they do not fit within this year's budget?

SUMMARY

1. Scholars of the past sought to understand the natural laws that govern physical and social environments. The economic theory of the market system and the political theory of democracy developed together. Both depended on the free exercise of individual rights and responsibilities.

2. Economics deals with the economic problem: scarce resources and unlimited wants. Land, labor, capital, and management or entrepreneurial ability are scarce resources.

3. An economic system is necessary for organizing scarce resources for producing the goods and services the community wants. An economic system answers the questions *what* to produce, *how* to produce it, and *for whom* to produce it.

4. An economic system may be based on tradition, command, or free markets. Adam Smith's *Wealth of Nations* described the operation of a free market system.

5. The U.S. economy is based primarily on free markets. We believe a free market economy is most efficient, in terms of both technical and allocative efficiency.

6. However a society chooses to answer the three economic questions, it will suffer opportunity costs. Opportunity costs are the sacrifice of other choices that might have been selected. Economics helps us compare the benefits of each choice with its costs.

7. Graphs are useful in economics. The graph of production possibilities illustrates the problem of scarce resources and the inevitability of opportunity costs.

TERMS TO REMEMBER

free resources: resources in such abundance that their price is zero

economic problem: the problem of scarce resources and unlimited wants that every society faces

land: the original and nonreproducible gifts of nature

labor: the productive activity of human beings

capital: produced means of production, like buildings, tools, and machines

management or entrepreneurial ability: the resource that combines other resources in production

economic system: an arrangement by which a society chooses the allocation of its resources

technical efficiency: using resources to produce the maximum possible output with scarce resources and available technology

allocative efficiency: using resources to produce the goods and services people want

opportunity costs: the goods and services we give up when we choose to use resources in one way rather than another

economic model: a simplified view of reality for explaining the economic environment

production possibilities curve: a graph showing the maximum quantities of output a society can produce, given its scarce resources and available technology

price inflation: a general increase in prices; a rise in some prices that is not offset by a fall in other prices

marginal analysis: a way of making decisions based on comparing the costs and benefits of one more unit of something

direct relationship: for two values, when one increases, the other increases; when one decreases, the other decreases

inverse relationship: for two values, when one increases the other decreases

TOPICS FOR DISCUSSION

1. The following terms were used frequently in this chapter. They are not strictly economic terms but are used in everyday conversation. Explain how they are involved in the study of economics.

> Law or principle
> Costs and benefits
> Efficiency and model

2. Explain how the three fundamental economic questions are involved in a nation's decision to increase production of military equipment and reduce financial support for education.

3. A famous soprano can earn $100 an hour recording operatic arias. However, she has a taste for home-grown tomatoes and spends many hours cultivating her garden when she could be performing. How would you determine the cost of her tomatoes?

4. Use a production possibilities curve to illustrate limited time for study. Suppose you must prepare lessons in mathematics and Spanish, and you have only 10 hours to work. If you devote the entire time to mathematics, you can work 50 problems. If you devote the entire time to Spanish, you can translate 25 pages. Other possibilities are:

Spanish (in pages)	0	8	15	20	25
Mathematics (problems)	50	45	40	25	0

Construct a production possibilities curve using these quantities. Label the horizontal axis "Spanish" and the vertical axis "mathematics" and graph the appropriate quantities. (Remember to move along the horizontal axis first, then up the vertical axis.)

Is your curve bowed out in the center? What is the opportunity cost of the first 8 pages of translation? The first 25 problems? What is the maximum total work you could accomplish in the limited time? Based on your experience, can you make a reasonable decision how to allocate your time? If you need a good grade in Spanish to pass the course, will this influence your decision?

Suppose you purchase an electronic calculator and your production possibilities increase as shown below:

Spanish	0	8	15	20	25
Mathematics	75	70	65	40	0

Show your new production possibilities curve on the same graph. You have experienced technological progress!

5. Most married women now work outside the home. Their decision to accept a job involves marginal analysis. They must compare the benefits with the costs of their jobs. Some benefits and costs are listed below. Can you add others?

BENEFITS	*COSTS*
Salary	Income taxes
Opportunities for advancement	Transportation costs
	Home-cleaning costs
Intellectual stimulation	Loss of social contacts
New social contacts	Loss of time for cultural or physical development

What social and technological changes in recent years have changed the nature of benefits and costs? What personal changes may have changed the relationships between benefits and costs for particular women?

6. Consult current newspapers or magazines for information regarding the attempts of the USSR and Eastern European nations to change their economic systems from central planning to a market system. Report on your findings.

ANSWERS TO TEST YOURSELF

(p. 18) Twenty tons and 400 bushels; any combination on the production possibilities curve.

(p. 21) 1. A backward shift of production possibilities.
2. Increased production possibilities for food and other agricultural products.
3. Increased production possibilities for goods and services using relatively large quantities of labor.
4. Whether production possibilities decrease or increase depends on whether rebellious attitudes result in lower or higher worker productivity.
5. Increased production possibilities.
6. Incentives to expand production to satisfy the larger market.
7. Reduced production possibilities for goods requiring relatively large quantities of restricted resources.
8. Reduced production possibilities for goods and services using the restricted resource.

(p. 24) Ratios are as follows: Education—3, 1.25, 1.5; transportation—2, 0.75, 3.5; recreation—1.33, 0.5, 2.4. The community should choose the school, the driver-training course, the highway, the bus service, and the pool. The gymnasium and the stadium are also worthwhile. The rapid-transit service and the golf course are definitely not recommended.

Chapter

Demand and Supply:
The Basics

or The Customer Is Always Right

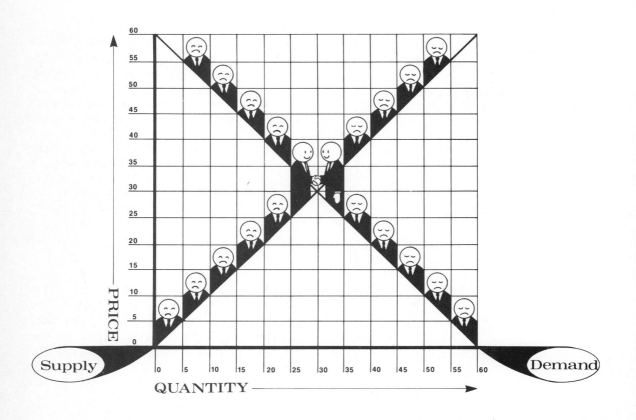

Tools for Study

LEARNING OBJECTIVES

After reading this chapter, you will be able to:

1. Describe the four characteristics of competition.
2. Explain and illustrate the laws of demand and supply.
3. List factors affecting demand and supply and explain their effects.
4. Explain the meaning of market equilibrium.

CURRENT ISSUES FOR DISCUSSION

What are the advantages and disadvantages of government intervention in markets?

People "in the ordinary business of life" was how early economists described the subject matter of economics. Producing goods for exchange, responding to market incentives, and adjusting to changing market conditions became the subject of the social science of economics.

THE INVISIBLE HAND

The economist Adam Smith was a great admirer of the market system. Smith described how free markets answer the question "What?" and produce the things consumers want. Free markets provide the highest levels of living possible with the community's scarce resources and available technology.

All this is accomplished by what Smith called the "invisible hand." Buyers and sellers seek their own individual self-interest, without any need for government intervention. In doing so, they are led, as if by an invisible hand, to decisions that yield the maximum possible output of wanted goods and services.

To understand this, suppose Consumer A wants something that Consumer B produces. In exchange for Consumer B's product, Consumer A must produce something Consumer B wants. Both consumers give up something of less value to themselves than what they receive in return; therefore, both gain. By pursuing their own self-interest, they increase their total welfare.

Indeed, Adam Smith had a certain reverence for the system that he believed promotes the fullest possible living standards for all people.

COMPETITION IN THE MARKET

If Adam Smith's ideal market is to work, there must be competition in the marketplace. Perfect competition has four characteristics:

1. There must first be *many buyers and sellers,* all seeking their own advantage. Furthermore, buyers and sellers must be small relative to the size of the market. Small buyers and sellers cannot affect market price by buying more or less or by offering to supply more or less for sale. In competition, every buyer and seller is a **price taker**.
2. There must be *perfect information* regarding selling conditions throughout the market. No single buyer should unknowingly pay a higher price or a seller charge a lower price than prevails throughout the market.
3. There must be *ease of mobility* to the most favorable market for buying or selling. Thus, buyers must be able to seek the lowest prices, and sellers the highest prices for their goods. Owners of productive resources must be free to move their resources into markets where they are most wanted and where they can be employed most efficiently.
4. Finally, in competition the products of one seller must be *just like those of all other sellers* in a particular market. Unless products are identical, some buyers might be willing to pay a premium price for the unique products of a particular seller. Autos, soft drinks, and cigarettes, for example, must have no real or apparent differences, making one seller's product more desirable than another's.

Perhaps you have heard the story of the gentleman who decided to play a joke on the clerk in the pet shop. He asked to purchase a canary, and while the clerk was ringing up the sale, she chatted about what a nice pet the bird would be. The gentleman smiled and explained that he really didn't need a pet, already owning a nice cat. Occasionally, however, the cat liked to have a little fun and exercise and so . . . . The clerk drew back in indignation and ordered the gentleman from the premises. Chuckling inwardly at the success of his joke, the gentleman headed for the door where an elderly lady had been listening to the entire conversation. She tugged at his sleeve to get his attention and whispered, "They're fifty cents cheaper down the street."

> **TEST YOURSELF**
> Explain how this story illustrates the four characteristics of competition. How do you know competition is not really perfect in the story? Can you suggest other markets where competition is more nearly perfect?

BUILDING A MARKET MODEL

Adam Smith's "invisible hand" guides behavior in markets, where buyers and sellers meet to exchange goods and services. The study of how individual markets work is called **microeconomics.** Consumers enter markets to purchase particular goods and services. Business firms respond by producing the goods and services consumers want. Microeconomics, therefore, is the study of individual markets, where producers respond to consumers' wants.

The quantities consumers are willing and able to buy at various prices constitute **market demand**. The quantities business firms are willing and able to sell at various prices constitute **market supply**. Combining market demand and market supply for a particular good or service yields an economic model of the market. As we consider demand and supply in this chapter, we will assume that markets are perfectly competitive; that is, the four characteristics of Adam Smith's ideal market are true. In chapter 5, we will relax the assumption of perfect competition and describe the operation of markets when competition is not perfect.

Market Demand

Consumers buy goods and services because of their own tastes or preferences and their income or ability to pay the price. Given an individual consumer's tastes and income, there are certain quantities he or she would want to buy at various prices. An individual consumer's own wants are shown in his or her demand schedule for a particular good or service. The wants of all consumers in a particular market combine to form the market demand schedule for that particular good or service.

Table 2.1 gives demand schedules for two hypothetical consumers and for all consumers taken together in the market for compact discs. Columns (2) and (3) show that at lower prices consumers Andy and Barbra would purchase larger quantities than at higher prices. Column (4) shows the market demand schedule. It is the sum of the quantities all consumers want to buy at the prices shown in Column (1).

Figure 2.1a is a graph of consumer Andy's demand schedule. The line on the graph is Andy's demand curve. The demand curve shows that Andy would buy three compact discs at a price of $8 and ten at a price of $3. Figure 2.1b is a graph of consumer Barbra's demand schedule. Note that Barbra's tastes or income permit her to purchase more compact discs than Andy, whatever the price.

Figure 2.1c is a graph of market demand. A market demand curve shows the quantities all consumers in the market would be willing and able to buy at various prices. At a price of $8 all the consumers in this market would buy a total of 13,000 compact discs per month, and at $3 consumers would buy a total of 33,000.

TEST YOURSELF
It is possible to show on Figure 2.1c the total expenditure or total revenue from the sale of compact discs at any price. This is done by drawing a rectangle whose northeast corner touches the demand curve at the indicated price. Can you explain why?

Table 2.1 Hypothetical Demand Schedules for Compact Discs (per month).

(1) Price	(2) Consumer Andy's Demand	(3) Consumer Barbra's Demand	(4) Sum of Consumer Demands = Andy + Barbra + . . . + n = Market Demand
$8	3	6	13,000
7	4	7	17,000
6	5	8	21,000
5	6	9	25,000
4	8	10	29,000
3	10	12	33,000

Figure 2.1   Demand for Compact Discs.

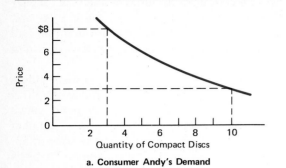

a. Consumer Andy's Demand

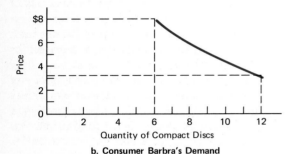

b. Consumer Barbra's Demand

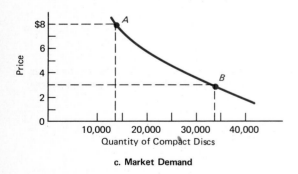

c. Market Demand

The Law of Demand

Consumer demand helps answer the question What? An individual consumer's demand curve shows the quantities of a particular good or service that consumer would buy at various prices. A consumer is normally willing to pay a high price to acquire one unit, and perhaps even the first few units, of a good or service. Eventually, however, more units are not as useful as the first. This means that the consumer will buy more units only if the price is lower.

A consumer's demand for compact discs (and pizzas and all other goods and services) is said to be *inversely* related to price. At high prices a consumer wants to buy fewer units than at low prices. The inverse relationship between price and quantity demanded is known as the **law of demand**.

The Difference Between Quantity Demanded and Demand

Economists mean quite different things when they say "quantity demanded" and "demand." Remember that a demand curve shows the quantities consumers are willing and able to buy at various prices. A change in the price of a good causes a change in **quantity demanded**. A change in quantity demanded is shown as a movement along the demand curve for that good. In Figure 2.1c a reduction in price from $8 to $3 causes a movement along the demand curve from point A to point B. This is an increase in quantity demanded: from 13,000 units at a price of $8 to 33,000 units at a price of $3.

Factors other than price affect consumers' decisions to buy. Other factors affecting consumer choice are held constant while drawing a single demand curve. Changing the other factors that affect consumer demand would cause a change in the entire demand curve. Economists say there is a change in **demand.** The next section will describe the factors that cause a change in demand and a shift in the entire demand curve.

Determinants of Demand

Some factors that can cause a change in demand are changes in:

1. The incomes of buyers.
2. The number of buyers in the market.
3. Consumers' tastes and preferences.
4. The prices of related goods.
5. Consumers' expectations about future prices.

1. To understand how changes in other factors can change demand, first suppose consumer Andy's *income* doubles. Now Andy is willing and able to buy twice as many compact discs at every price level as before. Andy's old and new demand schedules are shown in Table 2.2, and both schedules are graphed on Figure 2.2. Notice that Andy's new demand curve lies to the right of the old one. There has been a change in demand. In this case, there has been an increase in demand, as shown by a shift of the demand curve to the right. At each and every price, Andy is willing and able to buy a larger quantity than before. (If Andy's income had been cut in half, we would expect his demand

Table 2.2 Consumer Andy's Demand Schedule for Compact Discs (per month).

Price	Old Demand Schedule	New Demand Schedule
$8	3	6
7	4	8
6	5	10
5	6	12
4	8	16
3	10	20

to fall. At each and every price, Andy would be willing and able to buy fewer compact discs than before. A decrease in demand is shown by a shift of the demand curve to the left. Pencil in a decrease in demand on Figure 2.2.)

Remember that we described a change in quantity demanded as a movement along a demand curve caused by a change in the price of a good. In contrast, a change in demand is a shift of the entire demand curve caused by a change in a

Figure 2.2 Change in Demand.

An increase in income causes an increase in Consumer Andy's demand for compact discs. An increase in demand is shown by a shift of the entire demand curve to the right. At a price of $5 Andy is now willing to purchase 12 compact discs.

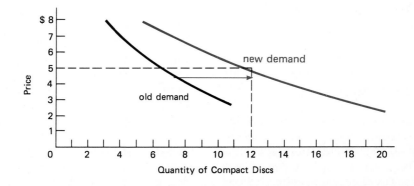

factor other than the price of the good. An increase in demand shifts the demand curve to the right, a decrease, to the left.

TEST YOURSELF

In 1990, certain auto manufacturers offered rebates in the hope of increasing car sales. Do rebates cause a change in quantity demanded or a change in demand?

2. The other factors that affect demand have similar results. If the *number of buyers* in the market should increase, for example, we can expect demand for a particular good to increase. Merchants are generally pleased when a new highway is built, bringing more tourists into their shops and shifting demand curves to the right. On the other hand, when a major local manufacturing plant closes, fewer buyers remain in the area, and many merchants are distressed to see their demand curves shift to the left.

3. A change in *consumer tastes* also affects demand. Suppose consumers decide that reading or going to the movies is a better way to spend their leisure time than listening to music. The demand curve for compact discs would shift to the left. (On the other hand, demand for books or movie tickets would shift to the right.) Can you think of other goods that have enjoyed an increase in demand (or suffered a decrease in demand) because of changes in consumer tastes?

4. The fourth factor affecting demand is *prices of related goods*. Some goods are **substitutes** in consumers' budgets. Substitutes are goods that are similar to or can be used in place of another—like pizza and hamburgers, cars and mass transportation, rock concerts and sporting events. An increase in the price of one good normally reduces quantity demanded for that good. Purchasing less of this good causes

an increase in demand for its substitute. (What would you expect to happen to the demand for compact discs if the price of concert tickets should fall?)

Some goods are **complementary** in consumers' budgets. Complementary goods are goods that "go together"—like cars and gasoline, compact discs and CD players, beer and pretzels. If the price of CD players should rise, we might expect the demand curve for CDs to shift to the left.

5. Finally, consumers' *expectations* about future price changes affect demand. Expected price increases encourage consumers to "buy now to beat the price rise." Expected price reductions discourage current purchases. During the inflation of the 1970s, U.S. consumers grew painfully aware of the former kind of expectations, and many market demand curves shifted to the right.

TEST YOURSELF

What would you expect to happen to market demand curves for air travel during the week before announced rate reductions are scheduled to take effect?

Market Supply

Many people say it is impossible to wash one hand without also washing the other. Economists say it is just as impossible to think about demand without also thinking about supply. Supply describes the willingness and ability of business firms to offer goods and services for sale. The quantities a firm would offer at various prices constitutes the firm's supply schedule. The quantities supplied by all firms in a particular market combine to form the market supply schedule for that particular good or service.

Table 2.3 Hypothetical Supply Schedules for Compact Discs (per month).

Price	Metro Music's Supply	Jive Town's Supply	Sum of Firm Supply = Metro + Jive + . . . + n = Market Demand
$8	8500	11,000	55,000
7	7500	10,000	45,000
6	6500	9000	35,000
5	5500	8000	25,000
4	4500	7000	15,000
3	3500	6000	12,000

Table 2.3 gives supply schedules for Metro Music and Jive Town and for all firms taken together in the market for compact discs. Columns (2) and (3) show that at higher prices the firms would supply larger quantities than at lower prices. Column (4) shows the market supply schedule, the sum of quantities all firms would supply at the prices shown in Column (1).

Figure 2.3a is a graph of Metro Music's supply schedule. The line on the graph is Metro Music's supply curve. It shows that Metro Music would supply 5500 compact discs at a price of $5 but only 3500 if the price were as low as $3. Figure 2.3b is a graph of Jive Town's supply schedule. Note that Jive Town's resources or technology enable that firm to produce more compact discs than Metro Music at every price.

Figure 2.3c is a graph of market supply. The market supply curve shows the quantities all firms in the market would offer for sale at various prices. At a price of $8 all firms in this market would supply a total of 55,000 compact discs per month, and at a price of $3 all the firms would supply a total of 12,000.

The Law of Supply

When we drew our demand curves, we saw that there is an *inverse* relationship between price and the quantity that would be demanded by consumers. Now we see that there

is a *direct* relationship between price and the quantity that would be supplied by producers. At low prices, few units would be supplied. At high prices, a larger quantity would be supplied. The direct relationship between price and quantity supplied is known as the **law of supply**.

The Difference Between Quantity Supplied and Supply

As with demand, it is important to distinguish between quantity supplied and supply. A change in the price of a good causes a change in **quantity supplied**, shown on a graph as a movement along the supply curve. In Figure 2.3c a decrease in price from $8 to $3 causes a movement down the market supply curve from point A to point B. The decrease in quantity supplied is from 55,000 units at a price of $8 to 12,000 units at a price of $3.

Factors other than price also affect firms' decisions to supply goods for sale. Other factors affecting supply are held constant while drawing a supply curve. Changing the other factors causes a **change in supply**, shown as a shift in the entire supply curve.

Other factors that can cause a change in supply are changes in:

1. The *costs* of resources used in the industry.
2. The *number of firms* in the industry.

Figure 2.3 Supply of Compact Discs.

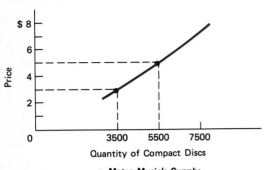

a. Metro Music's Supply

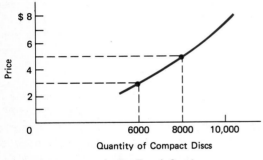

b. Jive Town's Supply

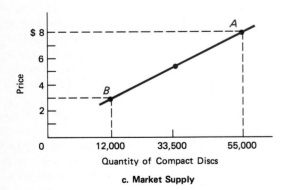

c. Market Supply

3. The state of *technology* used by firms in the industry.
4. *Prices of related goods.*
5. *Expectations* of future price changes.

How do these other factors affect supply?

First, suppose the cost of an important resource used in the production of compact discs increases. As a result, the cost of producing all units increases, so that Metro Music produces fewer units at every price level. (Another way of saying this is that higher prices are required for every quantity.) The old and new supply schedules are shown in Table 2.4, and both schedules are plotted on Figure 2.4. The graph shows that there has been a change in supply. The new supply curve lies to the left of the old curve because there has been a decrease in supply. (An increase in supply would be shown by a shift to the right.) At every price Metro Music supplies fewer compact discs than before.

To summarize: A change in **quantity supplied** is a movement along the supply curve, brought about by a change in price. A change in **supply** is a shift of the entire supply curve to a new position, brought on by a change in some factor other than price.

TEST YOURSELF
A rise in the price of American grain increases the cost of producing beef cattle. Do higher grain prices cause a change in quantity supplied or a change in supply?

Now suppose the number of firms in the industry changes. If the number of producing firms increases, we might expect the supply of a good or service to increase. A recent example is the market for home computers. Profits from the sale of home computers have encouraged many new firms to move into the industry. As a result, the market supply curve for home computers has shifted to the right. A change in technology also affects supply. The improved technology of producing video cassette recorders has helped reduce their costs of production and increased supply. Can you give examples of industries in which a decrease in the number of firms or a change in

Table 2.4 Metro Music's Supply Schedules for Compact Discs (per month).

Price	Old Supply Schedule	New Supply Schedule
$8	8500	7500
7	7500	6500
6	6500	5500
5	5500	4500
4	4500	3500
3	3500	2500
2.67	3000	2000

technology has caused supply to fall?* What has happened to the market supply curve?

What are the effects of changes in other prices and expectations of price changes? A decrease in the price of wheat generally causes the supply of soybeans to increase, as farmers replant their fields with the higher-priced crop. On the other hand, *expectations* of falling wheat prices generally cause the sup-

* Black and white television sets; luxury autos.

Figure 2.4   Change in Supply.

An increase in the cost of electric power reduces Metro Music's supply of compact discs at every price level. A decrease in supply is shown by a shift of the entire supply curve to the left.

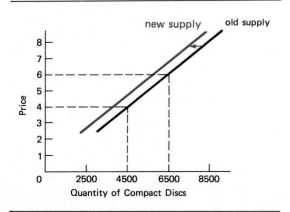

ply of wheat to increase, as farmers try to unload their existing stocks before prices fall. Can you illustrate each of these market changes graphically?

MARKET EQUILIBRIUM

In free, competitive markets the interaction of demand and supply determines the price of a good. In our hypothetical market for compact discs, many consumers (demanders) enter the market to purchase CDs. Many producers (suppliers) respond by offering CDs for sale. Consumers and producers must agree on a market price. When a price is established at which all the CDs offered for sale are bought, we say the market has reached equilibrium.

Through a process of bargaining, bidding, and asking prices, a price is determined that just "clears the market." It is the price at which all the quantity offered for sale will be bought.

Figure 2.5 is a model of the market for compact discs. Consumer demand and producer supply are shown together in the market. At a price of $5, 25,000 CDs would be supplied and 25,000 CDs would be demanded. Therefore, the equilibrium price that clears the market is $5; the equilibrium quantity sold is 25,000. Buyers of the 25,000 CDs are satisfied with the price of $5; firms producing CDs are willing to supply 25,000 at a price of $5.

Figure 2.5 Market Equilibrium.

At a price of $5, quantity demanded equals quantity supplied. There are no surpluses or shortages, and the market is in equilibrium.

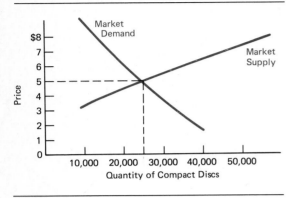

Figure 2.6 Surpluses and Shortages.

If price is higher than the equilibrium price, quantity supplied is greater than quantity demanded, and there is a surplus. If market price is lower than the equilibrium price, quantity demanded is greater than quantity supplied, and there is a shortage.

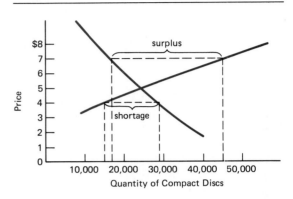

Surpluses and Shortages

What would happen at a price higher or lower than the equilibrium price of $5? As shown on Figure 2.6, at a price of $7, quantity supplied is 45,000 CDs, and quantity demanded is only 17,000. At a price higher than equilibrium there is a surplus of 45,000 − 17,000 = 28,000 CDs. In competition, suppliers compete with each other to sell their surplus CDs and drive price down to the equilibrium level.

Figure 2.6 shows that at a price of $4, quantity supplied is 15,000 CDs, and quantity demanded is 29,000. At a price lower than equilibrium there is a shortage of 29,000 − 15,000 = 14,000 CDs. This time, consumers bid against each other for the limited supply and drive price up to its equilibrium level.

Only at a price of $5 are there no surpluses or shortages. Quantity demanded is equal to quantity supplied, and the market is in equilibrium. Each consumer purchases the quantity at which his or her personal desire for CDs is high enough to justify the equilibrium price.

Each producer supplies the quantity at which the equilibrium price is sufficient to justify producing it.

Changes in Equilibrium

Changing conditions in the market cause changes in demand and supply. Changing consumer tastes or incomes shift demand curves to the right or left. Changes in production costs or technology change supply, shifting supply curves. Changes in the number of firms or consumers also shift supply and demand curves. As curves shift, the market moves toward a new equilibrium price.

Figure 2.7 shows how shifts in demand or supply have affected equilibrium price in various markets. Can you cite other examples from your own experience in which supply or

Figure 2.7 Changes in Equilibrium Price and Quantity.

a. The demand for wheat increased as Russian and Chinese buyers entered the U.S. market for grain. Producers attempted to satisfy the increased demand, but production costs rose, and prices rose also.

b. Improved technology reduced the cost of producing pocket calculators and increased supply. Consumers moved down their demand curves and purchased more calculators at lower prices.

c. The increased price of imported oil raised the cost of producing chemical fertilizers and reduced supply. Farmers moved up their demand curves and purchased less at higher prices.

d. Consumers' tastes changed and they preferred roller skating to bowling. The demand for games of bowling dropped and the price fell.

e. Higher incomes allowed more Americans to take vacation trips. The demand for rooms in ski lodges increased and the price increased.

f. The high price of beef caused consumers to shift to more fish in their diets. Increased demand for fish pushed its price up, too.

g. Changing hair styles reduced the profitability of barber shops. Many barbers left the market, causing a decrease in supply. Consumers purchased fewer haircuts at the higher price.

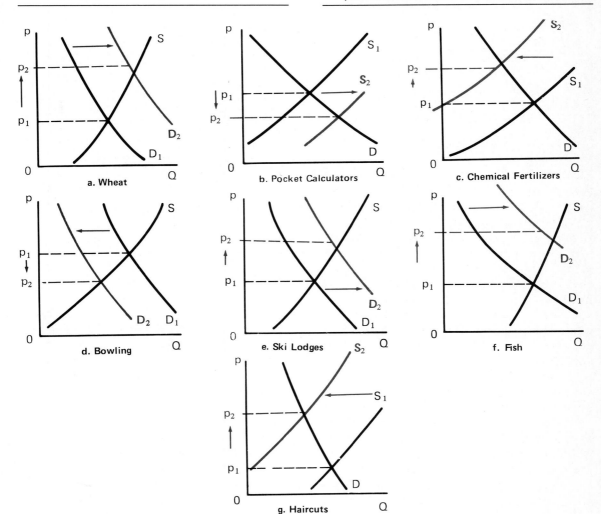

How Things Have Changed

WHAT IT COST

	1974	*1990*
Ford's smallest-model car	$2,600	$4,600–$7,200
One-way air ticket to Montreal	105	199
Alka-Seltzer (25 tablets)	.44	3.59
Right Guard deodorant (7 oz)	.79	2.19
9-volt transistor battery	.14	3.49
Aqua Net hair spray	.39	1.29
One-quart thermos bottle	1.99	4.99
Nylon bikini	16	35
Ladies' sandals	1.99	9.99
Pantyhose	.50	3.59
Central air conditioning	1,199	1,300
Ground beef (1 lb)	.68	1.79
Sliced bacon (1 lb)	.78	1.39
Top round steak	1.48	3.59
Watermelon	.98	3.89
Pocket calculator:		
Add, subtract, multiply, divide	34.95	4.96
Reciprocals, squares, square roots	89.95	9.96
19.9 cubic foot refrigerator-freezer		
with ice maker	499	679
Small room air conditioner	134	199
Bahamas Trip (per person,		
double occupancy):		
5 days, from West Palm Beach	89	
4 days from Atlanta		359

demand curves have shifted to the right or left? What was the effect of each shift on equilibrium price and quantity?

The remainder of this chapter will consider the consequences of government intervention in markets, particularly with respect to the effect of government intervention on the existence of surpluses and shortages.

1. **Perfect competition does *not* depend on:**
   a. A large number of buyers and sellers.
   b. Information about market conditions.
   c. Distinguishing characteristics of the product.
   d. Ease of movement among markets.
   e. Small size of firms relative to size of the market.

2. **For most goods and services:**
   a. Quantity demanded is low at low prices.
   b. Quantity demanded is high at high prices.
   c. Demand is based on costs of production.
   d. Quantity demanded is inversely related to price.
   e. Quantity demanded is directly related to price.

3. **Which of the following is not an example of a change in supply?**
   a. Improved technology of sound reproduction reduces the equilibrium price of recordings.
   b. A rising price for natural gas encourages existing firms to produce more.
   c. Cereal manufacturers shift from producing corn flakes to producing oat bran.
   d. Foreign car manufacturers sell their products in the United States.
   e. Competition from Brazilian farmers causes U.S. farmers to stop producing soybeans.

4. **Which of the following is an example of a change in quantity demanded?**
   a. Consumer tastes shift away from Kentucky Fried Chicken and toward Mexican dinners.
   b. All consumers who want CB radios already have them.
   c. A major discount firm conducts a "One-Third Off Sale."
   d. High gasoline prices reduce automobile sales.
   e. Unemployed auto workers must reduce their living standards.

5. **Which of the following is not true of market equilibrium?**
   a. The price "clears the market."
   b. Everyone who wants the product can buy it.
   c. There is no surplus or shortage.
   d. Price is high enough to satisfy those who supply the equilibrium quantity.
   e. Quantity supplied is equal to quantity demanded.

6. **Which of the following pairs does not belong with the others?**
   a. Paper and pen.
   b. Turkey and liverwurst.
   c. Hammer and nails.
   d. Bread and jam.
   e. Shoes and stockings.

Theory in Practice

PRICE CEILINGS AND PRICE FLOORS

We have seen how the laws of demand and supply work to allocate scarce resources among alternative uses. The individual decisions of consumers and producers combine to answer the question: What is to be produced, how much, and at what price?

In the real world, most markets are not entirely free to operate in precisely the way we have described. Our economic system is actually a mixed system: primarily a free market system, but with some elements of command and even some tradition. Our government intervenes in the market in a number of ways to establish the prices and quantities of particular goods and services.

One reason government fixes prices involves changes in demand or supply that yield abnormally high or low prices for certain goods or services. Abnormally high prices may unfairly reward and punish particular groups in our society. To avoid abnormally high prices, government may set a **price ceiling** above which market price may not rise. Abnormally low prices unfairly punish other groups. To avoid abnormally low prices, government may set a **price floor**, below which prices may not fall. In both cases, government fixes prices at a level that satisfies voters' view of fairness, or equity, in the distribution of goods and services.

A disadvantage of price ceilings and price floors is that they prevent markets from moving to equilibrium. They tend to cause surpluses and shortages to linger longer than when the market is allowed to push prices up or down.

To illustrate the problem, we will consider government price fixing in the markets for natural gas and farm commodities.

Price Ceilings for Natural Gas

More than 30 years ago, the United States government became concerned about conditions in the market for natural gas produced in the southcentral United States. Increasing demand for natural gas had caused the market demand curve to shift to the right; increasing production costs had caused the supply curve to shift to the left. The result was rising prices, with worsening hardships for households and industrial users of this clean fuel. A price ceiling was put in place to hold the price of all natural gas traded in interstate markets to $.50 per thousand cubic feet.

The market for natural gas is shown in Figure 2.8. According to Figure 2.8 the equilibrium price that clears the market is $1.50 per 1000 cubic feet. Price was not allowed to rise above the $.50 ceiling, however. At the artificially low price, consumers and business firms wanted to buy larger quantities of natural gas to heat their homes and to operate manufacturing processes. Quantity demanded

Figure 2.8   The Market for Natural Gas.

A price ceiling creates a shortage of natural gas.

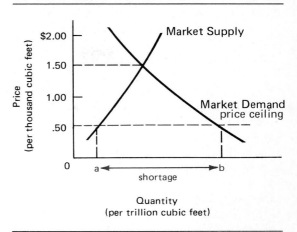

at the low ceiling price remained as high as *0b*. Meanwhile, at the artificially low price producers of natural gas were willing to supply only the quantity shown at *0a*. With a government-imposed price ceiling, the market could not move toward equilibrium, and there was a shortage of natural gas. The shortage is shown on Figure 2.8 as *ab*, the difference between quantity demanded (*0b*) and quantity supplied (*0a*).

Some Americans grew accustomed to a cheap supply of natural gas and used it wastefully. Others could not buy any natural gas at all and turned to other fuels, increasing the demand for other energy resources and causing their prices to rise as well. With fewer producers in the market for natural gas, the country faced a potential crisis of supply. The result of price ceilings can be disastrous shortages!

TEST YOURSELF
Are natural gas and other fuels substitutes or complements?

When government fixes prices below the equilibrium level, the smaller quantity supplied must often be rationed among the large numbers of would-be buyers. Rationing requires a large bureaucracy and raises questions regarding fairness of distribution.

In 1978 Congress and President Carter decided to work toward removal of the ceiling price on natural gas. Immediate removal would have sharply raised prices for many consumer and industrial users of gas. It would have transferred large amounts of purchasing power from consumers of natural gas to owners of existing supplies. The final decision was to raise the ceiling price by some amount each year until by 1985 the ceiling was removed completely. Rising prices were expected to encourage producers of natural gas to supply more and consumers to demand less until finally quantity supplied would be equal to quantity demanded.

Price Floors for Farm Commodities

Fifty years ago in the Great Depression of the 1930s American farmers were suffering severe hardships because of the sharp drop in farm prices. New scientific techniques and advanced agricultural equipment had increased food production faster than the American public wanted to buy. As a result, supply curves for farm commodities had shifted to the right faster than the rightward shift of demand, and farm prices and incomes had fallen.

The voting power of the farming sector was strong. In response to farmers' demands, Congress passed laws setting price floors for certain farm commodities including corn, wheat, rice, cotton, tobacco, and peanuts.

The market for corn is shown in Figure 2.9. According to Figure 2.9 the market equilibrium price is $2.00 per bushel, but price was not allowed to fall below the government-supported price of $4.00. At the artificially high

Figure 2.9   The Market for Corn.

A price floor creates a surplus of corn.

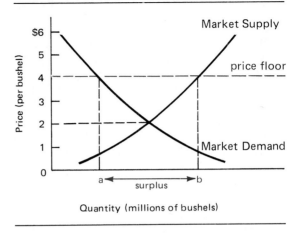

Quantity (millions of bushels)

price consumers wanted to buy less corn for cooking; ranchers wanted to buy less corn for livestock feed. At the artificially high price quantity demanded was only 0a at a price of $4.00, but farmers were willing to supply as much as 0b. In fact, many farmers converted their fields from other crops to produce even more corn. The result of the government-supported price was a surplus of corn, shown on Figure 2.9 as ab, the difference between quantity supplied and quantity demanded.

U.S. farmers grew accustomed to government-supported prices for their grains. They continued to expand output or, at least, failed to cut production or to leave farming for occupations that would earn sufficient income at free market prices. The U.S. government made crop loans to farmers based on the artificially high support price. Farmers who were unable to sell their grain at that price defaulted on their loans and turned their crops over to the government. The result of a price floor can be embarrassing surpluses!

For many years, surplus farm products were acquired and stored by the government at great expense to taxpayers. However, surpluses were used up during war years and in years when crop failures brought on famine in other nations. By the mid-1970s, surplus stocks of grain in the United States had practically disappeared.

Grain stocks began to increase again late in the 1970s. Farmers had taken advantage of rising worldwide demand to expand production significantly. Many farmers borrowed from banks to purchase high-priced land and equipment. When grain prices failed to keep up with their rising costs, many farmers defaulted on their bank loans, and some lost their farms. There was much unrest, and a farmers' strike was threatened.

Farm legislation expires every five years, and Congress decides on a new policy appropriate to current conditions. Recent farm legislation has had as its objective to stabilize farm incomes while interfering as little as possible with markets for farm products. Today's farm legislation sets **target prices**, prices that are designed to be just below equilibrium prices in normal crop years and to cover farmers' basic costs of seed, fertilizer, labor, and machinery. In years of high demand relative to supply, farmers can sell their grain in free markets at the market equilibrium price. In years of low demand relative to supply, price tends to fall below the target price; then government pays farmers the difference between the low market price and the target price. Government payments allow farmers to stay in business while enabling consumers to continue to enjoy low food prices at the supermarket.

A second part of the current farm law is aimed at stabilizing the supply of farm commodities. Under the **set aside** provision of the law, farmers are asked not to cultivate a portion of their land when particular crops are expected to be in surplus. A food grain reserve purchases surplus grain in years of plenty for resale in years of shortage.

Has Government Price Fixing Been a Blessing or a Curse?

Certainly government intervention in these markets originated with the best intentions. Our political system helps ensure that government policies reflect the wishes of voters. Often, however, price ceilings and price floors have benefited particular groups of voters while at the same time reducing efficiency for the economy as a whole.

Look again at the market for natural gas in Figure 2.8. A higher free-market price for gas would have discouraged nonessential uses and conserved our nation's supplies of this valuable resource. Moreover, the higher price would have encouraged new and existing firms to seek out and develop new sources of natural gas. An increase in supply would have helped bring prices down in the future. The result of free market pricing might have been a more balanced use of all available fuel in American homes and business firms.

In the farming sector, lower free-market prices for farm commodities would have meant temporary hardships for some farmers. Some would have left farming to seek better jobs in manufacturing firms. With fewer farmers in the market, the supply of farm commodities would have shifted to the left. Prices would have risen until finally the remaining farmers were earning enough income from their crops to pay the full costs of farming.

Most economists believe that free-market prices help ensure technical and allocative efficiency in the use of our scarce resources: that is, production of the largest quantities of what we want with the smallest quantities of land, labor, capital, and entrepreneurship. Free-market prices avoid the shortages and surpluses associated with price ceilings and price floors. Occasionally, government may need to intervene in certain markets to ease temporary hardships for particular groups. Over the long run, however, the free market generally provides a better answer to the question What?

Government price fixing can have other side effects. Artificially low prices can encourage excessive use of a commodity. Throughout most of the 1970s the price of crude oil produced in the United States was controlled by a low ceiling price. The price ceiling made gasoline cheap to American drivers and encouraged the use of private automobiles. In addition, the price of parking in downtown areas is often held below equilibrium by downtown department stores, and the cost of building highways is often paid by the federal government at low cost to local taxpayers. Artificially low prices for all these complementary goods and services have contributed to the rise of automobile traffic in the United States.

Remember that the opportunity cost of using land as a parking lot or highway is the other things for which the land could have been used: department stores, restaurants, factories, homes, parks, and so forth. It is perhaps correct to say that the artificially low price for gasoline cost us the opportunity to use land for homes, businesses, and recreational areas.

SUMMARY

1. Adam Smith developed the body of theory that explains economic activity in competition. When markets are free and competitive, the economy will achieve the greatest possible output from its scarce resources.
2. Perfect competition requires many small buyers and sellers, perfect knowledge of market conditions, ease of mobility to favored locations, and products that are identical.
3. The free market system is based on the preferences of consumers who evaluate the usefulness of goods and services. The result is many consumer demand schedules that are added together to form market demand. Demand curves slope downward because larger quantities are bought only at lower prices.
4. Changes in income, tastes, number of buyers, prices of related goods, and expectations of price changes cause changes in market demand.
5. The quantities of a good or service that a business firm would offer for sale at various prices constitute the firm's supply schedule. Adding together the supply curves of all firms in a market yields market supply. Supply curves slope upward because larger quantities will be supplied only at higher prices.
6. Changes in the number of firms in the industry, the costs of resources used in the industry, the state of technology, related prices, and price expectations cause supply curves to shift to the right or left.
7. Market equilibrium is the price at which the quantity demanded by consumers is just equal to the quantity supplied by producers. At prices higher than the equilibrium price, quantity supplied is greater than quantity demanded, and there is a surplus. At prices lower than the equilibrium price quantity demanded is greater than quantity supplied, and there is a shortage.
8. Government may intervene in free markets to ease temporary hardships created by shifts in demand or supply. It may establish a price ceiling or price floor when market price is believed to be too high or too low. A price ceiling is likely to cause a shortage; a price floor, a surplus.

TERMS TO REMEMBER

microeconomics: the study of how individual economic units help answer the questions What? How? and For whom?

market demand: the quantities all consumers would buy at various prices

demand schedule: the quantities a particular consumer is willing and able to buy at various prices

the law of demand: the relationship between price and quantity demanded is inverse; that is, as price increases, quantity demanded decreases, and as price decreases, quantity demanded increases

change in demand: a shift in a demand curve in response to a change in some factor other than price

change in quantity demanded: a movement along a demand curve in response to a change in price

substitute goods: goods that can easily be used in place of one another (hamburger or pizza); as the price of one good changes, demand for the substitute changes in the same direction

complementary goods: goods that are normally used together (beer and pretzels); as the price of one good changes, demand for the complementary good changes in the opposite direction

supply schedule: the quantities a particular firm is willing to supply at various prices

market supply: the quantities all firms would supply at various prices

quantity supplied: the quantity that would be supplied at a particular price

market equilibrium: the point on the demand and supply curves at which quantity supplied is equal to quantity demanded

surplus: the difference between quantity supplied and quantity demanded when price is above the equilibrium price

shortage: the difference between quantity demanded and quantity supplied when price is below the equilibrium price

price ceiling: a price set by government, above which market price is not allowed to rise

price floor: a price set by government, below which market price is not allowed to fall

TOPICS FOR DISCUSSION

1. Which of the following markets are likely to be most competitive? Explain your answer.

Barber shops	Hair stylists
T-shirts	Alligator shirts
Electric power	Concrete

2. What are the characteristics of a competitive market? Which characteristics are present or absent in each of the following markets: personal computers, weight machines, avocados, home-delivered milk?

3. Explain why it is important to draw a demand curve for a particular period of time. Then explain how demand curves are likely to change as the period of time lengthens.

4. List substitutes and complements for each of the following: movies, motorcycles, gold chains, wallpaper.

5. Demonstrate graphically the effect of high gasoline prices on demand curves in markets for other goods and services.

6. A certain auto manufacturer reduced the price of its compact model because of a bad safety record, but still sales fell. Does this result contradict the law of demand? Explain.

7. During a period of rising food prices, I went to the supermarket for a head of lettuce. The lettuce bin was not sporting its customary price sign. Because lettuce prices had been fluctuating between 69 and 99 cents, I asked the produce manager what the price was that day. He whispered the answer: 69 cents. Of course, I took advantage of the low price to buy several heads. Then the produce manager explained the reason he hadn't put a sign over the bin.

   "If I put out a sign saying '69 cents' I'd be all out of lettuce before noon," he said. "If I had plenty and the price was 99 cents, I'd put out a big sign. But this way I can save what I've got and make it last all day."

   Was this grocer using the price system to allocate a scarce commodity among his customers? Why do you think he acted the way he did? Can you suggest a better approach to his problem?

8. Consumer boycotts are occasionally used to protest high food prices. An effective boycott can be shown as a backward shift of the demand curve. Our understanding of free markets should give us some clues as to the reaction of suppliers to lower demand (and lower prices). How do you think a boycott will affect food prices after several months, during which farmers have had time to adjust to the new conditions? How will the "invisible hand" change farm output? Show your answer graphically.

9. Changing life-styles and the changing age mix of the U.S. population have brought on an increase in wine sales. As a result, prices have risen from 25 to 200 percent (depending on the quality of the wine). California vintners have expanded cultivation of grapes, and wine lovers hope that prices will soon stabilize.

   Comment on the information given above. Use a series of graphs to illustrate changes in consumer demand and equilibrium price. Then show how producers are adjusting to changes in market conditions.

10. Some local governments in the United States have imposed rent controls on city apartments. Discuss the purpose of this kind of price ceiling and list as many consequences as you can.

11. National concerns regarding the harmful effects of alcohol consumption are contributing to a shift in demand curves. Describe the consequences for equilibrium prices, total expenditures for alcoholic beverages, and resource allocation. How would a famous eighteenth century economist have described these changes?

ANSWERS TO TEST YOURSELF

(p. 30)   Other sellers, information about prices, buyer's ability to walk down the street, and identical canaries. In perfect competition, the prices would be equal.

(p. 31)   Total revenue is price times quantity. The area of a rectangle is height times base. A rectangle formed under the demand curve has price for its height and quantity for its base. Therefore, the area of the rectangle = height × base = price × quantity = total expenditure or total revenue.

(p. 34)   A change in quantity demanded.

(p. 34)   A shift to the left.

(p. 36)   A change in supply.

(p. 43)   Substitutes.

More about Demand: Price Elasticity

or "It Costs How Much?"

Tools for Study

LEARNING OBJECTIVES

After reading this chapter, you will be able to:

1. Explain the differences in consumers' responsiveness to price changes for particular goods or services.
2. Describe different kinds of demand curves in terms of their responsiveness to price changes.
3. Explain how consumers' responsiveness affects a firm's total revenue from sales.
4. Describe the basis for price discrimination.

CURRENT ISSUES FOR DISCUSSION

What difference does price elasticity make: to consumers? to business firms? to government?

Most people are interested in prices. One of the first things we learn to say when studying a foreign language is "What is the price?" We want to have the things we want at the lowest possible price.

Prices are often confusing, however. Even when price is clearly stated, the basis for the price may not be obvious. For example, it is not obvious why air fares between the same two cities are different for different passengers or at different times of the day or week. It is not obvious why a textbook should cost more than a popular novel!

In Chapter 2 we constructed a basic market model of supply and demand. We saw how the interaction between demand and supply determines the equilibrium market price. The **equilibrium price** is the price at which the quantity offered for sale is just equal to the quantity consumers want to buy. Thus, there is no surplus or shortage.

In this chapter we will look more closely at demand and the factors that influence demand curves. We will show how the shapes of demand curves differ and how their differences affect the seller's total revenue from sales. Finally, we will see that achieving the maximum possible revenue from sales requires a particular pricing policy. Then we will be able to clear up some of the confusion regarding air fares and textbook prices!

PRICE ELASTICITY OF DEMAND

In chapter 2 we saw that the positions of demand curves differ according to incomes and numbers of buyers, consumer tastes, prices of

Viewpoint

DEMAND ELASTICITY IN THE MARKET FOR PETROLEUM

Price elasticity of demand measures the percentage change in quantity demanded associated with a percentage change in price. Demand elasticity for some goods depends strongly on the physical circumstances necessary for consuming it; that is, the buildings and equipment or the social arrangements surrounding the goods' use. Physical surroundings change slowly, with the result that quantity demanded responds slowly to price changes.

Consider the response of U.S. consumers to changes in the price of energy. The 1973 OPEC oil embargo raised the price of a barrel of crude oil from $2.50 to $12.50. Most Americans continued to drive their automobiles, heat and cool their homes and office buildings, and purchase petroleum-based plastic products and synthetic materials. (Given their existing stock of equipment and existing social arrange-

ments, they had no other choice.) Quantity demanded remained high, and the total cost of imported petroleum and petroleum products rose from $8.4 billion in 1973 to $26.6 billion in 1974. As a fraction of the U.S. total import bill, purchases of petroleum increased from 12 to 26 percent.

For several years the cost of imported petroleum increased at an average rate of more than 12 percent a year. Not only were short-range demand curves for petroleum relatively inelastic, but fairly strong economic growth was causing demand curves to shift to the right. Then in 1979, the price of petroleum increased again to almost $30 a barrel. The U.S. import bill leaped by 43 percent, and prices of goods and services related to petroleum (almost everything is!) rose sharply, too. In 1980 the nation suffered a recession, and growth was slow until 1982, when a new

related goods, and expected future prices. The shapes of demand curves differ also. The shape of a demand curve reflects price elasticity of demand.

Price elasticity of demand may be reflected in the slope of the demand curve. Because the usefulness of some goods diminishes quickly, their demand curves slope downward rather sharply as we acquire more units during a particular period of time. Salt is an example of a good of which the first unit bought is useful, even essential. Further purchases in any one time period, however, could become a nuisance. Consumers would not buy much more

salt even if price should fall drastically, and they would not buy much less if price should rise.

Economists describe demand for such goods as **price inelastic:** They mean that quantity demanded is not very responsive to price changes. Necessities with few substitutes generally have relatively inelastic demand. These are items that we must buy in some certain quantity, but we have little use for more than that quantity.

Demand for certain other goods is **price elastic:** For these goods, quantity demanded is quite responsive to price changes. Luxuries

recession took hold that became the most severe (in terms of unemployment) since the Great Depression of the 1930s.

By 1983, a decade of high petroleum prices had forced changes in many physical facilities and in social arrangements involving the consumption of petroleum. The most noticeable was a shift in buying habits from large, gas-guzzling "luxury" automobiles to smaller, more fuel-efficient compact cars. Another was a change in building construction to use natural sources of heat, light and shade more effectively. Finally, many U.S. families moved closer to their places of work or school, and some organized carpools.

Business firms also made changes in response to high petroleum prices. Many firms re-organized their production processes to improve efficiency. Some eliminated product lines that consumed large amounts of energy, and some went out of business.

How have all these developments affected price elasticity of demand for petroleum and petroleum-based products? From relatively price inelastic demand in 1973, demand curves for petroleum gradually became more elastic. New physical facilities and social arrangements became more flexible, so that consumers could vary quantities of petroleum used as the price of petroleum changes. By 1990, however, more plentiful supplies and lower prices for petroleum were encouraging increased consumption, and some consumers were returning to the wasteful ways of the early 1970s. The threat of renewed hostilities in the Middle East raised fears of a new oil crisis.

and goods with many substitutes often have relatively elastic demand. Consumers can decide to buy or not depending on price.

Can you think of examples of goods or services with elastic and inelastic demand? How do you think consumers respond to changes in the price of dental care, meat, doughnuts, airline tickets, wallpaper, and gasoline? (As is often true in economics, an acceptable answer is "it depends.")

Price elasticity of demand affects consumers' total expenditure for a good. If market demand is relatively price elastic, consumers respond significantly to price changes. Thus,

with elastic demand a price increase causes a greater decrease in sales, and total expenditure falls. On the other hand, a price reduction causes a greater increase in sales, and total expenditure increases. Henry Ford discovered this result in the early days of the automobile industry. Ford found he could increase his firm's total revenue from sales by reducing the price of his autos. (Can you explain this result in terms of price elasticity of demand?)

If market demand is price inelastic, consumers do not respond very much to price changes. They buy roughly the same quantities regardless of price. In this case, a price increase does not cause sales to fall very much, so that total expenditure increases. On the other hand, a price decrease does not cause sales to increase very much, so that total expenditure falls. OPEC oil-producing nations understand price elasticity of demand quite well. During the 1970s they discovered they could increase their countries' total revenue from oil sales by increasing oil prices. (Explain this result in terms of price elasticity of demand.)

What Determines Price Elasticity of Demand?

Price elasticity of demand depends on these three characteristics:

1. The availability of substitutes.
2. The importance of the item in the consumer's budget.
3. The time it takes to develop or discover a substitute.

When there are many substitutes, consumers can change buying plans freely. A small increase in the price of a good causes a large decrease in quantity demanded, as consumers substitute similar but lower-priced goods. Likewise, a small decrease in price causes a large increase in quantity demanded, as consumers purchase the cheaper good rather than its higher-priced substitutes. For these reasons, goods with many substitutes generally have price elastic demand. Essential goods with no substitutes have price inelastic demand.

When purchasing a particular good requires a relatively large part of a consumer's budget, quantity demanded responds significantly to a change in price. In contrast, if the good is a small item in a consumer's budget or if its price is very low, consumers do not

change their buying plans very much. Hence, a large item generally has elastic demand, and a small item, inelastic demand.

Finally, demand is generally more price elastic over longer periods of time. Over time, consumers can find substitutes to take the place of goods whose prices have risen, and they can find new ways to use goods whose prices have fallen. After years of struggling to adjust to higher gasoline prices during the 1970s, U.S. consumers finally cut their purchases of gasoline in the 1980s. Many consumers turned to public transportation, and their demand curves for gasoline became more price elastic. (Consumers faced a different sort of budget crisis in the mid-1980s when a bad crop year pushed up the price of peanut butter. For peanut butter lovers who refuse to accept substitutes, demand curves will remain price inelastic for a very long time!)

Different consumers may have different price elasticities of demand for the same good. A particular consumer's price elasticity of demand depends on whether he or she considers the good essential (few substitutes) and how important the good is in the consumer's own budget.

CALCULATING PRICE ELASTICITY OF DEMAND

Business firms devote much effort to estimating price elasticity of demand for their products. Consumers' responsiveness to price has a lot to do with total expenditure for a good and, ultimately, a firm's total revenue from sales.

We measure price elasticity of demand as the percentage change in quantity demanded relative to the percentage change in price; $\%\Delta Q_d / \%\Delta p$.* If $\%\Delta Q_d$ is greater than $\%\Delta p$,

*The symbol Δ (Greek Delta) is used to denote "change in."

How Things Have Changed . . .

AVERAGE ANNUAL INCOME AND EXPENDITURES, 1986

	All Families	Under Age 25	Between Ages 45 and 54
Income before taxes	$25,481	$12,445	$33,447
Food	3,363	2,026	4,439
Alcoholic beverages	273	335	325
Housing: Shelter	3,986	2,654	4,966
Fuel, utilities, and public services	1,646	795	2,050
Household appliances and furniture	1,256	672	1,432
Apparel and service	1,149	871	1,581
Vehicles	2,340	1,675	3,405
Gas and motor oil	916	655	1,219
Other transportation	1,559	1,006	2,214
Health care	1,062	336	1,172
Life insurance	293	63	444
Retirement, pension, social security	1,836	777	2,918
Other	3,031	1,897	4,412
Personal taxes	2,290	919	3,360

Statistical Abstract of the United States, 1989.

Figure 3.1a   Elastic Demand.

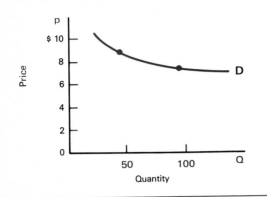

Figure 3.1b   Inelastic Demand.

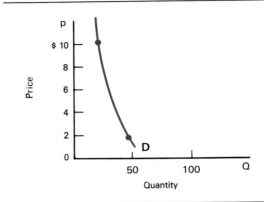

we say that demand is price elastic; consumers respond significantly to price change. If $\%\Delta Q_d$ is less than $\%\Delta p$, we say demand is price inelastic; consumers respond only slightly to price change. If $\%\Delta Q_d$ is precisely equal to $\%\Delta p$, we say that price elasticity of demand is unity, or one.

Differences in price elasticity are sometimes reflected in the shapes of demand curves. Look at Figure 3.1a. In Figure 3.1a a small percentage change in price (from $9.00 to $8.00) causes quantity demanded to change by one-half. Demand is relatively price elastic over this range of the demand curve, and the curve is relatively flat. Now look at Figure 3.1b. In Figure 3.1b a large percentage change in price (from $10.00 to $1.00) causes quantity demanded to change only slightly. Demand is relatively price inelastic over this range, and the curve is relatively steep.*

In some markets quantity demanded responds in extreme ways to price changes. This

is true of the demand curves in Figures 3.2a and 3.2b, which are described as infinitely price elastic and perfectly price inelastic, respectively.

Most demand curves reflect different price elasticities at different price levels. Look at Figure 3.3. The demand curve in Figure 3.3 is called a **linear demand curve** because its slope is constant over its entire length. Along any small segment of the curve, price elasticity of demand is computed according to the following ratio:

e_d = percentage change in quantity
demanded/percentage change in price
= $\%\Delta Q_d / \%\Delta p$

Notice that both numerator and denominator of the elasticity ratio are in percentage terms. To calculate a percentage change it is necessary first to measure the actual change and then compare the actual change with a total, or base, value. Because the base value changes with movement along the demand curve, it is appropriate to use as a base the average of the two values before and after the change. Thus, a price reduction from $500 to $400 represents an actual change of $(p_1 - p_2)$ = $500 - $400 = $100. In percentage terms a $100 price reduction is

*The slope of a demand curve does not always reflect price elasticity of demand. In fact, the slope of a demand curve depends also on the horizontal scale of the graph. Can you demonstrate how changing the horizontal scale can change the slope of a demand curve?

Figure 3.2a   Infinitely Elastic Demand.

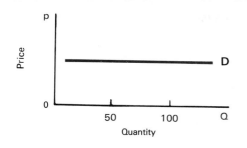

Figure 3.2b   Perfectly Inelastic Demand.

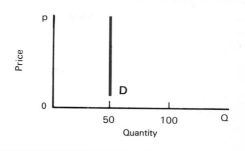

$$\%\Delta p = (p_1 - p_2)/[\tfrac{1}{2}(p_1 + p_2)]$$
$$= (500 - 400)/[\tfrac{1}{2}(500 + 400)]$$
$$= 100/450 = 0.22 = 22 \text{ percent}$$

Thus, $\%\Delta p = 22$ percent. Again from Figure 3.3, a price reduction of \$100 causes quantity demanded to increase from zero to 100 units. In percentage terms the change in quantity is

$$\%\Delta Q_d = (Q_1 - Q_2)/[\tfrac{1}{2}(Q_1 + Q_2)]$$
$$= (0 - 100)/[\tfrac{1}{2}(0 + 100)]$$
$$= -100/50 = -2.00 = -200 \text{ percent}$$

Thus, $\%\Delta Q_d = -200$ percent.

Figure 3.3   Computing Price Elasticity of Demand.

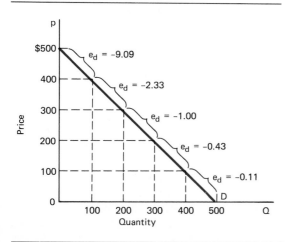

With $\%\Delta p = 22$ percent and $\%\Delta Q_d = -200$ percent, price elasticity of demand along this segment of the demand curve is

$$e_d = \%\Delta Q_d/\%\Delta p = -200/22 = -9.09$$

This value has been written alongside the linear demand curve in Figure 3.3.

Other price elasticity computations were performed similarly and the results added to the figure. (We performed the computations as if price is to be reduced and quantity increased, but the results would be the same if we reversed the direction of price and quantity.)

Notice that all the values for price elasticity of demand have a negative sign. Price elasticity of demand is almost always negative, because price reductions almost always cause quantity demanded to increase. Likewise, price increases almost always cause quantity demanded to fall. The result is that the numerator and denominator of the elasticity ratio will almost always have opposite signs, making the ratio negative. In general, the sign of the elasticity ratio is less important to business planners than its magnitude, so we will generally omit the minus sign and just remember that price elasticity of demand is almost always negative.

Notice also that price elasticity of demand varies along the linear demand curve from a high value at high prices (where demand is price elastic) to a low value at low prices (where demand is price inelastic). Along one very small segment of a linear demand curve price elasticity of demand is precisely equal to one. That is, percentage change in quantity demanded is precisely equal to percentage change in price, and price elasticity of demand is unity.

Variations in price elasticity of demand affect consumers' total expenditures and business firms' total revenue from sales. The demand curve in Figure 3.3 has been reproduced as Figure 3.4a to illustrate the effect on total revenue of price changes when elasticity varies along the curve. Figure 3.4b shows total revenue at combinations of price and quantity taken from the demand curve. The horizontal axis of Figure 3.4b corresponds to that of Figure 3.4a and represents quantity sold at various price levels. The vertical axis represents total revenue, calculated by multiplying price times quantity at various points on the demand curve:

$$\text{total revenue} = TR = p \times Q$$

Look first at the demand curve at a price of $500 where quantity demanded is zero. Then look at a price of $0 where quantity demanded is 500 units. Total revenue associated with both points is zero, plotted accordingly on Figure 3.4b. Now select other points on the demand curve, calculate total revenue, and plot the point: At $p = \$400$, $Q = 100$, and $TR = \$400 \times 100 = \$40,000$; at $p = \$300$, $Q = 200$, and $TR = \$60,000$; at $p = \$200$, $Q = 300$, and $TR = \$60,000$; at $p = \$100$, $Q = 400$, and $TR = \$40,000$.

Note carefully the shape of the total revenue curve in Figure 3.4b. The total revenue curve in Figure 3.4b is typical of TR curves associated with linear demand curves. All such TR curves have maximum total revenue in the midrange of price and quantity and declining total revenue, outside that range. Compare the TR curve with the values for price elasticity of demand shown on Figure 3.3 and note that maximum total revenue occurs when price elasticity of demand is equal to one: $e_d = 1$. Along the corresponding small segment of the demand curve a percentage change in price causes an equal percentage change in quantity demanded, so that total revenue neither rises nor falls.

The result is different along other segments of the demand curve. To see why, begin high on the demand curve where we found price elasticity to be $e_d = 9.09$. With $e_d > 1$,

Figure 3.4a   A Linear Demand Curve.

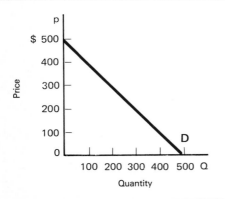

Figure 3.4b   Total Revenue Associated with a Linear Demand Curve.

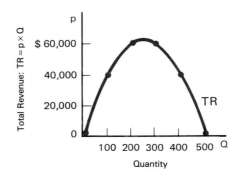

price reductions cause substantially greater percentage increases in quantity demanded, and total revenue increases. Similarly, price increases cause substantially greater decreases in quantity demanded, so that total revenue falls. The behavior of total revenue along this segment of the demand curve reflects the relatively greater responsiveness of quantity demanded to price changes.

Now look at the lower segment of the demand curve where $e_d = 0.11$. Percentage price reductions cause only slight increases in quantity demanded, and total revenue falls. Price increases cause only slight decreases in quantity demanded, and total revenue increases. This time, the behavior of total revenue reflects the relatively smaller responsiveness of quantity demanded to price change.

These results suggest certain conclusions. If a firm has the power to set its own price, it might seek a revenue-maximizing price and quantity at the point on its demand curve where $e_d = 1$. Reducing price to this level causes greater percentage increases in quantity demanded and increases TR. Or, alternatively, raising price to that level causes smaller decreases in quantity demanded and increases TR. Most firms do not have the power to set price, of course. In fact, in this chapter we have assumed that competition exists in the market so that no firm can affect price at all. (We will relax that assumption in Chapter 5.) Moreover, for most firms maximum revenue is not itself an appropriate goal. Firms must consider production costs, too (the subject of Chapter 4), and the profit remaining after all costs are paid. This makes maximum profit a more appropriate goal than maximum revenue. We will have more to say about this concept later.

Self-Check

1. **Consumer A's demand for pizza is relatively price inelastic. This means that A:**
   a. prefers hamburger to pizza.
   b. buys all the pizza she or he could afford.
   c. will not buy pizza if its price increases.
   d. buys roughly the same amount regardless of price.
   e. responds significantly to price changes for pizza.

2. **Most consumers probably have relatively inelastic demand for:**
   a. Oranges.
   b. Gasoline.
   c. College textbooks.
   d. Filet mignon.
   e. Magazines.

3. **Which of the following has no effect on price elasticity of demand:**
   a. The availability of substitutes.
   b. Total expenditure for the good.
   c. The importance of the good in the consumer's budget.
   d. The time required to develop a substitute for the good.
   e. Whether the good is essential or a luxury.

4. **Price elasticity of demand of −0.5 suggests that:**
   a. Decreasing price would cause total revenue to increase.
   b. The item has many substitutes.
   c. Quantity demanded changes by half the percentage change in price.
   d. Percentage change in price is less than percentage change in quantity.
   e. All are correct.

5. **Which of the following is incorrect:**
   a. A linear demand curve has a price elasticity of one.
   b. A horizontal demand curve is infinitely price elastic.
   c. A vertical demand curve is perfectly price inelastic.
   d. Price elasticity may differ at different points on a demand curve.
   e. Equal percentage changes in price and quantity yield a price elasticity of one.

6. **Total revenue from sales:**
   a. Increases as you move down a linear demand curve.
   b. Decreases as you move down a linear demand curve.
   c. Can be represented by a rectangle drawn beneath a demand curve.
   d. Is zero when the price elasticity is one.
   e. None of the above.

PRACTICE WITH PRICING

We have described how a firm's pricing policy affects its total revenue from sales. Competitive firms normally lack the power to set price. However, there are circumstances where a firm can separate its markets and set different prices according to price elasticity of demand in the separate markets. Imagine a clothing retailer who sells in consumer markets in different parts of town. Currently the retailer sells 200 units a day at a unit price of $25, for total revenue of $TR = p \times Q = \$25 \times 200 = \$5000$. However, she suspects that consumers differ in the different neighborhoods with respect to tastes, incomes, por-

tion of income spent for clothing, and willingness to accept substitutes. In fact, consumer demand in one neighborhood might be described as relatively price inelastic: Consumers will continue to buy substantially the same quantities regardless of price, so that price elasticity of demand at a unit price of $25 is only $e_d = 0.5$. Consumer demand in the other neighborhood is more price elastic: Consumers respond significantly to price change, so that price elasticity at a price of $25 is $e_d = 1.5$.

Demand curves representing the two neighborhoods are shown in Figures 3.5a and 3.5b. For simplicity, we have assumed that half of daily sales are currently being made in

Figure 3.5a   Price Discrimination; First Market for Clothing.

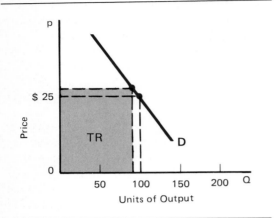

Figure 3.5b   Price Discrimination; Second Market for Clothing.

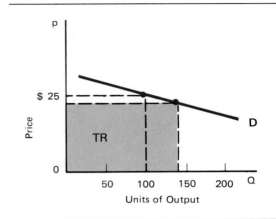

each market at the $25 price, for equal revenues of $2500.

Now let us change the prices in the two neighborhoods and calculate the effect on total revenue. In the first market, price is below the level of maximum total revenue. (We know this because price elasticity of demand is less than one.) With $e_d = 0.5$, increasing price by 10 percent in this market should reduce quantity demanded by only 0.5(10 percent) = 5 percent. Total revenue in this market becomes $TR = p \times Q = 1.10$ ($25) $\times$ 0.95(100) = $2612.50.

In the second market, price is above the level of maximum total revenue. (How do we know this?) With $e_d = 1.5$, reducing price by 10 percent should increase quantity demanded by 1.5(10 percent) = 15 percent. Total revenue in this market becomes $TR = p \times Q = 0.90$($25) $\times$ 1.15(100) = $2587.50.

The shaded rectangles in Figures 3.5a and 3.5b show how total revenue increases when markets are separated and prices are set according to price elasticity of demand. The retailer's new price policy earns total revenue of $2612.50 + $2587.50 = $5200 for an increase

of $200 each day. The decrease in quantity demanded in the first market is less than the increase in the second, so that the retailer's total sales increase to 210 units.

TEST YOURSELF:
What does this example suggest about pricing policies for textbooks versus novels? Explain the difference.

PRICE DISCRIMINATION

Setting different prices for different buyers is known as **price discrimination.** Retailers frequently practice price discrimination, reducing price in markets with relatively elastic demand and increasing price in markets with relatively inelastic demand. In this way they approach the point of maximum total revenue in every market.

There is another form of price discrimination when firms separate consumers even more precisely and set different prices for different segments of a single demand curve. Price differentials of this sort are common for tickets to cultural and sporting events. The basis for separating consumers may be the location of the seats or the age or sex of the consumer!

Many of the nation's airlines have been experimenting with price discrimination as a way to increase total revenue. Throughout the 1980s airlines faced rising costs for labor, fuel, and capital equipment. Revenues did not increase fast enough to pay a satisfactory return on funds invested in the industry. Today many airline firms charge lower fares for passengers who are willing to give up some service. The airlines hope that enough new passengers will buy the lower-priced tickets to offset the lower price each passenger pays.

Figure 3.6 shows a hypothetical demand curve for seats on an airplane. There are 200 seats, and the airline would like to "sell" the seats at prices that will yield the most revenue. Let 50 seats be designated "first class" and provide first-class passengers with plenty of comfortable leg room, champagne and lobster for dinner, and attentive stewards. Some passengers will be willing to pay $100 for first-class service. Designate the remaining seats "tourist class" and serve tourist-class pas-

sengers baked chicken for a price of $75. Total revenue is $TR = \$100 \times$ number of "first-class" passengers (maximum 50) plus $75 $\times$ number of "tourist class" passengers (maximum 150), for maximum revenue of $16,250.

Notice that maximum total revenue is represented by the shaded rectangles under the demand curve in Figure 3.6. Total revenue is price times quantity sold, shown by the height and width of the two rectangles.

Unless all the seats are sold, total revenue will be less than the maximum. In fact, if demand is relatively price inelastic over this price range, only a certain number of tickets will be sold regardless of the difference in ticket prices. In Figure 3.7 only 30 first-class passengers and 100 tourist-class passengers yield total revenue of ($100 $\times$ 30) + ($75 $\times$ 100) = $10,500. Notice the smaller shaded area when only 130 seats are sold.

Consider the situation if demand is relatively price elastic at lower prices. Let the regularly scheduled passengers fly at the stated rates and then open the remaining seats to "no-frills" passengers at a price of only $50. No-frills passengers are unceremoniously dispatched to the rear of the plane and served

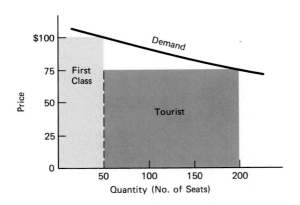

Figure 3.6 Airline Revenues with "First Class" and "Tourist" Fares.

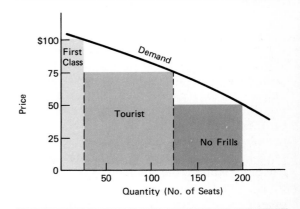

Figure 3.7 Airline Revenues with "First Class," "Tourist," and "No Frills" Fares.

no food or drink at all. If the remaining seats are filled at the lowest rate, revenue increases by $50 × 70 = $3500, for a total of $10,500 + $3500 = $14,000. Unless the firm can fill its planes with first-class and tourist passengers, it would seem to be an advantage to offer no-frills tickets. Total revenue will increase by the added rectangle in Figure 3.7.

The experiment in pricing turned out well for some firms. The results seemed to show that demand for air travel is relatively price inelastic at high prices and price elastic at low prices. Some travelers must purchase tickets regardless of price, but many travelers decided to take a trip just because air fares were reduced. (Why? Remember the factors that determine elasticity.) The airlines were able to fill most of their seats with passengers paying various rates, and total revenue increased.

Experiments with elasticity can be profitable!

PRACTICE DECIDING TAX POLICY

Governments consider price elasticity of demand when they add an excise tax to the price of a consumer good. Generally, the taxed item should have price inelastic demand. Otherwise consumers will not buy at the higher price, and the government will not collect any revenue.

How would you describe price elasticity of demand for cigarettes? Are smokers likely to respond to price changes by buying either substantially more or fewer cigarettes?

Apparently governments believe that the demand for cigarettes is relatively price inelastic. The demand curve in Figure 3.8 is drawn on the assumption that smokers will not respond very much to price changes. At a price of $14 per carton quantity demanded is 4000 cartons. Notice the rectangle representing total expenditure at $14: total expenditure = quantity demanded × market price = 4000 × $14 = $56,000.

Figure 3.8   Hypothetical Demand Curve for Cigarettes.

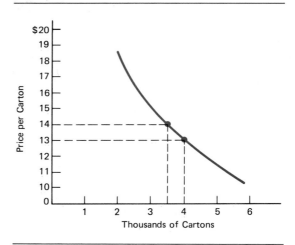

Now suppose government imposes a tax that adds $1 per carton to the price. At the new price of $15, quantity demanded is 3800 cartons. Notice the rectangle representing total expenditure: 3800 × $15 = $57,000. Mark off the rectangle that represents government's tax revenue: tax revenue = quantity demanded × tax = 3800 × $1 = $3800.

With the excise tax, consumer expenditures for cigarettes increase from $56,000 to $57,000, but producers' share of revenue falls. Producers still receive $14 per carton, but they sell only 3800 cartons for revenue of 3800 × $14 = $53,200. Mark off the rectangle representing producers' revenue before the tax and the rectangle representing consumer expenditures after the tax.

TEST YOURSELF
Compare government tax revenue from a cigarette tax with tax revenue from a tax on a good with relatively price elastic demand (like cheese). How might the demand curve for cheese differ from the demand curve for cigarettes? How would you describe the tax-revenue rectangle?

SUMMARY

1. Price elasticity of demand measures the responsiveness of consumers to price changes. It is computed as percentage change in quantity demanded relative to a percentage change in price.
2. Price elasticity of demand depends on the availability of substitutes for the good or service, the importance of the item in the consumer's budget, and the time it takes to develop a substitute.
3. A horizontal demand curve has zero percentage change in price; therefore, its price elasticity of demand is infinite. A vertical demand curve has zero percentage change in quantity; therefore, its price elasticity is zero, or perfectly elastic.
4. On a linear demand curve, price elasticity varies from high (at high prices) to low (at low prices). Maximum total revenue occurs at the price and quantity where $e_d = 1$. A revenue-maximizing firm observes the following rule: If $e_d > 1$, reduce price for greater total revenue; if $e_d < 1$, increase price for greater total revenue.
5. Some firms practice price discrimination in separate markets to take advantage of differences in price elasticity. In markets where price elasticity of demand is less than one, firms increase price to increase total revenue; in markets where price elasticity is greater than one, they reduce price to increase total revenue.
6. Some firms increase total revenue by setting not one single price but a series of prices. Their objective is to collect all (or almost all) of the revenue represented by the area beneath the demand curve.
7. Governments consider price elasticity of demand when imposing a tax. Because demand for cigarettes is relatively price inelastic, cigarettes are often taxed.

TERMS TO REMEMBER

price elasticity of demand: the responsiveness of quantity demanded to changes in the price of a good or service

elastic demand: condition in which percentage change in quantity is greater than percentage change in price

inelastic demand: condition in which percentage change in quantity is less than percentage change in price

total revenue: price times quantity sold; or the sum of all prices times quantities sold at various prices

elasticity ratio: $\%\Delta Q_d / \%\Delta p$

price discrimination: the practice of setting different prices in different markets, generally on the basis of differences in price elasticity of demand

cigarette tax revenue: number of units sold times tax levied on each unit

TOPICS FOR DISCUSSION

1. The data below describe a linear demand curve. Calculate price elasticity of demand at four intervals along the demand curve. Then locate the price at which total revenue would be maximized. Explain your answer.

PRICE	QUANTITY
10	10
8	14
6	18
4	22
2	26

2. What characteristics of each of the following would determine its price elasticity of demand:

    insulin
    automobile tires
    fresh fruit
    house paint
    soft drinks
    a visit to the dentist's office
    vintage wine
    sports cars

3. Explain the basis for the distinctive shape of the total revenue curve associated with any linear demand curve.

4. Make a list of items whose purchase is generally taxed. What economic characteristic do such items share? Illustrate your answer graphically and explain.

5. Old Reliable Air Service reduced its intercity fare from $37.50 to $35.00 and increased ticket sales from 120 to 160 for the week. Compute Reliable's price elasticity of demand. Was the price change a wise move? Explain. Should Reliable continue to reduce price? Why or why not?

6. What circumstances must be true for price discrimination to benefit a retailer? Why?

7. What considerations might affect a city's decision to levy a sales tax? Why might the city decide to exempt food from the tax? Medicine?

8. Compare price elasticity of demand for various kinds of restaurant meals: fast foods, ethnic foods, elegant dining. What steps do restaurants take to affect price elasticity of demand?

ANSWERS TO TEST YOURSELF

(p. 62)   Because textbooks are typically assigned for the course, their demand curves are relatively price inelastic. Price may be set higher than the price of a comparable novel, which consumers can buy or not as they choose.

(p. 64)   If demand for cheese is relatively price elastic, the higher price causes a greater percentage decrease in quantity demanded. The result is lower total expenditures for cheese and lower tax collections for the government.

Chapter

More About Supply: Costs of Production and Price Elasticity of Supply

or The Case of the Invisible Hand

In Chapter 3 we examined demand curves in detail. We described the circumstances that affect the shape and position of demand curves. The circumstances that affect supply curves are also important, particularly for understanding how the invisible hand works.

Remember we described the invisible hand as guiding business firms to produce the things consumers want with the least expenditure of scarce resources. (We called that result *efficient*.) In order to do its job, the invisible hand must have information about costs of production. Costs of production reflect a firm's use of scarce resources and define the price a firm must receive for its product.

As you read this chapter, think about the signals the invisible hand receives from costs of production—and the signals it sends to producing firms.

MARKET SUPPLY

A producer's response to consumer demand is shown by his or her supply schedule. A **supply schedule** shows the quantities of a good or service that would be offered for sale at various prices.

Every firm in the industry may be expected to have a supply schedule that, together with the supply schedules of all other firms, constitutes **market supply.** When a supply schedule is plotted on a graph, the result is a supply curve.

Deriving a Firm's Supply Curve

Understanding economic costs is essential for understanding a firm's supply curve. (Production cannot be carried on for long unless price is high enough to pay the firm's costs of production.) In this section we will look at economic costs in detail.

To begin, we must note that economic costs behave differently according to the time spans in which they occur: the short run or the long run. The **short run** is a period of time in which certain resources are fixed in quantity and quality and cannot be changed. Buildings and equipment are generally considered fixed in the short run. They are fixed, but they can be combined with various quantities of other resources—such as labor, materials, and electric power—to produce a certain quantity of output. The **long run** is a period of time in which no resources are fixed. The quantities of buildings and equipment can be increased or decreased, along with the quantities of labor, materials, and electric power.

In the following sections, we will discuss the behavior of economic costs in the short run.

Economic Costs and Economic Profit

Economic costs comprise the sum of all payments to persons who provide resources for use in production:

Workers must be paid wages or salaries.
Owners of land must be paid rent.
Suppliers of capital must be paid interest.
Entrepreneurs must be paid profit.

To understand economic costs, it is important to distinguish between the necessary profit that must be paid to an entrepreneurial resource and a payment over and above the necessary profit. Some level of profit is necessary to compensate entrepreneurs for assuming the risks of remaining in a particular business. The necessary profit is called **normal profit,** and an extra profit over and above the necessary amount is

what economists call **economic profit.** Because normal profit is a necessary payment to the entrepreneurial resource, it is considered a part of **economic costs.** Thus, when economists talk about costs, they are talking about wages and salaries, rent, interest, and normal profit:

$$\text{economic costs} = \text{wages} + \text{rent} + \text{interest} + \text{normal profit}$$

If a firm's total revenue from sales exceeds its economic costs, we say that the firm has received economic profit:

$$\text{total revenue} - \text{economic costs} = \text{economic profit}$$

Most firms have as an objective to maximize economic profit. Maximum economic profit occurs when the firm follows the profit-maximizing rule:

> To maximize economic profit, a firm must expand production until production and sale of the last unit increases total revenue by just enough to offset the increase in total cost.

Let us illustrate the profit-maximizing rule in more detail.

To begin, we will look more closely at economic costs. Economic costs can be classified in two ways, depending on their behavior as output increases. The two kinds of costs are fixed costs and variable costs. Fixed costs remain the same in the short run, no matter how many units of output are produced. Variable costs are different in that they change as quantity of output changes.

Fixed Costs

Fixed costs are costs that occur only in the short run. Remember that the short run is a period of time in which certain of a firm's resources are fixed—resources like buildings, equipment, and managerial personnel. Buildings and equipment are owned or leased for a particular period of time, and managerial personnel have contracts for work over a particular period. Whether or not the firm produces any output at all during this period of time, the costs of its fixed resources must be paid. Increasing the quantity of output above zero during the short run permits the firm to spread its fixed costs over larger and larger quantities of output. The result is that average fixed cost (or fixed cost for each unit of output) falls.

The concept of fixed cost is illustrated in Figure 4.1, using Metro Music, producer of compact discs, as an example. During the short run Metro Music has fixed resources for which charges of $1000 must be paid, as shown in Figure 4.1a. For any quantity of compact discs produced during this period of time, average or unit fixed cost is AFC = FC/Q, as shown in Figure 4.1b. Average fixed cost is high for small quantities and diminishes for larger quantities of output Q.

Variable Costs
Variable costs are payments for the variable resources that are used along with the firm's existing fixed resources. Examples of variable resources are labor, materials, electric power, and water. Increasing production above zero in the short run requires the firm to purchase additional quantities of variable resources.

Generally, there is some range of production over which additional units of output require proportionally smaller additional quantities of variable resources. The reason has to do with the design of the firm's fixed plant and equipment. Most manufacturing plants are designed so that variable resources can be used more efficiently over a certain range of output. Over this efficient range of production, variable resource requirements per unit of output are low, and average variable cost is low as well. If production is expanded beyond the efficient range of production during the short run, variable resource requirements increase more than proportionally to output, and average variable cost tends to increase.

The typical behavior of average variable cost in the short run is shown in Figure 4.2. Variable cost per unit tends to fall in the short

Figure 4.1a   Fixed Cost.

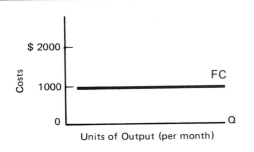

Figure 4.1b   Average Fixed Cost.

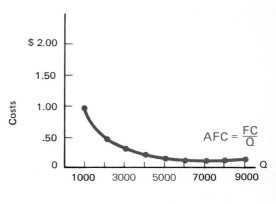

HYPERMARKETS

What's bigger than a supermarket? Would you believe a hypermarket?

About a dozen U.S. cities now have grocery stores as large as eight times ordinary supermarkets—stores so big they could hold almost six football fields. (A typical supermarket would hold only about two-thirds of a football field.)

Such hypermarkets provide customers with tremendous variety in fresh vegetables, meat and seafoods, prepared foods, baked goods, and desserts. They have the disadvantage that they are expensive to build, staff, and stock. To pay their high fixed costs requires a large volume of business: at least 500,000 customers within a 20-minute drive. Most metropolitan areas lack the potential market to make a hypermarket profitable.

To offset its many food items that earn low-unit profits, a hypermarket must stock many items that earn high-unit profits. It must also turn over its low-profit items frequently, so that the large volume of sales creates large total profits.

How would the cost curves of a hypermarket differ from the typical cost curves shown in your text? Why might it profit a hypermarket to have a restaurant, even if the restaurant loses money?

---

run as quantity of output increases and production becomes more efficient. The most efficient, lowest-cost level of production for Metro Music's plant appears to be around 3000 compact discs per month. Variable cost per unit tends to increase as quantity of output increases beyond 3000 units in the short run.

When average fixed cost in Figure 4.1b is added to average variable cost in Figure 4.2, the result is average total cost, shown in Figure 4.3.

Cost Data

The data for drawing Figures 4.1, 4.2 and 4.3 are listed in Table 4.1. Column (2) lists Metro Music's total fixed cost for all levels of output (Q) in the short run. Column (3) shows how

Figure 4.2   Average Variable Cost.

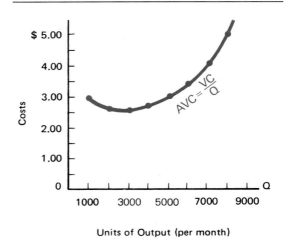

Units of Output (per month)

Figure 4.3   Average Total Cost.

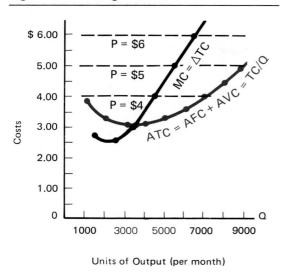

Units of Output (per month)

average fixed cost declines for larger quantities of output shown in Column (1). Column (4) shows total variable cost for various levels of CD production, and Column (5) shows average variable cost $AVC = VC/Q$.

Study the cost data carefully. Notice that average variable cost declines as production increases to 3000 CDs. The design of fixed

plant and equipment makes production most efficient at about 3000 units per month. Beyond production of 3000 CDs production becomes less efficient, and average variable cost rises. Total cost in Column (6) is the sum of Columns (2) and (4).

Average total cost in Column (7) is $ATC = TC/Q$ or $AFC + AVC$. Notice the behavior of average total cost. The decline and eventual rise of ATC is a result of the continuous decline in AFC and the eventual rise in AVC. Average total cost is significant for determining a firm's economic profit (or loss) per unit of output. The difference between selling price and average total cost is average, or unit, economic profit. Thus;

$$p - ATC = \text{average economic profit (or loss)}$$

Marginal Cost

Column (8) in Table 4.1 introduces a new cost concept that is significant for determining supply in the short run: marginal cost. **Marginal cost** is the change in total cost associated with producing a single additional unit of output: $MC = \Delta TC/\Delta Q$. The values in Column (8) are calculated by subtracting successive TC values in Column (6) and dividing by $\Delta Q = 1000$ units from Column (1). Because MC is associ-

Table 4.1   Metro Music's Cost Data.

(1) Q Output per Month	(2) FC Fixed Cost	(3) AFC Average Fixed Cost	(4) VC Variable Cost	(5) AVC Average Variable Cost	(6) TC Total Cost	(7) ATC Average Total Cost	(8) MC Marginal Cost
1000	1000	1.00	2900	2.90	3900	3.90	
2000	1000	.50	5500	2.75	6500	3.25	2.60
3000	1000	.33	8000	2.67	9000	3.00	2.50
4000	1000	.25	11,000	2.75	12,000	3.00	3.00
5000	1000	.20	15,000	3.00	16,000	3.20	4.00
6000	1000	.17	20,000	3.33	21,000	3.50	5.00
7000	1000	.14	26,000	3.71	27,000	3.86	6.00
8000	1000	.125	33,000	4.13	34,000	4.25	7.00
9000	1000	.11	45,000	5.00	46,000	5.11	12.00

ated with changes in quantity, data are entered between the lines in the table.

A marginal cost curve has been added to Figure 4.3. Notice that *MC* declines as the level of production increases from zero to some relatively small quantity. As production approaches the most efficient, lowest-cost quantity of output at $Q = 3000$, *MC* begins to rise. However, until production reaches $Q = 3000$, *MC* is less than *ATC* and pulls *ATC* down. When production expands beyond the most efficient level, *MC* rises above *ATC* and begins to pull *ATC* up.

The behavior of *MC* reflects changes in variable resource requirements associated with production at less than or greater than the most efficient operation of the firm's fixed plant and equipment.

Marginal Revenue and Quantity Supplied

Now we are ready to derive Metro Music's supply curve for compact discs. Remember the profit-maximizing firm's rule for determining supply:

> To maximize economic profit, a firm must expand production until production and sale of the last unit increases total revenue by just enough to offset the increase in total cost.

Marginal cost is important for the supply decision, because marginal cost represents additional cost. Any quantity of output that adds more to revenue than it adds to cost increases Metro Music's economic profit for the month and should be produced. In fact, a profit-maximizing firm like Metro Music should increase production as long as the marginal cost of an additional unit is less than the added revenue it brings in.

We may define a firm's additional revenue from sales as its marginal revenue. **Marginal revenue** is the change in total revenue associated with production and sale of a single additional unit: marginal revenue $= MR =$ $\Delta TR/\Delta Q$. For firms in competition, the additional revenue from increased production is price. This is because in competition price is set by the market, and no firm is large enough to affect price. Understanding this allows us to say:

$$\text{additional revenue} = \text{marginal revenue}$$
$$= \text{price and}$$
$$MR = p$$

Comparing marginal cost with marginal revenue enables Metro Music to make its supply decision. In fact, if $MR > MC$, Metro Music should follow the profit-maximizing rule and increase production. This is because marginal revenue greater than marginal cost indicates that the last unit sold adds more to revenue than it adds to total cost. Therefore, producing the last unit causes the firm's economic profit to increase. On the other hand, if $MR < MC$, Metro Music should follow the profit-maximizing rule and reduce production. Marginal revenue less than marginal cost indicates that the last unit adds less to revenue than it adds to total cost. Therefore, producing the last unit causes the firm's economic profit to fall. Finally, only if $MR = MC$ is Metro Music producing the profit-maximizing quantity of output. Marginal revenue equal to marginal cost indicates that the last unit sold adds just enough revenue to cover its additional cost. This is the profit-maximizing quantity of output.

We can summarize the profit-maximizing conditions this way:

If $MR > MC$, increase production.
If $MR < MC$, reduce production.
If $MR = MC$, continue to produce at this level.

Look again at Figure 4.3 and Metro Music's *MC* curve. Horizontal lines drawn at $4, $5, and $6 indicate possible selling prices for compact discs when they are sold in competitive markets. The profit-maximizing quantity at each price is the quantity shown on the MC curve where $p = MR = MC$. Thus, at a price of $p = \$4$ Metro Music should produce $Q = 4500$ CDs; when $p = \$5$, $Q = 5500$; when $p = \$6$, $Q = 6500$; and so forth. For any other price not indicated by a horizontal line ($p = \$6.50, \$5.75, \$4.25$, etc.) the profit-maximizing quantity may be read from the MC curve.

The Shutdown Point

Reading quantity from the MC curve allows us (almost) to treat MC as Metro Music's short-run supply curve. The reason this is not entirely correct is that certain points on the MC curve would involve unacceptable losses. The firm would shut down rather than increase its losses with every unit of output produced.

To understand this, first consider production of 2500 CDs at a price of $p = \$2.50$. With price less than $ATC = \$3.12$, the firm would experience economic loss of $\$2.50 - \$3.12 = -\$.62$ for each unit produced and sold. Losses may be acceptable in the short run under certain conditions.* The important condition is that price must be high enough to cover average variable cost.

Remember that fixed costs must be paid in the short run, regardless of whether the firm earns economic profit. To produce no output at all would involve short-run losses amounting to the entire fixed costs: $FC = \$1000$. However, production of any quantity of output for which price at least covers AVC might yield some revenue for reducing the loss associated with fixed costs. Therefore, a price of $\$2.50$ is not necessarily unacceptable in the short run. The question is whether $p = \$2.50$ does, in fact, cover Metro Music's average variable cost.

Look at Table 4.1 at about $Q = 2500$ where $MC = \$2.50$. Production of 2500 units

---

* A number of firms experienced short-run losses in the 1980s: Chrysler, Ford, Pan American Airlines.

per month would involve variable cost of between $\$2.67$ and $\$2.72$. This means that in addition to losses of $FC = \$1000$ each month, Metro Music would incur losses of about $\$.20$ for each CD produced, attributable to average variable cost. With price less than average variable cost, production should not be carried on. In fact, the lowest price for which Metro Music should produce CDs in the short run would be $\$2.67$, a price that just covers average variable cost. At a price of $\$2.67$ the firm's entire economic loss would be fixed cost of $FC = \$1000$ per month.

We might identify $p = \$2.67$ as Metro Music's shut down point in the short run. Production will be carried on in the short run only if price is at least as great as $\$2.67$, with the profit-maximizing quantity identified where p crosses the $MC =$ supply curve. Prices greater than $\$3.00$ would enable Metro Music to earn economic profit. Prices between $\$2.67$ and $\$3.00$ would involve economic loss, but short-run losses would not exceed $FC = \$1000$. This allows us to use a portion of Metro Music's MC curve as its supply curve: the portion that lies above Metro Music's minimum acceptable price at its shutdown point.

At the end of Metro Music's short run, for which certain resources are fixed, the firm would want to reevaluate its position in this market. If short-run losses have occurred and are expected to continue, Metro Music should consider discontinuing this operation. Continuing losses would indicate that the firm's resources might be better employed elsewhere. On the other hand, if production has yielded economic profit, Metro Music might want to expand its productive capacity.

Decisions to expand or contract a firm's productive capacity are called **long-run decisions.** Long-run decisions involve increasing or decreasing the firm's fixed resources and depend on the firm's expectations of market conditions in the long run. We will have more to say about long-run decisions later.

The Market Supply Curve

Metro Music's short-run supply curve from Chapter 2 has been drawn again as Figure 4.4. At prices less than $2.67 the firm will produce zero output and suffer losses equal to fixed costs of $1000. At a price of $2.67, the firm will produce and sell 3000 CDs per month. It will produce and sell as many as 5500 CDs if price is at least $5.00.

PRICE ELASTICITY OF SUPPLY

In Chapter 3 we described demand curves in terms of price elasticity of demand. As you might have expected, it is also possible to describe supply curves in terms of price elasticity.

Price elasticity of supply measures the responsiveness of suppliers to changes in the price of a good or service. It is defined as the percentage change in quantity supplied relative to a percentage change in price:

price elasticity of supply $= e_s = \%\Delta Q_s / \%\Delta p$

Figure 4.4 Metro Music's Supply Curve.

Metro Music's supply curve is its marginal cost curve above the shutdown point.

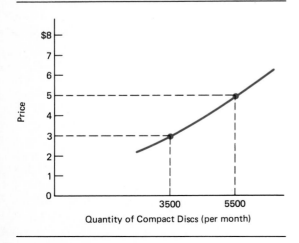

Quantity of Compact Discs (per month)

Because quantity supplied in the short run depends on marginal cost, the responsiveness of suppliers to price changes depends strongly on the behavior of marginal cost. For some goods, marginal cost rises fairly quickly as more units are produced. This means that larger quantities can be offered for sale only if price rises substantially, making suppliers not very responsive to small price changes. In such cases, percentage change in quantity is low relative to percentage change in price. Economists describe supply for such goods as **price inelastic:** quantity supplied is not very responsive to price changes. When supply is price inelastic, supply curves slope upward rather steeply.

For other goods, quantity supplied can be increased with little increase in marginal cost and correspondingly smaller increases in price. Percentage change in quantity supplied is large relative to percentage change in price. When suppliers respond readily to small price changes, supply is said to be **price elastic**. Supply curves slope upward less steeply for price elastic goods.

What Determines Price Elasticity of Supply?

Price elasticity of supply depends on how quickly firms can change output when price changes. We have seen that the responsiveness of suppliers to price depends strongly on marginal cost; that is, the additional cost of increasing production with the fixed resources owned by the firm. Here are some other factors that affect price elasticity of supply:

1. Price elasticity of supply also depends on the time required to increase or decrease fixed resources or to enter or leave the industry. It takes longer to build a steel mill than a fast-food restaurant; therefore, we would expect firms producing fast

How Things Have Changed

COMPOSITE MATERIALS

In just the past 10 years, composite materials have quadrupled their share of the weight of U.S. autos (from less than 2 to 8 percent). Composite materials consist of layers of fibers woven or bonded into sheets of plastic, metal, or ceramics. For years, tennis rackets, golf clubs, and recreational boats have been made of composites. Today, missiles and aircraft—tomorrow bridges and houses. Composites are light and strong, but their high labor costs keep average total cost higher than traditional steel or aluminum. Foreign manufacturers are moving aggressively into research and development of composite materials and threatening the U.S. lead.

foods to respond more readily to price changes than firms producing steel.

2. Price elasticity of supply depends strongly on the storability of the item. A product's storability determines whether it can be stockpiled when price is low and brought to market later when price is higher; therefore, storability determines how quickly firms can change quantity when price changes.

TEST YOURSELF

Consider the following groups of items. How would you describe the responsiveness of supply to changes in price? Ask yourself: Can firms produce much more if price rises or less if price falls? How flexible are production plans of suppliers? Is the product easily storable?

1. Strawberries, milk, eggs, beef.
2. Sweaters, autos, potato chips.
3. Gold, coal, lumber.
4. Transistors, screwdrivers, stained-glass windows.
5. Autos in the 1920s and autos in the 1990s.

Self-Check

1. **Economic costs include all but which one of the following?**
   a. Charges for repairing the firm's truck.
   b. Interest on a loan from the company president's father.
   c. Rent on a warehouse owned by the company president.
   d. A required payment to the entrepreneur who set up the company.
   e. An extra return resulting from abnormally high product prices.

2. **Which of the following statements is correct?**
   a. If $MC > MR$, the firm should expand production.
   b. As long as $MR > MC$, the firm should expand production.
   c. Production should not be carried on if $p < ATC$.
   d. Shutdown will occur if p falls below AFC.
   e. A firm may decide not to pay fixed costs in the short run.

3. **Fixed costs**
   a. Occur only in the long run.
   b. Decrease with quantity of output.
   c. Depend on quantity of output in the short run.
   d. All of the above.
   e. None of the above.

4. **XYZ Pizza Parlor's supply of pizza is price elastic. This probably means:**
   a. It has facilities for producing large quantities.
   b. Supply is responsive to price changes.
   c. It would cut back production significantly if price fell.
   d. Increasing production would not significantly affect unit costs.
   e. All of the above.

5. **Average economic profit, or loss,**
   a. Is equal to $AVC - p$.
   b. Is equal to $p - MC$.
   c. Is the change in profit associated with a unit change in output.
   d. Increases with quantity of output.
   e. Is the difference between price and average total cost.

6. **Maximum profit occurs where $MC = MR$ because**
   a. Additions to total revenue are greater than additions to total cost.
   b. Average total cost is lowest.
   c. Marginal cost is lowest.
   d. Total revenue is greatest.
   e. Additions to total cost are equal to additions to total revenue.

Theory in Practice

PRICE ELASTICITY AND PRICE FIXING

When government sets price ceilings and floors, it is important to consider price elasticity of demand and supply. Recall our two examples of government price fixing: natural gas and farm commodities. How do you think price elasticity has affected markets under price fixing? How would removal of price controls affect markets?

In the market for natural gas, the artificially low price caused buyers to move down their demand curves. They responded to lower prices for natural gas by demanding substantially larger quantities. We would say that demand was relatively price elastic. When demand is price elastic, removal of a price ceiling sharply curtails quantity demanded, limiting sales of natural gas to only the most urgent uses.

TEST YOURSELF
What characteristics of natural gas help make demand relatively price elastic? Refer to the determinants of price elasticity of demand in Chapter 3 if you need help.

Price elasticity of supply is important, too. Price ceilings on natural gas clearly reduced incentives to increase production of this clean, efficient fuel. Will a free market price encourage much greater production? No one really knows for certain how much natural gas remains in underground reservoirs or how much it will cost to get it out. This makes a clear answer impossible. To the extent that convenient sources of natural gas exist, supply will be price elastic, and a free market price will not be substantially above a government-controlled ceiling price. However, as sources become depleted, supply will eventually become less elastic, and price will rise sharply. At the higher price, little additional fuel will be available, and only the most urgent needs will be satisfied.

TEST YOURSELF
Illustrate graphically the market for natural gas under the assumption of relatively elastic demand and inelastic supply. Show the government's price ceiling. Then discuss the consequences of removing the price ceiling.

Price elasticities are different in the markets for farm commodities. Demand for farm products is relatively price inelastic: consumers' response to small price changes is not as great as for natural gas. This is because families must buy food items in roughly constant quantities regardless of price. Artificially high support prices for food do not substantially reduce quantity sold—at least in the immediate period. Nor would lower free market prices increase food purchases very much.

Price elasticity of supply of food varies, depending on the length of time for responding to price change. Over short periods supply is relatively price inelastic. However, modern technology has made supply of farm products relatively price elastic over time periods long enough for grain to ripen, calves to mature, and so forth. An artificially high support price encourages excess production. On the other hand, a small drop in prices from high support levels might reduce farm production sharply. Many farmers would leave the farm for jobs in

industry. The fewer remaining farmers would have to supply our entire food requirements in good years and bad. Widespread crop failures in any one year would make supply curves quite price inelastic and lead to significant price increases.

All these considerations (and more) are involved in government's decision to control prices or to remove controls. The issue of government price fixing is not a simple one.

TEST YOURSELF
Illustrate graphically the market for farm commodities under the assumption of fairly inelastic demand and elastic supply. Show government's support price. Then discuss the consequences of removing price supports.

Price Elasticity of Supply over Time

The prices we pay for the essential things of life depend strongly on supply. The location and shape of supply curves depend on decisions to produce goods and services. Many firms assemble the resources and organize production for the market. They offer goods for sale as long as market price is high enough to cover full costs of production.

Production costs behave differently over the long run. This is particularly true in the home building industry. Today most homes are built by small, privately owned construction firms. For such firms, capacity to increase production is limited in the short run. Increasing production would stretch their managerial staff too thin and require their skilled workers to work overtime; it would overwork capital equipment and make it more subject to breakdowns. As a result, an increase in the market price for housing brings forth little increase in quantity supplied in the short run. With inelastic supply, shifts in demand can bring wide savings in price.

Over a longer time, conditions are likely to be different. If higher prices continue beyond the short run, more firms will enter the housing industry. More new homes can be offered for sale, and prices will not rise as much. We would say that supply is more price elastic over the long run.

What about supply over a very long time? The housing industry is a good example of what can happen to supply curves if there is plenty of time for responding to price changes.

In recent years, wide swings in home prices have brought on major changes in the housing industry. The structure of the industry has been changing from a fragmented industry of many small firms to one of fewer, larger firms. Larger firms can use modern production techniques and equipment for producing more houses at lower costs. For example, a large firm can assemble wall sections and roof panels at a centrally located factory. On an ordinary assembly line, low-skilled workers can nail building sections together according to a standard pattern. Even electric wiring and plumbing can be installed at a central location. Then flatbed trucks can carry the preformed parts to building sites in a particular neighborhood. Only a few skilled workers may be needed to complete the construction. Finally, a large firm can deliver appliances to an entire tract of houses at one time.

Technological development of this sort can make supply curves even more price elas-

Figure 4.5   Hypothetical Supply Curves in the Market for Housing.

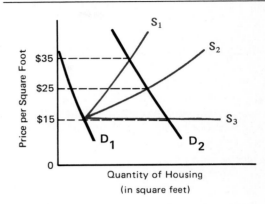

S_1: Supply over a short time period
S_2: Supply over a longer time period
S_3: Supply over a very long time period

tic over the very long run. Figure 4.5 shows a range of hypothetical supply curves for the immediate time period, a longer time period, and a very long time period. Explain the effect on price as the time for adjusting to increased housing demand lengthens.

Could a supply curve ever slope downward to the right? Under what conditions might this occur? (Refer to the section What Determines Price Elasticity of Supply.)

Viewpoint

FINANCING A NEW BUSINESS

Many Americans have as their goal to start their own business. To organize a new business firm requires, first, the acquisition of funds. Funds can be acquired in several ways: by borrowing or by selling stocks and bonds.

Most firms begin by selling stocks and bonds to interested investors. When a firm sells common or preferred stocks, it is essentially selling shares of ownership. Common stockholders understand that, as part owners, they will participate in the fortunes (whether good or bad) of the firm. That is, they will receive a share of economic profit in the form of dividends when times are good. When times are bad, they may receive no dividends at all. They have the right to vote for a board of directors, which selects the firm's managers. They may also sell their shares at any time. If the firm has paid large dividends (or is expected to in the future), stockholders may find the value of their stock increasing. Unfortunately, the reverse is also true.

Whereas holders of common stock

risk the ups and downs of business along with the fortunes of the firm, holders of preferred stock have a more certain prospect. Preferred stockholders are guaranteed a certain dividend, if any dividends are paid at all. However, preferred stockholders are normally not entitled to participate in selecting the firm's managers.

Bonds differ from stocks in that they are essentially loans from investors, with a definite schedule of interest payments and a definite date of maturity when the principal is to be repaid. In general, the assets of the firm are used as collateral (a pledge for the fulfillment of the loan contract). If the firm is very profitable, bondholders will receive no more than the agreed amount. If the firm is not profitable, bondholders must be paid before dividends are paid to preferred or common stockholders. Like stockholders, bondholders may also sell their bonds to other investors before maturity.

A new firm may also acquire funds by borrowing from banks or other financial in-

SUMMARY

1. A firm's supply schedule is based on economic costs, which include all necessary payments to owners of the resources used in production. Economic profit is profit above the necessary normal profit paid to people who supply entrepreneurial ability.

2. Payments to fixed resources must be paid in the short run, regardless of quantity of production; payments to variable resources depend on quantity of production.

3. Quantity supplied can be read from a firm's marginal cost curve, because $MC = MR = p$ defines the profit-maximizing quantity for a firm in competition. The shutdown point occurs where price is equal to average variable cost.

stitutions, subject to the credit policies of particular institutions.

Most new business firms seek a combination of funding through stocks, bonds, and borrowing that satisfies their particular objectives. Bond sales and borrowing have the advantage that interest payments are deductible from the firm's income before taxes are assessed. They have the disadvantage that agreed interest and principal payments must be paid, even if the firm's income is low. Stock sales have the advantage that dividends may or may not be paid, depending on the fortunes of the firm. They have the disadvantage that dividends are paid from income that has already been taxed and are taxed a second time as part of stockholders' income. Another disadvantage of selling stocks is that as more stocks are issued, the share of the firm's income that can be paid to a single stockholder decreases.

In the 1980s a popular way to set up a business was to purchase an existing business through a leveraged buyout

(LBO). **Leverage** refers to borrowed funds. Thus, a LBO was the purchase of a firm's stock using borrowed funds. In general, the assets of the purchased firm were used as collateral for the loan. Interest and principal payments on the loan were made by operating the acquired firm profitably or by selling off some of its assets.

Some LBOs turned out to be very profitable, as the firm's new owners cut costs and operated the firm more efficiently than the previous owners. Some LBOs ran into difficulty when profits or asset sales, produced insufficient funds to make the heavy interest and principal payments on large debt. In 1989 interest payments amounted to more than half the average firm's profits, versus only 2 percent 25 years ago.

Why do you suppose LBOs are feared by managers of many business firms? What are the possible effects on the nation's productivity when business firms face the threat of an LBO?

---

4. Price elasticity of supply measures the responsiveness of producers to price changes and reflects the behavior of marginal costs. Other determinants of price elasticity of supply include the time required to increase fixed resources or to enter or leave the industry, and the storability of the product.
5. Price elasticity of demand and supply influences the range of price and quantity changes when government price controls are removed.

TERMS TO REMEMBER

economic costs: necessary payments to owners of productive resources

normal profit: a necessary payment for the use of entrepreneurial ability

economic profit: a payment greater than normal profit

fixed costs: costs that are constant in the short run regardless of quantity of output

variable costs: costs that vary with quantity of output

marginal cost: the change in total cost associated with a change in quantity of output

marginal revenue: the change in total revenue associated with a change in quantity of output; in competition marginal revenue is the same as price

shutdown point: the point on the marginal cost (supply) curve at which price is equal to average variable cost

price elasticity of supply: the responsiveness of quantity supplied to changes in price

TOPICS FOR DISCUSSION

1. Explain why it is important to draw a supply curve for a particular period of time. Then explain and demonstrate market changes that could cause changes in the position and/or slope of market supply.
2. Complete the table below. Then perform the exercises that follow.

Q	FC	AFC	VC	AVC	TC	ATC	MC
1	100	100	10	10	110	110	10
2	—	—	18	—	—	—	—
3	—	—	24	—	—	—	—
4	—	—	34	—	—	—	—
5	—	—	48	—	—	—	—
6	—	—	66	—	—	—	—
7	—	—	90	—	—	—	—
8	—	—	118	—	—	—	—
9	—	—	150	—	—	—	—
10	—	—	186	—	—	—	—

a. The firm's shutdown price is _____.
b. The firm receives economic profit for any price greater than _____.
c. When price is $14, the profit-maximizing quantity is _____. Economic profit is _____.
d. When price is $32, the profit-maximizing quantity is _____. Economic profit is _____.
e. Draw the firm's supply curve.
3. Since World War II, the electronics industry has produced many exciting and innovative products. One of the most recent has been the video recorder for recording television programs. Initially, only two Japanese firms supplied the entire market. How would you describe elasticity of supply in the short run, over a 5-year period, and over a 25-year period? What would you expect to happen to price?
4. Some local governments in the United States have imposed rent controls on city apartments. Discuss the purpose of this kind of price ceiling and list as many consequences as you can.
5. Oil spills near the U.S. coast are increasing pressure for corrective actions by firms operating oil tankers. Describe the likely chain of events that will follow such actions and the ultimate consequences for U.S. consumers.

ANSWERS TO TEST YOURSELF

(p. 77) There are substitutes. It is a relatively large part of consumers' budgets.

(p. 79) Removing the price ceiling will cause a significant reduction in quantity demanded but little increase in quantity supplied.

(p. 80) Removing price supports for farm commodities will cause little increase in quantity demanded and a substantial decrease in quantity supplied.

(p. 80)   The time for responding to price changes is probably shortest for eggs, sweaters, potato chips, transistors, screwdrivers, and autos in the 1990s. The technology is fairly simple and flexible for these items making their supply curves relatively price elastic. Beef requires longer to produce and stained-glass windows require specialized craftsmanship, making their supply curves less elastic. Milk, gold, coal, and lumber can be stored, so that supply is relatively elastic. Strawberries cannot be stored or quickly produced, making supply extremely inelastic.

Chapter

Imperfect Competition and Inefficient Outcomes

or What's Good for GM Is Good for GM

Tools for Study

LEARNING OBJECTIVES

After reading this chapter, you will be able to:

1. Describe how competition eliminates economic profit and increases efficiency.
2. Define monopoly, oligopoly, and monopolistic competition and give examples of each.
3. Explain why imperfect competition brings economic profit and economic inefficiency.
4. Discuss the laws that enforce competition.

CURRENT ISSUES FOR DISCUSSION

How does monopoly affect us? How do some natural monopolies set prices?

Adam Smith and the Classical economists that followed him described how markets work when there is perfect competition. As you learned in Chapter 2 perfect competition depends upon:

Many buyers and sellers, each too small to affect market price.

Products so similar that no one producer can insist on a price higher than the equilibrium price.

Complete information about market conditions.

Ease of movement into the most favorable markets.

In perfect competition, many individual firms compete for the consumer's dollar. An invisible hand guides firms to produce the goods and services consumers want.

In Chapters 2, 3, and 4 we described the market model that illustrates the Classical theory of free, competitive markets. In the Classical theory, consumer demand schedules combine to yield a market demand curve. Business firms' decisions to supply goods and services combine to yield market supply. The interaction between market demand and supply determines market equilibrium. At equilibrium, price is such that quantity demanded is equal to quantity supplied, and there is no surplus or shortage.

In the short run, the competitive price may yield economic profit or loss for firms in a particular market. Economic profit or loss occurs because of the existence of fixed resources and because of the difficulty of quickly expanding or contracting the industry's fixed plant and equipment. Thus, in the short run, supply may not increase or decrease readily in response to changes in demand, and price may be greater or less than average total cost. In the long run, however, the industry's fixed plant and equipment can be expanded or cut back. New firms can enter the market, so that supply curves shift to the right or left.

In this chapter we will see how changes in supply can cause price to rise or fall to the level of average total cost, eliminating economic profit or loss. This result occurs only in competition, however. Without competition, firms may choose not to increase supply, so that economic profit continues. The existence of economic profit indicates inefficiency in the use of the nation's scarce resources.

DECIDING PRICE AND OUTPUT IN COMPETITION

Adam Smith described how competitive markets respond to a kind of invisible hand. The invisible hand encourages new firms to enter markets where they can earn economic profit. As new firms add their output to that of existing firms, market supply increases, pushing the market equilibrium price down until it just covers full costs, including wages and salaries, rent, interest, and normal profit. At the lower price there is no excess return or economic profit.

Figure 5.1 illustrates the invisible hand at work in a competitive market. New firms entering the market cause an increase in market supply, shown as a rightward shift in the supply curve and creating a surplus at the current price. As all the firms in the market compete to sell their surplus output, price falls and a new, lower equilibrium price is reached. If the new price includes economic profit, still more firms will enter the market, continuing to push price down until price is equal to average total

Figure 5.1   An Increase in Supply in a Competitive Market.

Where there is economic profit, new firms enter the market. Market supply increases and price falls until economic profit is eliminated.

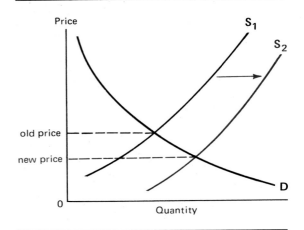

cost. When $p = ATC$, there is no economic profit and no further incentive for new firms to enter the market. After all these adjustments have taken place, the new price is just high enough to cover full economic costs, including normal profit but not economic profit.

Competition ensures both technical and allocative efficiency in the long run. Competitive markets are technically efficient because they force price down to the lowest possible level for which the good or service can be produced. Why is this so? Firms in competition are compelled to construct their plants according to the most efficient design, and they must operate their plants at the best possible rate for holding down average total cost. Competitive markets achieve allocative efficiency, too, because they satisfy consumers' wants at prices just high enough to pay the minimum necessary cost of scarce resources.

Economic loss calls for the opposite kind of adjustment. When the market equilibrium

How Things Have Changed . . .

CONCENTRATION RATIOS IN MANUFACTURING: 1982

Industry	Number of Companies	Percentage of shipments, ranked by company size			
		4 Largest	8 Largest	20 Largest	50 Largest
Petroleum refining	282	28	48	76	93
Motor vehicles and car bodies	284	92	97	99	99+
Meat-packing plants	1658	20	43	61	75
Electronic computing equipment	1520	43	55	71	82
Radio and TV communications equipment	2083	22	35	57	73
Aircraft	139	64	81	98	99+
Pharmaceutical preparations	584	26	42	69	90
Photographic equipment and supplies	723	74	86	91	94
Bottled and canned soft drinks	1236	14	23	39	56
Telephone, telegraph apparatus	259	76	83	92	97
Bread, cake, and related products	1869	34	47	60	73
Cigarettes	8	Withheld to avoid disclosure			
Construction industry	817	42	52	69	81
Tires and inner tubes	108	66	86	98	99+
Soap and other detergents	642	60	73	83	90

Compare the percent of shipments made by the 50 largest companies with the total number of firms in the industry to get an idea of the structure of the industry.

Statistical Abstract of the United States, 1989.

price is below average total cost, total revenue from sales is less than total cost, and firms suffer negative economic profit or loss. Negative economic profit also acts like an invisible hand, in this case encouraging firms to leave the market. As firms leave, supply decreases, and price rises to cover average total cost.

Figure 5.2 shows how competitive markets adjust to negative economic profit or loss. In Figure 5.2 a decrease in supply causes a leftward shift of the supply curve and creates a shortage at the current price. Buyers bid against each other for the limited supply and force price up. Finally, a new equilibrium is reached with a higher price and a smaller quantity sold. The new equilibrium price is just high enough to cover average total cost, including normal profit but not economic profit. Again, the new equilibrium price is the minimum price for which this product can be produced.

We say that firms in competition are **price takers**. Every competitive firm faces an equi-

Figure 5.2   A Decrease in Supply in a Competitive Market.

Where there is negative economic profit, firms leave the market. Market supply falls and price rises until negative economic profit (loss) is eliminated.

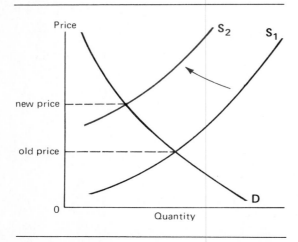

librium price that it is too small to affect. It can sell any quantity at the market equilibrium price, but it can sell nothing at a higher price. In the long run, a competitive firm will supply output as long as market price is at least as great as average total cost. When all firms follow this rule, price is forced to a level that includes neither economic profit nor loss.

It is understandable that Adam Smith regarded free markets with a kind of reverence. In free markets, consumer demand curves act as signals, informing producers of the preferences of buyers for particular goods and services. Producers, in turn, seek the least costly way to satisfy consumer wants. The result is efficient production: the minimum expenditure of limited resources and the maximum production of goods consumers want. When production is efficient, opportunity costs are held to a minimum.

Adam Smith realized that competition might not be perfect in the real world, however. In the real world, some business firms may try to control the output of particular goods and services. They may look for ways to maintain high prices so that they can continue to receive economic profit. They may prefer not to "flood the market" with increased quantities but instead limit supply and keep price high. Without competition, firms are not forced to produce the maximum quantities of the things consumers want at the minimum expenditure of productive resources. Thus, to the extent that competition is not perfect, our market system is not efficient.

MONOPOLY

Remember that one of the characteristics of competition is many small sellers producing identical products. In the real world, there are not many markets that have many small sellers, and there are not many products that are identical to all other products in the market. In fact, many real-world markets have only a few

Viewpoint

MONOPOLY IN MONOPOLY

It's not whether you win or lose, it's how you name the game! That's the problem in the antitrust dispute over Monopoly.

You won't find many Americans who aren't familiar with the game of Monopoly. Legend has it that the game was devised around the turn of the century by a Virginia Quaker, Elizabeth Magee. It was known as "The Landlord's Game." For years, several versions were played on painted oilcloth.

In 1933 a retired hotel manager from Georgia became interested in the game and bought rights to the idea. After updating and standardizing the rules, he sold the patent and trademark to Parker Brothers. Today Parker Brothers is the world's largest producer of games, and Monopoly is its star. More than 80 million games of Monopoly have been sold worldwide.

Such success could not forever go unchallenged. Many other manufacturers have come up with similar ideas, hoping to grab a share of this profitable market, but Parker Brothers has fought them all. It has generally been successful in preventing other firms from using any ideas similar to the original, one-and-only Monopoly. It was successful, that is, until 1973 when an economics professor from California came out with a new game he called Anti-Monopoly.

Professor Ralph Anspach is a specialist in antitrust law. His new game is similar to the original Monopoly, but instead of building monopoly its objective is to break it up. His idea caught on, and in the first two years he sold 280,000 games for total revenue of about $1 million. All this after investing only $5000 to set up his own company!

By law the Monopoly trademark belongs exclusively to Parker Brothers. Theirs is a legal monopoly. Therefore, Parker Brothers sued professor Anspach for illegal use of their property. In turn, the professor sued Parker Brothers over the validity of the trademark itself. He pointed out that some trademarks eventually become a part of the language itself and are free to be used by any firm. Kleenex, Kodak, aspirin, and even checkers are examples of terms that used to be brand names but now refer to whole classes of products. Besides, he said, Anti-Monopoly does not involve competition with Monopoly at all.

Apparently the court agreed. Anspach won his case.

large sellers producing unique products. In such markets, the efficient results of Adam Smith's competitive model may not occur.

If there is only one large seller in a market, the firm is said to be a **monopoly**. Except for monopolies achieved through patents, franchises, or government regulation, most monopolies are illegal in the United States. Still, there are many markets where a few large firms behave like a monopoly and achieve results like a monopoly. When we speak of monopoly in this text, we are referring to groups of firms that behave like a single monopoly firm and have the power to affect market price. Such groups of firms are sometimes called **shared monopolies**.

A monopoly can be achieved in several ways. The monopoly may be the first firm (or firms) in the industry; it may buy out smaller rival firms; or it may drive weaker competitors out of business. A monopoly must keep out competitors in order to limit supply and keep price from falling; and it will try to increase demand so that there will be buyers at profitable prices.

A country fellow in the rural South had learned this lesson quite well—without ever attending business school! Some tourists were driving along a detour far off the main road when they became hopelessly mired in the mud. A humble shack was the only sign of civilization, and the farmer's tractor was available (at a price) to pull their car from the ditch. As he handed the fellow a $50 bill, the tourist observed, "I'll bet you're busy night and day pulling cars from this mud, aren't you?"

"Nope," replied the farmer. "Night's when we haul the water."

(How would you describe the tourists' price elasticity of demand for towing assistance?)

Gentlemen's Agreements

In years past, achieving monopoly often occurred through gentlemen's agreements. With only a few large firms in a particular industry, the firms would agree among themselves to behave like monopolists. They would agree not to reduce price, and they would establish market shares for each firm. In this way, each firm enjoyed control over supply in a protected market. Firms like these are said to be **price makers**. Price makers are distinguished from price takers because they have power to affect market price.

(Gentlemen's agreements are a little like the cartoon showing two donkeys tethered at the ends of a strong rope. Each donkey is struggling to eat a bale of hay just beyond his reach at the end of the rope. When the donkeys agree to cooperate, they are able to eat first one bale and then the other, and both are satisfied.)

Horizontal and Vertical Monopolies

There are two kinds of monopolies. One kind includes firms that provide the same good or service and is called a **horizontal monopoly**:

supermarket—supermarket—supermarket
auto plant—auto plant

Another kind includes firms that process a single product from start to finish—from its raw form to its distribution to the final consumer—and is called a **vertical monopoly**:

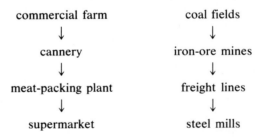

It is easy to see the advantages that come from controlling production of a product from raw material to finished good.

OLIGOPOLY

True monopoly is rare in U.S. markets, but oligopoly is fairly common. An **oligopoly** is a market in which a few large firms supply most of the output, but some small firms produce for certain small segments of the market. Oligopolies typically occur in industries that require a large initial capital investment. In such industries, fixed costs may be too high for small firms to get started, or market demand may be too small for many firms to operate efficiently.

When a few large firms dominate a market, the results are similar to monopoly. Oligopoly firms may not actually agree to limit output and raise prices, but because their production costs are similar, they arrive at similar price and quantity decisions without outright agreements. Like monopolists, they become price makers.

Some examples of markets long dominated by a few large firms are automobiles (dominated by General Motors, Ford, and Chrysler), steel (dominated by U.S. Steel, Bethlehem, and Republic), rubber tires (dominated by Goodyear, Uniroyal, Firestone, Goodrich, and General), and meat packing (dominated by Swift, Armour, Wilson, and Cudahy).

MONOPOLISTIC COMPETITION

Other markets in the United States are described by a term that suggests characteristics of both monopoly and competition: **monopolistic competition**.

Monopolistic competition is similar to monopoly because each firm claims to produce a distinctly unique product: the only socially accepted toothpaste or shampoo, the only truly tasty soft drink, the only fully nutritious breakfast cereal. Even though their products are similar, monopolistically competitive firms try to make them seem different, so as to achieve a monopoly in a particular small market. They achieve product uniqueness through differences in style or packaging or simply through clever advertising. Product uniqueness enables a firm to raise price above the

competitive level and still hold on to customers who are loyal to its product. It is a price maker, but in a more limited sense than a true monopolist or oligopolist.

Monopolistic competition is similar to competition because there are generally many firms in the industry. In fact, there are so many firms that each firm tends to produce a smaller quantity than is technically efficient. The best example of this kind of inefficiency is when four fast-food restaurants crowd into a single block. Each one promises special "service with a smile," but together they divide a market that might be served more efficiently by two larger firms.

Monopolistic competition occurs often in retail trade and personal services such as delicatessens, fabric shops, laundries, and barber shops. Initial capital investments for these types of businesses are low, making it easy for many small firms to enter the market.

The three kinds of imperfect competition can be summarized as follows:

Monopoly
  One seller
  Difficult to enter
  Unique product
  Control over price
  Higher price, lower quantity than
    competition

Oligopoly
  Few sellers
  Somewhat difficult to enter
  Identical or differentiated product
  Similar prices
  Somewhat higher price and lower
    quantity than competition

Monopolistic Competition
  Many sellers
  Easy to enter
  Differentiated product
  Some control over price
  Slightly higher price than competition
    and probably higher costs of production

Viewpoint

TWO MONOPOLIES IN AMERICAN HISTORY

During the earliest stages of industrialization in the United States following the Civil War, there was cutthroat competition among American business firms. (The donkeys were still struggling to get at the hay.)

In the building of the railroads, early industrialists like Cornelius Vanderbilt fought ruthlessly to drive their competitors out of business. Where a competing railroad served the same two cities as Vanderbilt's line, Vanderbilt would reduce fares below average total cost. He would make up the loss by increasing fares on other routes where he faced no competition. When the competing railroad was forced into bankruptcy, Vanderbilt would buy it cheaply, so that eventually he controlled freight service over most of the northeastern United States.

In the petroleum industry, John D. Rockefeller began with several small oil refineries. However, Rockefeller realized that he could increase his market power if he controlled the oil from well to final distributor. Rockefeller's Standard Oil Company was able to buy the major oil pipelines and establish a monopoly in the transport of crude oil. As the only buyer of oil from well owners, Rockefeller would offer a low price. Then the oil would be transported over Standard Oil's pipelines. Finally, as the only seller of delivered oil to refiners, Rockefeller would insist on a high price.

Low prices for crude oil, on the one hand, and high prices for delivered oil, on the other, forced well owners, refiners, and distributors out of business. Then Rockefeller bought them up and eventually brought a major part of the petroleum industry under the control of Standard Oil. Whenever Rockefeller's rivals could not be forced out of business or could not be merged with Standard Oil, they could often be persuaded to enter into a gentlemen's agreement. (The donkeys agreed to share the hay!)

These two cases illustrate vertical and horizontal monopoly. Can you identify each?

Can you name local examples of the three kinds of imperfect competition?

DECIDING PRICE AND OUTPUT IN IMPERFECT COMPETITION

When competition is imperfect, markets do not adjust to economic profit or loss as smoothly as Adam Smith predicted. Without competition, firms are not forced to supply maximum quantities at prices just high enough to cover average total cost. If imperfectly competitive firms can prevent the entry of new competition, they can continue to collect economic profit.

Remember that firms in perfect competition are price takers, free to sell any quantity but unable to affect the market equilibrium price. In imperfect competition, firms become price makers. Facing the entire demand curve for its product, a firm in imperfect competition can set any price on the demand curve and sell the corresponding quantity. To sell a larger quantity requires a movement down the demand curve to a lower price. Setting a higher price requires a movement up the demand curve to a smaller quantity.

What price will the imperfectly competitive firm set? The answer depends, first, on the effect of price changes on the firm's total revenue and, second, on the effect of quantity changes on the firm's total costs. (These topics were the subject of Chapters 3 and 4, respectively.) Changes in total revenue and total cost affect a firm's economic profit and determine the profit-maximizing quantity and price.

Let us look first at the effect of price changes on a firm's total revenue. Suppose an imperfectly competitive firm is selling five shirts a day at a price of $15.00. Total revenue is $TR = Q \times p = \$75$ per day. Suppose the firm can sell six shirts if it reduces price to $14.00 (for $TR = \$84$) or four shirts if it raises price to $16.00 (for $TR = \$64$). What is the effect of price changes on the firm's total revenue? In this case, the firm can increase total revenue by reducing price and increasing the number of units sold. In fact, if demand is elastic at the current price, reducing price will always yield an increase in total revenue. (Remember that when price elasticity of demand is greater than one, percentage change in quantity demanded is greater than percentage change in price.)

Table 5.1 shows the imperfectly competitive firm's total revenue from sales at various prices.

Figure 5.3 is the demand curve associated with the prices and quantities in Table 5.1. The imperfectly competitive firm can select any price on the demand curve and sell the corresponding quantity.

Now let us look at the effect of quantity changes on total costs. Like a competitive firm, the imperfectly competitive firm seeks to

Table 5.1   Total Revenue at Various Prices.

Quantity Demanded	Price	Total Revenue
5	$15	$ 75
6	14	84
7	13	91
8	12	96
9	11	99
10	10	100

achieve maximum economic profit. Because economic profit is the difference between total revenue and total cost, the imperfectly competitive firm wants to set a price that maximizes the difference between total revenue and total cost. It looks for the point on its demand curve at which price and quantity sold satisfy this objective.

Selecting price and quantity in the imperfectly competitive firm is similar to competition in another respect. Like the competitive firm, the imperfectly competitive firm follows

Figure 5.3   A Demand Curve in Imperfect Competition.

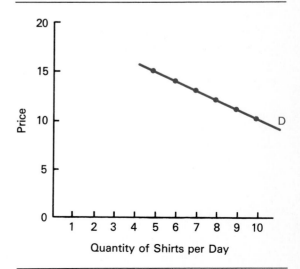

the profit-maximizing rule and selects quantity where marginal revenue is equal to marginal cost: $MR = MC$. The reason is that when $MR = MC$, the last unit sold adds just enough to revenue to cover what it adds to cost. When the last unit sold adds the same to revenue as it adds to cost, economic profit is maximum.

Now we come to the significant difference between pricing with and without competition. The difference has to do with marginal revenue. Although marginal cost of production may be the same whether or not there is competition, marginal revenue is not the same. Remember that the firm in imperfect competition faces the entire market demand curve. This means that in order for the firm in imperfect competition to sell an additional unit it must reduce price. Selling all units at the lower price means that marginal revenue for the firm in imperfect competition is less than price.

Consider again the imperfectly competitive supplier of shirts we discussed above. Selling five shirts at $15 yields total revenue of $75. Selling six shirts at $14 yields total revenue of $84. The increase in revenue associated with a one-unit increase in quantity is $MR = \$84 - \$75 = \$9$. With $p = \$14$ and $MR = \$9$, marginal revenue $MR = \$9$ is less than price $p = \$14$.

Table 5.2 is the same as Table 5.1 with an additional column showing marginal revenue. Because marginal revenue is associated with

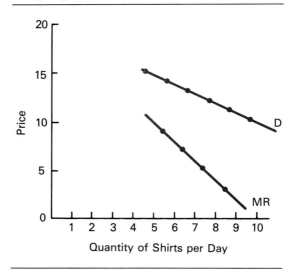

Figure 5.4a   Marginal Revenue in Imperfect Competition.

changes in the number of units sold, it has been written between the lines in the table.

Figure 5.4a shows points for marginal revenue associated with the prices and quantities shown in Table 5.2. For every price and corresponding quantity, marginal revenue is less than price. Now look at Figure 5.4b, which includes a typical marginal cost (MC) curve. Use the profit-maximizing rule to locate the price and quantity where $MR = MC$. Note that marginal revenue is equal to marginal cost when $Q = 6$ shirts per day. Find the

Table 5.2   Total Revenue and Marginal Revenue in Imperfect Competition.

Quantity Demanded	Price	Total Revenue	Marginal Revenue
5	$15	$ 75	
6	14	84	$9
7	13	91	7
8	12	96	5
9	11	99	3
10	10	100	1

Figure 5.4b The Profit-Maximizing Price and Quantity in Imperfect Competition.

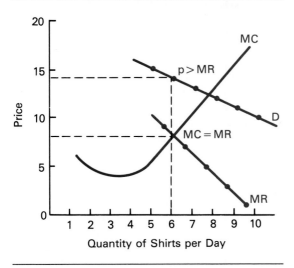

Quantity of Shirts per Day

characteristic in imperfect competition is the power to affect price.

A firm's power to set price depends on the shape of the firm's demand curve and, in particular, price elasticity of demand at the current price. Firms with greater market power face demand curves that are relatively price inelastic: percentage changes in price yield smaller percentage changes in quantity demanded. In this case, some consumers want the product so badly they are willing to pay a higher price than the price in competition. (Remember the tourists.) Firms with less market power face demand curves that are relatively price elastic: Percentage changes in price yield larger percentage changes in quantity demanded. In this case, consumers have greater choice and can decide to buy or not, depending on price. (Can you give an example from the fast-food industry?)

selling price for $Q = 6$ by looking at the demand curve where $p = \$14$.

Now we can see the significant difference between pricing in competition and pricing in imperfect competition. In perfect competition $p = MR$. Therefore, the profit-maximizing quantity occurs where $p = MR = MC$. In imperfect competition $p > MR$. Therefore, the profit-maximizing quantity occurs where $p > MR = MC$. Price is greater than marginal revenue and marginal cost, providing the imperfectly competitive firm the opportunity to collect economic profit.

To Summarize

To summarize, the result of monopoly, oligopoly, and monopolistic competition is economic inefficiency, both in the failure to produce what people want (allocative efficiency) and in the failure to produce at lowest cost (technical efficiency). The significant

THE RESULTS OF IMPERFECT COMPETITION

Imperfect competition has harmful effects, both in the present and in the future. With monopoly, oligopoly, or monopolistic competition, prices tend to be higher than in competition, and quantity sold tends to be lower. Barriers to entry prevent new firms from responding to market signals. When consumers must pay more for wanted goods, they have less income left to spend for other things, which slows the development of other industries.

Often, firms that sell to imperfectly competitive firms must accept low prices for their products. Workers and suppliers of materials and component parts may have no choice but to accept low prices from a monopolistic or oligopolistic firm.

Higher prices and lower quantity make our economy less efficient than it would be in competition. In competition, economic profit

Contemporary Thinking about Economic Issues

HOW SHOULD WE THINK ABOUT ANTITRUST?

Robert Katzmann is worried about current thinking on antitrust.

It used to be that the emphasis in antitrust activity was on the power that monopolies could wield over small business and consumers. "Trust busters" like President Theodore Roosevelt were concerned that powerful monopolies could squeeze small businesses and stifle "entrepreneurialism, individualism, and economic self-reliance." Not only would powerful monopolies damage the efficiency of the nation's economy; through their concentration of economic power, they would "undermine democratic government."

Over the past decade, the emphasis has changed, and today antitrust activity concentrates more on economic efficiency as a guide to enforcement of antitrust laws. With the emphasis on economic efficiency, antitrust activity has diminished. One reason is that large businesses are frequently *more* efficient than small businesses. Economists at the University of Chicago point out that large firms are better able than small firms to take advantage of economies of scale; and the large profits of such firms are a result not of exploitation of small firms but of greater efficiency.

Another reason for the decline in antitrust is the seriousness of other problems facing the nation today. The problems of inflation, unemployment, high interest rates, and international competition call into question the allocation of resources to fight business firms that are only trying to do a good job in the market. The dominance of this philosophy in the Reagan administration led to a decrease in the budget of the antitrust enforcement division of the Federal Trade Commission (FTC). As a result, the FTC now allows more vertical and conglomerate mergers and is more lenient regarding horizontal mergers, as well.

Katzmann worries about these developments. Giving such emphasis to the economic aspects of mergers, he says, implies neglect of the social and political consequences of economic power. Although it is correct to consider economic efficiency in ruling on merger activity, we should not forget all those fundamental values associated with competition: the stimulus to economic growth and employment and the pressures toward price stability and technological progress. To fail to enforce the antitrust laws would be to abandon our founding fathers' "social and moral vision of America."

Robert A. Katzmann, *Regulatory Bureaucracy: The Federal Trade Commission and Antitrust Policy*. 1979, MIT Press, Cambridge, MA.

serves as a signal to expand production. Without competition, it is doubtful that a firm will use its economic profit to improve its production techniques or its product. The result for the economic system as a whole may be slower growth and lower productivity.

The harmful effects of imperfect competition are especially damaging in international trade. Higher prices and lower incentives to improve product quality have caused U.S. auto and steel manufacturers to lose markets to foreign suppliers. Monopolistically competitive firms have used scarce resources to make trivial product changes and have neglected major innovations. For all these reasons, imperfect competition has reduced the U.S. capacity for technological progress.

ANTIMONOPOLY LEGISLATION

Imperfect competition was not a serious problem early in our nation's economic development, but toward the end of the 1800s a great merger movement swept the nation's industries. In transportation and in industries producing and processing raw materials, business firms set up corporations.

In the corporate form of business, firms sell shares of stock to large numbers of investors. Buyers of stock become part owners of the corporation and receive a share of corporate profits. In theory, stockholders have the power to vote for directors and help decide company policy. In fact, few stockholders exercise their voting rights, leaving actual power in the hands of a few active stockholders. This makes it possible for a few individuals to control several firms just by buying a few shares of the outstanding stock of each. In the 1800s such arrangements were called **trusts*** and were able to monopolize production in certain

* Similar arrangements today are called **holding companies**.

key industries: sugar, meat packing, steel, rail transport, tobacco, and petroleum.

With a monopoly in the production of a good or service, a trust could pay low prices to its suppliers and charge high prices to its customers. The sugar trust, for example, could pay low prices for raw sugar, and a railroad could charge high prices to transport it. Trusts were particularly damaging to farmers. In the late 1800s, midwestern farmers combined to oppose the trusts and pressured Congress for legislation to outlaw them. Finally, in 1890 Congress passed the Sherman Antitrust Act.

The Sherman Antitrust Act

The Sherman Antitrust Act forbade any "contract, combination . . . or conspiracy, in restraint of trade." Any act to "monopolize, or combine or conspire . . . to monopolize" any market was prohibited.

The Sherman Act was so vague that it was difficult to decide precisely what actions were forbidden. The law's vagueness left plenty of room for interpretation by the courts. Also, although the act prohibited cooperative agreements among firms, it did not prohibit outright purchase of firms. The understandable result was a great round of business mergers.

Except for court action against the Standard Oil Company and the American Tobacco Company, the Sherman Act was used primarily against labor unions, which were regarded as monopolies in labor markets.

The Clayton Antitrust Act

In 1914, Congress passed the Clayton Antitrust Act to define more precisely certain practices that are harmful to competition. For example, the Clayton Act forbade price discrimination where the effect is to reduce competition. **Price discrimination** involves setting prices below costs in markets where there is competition. Low prices tend to force competing firms out of business, and the loss can be made up by setting higher prices in markets where there is no competition. The Clayton Act also forbade tying contracts, which required the buyer of a firm's products to buy a full line of products, thus closing out other suppliers. The law also forbade interlocking directorates, in which a single individual would serve on the board of directors of several related corporations, allowing the firms to coordinate their price and output policies and avoid competition.

Finally, the Clayton Antitrust Act forbade a firm to acquire voting stock in related corporations in order to operate them as one large firm (thus outlawing trusts). The act was later amended to forbid outright purchase of competing firms. Firms that want to purchase or to merge with a related firm now must request permission from the Antitrust Division of the U.S. Department of Justice.

Difficulties of Enforcement

Enforcement of the antitrust laws has been uneven and has depended largely on the particular philosophy and loyalties of the current U.S. president. Over the first 70 years of the antitrust laws, not one businessperson was sent to jail for a violation. Some fines were imposed, but fines were small compared to the expected profits from a "gentlemen's agreement."

In 1959, for the first time, business executives were sent to jail under the antitrust laws. Again in 1961 respected officials of major firms were sent to jail for conspiring to fix prices on electrical generating equipment.

In the 1970s executives of large corporations were found guilty of making illegal contributions to political campaign funds. It was suspected that the contributions were aimed at forestalling prosecution for antitrust violations. The most publicized case involved the purchase of several companies by International Telephone and Telephone Company. Following a large campaign pledge, ITT was allowed to keep the largest of its new acquisitions.

Recently the Antitrust Division has moved more vigorously to examine the pricing policies of highly concentrated industries. In 1981 executives of firms producing certain kinds of transparent paper were convicted of price fixing and sentenced to jail terms. In 1984, American Telephone and Telegraph Company agreed to break up into a number of regional telephone companies, while retaining control over subsidiary long distance and research and manufacturing operations.

CONGLOMERATES

The courts' crackdown on horizontal and vertical monopolies has led business firms to combine in new ways. In recent years corporations have formed **conglomerates**, in which the combining firms are from totally unrelated industries. A giant conglomerate may include firms producing such diverse products as dog food, whiskey, aerospace equipment, and Chinese food. Because the combining firms are in different industries, a conglomerate does not technically reduce competition. Still, it may represent a dangerous concentration of financial and political power.

The growth of conglomerates creates new problems for enforcement of the antitrust laws.

Viewpoint

THE DEBATE OVER BIGNESS

Economists disagree as to whether bigness in business is good or bad. On one side of the argument, John Kenneth Galbraith sees benefits from large scale business firms. Because average total cost tends to fall as output increases, large firms could mean lower prices for consumers. Moreover, Galbraith believes that large firms allocate more funds to research and development than small firms. Galbraith would allow large firms to operate, but he recommends government regulation of their price and output policies.

On the other side of the argument, Milton Friedman worries about market power, however it is used. He believes that large concentrations of financial (and political) power threaten individual freedom. Friedman recommends vigorous enforcement of the antitrust laws. He favors breaking up established market power and preventing further concentrations of power from developing.

For several decades early in this century, government relaxed its prosecution of the antitrust laws. The philosophy was: Bigness is not necessarily bad if market power is used fairly. As a result, competition diminished in many markets.

In 1945 a new philosophy took over. The Justice Department forced Alcoa Aluminum Company to separate some of its operations into competing firms. Alcoa was not accused of outright illegal practices—just growth through good management! The new philosophy seemed to be to stop monopoly before it developed.

The case of the Brown Shoe Company is another example. In 1962 Brown Shoe Manufacturing Company applied for permission to merge with Kinney Shoe Stores. Together they would have made up only a very small part of the shoe market. Still, the Justice Department decided that the merger would be a dangerous start down the road to monopoly, and it was not permitted.

A more recent antitrust issue has involved parallel practices: cooperative industry policies that shut potential competitors out of the market. The breakfast cereal industry, for example, includes three large firms whose combined market power may act to deny shelf space to small cereal manufacturers. The Justice Department would like to break up the firms into competing divisions, but the cereal firms are resisting the effort.

Self-Check

1. **Firms in perfect competition:**
   a. Produce identical products.
   b. Enter an industry in which there are economic profits.
   c. Expand or contract supply until price is equal to average total cost.
   d. Produce output at the lowest unit costs in the long run.
   e. All of the above.

2. **Monopolization is likely to result from:**
   a. Gentlemen's agreements.
   b. Repeal of the patent laws.
   c. Economic theory.
   d. Low initial capital requirements.
   e. Growing numbers of consumers in the market.

3. **Which of the following is not characteristic of an oligopoly?**
   a. A few large firms in the industry.
   b. Generally high capital requirements.
   c. Similar cost patterns.
   d. Ease of entry of new firms.
   e. Similar pricing policies.

4. **A product sold by a monopolistically competitive firm:**
   a. Has a lower price than under competition.
   b. Is identical with others in the industry.
   c. Is produced by a few large firms.
   d. May experience frequent model changes.
   e. Has characteristics similar to oligopoly.

5. **Antitrust laws forbid:**
   a. Tying contracts.
   b. Interlocking directorates.
   c. Price discrimination, if the effect is to reduce competition.
   d. Mergers harmful to competition.
   e. All of the above.

6. **When there is a monopoly in industry:**
   a. Excess economic profit serves as a signal attracting new firms.
   b. Price is the minimum for which the good can be produced.
   c. Output is greater than under competition.
   d. A larger volume of sales may mean a smaller total revenue.
   e. New firms can enter the industry with ease.

Theory in Practice

PRICING IN IMPERFECT COMPETITION

Probably the least competitive industry in the United States is the automobile industry. More precisely, the automobile industry is an oligopoly, with three firms supplying more than 70 percent of domestic production. Antitrust laws prevent the three firms from cooperating to limit output, raise price, or establish market shares. Still, after long years in the same business, each firm knows pretty well how the other firms will behave under current market conditions. As a result, their pricing and output decisions are often similar.

How does imperfect competition affect price and quantity in the market for automobiles?

Figure 5.5a shows a hypothetical demand curve for Super Cruisers. In a free, competitive market, many sellers would supply Cruisers, producing a market supply curve like the one shown in Figure 5.5b. Each seller would be forced by competition to charge the market price of $4000. The market price would be just high enough to cover all costs of pro-

Figure 5.5   The Market for Super Cruisers.

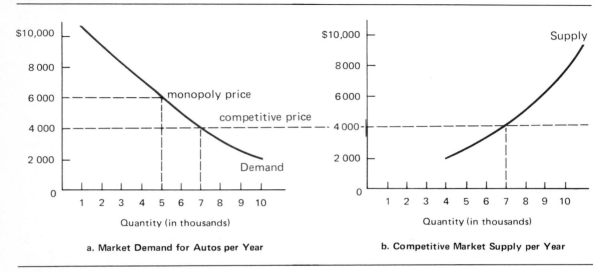

a. Market Demand for Autos per Year   b. Competitive Market Supply per Year

duction, including normal profit, and quantity supplied would be equal to quantity demanded. (What would be the equilibrium quantity of autos at a price of $4000?*)

If a single firm (or cooperating group of firms) has a monopoly in the market for Super Cruisers, there is no single market price. The single monopoly firm can charge any price on its demand curve and sell the corresponding quantity. Suppose the firm decides to set a price of $6000. At a price of $6000 the quantity of autos demanded is less than it would be at the competitive price, and production is lower in the automobile industry. (What is quantity demanded at a price of $6000?†) Furthermore, the monopoly price may include economic profit over and above the average total cost of producing automobiles. Without competition, economic profit cannot serve as a signal to attract new firms into the industry.

*7000 units.

†5000 units.

provide hypothetical data about market demand. If Super Cruisers are selling for $10,000, only 1000 units will be demanded, for total revenue of $10 million. At a price of $3000, 8000 Cruisers will be demanded, for total revenue of $3000 × 8000 units, or $24 million. Column (3) contains hypothetical cost data. Producing 1000 Cruisers costs an average of $ATC = $10,000. Total cost to the firm is $10,000 × 1000 units, or $10 million. Producing 8000 Cruisers costs an average of $5000, for total cost of $40 million.

Columns (4), (5), and (6) in Table 5.3 allow us to compare total revenue at every level of output with the cost of production. The difference between total revenue and total cost is economic profit.

Suppose you are the manager of a monopoly firm producing Super Cruisers. What quantity of output would you decide to produce? You could achieve maximum economic profit by producing 5000 units and selling them for $6000 each. (How much economic profit would you earn on each Cruiser?)

Table 5.3   Hypothetical Demand and Cost Schedules for Super Cruisers.

No. of Units Demanded per Year	Price	Average Total Cost	Total Revenue (millions)	Total Cost (millions)	Economic Profit (millions)
1000	$10,000	$10,000	$10	$10	$ 0
2000	9000	8000	18	16	2
3000	8000	6000	24	18	6
4000	7000	5000	28	20	8
5000	6000	4000	30	20	10
6000	5000	4000	30	24	6
7000	4000	4000	28	28	0
8000	3000	5000	24	40	− 16
9000	2000	7000	18	63	− 45

Now suppose this is a competitive industry. The existence of economic profit would encourage other firms to enter this market. Production and sale of Super Cruisers would increase. New firms would cut price in order to sell larger quantities.

TEST YOURSELF

What is the lowest price for which competitive firms will offer to produce and sell Cruisers? What quantity will be sold at that price? Why is it not a good idea to produce a larger quantity than this?

Practice in Oligopoly Pricing

The four largest tobacco companies in the United States were once a single monopoly firm: the American Tobacco Company. In 1911 the Supreme Court dissolved the American Tobacco Company and formed four separate firms: American Tobacco, Reynolds Tobacco, Liggett and Myers, and Lorillard. Sales of cigarettes grew steadily after that, and by the 1970s per capita consumption was 25 times what it had been in 1911. Sales of all four companies increased with the increase in demand, so that by the 1980s they controlled 84 percent of the U.S. cigarette market.

Today's cigarette industry is described as an oligopoly. Like most oligopolies, the four firms avoid price competition. They decide price through a system of price leadership, with Reynolds Tobacco Company the leader. Reynolds is big enough to discourage price cutting by the other firms. If another firm were to reduce price, Reynolds would cut below and gain a larger share of the market. If another firm were to raise price, Reynolds would refuse to follow the increase, again gaining market share. Thus, the other tobacco firms understand that it does not pay to set different prices, so they follow the price set by the leader.

Price leadership is possible because the major brands are regarded as fairly good substitutes. Many customers would switch from one brand to another if prices were different. (What does this tell you about price elasticity of demand for particular brands?) Price leadership enables all the firms to enjoy economic profits. Moreover, if average total costs were to rise and profits fall for the four cigarette firms, the three other firms would wait for Reynolds to make the first move. As soon as Reynolds increased price, the other firms would quickly follow.

Because of their control of supply, oligopoly firms tend to react to changes in demand differently from competitive firms. The result may be damaging to the economy as a whole.

Remember that competitive firms respond to an increase in demand by moving up their supply curves and supplying a larger quantity at a higher price. They respond to a decrease in demand by producing less at a lower price. The advantage in competition is that price changes help moderate the change in quantity, allowing production and employment in the industry to remain fairly stable. In oligopoly, on the other hand, more of the adjustment to a change in demand falls on quantity of output. This is because price remains constant, and production tends to rise or fall by the full amount of the change in demand.

The result for the economy as a whole is wide swings in production and employment. Workers in oligopoly industries may experience alternating periods of heavy overtime work followed by lay-offs. Furthermore, the power of oligopolies to maintain stable prices during recession may create inflation and make recovery from recession more difficult.

Practice with Natural Monopolies

We have seen that competitive markets tend to be more efficient than imperfectly competitive markets, but this is not always true. Some markets are more efficient when production is carried out by only one large firm. Such firms are called **natural monopolies**. A single firm may be able to produce electric power and transportation and communications services more efficiently, for example, than many competing firms. Firms that produce electric power and transportation and communications services for local markets are called **public utilities**. Most utilities are privately owned, but their prices are set by pub-

lic regulatory commissions to prevent them from behaving like ordinary monopolies.

A utility must invest millions of dollars in capital equipment. However, once its plant and equipment are in place, a utility can provide larger and larger quantities of output without much additional cost. This is because large-scale production allows a utility to spread its fixed costs over many units of output, so that average fixed cost is quite low.

A regulatory commission must decide what price and quantity of output would be fair to consumers and also fair to the owners of the utility. It is important to be fair to the owners or they will refuse to reinvest their funds in the firm. Then the utility's capital equipment cannot grow along with the needs of the community.

Consider the hypothetical market demand curve for electric power, shown in Figure 5.6. Market demand for power includes demand from households, retail stores, and factories.

Figure 5.6 Market Demand for Electric Power.

Some users are willing to pay as much as 10 cents per KWH for electric power. If the rate falls to 2 cents per KWH, quantity demanded is much greater.

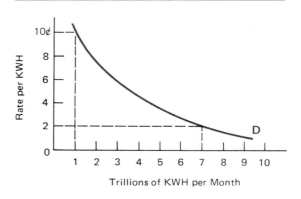

Viewpoint

THE END OF A NATURAL MONOPOLY

For almost a century, American Telephone and Telegraph Company has been regarded as a natural monopoly. Although small, independent companies have provided telephone service in some communities, the giant utility has generally controlled local and long-distance calls, equipment manufacture, and research in electronic communications. Pricing policies were regulated by public service commissions to enable the telephone company to cover its costs and to guarantee an acceptable level of profits for paying stockholder dividends. Regulated prices were set higher than full costs for business and long-distance calls so prices for local residential users could be set lower than full costs. To finance one type of service through profits earned on another type is called **cross-subsidization**.

Probably the most significant event for breaking up AT&T's communications monopoly was the development of communications satellites and microwave radio transmissions. The new technologies enabled new firms to enter the market for long-distance calls and provide the service more cheaply than the Bell System. The Justice Department and MCI Communications Company filed antitrust suits against AT&T, and in 1982 a consent decree was signed in which AT&T agreed to divest itself of its local operating companies. The operating companies were reorganized into seven regional companies, still to be regulated by local public service commissions. AT&T Information Systems was established to provide telephone equipment and services. Western Electric, Bell Labs, and long-distance calling remained with AT&T, and AT&T was given permission to enter new businesses, including businesses involving computers.

With deregulation, competition in long-distance calling was expected to bring those rates down. Computerized communications introduced new services, including electronic mail, video transmission, and data communication. New equipment manufacturers produced an array of new communications equipment.

Perhaps the breakup of AT&T was inevitable. Small, new firms were demanding the right to enter AT&T's markets, and AT&T needed authorization to explore and develop new markets. It appears no longer practical to allow a regulated monopoly to subsidize customers in competitive markets with profits earned in nonregulated markets. Still, there are problems. Without subsidies for local rates, many low-income households may be excluded from the communications network. Some form of government subsidy may be required for these households.

How Things Have Changed . . .

POWER TO THE PEOPLE

Small, independent power producers are challenging the "natural monopoly" status of many public utilities. They are supplying power to large factories over lines leased from power companies. They sell any excess power to the utility, thus providing the utility another source of power in periods of peak demand. Some utilities are setting up independent subsidiaries to produce power outside the normal regulatory system. Subsidiaries may be allowed to earn a higher rate of profit than a regulated utility, which is limited to a 13 percent to 24 percent return on investment.

Buyers whose demand for electric power is most urgent may be willing to pay as much as 10 cents per kilowatt hour (KWH). These buyers might include some homeowners and many manufacturing firms. According to Figure 5.6, the total quantity demanded at a price of 10 cents would be 1 trillion KWH per month.

Many homeowners and businesses would be willing to pay in the range of 5 cents per KWH for larger quantities of power. If the rate were as low as 2 cents, they would use even more. The result is a market demand curve for electric power that slopes downward like a typical demand curve.

Charging all consumers a single rate for power yields total revenue equal to a rectangle formed under the demand curve at the single rate. (Can you explain why?) The utility can increase revenue, however, by pricing according to a rate schedule. A rate schedule applies different rates to different groups of consumers, based on the amount of power they use.

With a rate schedule the utility can collect all the revenue under the demand curve for each group of consumers.

Price discrimination of this sort would be illegal for an ordinary monopoly. However, the regulatory commission may permit price discrimination if it enables the utility to cover full costs while increasing the quantity of power offered for sale.

Figure 5.7 shows total revenue collected with (a) a single rate for all consumers and (b) a rate schedule. In Figure 5.7 the rate schedule ranges from 2 cents to 10 cents per KWH. Notice the substantial increase in quantity and revenue with a rate schedule. Another advantage of a rate schedule is that it allows consumers far out at the right of the demand curve to enjoy the service even if the rate they pay is less than the cost of production! In effect, consumers at the left of the demand curve are helping pay for power used by those at the right.

The power company uses its revenue to

Figure 5.7   Total Revenue.

A rate schedule allows the company to collect all the revenue under the demand curve within the rate schedule.

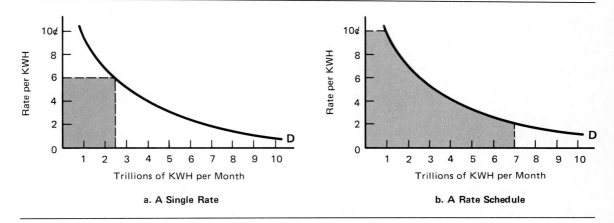

a. A Single Rate

b. A Rate Schedule

pay operating costs and to compensate all those who help finance the utility's investment in plant and equipment; that is, banks and holders of the firm's stocks and bonds. When operating and capital costs increase, the power company must ask the regulatory commission for permission to increase its rate schedule. If the commission approves the rate increase, all consumers will pay more for their electric power. Some consumers will move up their demand curves and use less power. If the power company has calculated correctly, however, it will collect greater total revenue to meet its higher costs.

Agreeing on a "fair" rate schedule is not easy. There are many users of electric power, all seeking lower rates. There are relatively few holders of stocks and bonds, seeking higher returns on their investments. The voting strength of the first group may influence elected commissioners to hold rates down. Or power companies may seek to ensure rate in-

creases by making campaign contributions to commissioners.

If rates are held down so that the return on invested capital falls, holders of the firm's stocks and bonds may decide to use their funds for other things. New power plants and equipment will not be built, and service will deteriorate. With revenues insufficient to cover full costs, a utility may need government help in the form of tax credits, subsidies, or outright government ownership.

Government involvement in the power industry has several disadvantages. Utility managers may be less concerned about holding costs down if they expect government to cover their costs. Also, a tax-supported subsidy would have to be financed by all the taxpayers while the benefits would go only to users of the service. Most economists believe it is more efficient and more equitable for users of electric power to pay for higher costs through higher rates.

Viewpoint

DEREGULATING THE AIRLINES

For half a century the U.S. air travel industry was regulated by the Civil Aeronautics Board (CAB). Air fares and routes were controlled to guarantee service to consumer markets at prices that would cover costs of production.

Many airlines operated on the "hub-and-spoke" principle. A major city would be designated a hub, with short spokes coming in to feed the long spokes going out to other hubs. Costs per passenger-mile were higher on the short spokes because fixed costs were spread over fewer units of output. The CAB allowed the airlines to set fares higher than average total cost on long spokes so fares could be lower than average total cost on short spokes.

Under the CAB, competition in the air travel industry was limited to airline "frills": attractive flight attendants, food and beverage service on flights, and advertising gimmicks. By the late 1970s, U.S. consumers were becoming concerned about high costs, excessive capacity, and general inefficiency in air travel. Congress directed the CAB to begin deregulating the industry and put itself out of business.

Competition brought tremendous changes in air travel. The major coast-to-coast lines focused their efforts on their long flights, cutting fares sharply to expand sales volume and keep their large planes filled. Some large airlines were unable to survive the fare wars and went out of business or cut back service. Small "commuter" airlines sprang up to serve short-haul passengers. Many were able to operate with limited terminal facilities and nonunion labor, so their costs were low and profits high. However, some small markets were found to be unprofitable, and air service to those areas was discontinued.

Many economists believe that the air travel industry is becoming more efficient. A variety of firms are emerging, each equipped with resources appropriate for serving a particular market. Competition is pushing air fares to the level of average costs (including normal profit) in each of a wide variety of consumer markets. Finally, total investment in the airline industry is beginning to reflect more accurately the actual requirements for service in air travel markets.

SUMMARY

1. Economic profit is an excess return over and above the full cost of resources used in production. In competition, economic profit serves as a signal attracting new resources into an industry. Negative economic profit, or loss, signals resources to leave an industry. As firms enter (or leave), price falls (or rises) until economic profit is finally eliminated.
2. The free movement of resources is difficult to achieve in the real world. Some industries become monopolized when conditions prevent the entry of new firms.
3. Pure monopolies are rare in U.S. industry. However, several firms have occasionally made gentlemen's agreements not to compete against each other.
4. Other forms of imperfect competition are oligopoly (dominated by a few large firms) and monopolistic competition (where many small firms produce differentiated products).
5. A monopoly may reduce output and raise price above the competitive level. If there are no competitors to force price down, a monopoly can continue to collect economic profit.
6. In the late 1800s political pressure was put on Congress to outlaw vertical and horizontal monopolies. The Sherman Antitrust Act of 1890 and the Clayton Antitrust Act of 1914 forbade certain practices aimed at reducing competition. More recently, competition has been threatened by conglomerates, combinations of firms in unrelated industries.
7. Very large firms may have an advantage in some types of production because of the low average total cost associated with a high volume of output. Firms in these industries are called natural monopolies.
8. Public commissions regulate price and output policies of natural monopolies. However, the job of regulating prices and profits is not an easy one.

TERMS TO REMEMBER

price takers: firms that can sell any quantity at the market price but no quantity at a higher price

monopoly: an industry supplied by one firm or by a group of firms acting as one

price makers: firms that can raise their prices by reducing their output

horizontal monopoly: a combination of firms, all producing the same type of output

vertical monopoly: a combination of firms, each involved in one stage of production of a particular good or service

oligopoly: an industry supplied by a few large firms

monopolistic competition: an industry supplied by many small firms, each producing a slightly different product

conglomerate: a combination of firms, each producing an entirely different good or service

cross-subsidization: the practice of financing one type of service through profits earned on another type

TOPICS FOR DISCUSSION

1. Explain the difference between the following pairs of terms:

   Vertical monopolies and horizontal monopolies.
   Competitive pricing and monopoly pricing.
   Price takers and price makers.

2. How is each of the following involved in the problem of enforcing the antitrust laws:

   Natural monopolies
   Price leadership
   Conglomerates

3. One area in which monopoly power may be of particular concern in the United States is the news media. The situation is especially threatening in towns where there is single ownership of newspaper, radio, and television facilities. The Antitrust Division of the Department of Justice has been pressuring the Federal Communications Commission to draw up rules to deal with monopolization of the news media. One proposal would require owners to sell or

swap properties in order to increase competition in the local market.

Can you suggest any advantages in single ownership of the news media? What are the disadvantages? What position would you take with respect to the proposal before the regulatory commission?

4. In the late 1800s, farmers of the midwestern states complained they were being squeezed between monopoly suppliers and monopoly buyers. They had to pay high prices to suppliers of agricultural machinery, freight service, and fuel, and they had to accept low prices from meat packers, grain dealers, and the sugar trust.

Do such problems exist today? How can the courts help reduce them? How are U.S. consumers affected?

5. Public utilities often face the problem of "peak loads" at particular times of the day or year. Power usage is greatest during the day (industrial plants) and in the summer (air conditioning). Telephone usage is greatest on weekdays (business calls). Mass-transit usage is greatest in the morning and evening rush hours. A public utility must invest in additional capital resources to fill exceptionally high demand, but its resources may be idle during other times of the day or year. Costs may also be higher during peak times if old, obsolete equipment is brought into service to satisfy higher demand.

How might a public regulatory commission deal with this problem? Would you favor price discrimination in such situations? How would price discrimination work?

6. Explain how the goal of technical and al-

locative efficiency is served under competition and without competition.

7. In 1980 the Federal Communications Commission (FCC) abolished rules regulating cable television rates but allowed cities to control entry into the cable television market. Federal law still forbids telephone companies to carry cable signals. Use your understanding of economic theory to predict the consequences of these restrictions for the cable television market. What are the potential dangers of a partnership between local governments and cable monopolies? Can you suggest an economically efficient arrangement for this market?

8. The McCarran-Ferguson Act of 1945 exempts insurance companies from the antitrust laws. Why do you suppose insurance companies were singled out for exemption? What are the possible consequences?

ANSWER TO TEST YOURSELF

(P. 105) The lowest price is determined by minimum average total cost: $ATC = \$4000$ with production of between 5000 and 6000 units. Producing more units would force price below ATC. Firms might produce for a price lower than ATC in the short run only if price at least covers average variable cost.

Chapter

Labor Markets and the Labor Movement

or You've Come a Long Way, Maybe

Tools for Study

Current Issues for Discussion

How efficient are resource markets? How do labor unions interfere with price and quantity decisions in labor markets? How does the collective bargaining process work? How are labor unions changing in response to changes in resource markets?

A first-grade teacher struggled through a long, rainy day to keep her squirmy dears quietly and constructively occupied (with no recess period for the children to release energies while the the teacher regained hers). At last, it was dismissal time, and appropriate mittens, hoods, and galoshes (last year's small-sized) had to be fitted, then exchanged, and often exchanged a second time. This was all accomplished amid great hilarity and confusion. One little boy amused himself in the hubbub by exploring the contents of the teacher's desk, where he found the brown window envelope containing her paycheck. He asked what it was, and upon hearing the answer, he queried, "Oh, do you work someplace?"

THE NATURE OF WORK

Most of us "work someplace"—whether or not we receive a paycheck. Indeed, in Western society the nature of a person's work is probably the clearest indication of his or her social status. Our work is essential to our emotional health and to the progress of our society. In a more immediate sense, however, work is essential to our material well-being and even survival. Lacking sufficient banana trees beneath which to repose as ripened fruit continuously satisfies our hunger, we are compelled to "rise and shine" and "put our shoulders to the wheel." We must cooperate to produce the goods and services we need for life. Someone must cultivate our grain, weave our cloth, build our homes, and, yes, even bury us.

Viewpoint

A DISADVANTAGE OF SPECIALIZATION AND DIVISION OF LABOR

There was a parlor game making the rounds several years ago in which the players were asked to answer the question, "Who are you?" with three responses. Supposedly, deep psychological insights could be gained from the answers and their sequence. For example, a man who answers, "I am a teacher, I am a father, I am a Democrat," reveals much of his personal sense of self.

How frightening it would be to have no answers to the question! Without a sense of self, one almost ceases to exist. Most of us in Western nations achieve our sense of self through our work. We do, therefore, we are!

When modern manufacturing jobs became simplified, workers began to lose some of the sense of self associated with particular jobs. Repeating one simple operation over and over tends to reduce a worker's pride and feeling of involvement in the finished product. At one time it may have been possible to reply in answer to the parlor question, "I am an automaker." However, it is not very satisfying to admit "I am a lever operator," "a wrench twister," or a "windshield lifter."

Karl Marx called this problem **alienation**. Alienation is the separation of a worker from the product of his or her work. Alienation diminishes a worker's sense of self and reduces opportunities for creative expression and personal growth. Alienation often leads to boredom on the job, deteriorating product quality, and reduced worker productivity.

The harmful effects of division of labor have caused some firms to change their manufacturing processes entirely, to change from making jobs more simple to making them more complex. These firms allow teams of workers to organize the manufacturing process as in the "old days" before the assembly line. They reward worker teams according to the quantity and quality of the product. Actual production may be somewhat less than under the assembly-line method, but there have been benefits in improved worker morale, lower turnover, and, frequently, improved product quality and lower supervisory costs as well.

The change from self-sufficiency to cooperation in work marked the beginning of economic development. When workers divided the necessary work and specialized in particular tasks, they could produce more than they could working alone. To illustrate the benefits of division of labor and specialization, Adam Smith told a famous story of a pin factory. When workers are assigned specific tasks on an assembly line, he said, they can produce many times more pins than if all of the workers concentrate on producing finished pins.

During the early 1900s two American businessmen, Frederick Taylor and Frank

Gilbreth, studied division of labor and specialization. They called their work **task management**: the separation of jobs into simple operations requiring little special training or effort. Henry Ford used division of labor in his first auto assembly lines.

The effect of specialization and division of labor is to expand dramatically the output produced per hour of work. Through specialization and division of labor modern societies can produce not only the necessities but also some of the luxuries that enrich life. Thus, modern consumers can enjoy an abundance of VCRs, running shoes, ice makers, and so on.

LABOR SUPPLY AND DEMAND

This chapter focuses on labor as a productive resource. Productive resources are bought and sold in markets similar to the markets for finished goods and services. We will begin our discussion with the assumption that resource markets are perfectly competitive; that is, that the four characteristics of competition prevail. Later, we will relax the assumption of competition and describe the effects of market power in resource markets. Although our discussion focuses on the market for labor resources, we should note that the principles that govern supply and demand for labor apply as well to supply and demand for land, capital, and entrepreneurial resources.

Resource supply shows the quantities of a resource that would be offered for sale at various market prices. Like any other supply curve, a resource supply curve is drawn for a certain period of time over which factors other than price are assumed to remain constant. Thus, the supply of labor is the quantities of labor that would be offered at various wage rates over a certain period of time. When the individual supply curves of all workers are added together, the result is a market supply curve of labor.

In general, the supply of labor obeys the law of supply; that is, workers tend to offer larger quantities of labor at higher wages.

Likewise, the demand for labor obeys the law of demand: Firms tend to employ larger quantities of labor at lower wages. Market demand for labor is the sum of all individual firms' labor demand curves. As we found in product markets, the intersection of demand and supply determines the equilibrium price and quantity: the wage rate and the quantity of labor that will be employed during the time period for which the supply and demand curves are drawn.

The supply curve in Figure 6.1 shows the quantities of labor that would be offered for employment in a particular market at various wage rates. The supply curve slopes upward to show that larger quantities will generally be offered at higher wage rates. The demand curve slopes downward because larger quantities will be employed only at lower wages. The equilibrium wage rate in Figure 6.1a is $6 per hour. At a wage of $6, a total of 1 million hours of labor will be employed in this market.

The Opportunity Cost of a Productive Resource

In a perfectly competitive resource market, the equilibrium price reflects the opportunity cost of using the resource in a particular way. Equilibrium price is higher when there are many alternative uses for a resource and lower when the resource is useful for producing only one product. Likewise, equilibrium price is higher when the resource is relatively scarce and lower when the resource is plentiful.

In labor markets, the equilibrium wage determines another result. For an individual firm the market wage determines the most efficient quantity of labor to employ with the firm's own fixed resources. To understand this point, let us look more closely at an individual firm's demand curve for labor.

Figure 6.1   A Market for Labor.

As the wage rate increases, hours of labor supplied increase, and hours of labor demanded fall.

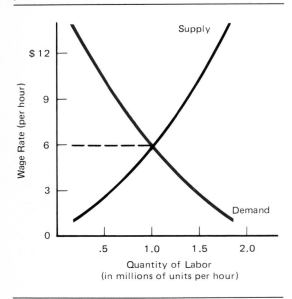

A Firm's Demand for Labor

Remember that a firm employs two kinds of resources: fixed resources and variable resources. **Fixed resources** are resources the firm cannot easily change in the short run. The firm cannot easily change the size of its plant and equipment in the short run, but the firm can vary the use of variable resources and, thus, the quantity of output from its fixed resources. **Variable resources** are such things as labor, raw materials, and the electric power necessary for operating the fixed plant.

The Law of Variable Proportions (or the Law of Diminishing Marginal Product)

As the proportion of variable resources to a firm's fixed resources changes, quantity of

output tends to change in particular ways. Adding the first units of variable resources to a firm's fixed resources generally causes quantity of output to increase by larger and larger amounts. We say that total product increases at an increasing rate. Eventually, however, adding more variable resources increases quantity of output by smaller and smaller amounts. We say that total product increases at a decreasing rate. At some quantity of variable resources, adding still more variable resources to a firm's fixed resources may cause total product to fall.

This principle is known as the **law of variable proportions**, or the law of diminishing marginal product. It states that there is some quantity of variable resources which, when used with a given quantity of fixed resources, yields the greatest increase in total product. We say that marginal product is at its maximum. Beyond this quantity (or range) of variable resources, each additional unit of the variable resource adds less to total product than the one before. We say that marginal product diminishes.

The Equilibrium Wage and Employment

There appears to be some quantity (or range) of variable resources that yields maximum marginal product when employed with a firm's fixed quantity of plant and equipment. If the firm employs too many or too few variable resources in relation to its existing fixed resources, additions to total product are smaller. To say that additions to total product are smaller is the same as to say that the cost of producing additional output is greater.

The firm does not normally employ precisely the quantity of variable resources that yields maximum marginal product. This is because, in the short run, the firm may sell its product for a price that is greater than (or less than) full costs of production. In fact, the firm must consider two kinds of market prices when making its employment decision:

1. The price of the finished product.
2. The price of the variable resource.

Thus, in the short run, an economically efficient firm decides resource employment according to the following rule:

> For efficient resource employment, a firm should employ units of a variable resource up to the point where the value of the output of the last resource unit hired is just offset by the resource's price.

As long as the firm follows this rule, it achieves maximum efficiency in the use of its fixed and variable resources.

Let us illustrate the resource-employment rule with a simple example. Table 6.1 provides hypothetical data for a grumpet firm that sells grumpets at a market price of $3. The firm owns a certain quantity of fixed plant and equipment and can employ various quantities of labor at an hourly rate of $6. Column (1) lists quantities of labor, and Column (2) lists total product per hour when various quantities of labor are employed. Notice that increasing employment of variable resources causes hourly production to increase, first, at an increasing rate, and then at a decreasing rate;

finally, if as many as seven workers are employed, hourly production will decrease.

Column (3) lists the market value of hourly production at various levels of employment, and Column (4) lists changes in the value of hourly production associated with changes in the level of employment. Column (5) lists the hourly wage.

How many workers should the firm hire? To hire one, two, or three workers would enable the firm to sell its grumpets and pay all the workers' wages. However, by hiring only one, two, or three workers, the firm sacrifices the gain from hiring the fourth worker at $6 and selling his or her additional output for $9. In fact, the firm should hire up to the fifth worker, whose additional production is worth just enough to pay his or her hourly wage.

Now, suppose the wage rate falls to $3. At a wage of $3, a sixth worker adds just enough to total product to pay his or her wage.

TEST YOURSELF
How many workers would the firm hire at a wage of $9?

Have you noticed that, given the behavior of marginal product in the short run when certain resources are fixed, the quantity of labor employed depends on the wage rate? In fact, we have just located three points on this firm's demand curve for labor: $w = \$9$ and

Table 6.1   Resource and Production Data (per hour).

(1) Number of Workers Q_L	(2) Total Product TP	(3) Value of Total Product $TP \times p$	(4) Value of Additional Production $\Delta(TP \times p)$	(5) Wage Rate w
1	2	6	6	6
2	5	15	9	6
3	9	27	12	6
4	12	36	9	6
5	14	42	6	6
6	15	45	3	6
7	14	42	-3	6

$Q_L = 4$; $w = \$6$ and $Q_L = 5$; $w = \$3$ and $Q_L = 6$. These points have been plotted on Figure 6.2 and connected to form this firm's demand curve for labor.

We can summarize resource demand as follows. Adding variable resources to a certain quantity of fixed resources eventually causes total product to increase at a decreasing rate. A firm calculates its own demand for a variable resource by measuring the value of the resource's contribution to total product. Then the firm employs the quantity of the resource at which the value of the marginal product of the last resource unit employed is just enough to pay the resource price. The firm's demand curve slopes downward because of the law of variable proportions (or the law of diminishing marginal product). The law says that when variable resources are added to fixed re-

sources, marginal product will tend to diminish. A firm will hire additional variable resources only if the value of the resource's marginal product is at least as great as the cost of hiring it.

Derived Demand

We describe the demand for a resource as a **derived demand**. A firm employs resources because there is demand for the products the resource can produce. It employs the quantity of any resource at which the value of the last unit's output is just enough to offset resource price. In competition all resources are paid a price equal to the value of the goods or services produced by the last unit hired. In fact, in competition all kinds of variable resources are paid according to the value of the output produced by the last unit.

After all variable resources are paid, the remaining revenue from the sale of output goes to the owners of fixed resources. Competition in resource markets will ensure that each type of resource is rewarded according to its own contribution to output.

Figure 6.2 A Firm's Demand for Labor.

A firm's demand curve for labor slopes downward because of the law of variable proportions (or the law of diminishing marginal product).

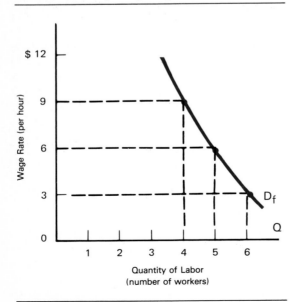

LABOR'S SHARE OF OUTPUT

Look again at Figure 6.1. Can you show on Figure 6.1 the space that represents the share of total output that is paid to labor? How does the size of the space reflect labor's productivity and market demand for labor's output?*

Of the four types of resources, labor receives the largest share of national income. One reason for labor's large share is the size and quality of the labor force. More and better workers have contributed to a growing eco-

---

* Labor's share is the rectangle formed beneath the demand curve at the equilibrium wage. It is determined by the equilibrium wage and the quantity of labor employed.

Contemporary Thinking about Economic Issues

TAKING CARE OF JUNIOR

Declining productivity growth and more slowly rising wages for male workers have pushed more mothers into the job market and increased the demand for day care for small children. The U.S. Congress has been considering proposals to expand the federal government's support of day care by about $27 billion over the next 5 years. The current intention seems to be a compromise between proposals to put more money in the hands of working parents and proposals to pay direct subsidies to day-care establishments.

The increasing demand for day care is increasing the derived demand for child-care workers. Child-care workers typically earn 30 to 60 percent less per hour than kindergarten or elementary school teachers.

Why? The wages of child-care workers are limited by the small number of children each worker serves, the revenue earned per child, and high overhead expenses of the establishment. Overhead costs include the costs of management, rent, equipment and supplies, insurance, payroll taxes, and interest or return on investment. Moreover, child-care workers are willing to accept low wages because they stay close to home and work part-time. They generally have less schooling than teachers, and they are not unionized.

Low wages reduce the quality of child-care workers. What can the nation do to improve the quality of day care?

Victor R. Fuchs, "Economics Applies to Child Care Too," *Wall Street Journal*, April 2, 1990.

nomic pie and a growing share for labor. From only 60 percent of total income in 1929, labor's share grew to 74 percent in 1989.* Rental income declined during that period from 6 percent to less than 1 percent, and interest earnings rose from 5 to 11 percent. Income of unincorporated enterprises, corporate profits, and farm income also declined, from 29 to 15 percent of total income.

In competition, differences in resource prices are the result of different supply and demand conditions in resource markets. For an especially productive resource in limited supply, resource price is relatively high. Less productive resources in more plentiful supply receive lower prices. Likewise, changes in resource supply and demand cause changes in resource price. Whether income shares increase or decrease with change depends on price elasticities of demand and supply, much as total expenditures in the markets for goods and services depend on price elasticities of demand and supply.

CHANGES IN DEMAND FOR LABOR

Growth in job opportunities has been uneven among industries. More workers have been needed in state and local government, retail

* Labor's increasing share is in part the result of a movement away from self-employment, where earnings would be reported as profit, to work for hire.

trade, transportation and public utilities, and services. The demand curves for these workers have been shifting to the right over the last decade, contributing to a rising equilibrium wage.

Employment opportunities have grown more slowly in the federal government, mining and construction, and manufacturing industries. The demand curves for these workers have shifted very little, so that their wage rates have not increased much in real terms.

Some examples of average hourly wage rates before taxes for workers in 1971 and 1987 are in Table 6.2. Data are from the *Monthly Labor Review*, published by the U.S. Department of Labor. Column (3) in the table

shows the gain in real wages—wages corrected for inflation—over the period shown.

HISTORY OF THE LABOR MOVEMENT

In the early years of the Industrial Revolution, two classes struggled to gain larger shares of national income: a small, well-organized, property-owning class of capitalists and a large, unorganized class of workers. Differences in the power of these two groups made for differences in their shares of income and living standards. According to Karl Marx, a nineteenth-century political and economic theorist, private ownership of capital re-

Table 6.2 Average Hourly Wages.

	Hourly Wage 1971	Hourly Wage 1987	Change in Real Wage (%)
Mining	$4.00	$12.52	− 18
Construction	5.56	12.69	− 14
Lumber and wood products	3.06	8.40	4
Furniture and fixtures	2.84	7.67	2
Stone, clay and glass products	3.55	10.25	9
Primary metal products	4.09	11.94	10
Fabricated metal products	3.67	10.00	3
Machinery, except electrical	3.90	10.70	4
Electrical and electronic equipment	3.43	9.88	9
Transportation equipment	4.44	12.95	10
Instruments and related products	3.48	9.71	6
Miscellaneous manufacturing	2.94	7.75	0
Food and kindred products	3.32	8.94	2
Tobacco Products	3.02	14.03	76
Textile mill products	2.54	7.17	7
Apparel	2.48	5.93	− 10
Paper products	3.58	11.43	21
Printing and publishing	4.08	10.28	− 5
Chemicals and allied products	3.84	12.37	22
Petroleum and coal products	4.49	14.59	23
Rubber and miscellaneous plastics	3.32	8.91	1
Leather products	2.58	6.08	− 11
Transportation and public utilities	4.08	12.03	12
Finance and real estate	3.24	8.73	2
Services	2.95	8.48	9
Wholesale and Retail Trade	2.83	6.53	− 13

How Things Have Changed

JOB SKILLS

The share of jobs requiring greater education has increased since 1970, from 21 percent to an estimated 28 percent in 1988. These jobs include white-collar jobs, such as professional, administrative, managerial, and technical jobs. Blue-collar jobs, including production workers, operative, and agricultural jobs, fell from 40 to 31 percent. Sales, clerical, and service jobs rose slightly and shifted more toward skilled jobs. Of workers in the service sector, 24 percent have college degrees, whereas only 11 percent of workers in goods-producing jobs hold college degrees. Fastest job growth in the 1990s will be in white-collar jobs, where 57 percent of workers have college degrees.

sources leads inevitably to class conflict and, ultimately, revolution. Revolution is followed by movement to a new, higher stage of historical development. Marx argued that the first great revolution moved Western nations from feudalism to capitalism, and the next would move capitalist nations to socialism. The greatest revolution of all would finally move socialist nations to communism.

When Marx was living, the possibility of class conflict and revolution was a real concern. During the Industrial Revolution in England, large landowners forced tenant farmers off the land so as to use their land to graze sheep to produce wool for the growing textile industry. Forced into the towns in great droves, the peasants sought jobs in the new factories and coal mines. Marx told stories of women and young children working long hours in sweat shops and dying of disease or malnutrition after a short and miserable life.

During any period of industrial development, a nation needs workers to build the capital resources necessary for producing more goods and services in the future. Producing capital goods requires a sacrifice of consumer goods. (Remember the production possibilities curve and the limits to total production.) The early capitalists found it relatively easy to require sacrifices from unorganized and desperate people, for whom any employment at all was better than starvation.

According to Marx, workers' hardships would eventually create class consciousness and rebellion. Violent revolution would destroy the capitalist class, and workers would seize the mines and factories. Afterward, the working class would operate capital resources in their interests alone.

Radical Unionism and Business Unionism

When the first labor unions were formed in Europe, radical Marxists thought they were the start of a new international brotherhood of labor that would overthrow capitalism and replace it with socialism. In the United States, however, the early revolutionary unions were soon replaced by **business unions**, unions that were concerned more with improving the material conditions of workers than with overthrowing the capitalists. U.S. workers did not think of themselves as part of a revolutionary class and were generally willing to cooperate with management to improve job conditions.

Rather than revolution, the most successful unions in the United States have emphasized specific problems in the workplace: wages, hours, sick leave, retirement, seniority, and fringe benefits. They have sought solutions to problems within the capitalist system. Contrary to Marxian expectations, the U.S. economy has provided higher standards of living both for the capitalists and for the workers. It has allowed many workers to become capitalists themselves, something else that Marx did not foresee.

Craft Unions and Industrial Unions

Eighteenth-century labor unions in the United States were typically craft unions, similar to the guilds of the Middle Ages. Their members specialized in skilled crafts such as shoemaking, carpentry, or printing. Most of the unions were small, and they quickly disbanded if employers objected. In fact, until 1842 unions were considered illegal conspiracies in restraint of trade.

As the Industrial Revolution spread, craft unions grew in number and size. However, a conflict arose over who should be eligible for union membership. Craft unions were exclusive organizations, limiting their membership to workers in the skilled crafts. Some workers wanted more inclusive unions, unions that would invite workers in an entire industry to join together under a single banner. An example of an industrial union was the Knights of Labor, which organized skilled and unskilled workers in particular industries into a nationwide federation of unions.

By 1886, the exclusive, craft formula was again dominating the labor movement. Cigarmaker Samuel Gompers organized the American Federation of Labor (AFL), and many local craft unions joined up. At the turn of the century, union membership comprised 750,000 workers, roughly 3 percent of the labor force. By 1920 membership had grown to 5 million, 12 percent of the labor force.

The 1930s

Union growth slowed during the 1920s because of general prosperity and economic progress. It declined further with the high unemployment of the Depression years. (Can you suggest a reason?*)

By the time of the Great Depression in the mid-1930s the U.S. economy was struggling with the problem of falling income, output, and employment. The Roosevelt administration was sympathetic to unions, and in 1935 Congress passed the Wagner National Labor Relations Act. The new law gave workers the right to organize and to bargain collectively with employers.

In the same year, the lingering conflict between the skilled, exclusive craft approach and the unskilled, inclusive industrial approach to union membership again divided the labor movement. Craft unions of skilled workers remained with the AFL. Industrial unions of unskilled workers left the AFL to form the more inclusive Congress of Industrial Organizations (CIO) under mineworker John L. Lewis. The CIO was a national federation of unions of unskilled, mass-production workers in modern automated industries.

By the time of World War II, union membership included almost one-fourth of the civilian labor force.

---

* When jobs are scarce, finding a job becomes more important than being a union member.

Postwar Labor Problems

Unions generally refrained from strikes and wage demands during World War II. After the war ended, however, their members insisted on higher wages to offset rising inflation, and a wave of strikes broke out. Congress reacted by passing the **Taft-Hartley Act** of 1947, which reduced the power of unions. The law guaranteed unions' bargaining rights but placed limits on strikes and certain "unfair labor practices." It granted the president the right to obtain an 80-day injunction to postpone a strike, and it outlawed certain union practices, including closed shop and secondary boycotts.

A **closed shop** requires employers to hire only union members at union wages. The Taft-Hartley Act replaced the closed shop with the **union shop**, in which workers can be required to join a union after they are hired. A **boycott** is a refusal to do business with a firm because of certain of its policies; this is generally legal. A **secondary boycott** is a boycott by one union because of a firm's policies toward another union; this is illegal.

Perhaps the most controversial part of the Taft-Hartley Act is Section 14B, which allows individual states to pass **right-to-work** laws. Right-to-work laws forbid the union shop within the state. Because workers are not required to join a union, right-to-work laws reduce unions' power over the work force. Twenty states, mostly in the South and Midwest, have right-to-work laws.

In 1955, the AFL and CIO buried their differences and merged into a single organization—the AFL-CIO. The two federations decided that by combining their strengths they would be better able to deal with growing public opposition to unions. Later, the Teamsters and United Auto Workers broke apart from the AFL-CIO. (The Auto Workers returned in 1981.)

Corruption in national unions in the 1950s prompted a congressional investigation by the McClellan Committee, and Congress passed new laws to regulate the internal affairs of unions. The **Landrum-Griffin Act** of 1959 required democratic election of union leaders and called for detailed reporting of union finances.

UNIONISM TODAY

Union membership in the United States has grown slowly in recent years. In 1950 about 15 million workers belonged to unions. By the end of the 1980s union membership had increased to more than 20 million. However, this number represents a diminishing share of the work force—from one-third in 1950 to less than one-fifth today.

In part, the relative decline in union membership is a result of the changing structure of the U.S. economy. We are becoming increasingly a service economy. Today more than half of consumer expenditures go for health, education, recreation, housing, and other services. Three-fourths of the nation's workers now work in service industries: transportation and public utilities; trade, finance, and real estate; and government. Many service occupations require skilled white-collar or professional workers. Such workers have traditionally been the most difficult to organize. Other service occupations are relatively unskilled and are difficult to organize because workers change jobs frequently, often leaving the labor force entirely for long periods of time.

In one sense, labor's weakness today is a result of its past successes. Wage increases won by unions have priced some union members out of the job market. High union wages have pushed some firms out of business and disrupted entire industries. In the U.S. automobile industry, for example, United Auto Workers' wages are generally higher than wage rates abroad. In some industries, nonunion workers have taken over jobs lost by

Contemporary Thinking about Economic Issues

FROM MANUFACTURING TO SERVICE JOBS

From rapid growth in manufacturing jobs in the 1950s and 1960s, in the 1970s the average annual increase in manufacturing jobs fell sharply. Then in the 1980s the absolute number of manufacturing jobs began to fall. More than a million jobs lost in the recession of 1981–1982 were never regained.

Some analysts say that's just fine. The United States is changing from a manufacturing economy to a postindustrial, service economy. In fact, while manufacturing employment has been shrinking, jobs in the service sector have increased to take up the slack. The optimists conclude that growth in the service sector will make for a cleaner, more challenging workplace, without the pollution and routine drudgery of manufacturing.

Of course, there are always pessimists, and Stephen S. Cohen and John Zysman have looked on the dark side of current trends. Cohen and Zysman point to the linkages that connect service jobs with manufacturing. Services such as programming, systems engineering, information processing, and designing are closely linked to underlying manufacturing industries. If the United States loses manufacturing, many service jobs will be lost as well.

Cohen and Zysman warn against confusing two kinds of trends. One trend includes the automation of one sector, which increases the productivity of labor and allows labor resources to be transferred into another, newly developing sector. This trend is favorable for promoting long-range growth and improved standards of living. The second trend includes the gradual disappearance of a sector and its relocation abroad. This trend is devastating to growth and threatens standards of living.

Manufacturing is the nation's primary generator of wealth. Our long-range prosperity depends on automating and increasing manufacturing. If we allow manufacturing to move abroad, we may lose more than just the smokestacks.

Stephen S. Cohen and John Zysman, *Manufacturing Matters*, Basic Books, Inc., New York, 1987.

high-cost union workers. This is particularly true in the building construction industry.

As their power has shrunk, unions have turned their attention to establishing a political climate favorable to labor's goals. They support government policies promoting high employment, federally supported job training, union wage scales for federal contractors, a legal minimum wage law, and national health insurance.

The largest unions are the Teamsters, the United Auto Workers, and the Steelworkers, each with more than a million members. Other strong unions are the Brotherhood of Electrical Workers, Retail Clerks, and Communication Workers. The fastest growing union today is the Association of State, County, and Municipal Employees, with more than a million workers.

Self-Check

1. **A significant force for economic development is:**
   a. Specialization.
   b. Division of labor.
   c. Interregional trade.
   d. All of the above.
   e. None of the above.

2. **The employment level of a variable resource is based on:**
   a. Its price.
   b. The price for which the final product sells.
   c. The availability of fixed resources.
   d. Both (a) and (b).
   e. All answers are correct.

3. **Karl Marx predicted that:**
   a. Tenant farmers would revolt against landowners.
   b. Violent revolution would redistribute property.
   c. Unions would make peaceful gains.
   d. Labor and management could work together profitably.
   e. Employment of labor would increase with advances in technology.

4. **Which of the following laws is most harmful to union interests?**
   a. Wagner National Labor Relations Act.
   b. Clayton Antitrust Act.
   c. Taft-Hartley Act.
   d. Landrum-Griffin Act.
   e. None is harmful to union interests.

5. **In 1989, union membership in the United States amounted to:**
   a. About one-third of the labor force.
   b. About one-fourth of the labor force.
   c. About one-fifth of the labor force.
   d. An insignificant fraction of the labor force.
   e. A large force of radical revolutionaries.

Theory in Practice

PRACTICE WITH RESOURCE MARKETS

We have focused on labor as the largest class of productive resource. Other resources are subject to the same kinds of demand and supply conditions that affect labor. Throughout the economic system, changes are constantly taking place in the availability of resources (supply) and in their productivity and the value of their output (demand). Resource buyers and sellers must constantly adjust to changes in the equilibrium price and quantity of land, labor, capital, and entrepreneurial ability.

Figure 6.3 illustrates an increase in resource supply and a fall in equilibrium price. How does a lower equilibrium price affect quantity employed? In general, we would expect a lower price to encourage buyers to employ more of this more plentiful resource. (They move down their demand curves and employ larger quantities.)

Figure 6.4 illustrates a decrease in resource supply and an increase in equilibrium price. The higher price discourages buyers from using this less plentiful resource. (They move up their demand curves and employ smaller quantities.) At the same time, the higher price encourages existing suppliers to

Figure 6.3   Increased Supply, Lower Price.

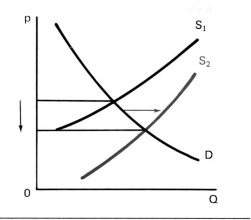

increase production, tending to increase quantity supplied.

When buyers and sellers adjust to changes in resource prices, the result is improved efficiency in resource employment. Throughout the economy, buyers substitute more plentiful (and cheaper) resources for less plentiful (and more costly) resources. Movement of buyers and sellers into and out of resource markets

Figure 6.4   Decreased Supply, Higher Price.

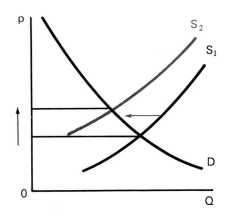

helps adjust supply to demand at competitive prices.

TEST YOURSELF
Trace the effects on resource supply of an increase in demand and a higher equilibrium price. What is the effect on economic efficiency? Now trace the effects on resource supply of a decrease in demand and a lower equilibrium price. What are the likely effects on the nation's total output of goods and services?

What productive resources are you developing as a student? Was your decision influenced by supply and demand in a particular resource market? How would changes in supply or demand affect your decision?

Now consider the following examples of changes in supply or demand. Explain the responses of buyers and sellers to each change. Then draw a graph of the affected resource market or markets and show the change in equilibrium price and quantity employed.

1. The Defense Department reduces its orders for military aircraft. What labor markets are immediately affected? Are there shifts in demand or supply? What other resource markets may eventually be affected?
2. A change in technology causes a reduction in the demand for long-playing records. How does a lower product price affect the demand for resources used to produce records?
3. Jamaica, a substantial producer of bauxite used in manufacturing aluminum, reduces its shipments to U.S. manufacturers. How does this change affect the market for aluminum used in the production of automobiles? What substitute or complementary markets may also be affected?
4. World famine increases the export price of American grain. How do higher grain prices affect the market for U.S. farmland and farm implements? Are there also effects in markets for suburban homes?

PRACTICE WITH A BACKWARD-BENDING SUPPLY CURVE

The supply curve of any resource depends on the willingness of resource owners to offer it in the market. The supply of labor is different from other resources because labor is inseparable from its owner. This sometimes makes for a peculiar supply curve.

We have said that the price of a resource reflects its opportunity cost: the value of the resource's output in an alternative employment. However, labor's opportunity cost includes also the cost of not working at all. Deciding to supply labor in production requires a wage that is high enough to offset the sacrifice of the worker's own leisure time.

In general, supplying small quantities of labor involves such a small sacrifice of leisure that a low wage is sufficient. Supplying larger quantities involves greater sacrifice and requires a higher wage. The result is a typical upward-sloping supply curve like the one we saw in Figure 6.1. If a worker reaches a very high level of material comfort, however, enjoying leisure may become more important to that worker than additional earnings, whatever the wage. When a worker reaches an income level adequate for his or her desired standard of living, the worker's supply curve becomes very steep and may even bend backward to the left.

Figure 6.5 illustrates a backward-bending supply curve. At a wage of w_1 a worker offers h_1 hours of work for total income represented by the rectangle formed by $0w_1 \times 0h_1$. If the wage rate rises to w_2, the worker can enjoy a higher income of $0w_2 \times 0h_2$ by supplying more hours of work. However, working only $0h_3$ hours yields the same income as before and leaves more hours for leisure. The higher wage could have the effect of reducing quantity supplied!

What is the actual level of wages at which workers begin to reduce hours worked? Of

Figure 6.5 A Backward-Bending Supply Curve of Labor.

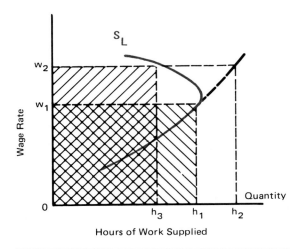

Hours of Work Supplied

course, this wage level differs for different workers. It depends on workers' current living standards relative to their desired living standards; and it depends on their attitudes toward work and leisure. For "workaholics" the backward bend in the labor supply curve would occur at a very high level of w. Workers in tropical climates probably experience the bend in labor supply at a lower level of w than workers in temperate climates. Can you explain why? Can you identify groups in the U.S. economy for whom the bend in supply might occur at a lower level than others? Might other resources also be subject to backward-bending supply curves? Why? (*Hint:* Consider crude oil or timber resources.)

UNION LABOR MARKETS

Unions affect resource markets in much the same way that imperfect competition affects product markets. In both cases, the goal is to control supply and keep price higher than it would be in a freely competitive market.*

Practice Determining Union Wage Rates

As we saw earlier in this chapter, a craft union is composed of workers with a particular skill, like the International Brotherhood of Electrical Workers or the International Ladies Garment Workers Union. In effect, members of a craft union represent the entire supply of a particular type of labor.

Historically, craft unions have tried to limit their membership, much as the American Medical Association and the American Bar Association have tried to limit the number of doctors and lawyers. Unions limit supply by establishing long apprenticeship programs and limiting access to the programs. Although many former discriminatory practices of unions are now illegal, unions still control the number of apprentices who are accepted for training in certain crafts.

The result of restrictions on membership is that there are probably fewer workers in these crafts than there would be under perfect competition. Thus, there is no competitive supply curve like the one in Figure 6.1. Instead, the supply curve for particular types of labor is a vertical line drawn at the quantity of labor supplied by the union. Look at Figure 6.6 and note the effect on the equilibrium wage rate for members of this craft union. Whereas the competitive wage rate would be about $7 per hour, the rate for unionized workers is about $11 per hour.

* Economist John Kenneth Galbraith believes that the trend toward union organization was actually a reaction to imperfect competition in product markets. He describes unions as ''countervailing power,'' labor power to balance the market power of industrial giants.

Figure 6.6 A Craft Union.

A craft union limits supply to raise the wage rate above the equilibrium wage.

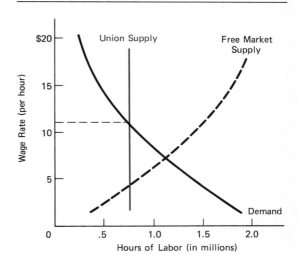

In contrast to a craft union, an industrial union represents all workers in an industry, whether skilled or unskilled. Again, control of the supply of labor enables the union to establish a higher wage rate. In this case, the union determines its wage rate through bargaining with management, keeping as an ultimate threat the possibility of a strike if a satisfactory wage agreement cannot be reached. Once a contract is signed, no labor will be supplied at a rate lower than the agreed-on wage. Thus, the supply curve becomes horizontal at that level, as shown on Figure 6.7. Firms can hire any quantity of workers shown on the horizontal portion of the supply curve. Firms can hire larger quantities by moving up the supply curve and paying a higher wage. Control of supply pushes the wage rate from the competitive wage of $7 to a union wage of $15.

Notice the effect of unions on total employment in Figures 6.6 and 6.7. When unions control supply, they prevent many willing

Figure 6.7   An Industrial Union.

An industrial union negotiates a wage rate higher than the equilibrium wage.

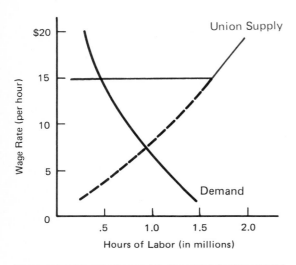

workers from entering certain markets. The result is a lower level of employment and higher labor costs than without a union. Lack of free competition interferes with the free flow of labor resources and reduces the efficiency of production.

TEST YOURSELF
In Figure 6.6 what is the difference in employment at a wage rate of $11 and $7? In Figure 6.7 what is the difference in employment at a wage rate of $15 and $7?

Unions, Wages, and Employment

In the real world, it is impossible to measure precisely the effect of labor unions on wages and employment. Why? Because it is impossible to separate the economic effects of unionism from the effects of other tendencies in the economic environment. For example, rising

wages may result not only from union power but also from:

1. A greater willingness of business firms to grant wage increases.
2. Government policies promoting full employment.
3. Oligopoly pricing, where large firms pass on higher wage costs to consumers in the form of higher prices.
4. The end of the nation's rural-to-urban migration, which formerly provided cheap labor and held wages down.

The combination of unionism with these other factors has probably kept wages higher during recessions than they would otherwise have been. In fact, although most prices tumbled during the Great Depression, wages of union members fell only slightly. When economic activity is on the upswing, on the other hand, union contract negotiations may lag behind price inflation, so that unions may actually slow the pace of wage increases. In both these cases, unions may keep income and total spending more stable than they might be otherwise.

During periods of economic growth and rising employment, union wages may rise faster than the prices of finished goods, squeezing business profits and discouraging new capital investment. Falling investment could become a problem, leading to low productivity growth and rising labor cost per unit of output.

The most powerful unions are those of skilled craftworkers for whom there are no clear substitutes. When there are no clear substitutes, demand is relatively inelastic, and firms must continue to employ necessary workers at higher and higher wage rates. This means that skilled workers can insist on higher wages with little fear of losing their jobs. Over the long run, however, substitutes can be developed for high-priced labor, so that labor

How Things Have Changed

WORK STOPPAGES

Year	Number	Workers Involved (×10³)	Days Idle (×10³)	Percentage Estimated Work Time
1960	222	896	13,260	0.09
1965	268	999	15,140	0.10
1970	381	2,468	52,761	0.29
1975	235	965	17,563	0.09
1980	187	795	20,844	0.09
1985	54	324	7,079	0.03
1986	69	533	11,861	0.05
1987	46	174	4,468	0.02

Statistical Abstract of the United States, 1989

demand curves become more elastic. Also, consumers can find lower-priced substitutes for goods produced by high-priced union labor.

The best example of labor substitution is in the bituminous coal-mining industry. A strong mine-workers' union in the 1940s and 1950s drove wage rates up to a point where mine owners and consumers sought substitutes. Mine owners developed coal-mining machinery to replace high-priced union labor, and consumers and business firms substituted cheap oil and gas for high-priced coal. Labor demand became more elastic, and the derived demand for labor fell. The result was increased unemployment for coal miners.

When high wages destroy jobs in unionized industries, unemployed workers must shift into nonunion jobs, increasing the supply of workers in these industries and causing wages there to fall. The result may be lower wages in the nonunion sector and lower average wages for the economy as a whole.

PRACTICE WITH COLLECTIVE BARGAINING

As a worker in U.S. industry, you may be invited (or required) to join a union. Periodically, your union leaders will negotiate a contract with management; the negotiating process is known as **collective bargaining**. A union contract covers wages, hours, fringe benefits, pension and insurance plans, and other conditions of employment. It may also include a no-strike provision for the life of the contract (generally from one to three years).

The wage clause guarantees a wage scale for various job classifications. It provides wage differentials for night work, supervisory responsibilities, hazardous or dirty work, and overtime work. It guarantees workers certain paid holidays and paid vacations depending on their length of service. It may allow the firm to collect union dues through automatic deductions from workers' paychecks. This is called a **union check-off clause**, and it increases the power of the union.

Beginning in the 1950s, high levels of inflation threatened the purchasing power of unions' pay scales. Inflation was a particularly serious threat when the life of a contract extended over several years. Unions insisted that clauses be added to contracts to guarantee cost-of-living increases* when prices rise. An example is a clause providing a 10 cent an hour increase in wages for each 0.5 percent increase in the consumer price index.

A typical union contract provides for pension and insurance benefits to be financed by employers, along with regular contributions withheld from employee paychecks. The employer's contribution is a tax-deductible expense—a cost of production similar to depreciation and other capital costs.

Firms in the auto, steel, and aluminum industries and some others have agreed to establish supplemental unemployment benefits financed entirely through employer contributions. With certain limitations, these funds provide cash benefits to workers laid off because of production cutbacks.

A union contract also includes provisions for job security. Generally, a unionized firm must give preference in layoffs and rehiring to workers with greater seniority (longer length of service). Seniority is less important in promotions, however, which are usually made on the basis of merit.

A union generally establishes procedures for disciplining or discharging workers for specified "good and proper" reasons. Proper reasons include violation of company rules,

* Cost of living adjustments are called **COLAs**.

excessive absenteeism, incompetence, or substance abuse. If a worker believes he or she was unjustly disciplined or discharged, the dispute may be taken to a grievance committee. Members of the grievance committee attempt to settle the dispute fairly through discussions with management.

During the process of negotiating a union contract, a mediator may be called in to help resolve differences between the bargaining parties. A **mediator** is an impartial outsider who helps the parties reach a compromise on particular issues; however, his or her recommendations are not generally binding.

If a conflict arises during the life of a contract, an arbitrator may be called in to settle the dispute. An **arbitrator** is an expert in the field of industrial relations. He or she is registered with the Federal Mediation and Conciliation Service and is expected to judge the situation impartially. The judgment of the arbitrator is binding on both sides.

There is no clear evidence to prove whether or not unions have actually raised the level of wages in U.S. industry. (It is impossible to know what wages might have been without unions.) It is probably correct to say that unions have helped stabilize wages and employment. To the extent that union leaders understand that increases in real wages depend on increases in productivity, they may persuade union members to improve their productivity before demanding higher money wages.

PRACTICE WITH PRODUCTIVITY

Increased labor productivity is important for two reasons. First, it enables us to enjoy higher standards of living. Second, it holds down production costs and helps reduce inflation. Since World War II, productivity of workers in private business has been increasing about 2.5 percent a year. Increases in productivity are the result of more and better equipment, more efficient use of resources, better management, and a better-educated work force.

Over the years, productivity growth has varied among industries, chiefly because of differences in the level of mechanization and standardization of production. The greatest gains have occurred in communications, electric power, gas, and sanitary services. Utilities like these are described as capital-intensive because each worker has a relatively large amount of capital equipment for increasing his or her productivity. Industries with few opportunities for mechanizing production are described as labor-intensive. Services like finance, real estate, and insurance fall in this category (although increased use of computers is increasing the capital intensity and productivity in these service industries, as well).

Table 6.3 shows the value of output produced (minus materials used) per dollar of la-

bor costs for various industries. Identify the capital-intensive and labor-intensive industries in the table.

Productivity growth slowed in the United States during the 1970s and continued low in the 1980s. One reason for the decline in productivity growth is a change in the composition of the labor force. More women and teenagers have joined the labor force, a result of the so-called baby boom that followed World War II. Many women and teenagers have had fewer opportunities for education and skill development, and their job performance has tended to be low. The quality of our capital stock has been changing also. New legislation requiring installation of environmental and safety equipment has reduced the measured output of goods per unit of resource employed. Finally, the U.S. economy has come increasingly to be dominated by service industries. Because service production cannot be significantly improved through the use of modern machinery, service industries offer fewer opportunities for productivity growth than manufacturing.

During the 1990s many of these conditions will change. Baby boom workers will reach their most productive years, and environmental and safety equipment will be fully operational.

Increasing productivity growth is an important goal for workers and for the nation as a whole. Slowing productivity growth brings slower growth in material standards of living. Rising labor costs push up prices. For these reasons it is important always to seek new methods for increasing productivity.

Table 6.3   Value Added Per Dollar of Payroll.
Value of output (net materials cost) per dollar of labor input

	1947	1973	1986
Tobacco	$3.10	$5.20	$9.36
Petroleum	2.70	4.51	4.15
Chemicals	2.75	3.80	4.22
Food	2.35	2.90	3.93
Instruments	1.60	2.55	2.70
Paper	2.25	2.35	2.73
Rubber	1.65	2.30	2.43
Lumber	1.80	2.25	2.15
Nonelectrical machinery	1.60	2.05	2.18
Transportation equipment	1.55	2.01	2.22
Textiles	1.85	1.98	2.16
Furniture	1.70	1.90	2.20
Apparel	1.75	1.90	2.28
Leather	1.75	1.85	2.14

PRACTICE IN POLITICAL ECONOMY

"Workers of the world unite. You have nothing to lose but your chains."

That was Karl Marx's message to indus-

Contemporary Thinking about Economic Issues

DECLINING PRODUCTIVITY GROWTH IN THE UNITED STATES

The foremost scholar of industrial productivity in the United States is Edward F. Denison of the Brookings Institution. Denison notes a marked slowdown in growth rates beginning in 1973, when the growth rate of potential national income fell from almost 4 percent to about $2\frac{1}{2}$ percent. **Potential income** is defined as production if unemployment were to be 4 percent and utilization of existing capital equipment appropriate for 4 percent unemployment. Actual national income per person employed fell even farther than potential income over the period Denison studied.

According to Denison, the fairly abrupt decrease in productivity growth in 1973 was followed by another in 1979. His research examines factors that contributed to growth both before and after the slowdown and then looks more closely at these six "residual factors" that may have been responsible for the change in growth:

1. Changes in the pace of technological advance probably did not contribute much to the growth slowdown. Spending for research and development (R&D) continued at almost the same rate as in the earlier period, but R&D efforts may have been subject to diminishing marginal product. Communication of new technological knowledge (both nationally and internationally) has probably improved.

2. A significant basis for slower productivity growth is a deterioration in performance of U.S. management. One reason is the diversion of attention away from efficiency in production toward legal and regulatory considerations. Wide fluctuations in market prices, stock prices, interest rates, and profits have required managers to focus more on short-term production decisions and have reduced the influence of persons knowledgeable in production technology. Furthermore, the reward system for U.S. managers does not compensate for attention to production processes that will become profitable only in the long run.

3. Denison found no significant evidence of a decline in work effort, although there was some indication of a decrease in job satisfaction.

trial workers more than a century ago. It was a call for revolution to overthrow the capitalist owners and managers of capital resources. Marx believed that history would move economic systems inevitably to communism, when the tools of capitalism would be owned ''in common'' and operated in the interests of workers.

What has been the actual outcome for capitalism? How correct were Marx's predictions?

The twentieth century has brought tremendous changes in manufacturing. Mass production has permitted greater specialization, with all the benefits of large-scale economies. Workers in industrialized nations have en-

4. There may be some misallocation of resources, which may be a result of restrictions against the use of testing in job placement and low minimum qualifications for employment. A misallocation of capital resources may be a result of a tax system that favored certain kinds of capital and may have distorted capital investment away from the most technically efficient kinds. Increasing barriers to trade may also have contributed to a misallocation of domestic resources.

5. The years of 1973 and 1979 were years of energy crises, but Denison found "no consistent relationship" between the use of energy and productivity growth. In fact, efforts to minimize the use of energy may have contributed to an increase in labor's productivity.

6. Other factors that contributed slightly to the productivity growth slowdown were inflation (by increasing the costs of information, prediction, and transactions), government regulations (by diverting labor and capital resources to comply with regulations), and delays resulting from legal problems and from the deterioration in the nation's highway system.

According to Denison, government's response to the productivity growth slowdown has focused too closely on investment, which is not primarily responsible for the problem. In the meantime, expenditures for growth-promoting activities (such as education) have not been increased and in many cases have been cut back. Moreover, government has not contributed to a business environment that promotes high and stable employment and price stability.

The initial response of business to the productivity growth slowdown has been to blame "Japanese competition." Fortunately, however, some business people are beginning to focus their attention on the long run, with greater incentives to production engineers and rewards for improved performance.

Edward F. Denison, *Trends in American Economic Growth, 1929–1982*, The Brookings Institution, Washington, D.C., 1985.

joyed more and better goods at lower relative prices than ever before in history.

The news has not all been good, however. Mass production has aggravated some of the problems that Karl Marx predicted. Remember Marx's prediction that large-scale production would lead to the alienation of the working class. As mere cogs in an impersonal capitalist machine, workers would lose the drive to achieve higher levels of craftsmanship, and their productivity would fall. They would grow bitter toward the system they felt oppressed them.

Fortunately—and this was not predicted by Marx—Western nations have been flexible enough to adjust to the human needs of workers. Democratic political institutions have provided the means for workers to express their job dissatisfaction in constructive ways.

Many Japanese and European firms have established innovative ways of dealing with problems at the workplace. In Germany, for instance, coal and steel firms have organized worker councils to consult with management on all decisions affecting jobs. Employees are represented along with stockholders on the board of every major corporation in the nation. Labor-management coresponsibility has long been in effect in other European nations, including socialist Yugoslavia.

Is the United States ready for this type of industrial democracy? In the 1970s Louis O. Kelso proposed an important change in labor-management relationships in the United States. Kelso proposed to "make every worker a capitalist"—but not in the way Marx predicted. Kelso's way is to enable workers to invest their own savings in industrial corporations.

In Kelso's "universal capitalism," a firm establishes an employee stock ownership trust—ESOT, for short. The ESOT obtains funds through bank loans and through the sale of stock to employees. Then the ESOT buys stock in the firm itself. It uses the dividends from the stock, first, to pay interest and principal on the bank loan and, ultimately, to pay dividends to worker-owners. In the meantime, workers and their representatives accumulate greater power to influence company policy and share in profits.

ESOTs have several advantages for a business firm and for the economy as a whole. The firm benefits from a work force that is committed to increased production; workers realize that their own prosperity depends on the company's prosperity and are less likely to make unreasonable wage demands. The economy benefits from a more equal distribution of income; modern technology can be capital-

intensive without depriving workers of adequate imcome.*

Now the question: Was Marx right? Or wasn't he?

SUMMARY

1. People achieve identity and status through their work. Primitive society took a great step forward when specialization and division of labor brought great increases in production.
2. Labor is a variable resource. Firms hire labor to use along with fixed resources to produce goods and services. An economically efficient firm employs labor up to the point where the cost of hiring the last unit of labor is just equal to the value of its product.
3. Two types of unions sought to organize workers in the United States. Craft unions were exclusive, each one consisting only of workers with a particular skill. Samuel Gompers' American Federation of Labor includes unions of this type. An alternative approach was industrial unions, which were inclusive and aimed at organizing all skilled and unskilled workers in an industry. The Knights of Labor was an example.
4. In 1935 the Wagner National Labor Relations Act was passed, guaranteeing labor's right to organize and bargain collectively. Also in the 1930s, unions under the leadership of John L. Lewis broke away from the AFL and organized unskilled, mass production unions into the Congress of Industrial Organizations.
5. After World War II public sentiment turned against unions. The Taft-Hartley Act was passed in 1947 to limit strikes and compulsory union membership.
6. Supply and demand for resources determines resource prices. A high price discourages the use of a relatively scarce resource and encourages its production. A low price encourages

---

* A disadvantage to workers is that their investment may be concentrated in one firm, with increased risk of loss.

use of a relatively plentiful resource and discourages further production.

7. Labor unions interfere with the smooth adjustment of supply in resource markets. The result may be a wage level that is higher than the free-market equilibrium wage. At the higher union wage, there is likely to be some unemployment of labor resources.

8. Through collective bargaining, a union draws up a contract with management. Provisions of the contract may include no strikes for the life of the contract, a guaranteed wage rate, an escalator clause, and pension and insurance plans.

9. Changes are taking place in the productivity of labor and of new types of capital equipment; labor is becoming more active in the ownership and control of business.

TERMS TO REMEMBER

division of labor: a system of production in which a job is divided into small tasks, and workers specialize in a small portion of the total job

fixed resources: resources (such as land and capital) whose quantities the firm cannot change in the short run

variable resources: resources (such as labor) whose quantities the firm can change, changing the level of output produced with the firm's fixed resources

law of variable proportions or **law of diminishing marginal product:** as more variable resources are added to a fixed quantity of plant and equipment, total product eventually increases by smaller amounts

business unions: unions that are concerned with job needs, such as wages, hours, and working conditions, rather than with radical politics

craft unions: unions whose members specialize in a particular craft or skill

industrial unions: unions whose members include all workers in a particular industry, skilled and unskilled alike

closed shop: an agreement made by a firm to hire only workers who are union members; outlawed by the Taft-Hartley Act of 1947

union shop: a rule, permitted in some states, in which workers must join the appropriate union after they are hired

secondary boycott: a boycott by a union against a firm because of its policies toward another union; outlawed by the Taft-Hartley Act of 1947

collective bargaining: the negotiating process between a union and management aimed at reaching an agreement on the union contract

capital or **labor intensive:** production processes using substantial quantities of capital or labor resources per unit of output

ESOT: employee stock ownership trust

TOPICS FOR DISCUSSION

1. Explain each of the following expressions and tell how it is significant in the use of labor resources:

   Specialization and division of labor
   Alienation
   Opportunity cost
   Countervailing power

2. Distinguish between each of the following pairs of expressions:

   Craft unions and industrial unions
   Fixed and variable resources

3. How did the following pieces of legislation contribute to the growth of the labor movement:

   Wagner National Labor Relations Act
   Taft-Hartley Act

4. Rising gasoline prices have been particularly hard on workers in the U.S. automobile industry. This may be a long-range problem that will require major adjustments in labor markets over the coming decades. What adjustments would you predict? Explain your answer in terms of demand, supply, and equilibrium price (wage). Include markets for

other types of labor as well as for automobile workers.

5. Some of the blame for declining productivity growth in the United States has been placed on labor. Even with all the advantages of large-scale technology, we may be failing to motivate U.S. workers to contribute their maximum effort to production. This is in sharp contrast to management techniques in Japan, which have apparently earned the loyal enthusiasm of workers for their jobs. It has been suggested that business firms should hire industrial engineers to be used as "vice-presidents of human productivity."

Imagine that you have accepted such a position in a large U.S. firm. How would you approach the problem of motivating workers? What production information would you need and how would you use it? What new programs or policies would you initiate?

6. Can you think of any disadvantages of joining a union? What are the advantages? Compare the advantages and disadvantages of unionism as a whole. What are the effects on society? Does your answer depend on the type of union and the quality of union leadership? Explain.

7. Rising energy prices have caused some policymakers to turn to new "soft" energy sources: sun, wind, biomass (organic waste). Discuss the implications in terms of the derived demand for resources.

8. Only about 30 of the nation's 15,000 banks are unionized. A small Minnesota bank suffered a long strike when eight female employees formed a union to protest discriminatory employment practices. Why do you suppose banks have been slow to unionize, and what do you expect will be the effect on other banks of the strike in Minnesota?

9. What do pecan rolls in Alaska's Westward Hotel have to do with traffic on the New Jersey turnpike? If you were the hotel pastry chef and you were offered double wages to leave the hotel and follow construction crews at work on the Alaskan pipeline to help provide eastern commuters with gasoline, you would be well aware of the connection. At a cost of at least $4.5 billion, the Alaskan pipeline turned out to be the largest construction job ever attempted. Discuss the probable effects of the pipeline project on these other markets:

> Pick-up trucks and hardware
> Crane operators
> Housing and linens
> Movies and radios
> Transportation services
> Illicit activities

10. Trace the effects on resource supply of an increase in demand and a higher equilibrium price. How are the results helpful to the economy? Now trace the effects on resource supply of a decrease in demand and a lower equilibrium price. What are the results for the economy as a whole in terms of the productivity of resources?

11. What productive resources are you developing as a student? Was your decision influenced by supply and demand in a particular resource market? How would changes in supply or demand affect your decision?

12. In what sense is the demand for oil transport a derived demand? Give other examples of derived demand. Illustrate graphically how increasing costs of a resource affect the market for a finished product.

13. Write a good definition for "productivity." Demonstrate mathematically how changes in the composition of the nation's output can affect average productivity of the nation as a whole. Give some reasons for low productivity growth in the service sector of the economy.

ANSWERS TO TEST YOURSELF

(p. 119) 4.

(p. 129) 1. Demand curves for engineers, designers, technicians, steel, and other raw materials shift to the left. Eventually demand curves for homebuilders and producers of consumer goods and services also shift to the left.

2. Resource demand curves shift to the left.

3. The supply curve of aluminum shifts to the left. Demand curves for substitute materials (tin, steel) may then shift to the right.

4. Demand curves for farmland and farm implements will shift to the right. Supply curves of suburban homes will shift to the left.

(p. 132) About 0.4 million workers; about 1.1 million workers.

Measuring Economic Activity

or How to Prove Anything with Statistics

We have used the concepts of supply and demand to describe markets for finished goods and for productive resources. The study of individual markets is called **microeconomics**. In this chapter we will focus on total production of all goods and services in the economy as a whole. The study of all markets taken together is called **macroeconomics**. To begin our study of macroeconomics we will show how to measure the value of all goods and services produced during the year, and we will make some judgments about how well our economic system is satisfying the needs of our people.

THE CIRCULAR FLOW OF SPENDING, PRODUCTION, AND INCOME

It is helpful to divide economic activity into two types of flows:

1. Spending flows paid to business firms for the goods and services consumers want to buy.
2. Income flows paid to households for business firms' use of productive resources— land, labor, capital, and entrepreneurial ability.

Flows of spending and income are shown in Figure 7.1, arranged to form a circle.

Flows of Spending

The upper loop of the circular flow in Figure 7.1 shows total spending in all the nation's

Figure 7.1 The Circular Flow of Spending, Production, and Income.

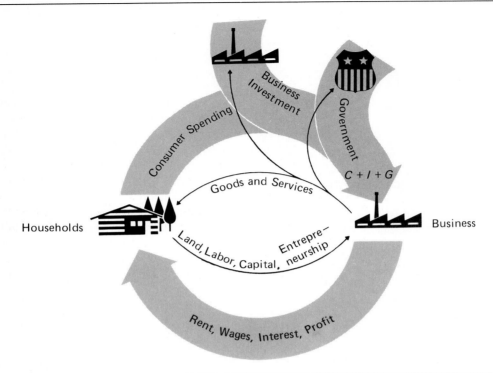

markets for goods and services. These are the markets we described in Chapters 2 through 5. In all these markets, spending flows in one direction, and newly produced goods and services flow in the opposite direction.

Notice that the largest part of spending comes from households. Households purchase consumer goods and services, such as autos, appliances, food, clothing, and recreation and health services.

Business firms also spend. They purchase raw materials, parts, equipment, buildings, and services from other business firms. Business spending for plants, equipment, and inventory is called **investment**.

The third major spender is government. Governments purchase goods and services to be used in the operation of government agen-

cies and for carrying on government programs. Only government purchases of goods and services are included in the spending flow. Not included are **transfer payments**—welfare checks, unemployment compensation, food stamps, and veterans' benefits—because such payments are not spending for new goods and services.

Foreigners also purchase goods and services produced by U.S. business firms, and U.S. consumers buy from foreigners. The net value of foreign spending is called **net exports**, which are becoming an increasingly important component of total spending in the U.S. economy. The complexity of international trade, however, calls for separate treatment. Therefore, we will omit net exports from our discussion of the circular flow at this point and consider foreign purchases in detail in Chapter 15.

Total spending by all these groups is a measure of all goods and services produced for sale during the year:

consumer spending
+
business *investment* spending
+
government purchases
= C + I = G =
total spending for new goods and services

Total spending is also a measure of business receipts from sales, which are available for distribution to the owners of resources used in production:

total spending for new goods and services
= business firms' income from sales

Flows of Income

Business firms use their income from sales to employ productive resources: land, labor, capital, and entrepreneurship. Productive resources are supplied by people in households, who receive income in return for the use of their resources. The lower loop of Figure 7.1 represents all the markets for resources. We discussed resource markets in detail in Chapter 6. We found that demand for a resource depends on demand for the things it can produce and that supply depends on the willingness of resource owners to sell various quantities of resources at various prices. In resource markets, land, labor, capital, and entrepreneurial ability flow in one direction; income, in the form of rent, wages, interest, and profit, flows in the opposite direction.

Not all spending received by business firms is actually paid to households as income. A portion of revenue from sales must be paid in taxes, and a portion is set aside in the form of business saving, including allowances for

depreciation of capital equipment. Only the remaining revenue—after taxes and business saving—is used to pay productive resources.

The sum of rent, wages, interest, and profit is national income. Strictly speaking, national income is income earned by productive resources. Thus, government transfer payments are not counted in national income, since they are not earned payments for contributions to production. The income that is actually received by individuals, including transfer payments, is called **personal income**. Personal income minus personal taxes (income tax, property tax, and inheritance tax) is the amount known as **disposable income**.

The derivation of disposable income can be summarized as follows:

total spending for new
goods and services = business revenue
− business saving
− business taxes

national income = $w + r + i + \pi$
(income earned)

+ transfer payments

Personal income (income received)
− personal taxes

disposable income

Most households save part of their disposable income. However, they spend the largest part for new consumer goods and services. Their new spending returns to the circular flow and becomes part of the flow of spending in the next period. The circular flow is complete.

GROSS NATIONAL PRODUCT

The circular flow represents a concept that is familiar to many of us: gross national product, or GNP. GNP is the final value of all goods and services produced for sale during the year: trucks, stereos, blue jeans, eggs, dental

Viewpoint

THE COMPOSITION AND GROWTH OF GROSS NATIONAL PRODUCT

As a nation develops, the composition of gross national product tends to change. The earliest type of production for exchange is typically production of *primary* products. Primary products are things that are "extracted" from a region's farms, forests, mines, and seas. Thus, they include food and animal products, lumber and fibers, ores and fossil fuels. Producing such goods requires a relatively low level of technology and little capital equipment. It uses the resources that are most abundant in nations at a low level of economic development: land and unskilled labor.

Primary products satisfy consumers' basic needs for food, clothing, and shelter. Once these needs are fully satisfied, consumers tend to want goods that improve the quality of life, and a region moves into production of *secondary* products. Secondary products are manufactured goods: furniture and appliances, transportation equipment, machines and tools. Manufacturing requires technology and capital investment at levels ranging from relatively sively than primary production does, and it employs a wider range of worker skills.

The third type of production for exchange is *tertiary* production; that is, the production of services. Services are activities performed on or for people and include personal services (like hairstyling, medical care, and entertainment) and business services (like financial accounting, investment consulting, and engineering design). Production of services requires a fairly high level of development in primary and secondary production because basic needs for material goods must be satisfied before labor can be released to perform services. Services improve the quality of life significantly, and their production offers workers many opportunities to develop creative and unique personal skills.

Over the years, the United States has moved through primary, secondary, and tertiary production. In 1975 production of services finally exceeded production of primary and secondary goods, and by 1990 spending for services was almost one-fifth

care, mail service, and so forth. GNP also includes finished goods and parts produced in the current year and held in business inventories to be sold in later years.

Note that GNP includes only the final value of current production and leaves out intermediate goods and materials such as steel for autos and flour for bread. Including intermediate goods would overstate the current value of GNP. If an auto, for example, sells for $8000 it may include a chassis worth, say, $4000, an engine worth $3000, $100 worth of

greater than spending for durable and nondurable goods. The total of wages and salaries for producing services has grown almost 10 percent annually since World War II, compared with less than 7 percent in manufacturing. Service employment has grown almost 4 percent annually, compared with less than 1 percent in manufacturing. In fact, manufacturing employment reached a peak in the United States in 1979 and declined throughout most of the 1980s.

The slow growth or decline of U.S. manufacturing industries has been a source of concern for some economists. Certain political leaders have begun calling for a new "industrial policy" aimed at revitalizing U.S. industries that have been unable to compete with newly developing manufacturing industries abroad. Their recommendations have included:

1. A central agency to decide industrial policy.

2. Councils of business, labor, and governmental leaders to gather information and recommend strategy for industrial development.
3. A federal development bank to invest in industries that need additional support.
4. Government aid to enable weak industries to adjust to new economic conditions.

Other political leaders have recommended greater reliance on free-market forces to encourage workers and investors to leave capital-intensive, labor-intensive, and resource-intensive industries and move into high-technology–intensive industries. Such industries require a high level of research and development spending relative to total output, but developing them would help maintain the competitiveness of U.S. industries relative to industries abroad.

electrical equipment, and a transmission worth $500. Including all these parts along with the car's final value would be double-counting.

GNP also leaves out sales of goods produced in earlier years. This means that sales of used cars, sales of existing houses, and sales from last year's inventory are not included. Stocks and bonds are not included either because they are not goods or services. The same is true of the sale of unimproved land.

Government transfer payments are not included in GNP because they are not payments for producing goods and services. (However, when consumers spend their transfer payments for consumer goods and services, those purchases are counted as consumer expenditures.) Nonmarket exchanges of goods and services are also omitted from GNP: gifts of homegrown vegetables, volunteer work, and the unpaid services of housewives. (It has been said that a man who marries his housekeeper reduces the nation's GNP. Can you explain why?)

We measure GNP in two ways:

1. *Spending on output.* GNP is the total value of spending for goods and services produced in the country in the current year. We have seen that purchases are made by consumers, business firms, and governments. Thus, GNP is the sum of spending flows in all product markets, as shown in the upper loop of Figure 7.1. It represents total demand in the economy, or aggregate demand:

$$\text{aggregate demand} = C + I + G = \text{GNP}$$

2. *Income of resources.* GNP is also total income received from current production of goods and services. Remember that a portion of business revenue from sales must be used to pay taxes and to save for future investment. However, the largest part is divided among resources employed in production, in the form of rent, wages, interest, and profit. Thus, GNP is the sum of income flows in all resource markets, as shown in the lower loop of Figure 7.1. Taken together business revenue from sales measures the value of all resources used in production and is, therefore, the value of total production or **aggregate supply**: GNP = $w + r + i + \pi$ + business taxes and saving = aggregate supply.

We can express these relationships with a simple formula:

$$\text{aggregate demand (spending)}$$
$$= \text{GNP} =$$
$$\text{aggregate supply (income)}*$$

You may say that total spending (aggregate demand) may not always equal total production (aggregate supply). In fact, a reduction in between current spending below current production can cause major headaches for business firms. Nevertheless, in a real sense the two values are always equal. The reason is the effect of inventories. Firms that are unable to sell all their current production to consumers or to government or other business firms in effect "purchase" their own output and add it to their inventory stocks. Whenever such "unplanned" inventory investment occurs, "planned" aggregate demand does indeed differ from aggregate supply. In this and the next chapter, we will distinguish between planned and unplanned investment expenditures and show how differences in "planned" spending and production may bring on changes in the level of economic activity.

The relationship between spending on output and income from production can be illustrated through a simple diagram. On the left side of the following equality are listed the components of aggregate demand: on the right are the components of aggregate supply. Note that the sums of the two columns are actually two ways of measuring the same quantity: GNP.

---

* The expression AD = GNP = AS is actually an identity: that is, the two sides of the expression measure essentially the same thing, approached from different directions.

$$\left.\begin{array}{c} \text{AGGREGATE DEMAND } (AD) \\ \text{consumer spending} \\ + \\ \text{government purchases} \\ + \\ \text{business investment spending} \\ + \\ \text{net exports} \end{array}\right\} = \text{GNP} = \left\{\begin{array}{c} \text{AGGREGATE SUPPLY } (AS) \\ \text{wages and salaries} \\ + \\ \text{rent} \\ + \\ \text{interest} \\ + \\ \text{profit} \\ + \\ \text{business saving} \\ + \\ \text{business taxes} \end{array}\right.$$

CHANGES IN THE CIRCULAR FLOW

Macroeconomics is concerned with the size of the circular flow. Most of us favor a steadily rising GNP for the rising standards of living that provides. We want GNP to grow fairly steadily, in line with our fairly steady growth in population and in the productivity of resources. If GNP grows more slowly than our nation's productive capacity, workers will be unemployed, and incomes will be lower than they might have been. The nation will be operating inside our production possibilities curve and failing to make efficient use of our scarce resources. When GNP fails to grow at all for two consecutive quarters, we say the nation is experiencing **recession**.

Too fast growth of GNP presents other problems. If GNP growth exceeds growth in our nation's productive capacity, we will be trying to produce outside our production possibilities curve. Too rapid growth could mean shortages of materials and skilled labor, with tendency for prices and wages to rise. The result of too rapid growth of GNP may be **price inflation**.

What determines the level of GNP and its rate of growth?

The level of total production depends on aggregate demand (*AD*). **Aggregate demand** is the sum of consumer spending, business investment spending, and government purchases ($AD = C + I + G$). If planned spending from any of these sources increases, the entire circular flow tends to expand. Profit-seeking firms will increase production in order to satisfy the higher demand for goods and services. On the other hand, if planned spending falls, the circular flow tends to contract. Business firms will cut back production to avoid losses on unsold goods and services.

The next sections describe how our economic system adjusts to changes in the spending plans of consumers, business firms, and government.

An Increase in Aggregate Demand

An increase in aggregate demand (*AD*) might begin with an increase in consumer spending (*C*). If many consumers become optimistic about the future, they may cut back on their savings in order to enjoy the "good life" now with little fear of hard times ahead. They may go on a spending spree and purchase a variety

Contemporary Thinking about Economic Issues

IMPROVING THE MODEL

Lawrence Klein won the 1980 Nobel Prize in Economics for his work in building a "model" of the U.S. economy. A model is a simplified view of reality, in which the important parts of the system interact to yield predictable results for the economy as a whole. Klein's model included hundreds of mathematical equations describing the behavior of consumer, business, government, and foreign spending. Putting the equations together and solving the model yields an estimated value for gross national product (GNP).

Today, Klein is worried about the "balance" of the U.S. economy: the balance between government defense spending and investment, the balance between consumer spending and saving, and the balance between foreign spending in the United States and U.S. spending abroad. Imbalances among all the various kinds of spending imply opportunity costs that, Klein believes, weaken our nation's capacity to compete and grow.

One source of imbalance is the enormous military buildup, which stresses military objectives at the expense of important economic and social goals. An opportunity cost of military spending is investment to increase the nation's productivity capacity. Instead of heavy military spending, Klein recommends a national industrial policy to encourage capital formation and create jobs. He believes that favorable tax rates for research and development and business investment would increase productivity and enhance the nation's competitiveness in world markets. Moreover, cooperative youth training programs involving the private and public sectors would increase the nation's "human capital" and help relieve the problem of unemployment. Such policies would bring on stronger economic growth, which would extend to the nation's smokestack industries and promote their revival.

Another source of imbalance is the emphasis on consumption, which reduces saving and reduces the capacity for private investment. Finally, the imbalances in foreign spending result in a transfer of the nation's wealth abroad. In both these cases, the opportunity cost of current consumption is the failure to construct capacity to produce more goods and services in the future.

According to Klein, correcting these imbalances would yield a more dynamic economy in the 1990s, displaying some of the vigor and strength of the 1960s. With emphasis on high-tech industries and high-productivity agriculture, he believes the nation could recapture some of its earlier prosperity.

U.S. News and World Report, January 31, 1983.

of new consumer goods: campers, video cameras, and hot tubs.

Another reason for an increase in aggregate demand might be an increase in business investment plans (I). Business firms may decide to invest in new products or new technical processes. Or faster population growth may encourage business firms to build new factories, rail lines, and power plants to satisfy expected growth in consumer demand. Some business firms may increase inventory investment in expectation of an increase in consumer spending.

Finally, an increase in aggregate demand might begin with an increase in government purchases (G). The federal government may decide to spend more for national defense or for research and development of new technologies. Or perhaps state and local governments may increase their spending for schools, roads, or parks.

Whatever the source of the increased spending, the result is greater incentives to produce goods and services, so as to satisfy the increased demand. More workers are hired, raw materials ordered, and factories built. The increased spending circulates throughout the economy, raising incomes of workers and suppliers. Workers and suppliers spend their higher incomes for consumer goods and services, and their increased spending adds to the incomes of other workers and suppliers. Thus, the initial increase in spending is magnified as rising incomes spread throughout the economy. An increase in spending increases the size of the circular flow, increases the production of goods and services, and increases employment of the nation's productive resources.

A Decrease in Aggregate Demand

Eventually the new spending that began the upward spiral in incomes will slow down. Unsold goods will pile up in inventories. When inventories begin to accumulate, retailers reduce their orders from manufacturers, and factories reduce production. They lay off workers, and the economy enters a slump. Cutbacks in spending circulate throughout the economy. More workers are laid off and cut back their own spending for consumer goods and services. The entire circular flow contracts.

A decrease in aggregate demand may begin with any of the three major groups of spenders we described earlier. Sometimes a decrease in aggregate demand is caused by consumers' decisions to spend less of their incomes. They may be overstocked with consumer goods, or they may be heavily burdened by debt and pessimistic about the future. Instead of spending all their incomes now, they may decide to put aside more savings for hard times ahead.

More often, a decrease in aggregate demand is caused by business firms' decisions to reduce their spending for new investment. If business firms have completed all desired new projects, they may not need additional productive capacity. They may be holding too many goods in inventories, gathering dust in warehouses.

Finally, a decrease in aggregate demand may be caused by government's decision to reduce spending for public projects. Government spending is tied to the production of community services and defense. Because these needs come along irregularly, government spending tends to fluctuate widely, adding to aggregate demand in some years and reducing it in others.

Whatever the source of the decrease in aggregate demand, the result is a decrease in the production of goods and services. Business firms want to avoid losses on unsold goods; so they cut back on orders for materials and lay off workers. They cancel plans for new buildings and equipment, and incomes of workers and suppliers fall.

As their incomes fall, workers are forced

How Things Have Changed

RESEARCH AND DEVELOPMENT EXPENDITURES (1987)

	France	West Germany	Japan	United Kingdom	United States
R&D expenditures ($ billions)	16.4	22.8	44.7	15.7	127.7
Percentage of GNP	2.4	2.8	2.8	2.4	2.8
Nondefense R&D ($ billions)	13.1	21.6	41.4	11.7	88.6
Percentage of GNP	1.8	2.6	2.8	1.8	2.0

A larger portion of U.S. research and development (R&D) is defense related. Still, to the extent that R&D produces knowledge with the same benefits regardless of the size of GNP, the United States' high expenditures for R&D provide substantial basis for technological advance. Average private returns on R&D investments are high: some say more than 20 percent a year. Moreover, there are external benefits of R&D that extend beyond the initial investor.

to reduce their spending for consumer goods and services. Then more business firms are forced to cut back production. The initial decrease in spending is magnified as falling incomes circulate throughout the economy.

INFLOWS AND OUTFLOWS

It is helpful to think of changes in the circular flow in terms of flows into and out of the spending stream. Spending by consumers, business firms, and governments constitutes inflows into the circular flow. Expenditures included in aggregate demand are received by business firms as shown in the upper loop of Figure 7.2.

Spending flows received by business firms are paid to households as income. Households use their incomes in any of three ways. Taxes must first be paid (T), a portion of income is saved (S), and the remaining income is spent for consumer goods and services (C). Consumer spending remains in the flow and continues to circulate, but taxes and saving flow out of the circular flow.

Outflows represent the part of consumer income not spent: autos, appliances, and clothing not bought, trips not taken, homes not built. In order for the circular flow to remain stable at the current level of income, some other groups must spend an amount equal to what consumers fail to spend. Government or business firms must purchase the new goods and services that are not bought by the household sector. In effect, outflows from the household sector must be balanced by new inflows from business or government.

Figure 7.2   Inflows and Outflows in the Circular Flow.

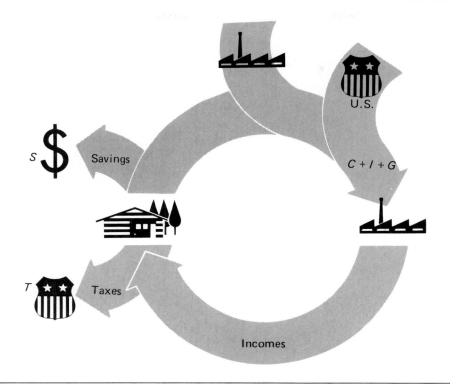

There are several ways outflows from spending might be replaced by new inflows. Saving outflows (*S*) may be returned to the circular flow by new investment spending (*I*) on the part of business firms; or tax outflows (*T*) may be returned by government spending (*G*). Or the sum of saving and tax outflows may be returned to the circular flow by some combination of new investment and government spending; thus,

$$S + T = I + G$$

If all outflows from spending are returned as new inflows, the circular flow remains stable. Aggregate supply is equal to aggregate demand at the current income level:

$$C + S + T = C + I + G$$
$$\text{means}$$
$$AS = AD$$

If outflows are not balanced by new inflows, there will be changes in the entire circular flow.

Consider first an excess of inflows over outflows: $I + G > S + T$. If inflows of new spending are greater than outflows from the spending flow, the level of GNP tends to increase. The higher level of aggregate demand encourages an increase in aggregate supply, and the circular flow expands. Now consider an excess of outflows over inflows: $S + T > I + G$. If outflows are greater than inflows,

GNP falls. Lower aggregate demand causes a drop in aggregate supply, and the circular flow contracts.

When inflows and outflows are precisely in balance, we say the economy has reached equilibrium. There is no tendency for GNP either to expand or to contract.

In the remainder of this chapter, we will look at GNP in more detail. In the next chapter we will develop an economic model that explains how aggregate demand determines the equilibrium level of spending, production, and income.

Self-Check

1. **Which of the following is included in GNP?**
   a. An appendicitis operation.
   b. An antique table.
   c. Wood flooring in a new house.
   d. Purchase of a U.S. Treasury bond.
   e. A gift of homemade cookies.

2. **The major groups of spenders are:**
   a. Consumers, savers, and investors.
   b. Consumers, business, and government.
   c. Land, labor, capital, and managers or entrepreneurs.
   d. Savers, investors, and government.
   e. Aggregate demand and aggregate supply.

3. **Productive resources:**
   a. Flow in return for consumer expenditures.
   b. Are outflows from the circular flow.
   c. Flow from households to business firms.
   d. Flow from business to government.
   e. Are rent, wages, interest, and profit.

4. **GNP is likely to grow if:**
   a. Consumers are pessimistic about the future.
   b. Business has completed all desired investment projects.
   c. Consumers are well stocked with goods.
   d. The government cuts back on its defense program.
   e. Population growth causes higher aggregate demand.

5. **The circular flow will stabilize at the level of spending and income at which:**
   a. Aggregate demand is equal to aggregate supply.
   b. $C + I + S = C + T + G$.
   c. New inflows of spending = outflows from income.
   d. All of the above.
   e. Both (a) and (c).

6. **Changes in consumer, business, or government spending:**
   a. Have no effect on production plans.
   b. Are a subject of microeconomics.
   c. May cause recession or inflation.
   d. Constitute aggregate supply.
   e. All of the above.

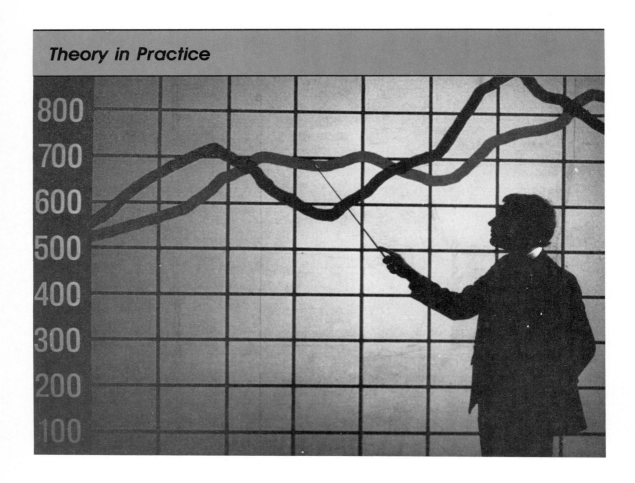

Theory in Practice

PRACTICE MEASURING GNP

In this section you will use recent data from the U.S. economy to measure actual GNP. (Data are altered slightly for simplicity.) Table 7.1 lists the components of GNP and income for 1989. Pencil the data into the appropriate places in the circular flow shown on Figure 7.3. Then answer the following questions. (Answers can be found at the end of Topics for Discussion.)

1. Calculate aggregate demand by measuring upper-loop spending on output. _____

2. Calculate aggregate supply by measuring lower-loop income from production. (Include business taxes and savings to ensure that aggregate supply is indeed equal to aggregate demand.) _____

3. Now calculate national income, or income earned by productive resources. _____

4. In addition to income from production, many households receive transfer payments from government. Transfer payments increase an individual's or family's personal income. Add transfer payments to national income to find personal income. _____

5. Now compute the following percentages:

    Consumer spending as a percentage of aggregate demand. _____
    Government purchases as a percentage of aggregate demand. _____
    Wages as a percentage of income earned in production. _____
    Profit as a percentage of income from production. _____

6. What percentage of personal income was saved in 1989? _____
7. What was the total value of outflows for 1989? _____ What was the value of new inflows? _____ (For this purpose, con-

Table 7.1   Summary Data from National Income Accounts, 1989

(Billions of Dollars)

Personal consumption expenditures	3540
Gross private domestic investment	780
Government purchases of goods and services	1017
Indirect business taxes (sales and excise taxes)	424
Business saving	570
Rental income	5
Wages and salaries	3230
Interest income	478
Profit income	630
Government transfer payments	616
Business and personal taxes	1675
Personal saving	206

Figure 7.3   Calculating GNP.

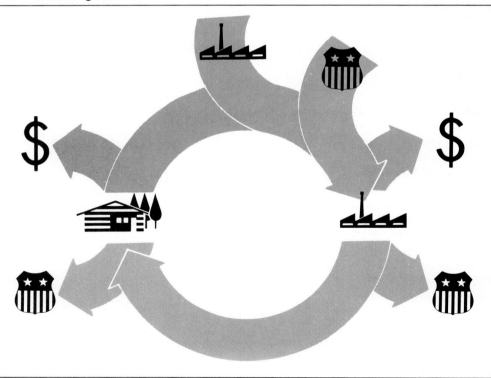

sider government transfer payments as a kind of "negative tax" and include them along with government purchases as a new inflow.)

These calculations should give you a better idea of how GNP is measured and of the quantities involved. *The Economic Report of the President*, published in January each year, supplies these data for the last 50 years. You may be interested in comparing data for the most recent year with earlier years.

PRACTICE MEASURING ECONOMIC GROWTH

Over the years, GNP has grown in the United States, bringing rising incomes and higher material standards of living. This is true both in terms of total production and on a per capita (per person) basis.

Money GNP and Real GNP

Not all increases in GNP bring these kinds of benefits, however. In fact, the dollar value of GNP can grow without any increase in the quantities of goods and services produced. This happens when inflation raises the prices of most goods and services.

To understand the effect of price changes, it is necessary to distinguish between money GNP and real GNP. Money GNP is GNP in dollars of the current year. Real GNP is GNP in dollars of constant purchasing power. If prices have risen, money GNP must be "deflated" to determine real GNP. For example, suppose total dollars spent on GNP increase from $10 billion to $11 billion in one year. Suppose also that prices during that year have increased by 10 percent. If this is true, the real quantity of GNP has not changed at all. With prices 10 percent higher, the $11 billion in expenditures has bought only $10 billion in

real goods and services. Money GNP has increased by $1 billion, but real GNP is the same as before.

Correcting money GNP for price changes requires the use of a price index.

Using a Price Index

A **price index** is a percentage comparison of current prices with prices in a base year. To illustrate, suppose a dollar's worth of goods in the base year included a loaf of bread, a bus ticket, and a pair of socks. Then suppose five years later the same collection of goods sells for $1.25. The price index for the current year is

$$PI = \frac{\text{current year price}}{\text{base year price}} = \frac{\$1.25}{1.00} = 1.25$$
$$= 125 \text{ percent}$$

With prices 25 percent higher, a worker must now earn 125 percent of what he or she earned in the base year in order to enjoy the same standard of living.

Suppose a worker can live comfortably in the base year on an income of $12,000. Five years later the price index has risen to 125. Income of $12,000 will be worth

$$\frac{\text{current income}}{PI} = \frac{\$12,000}{125 \text{ percent}} = \frac{\$12,000}{1.25}$$
$$= \$9600$$

In order to live as comfortably as before, the worker must now earn 125 percent of what his or her income was in the base year:

$$1.25 \times \$12,000 = \$15,000$$

TEST YOURSELF
Suppose the price index falls to 90 percent. This means that a worker needs only $.90 to buy what a dollar bought in the base year. How much is income of $12,000 worth now? How much would a worker have to earn to live as comfortably as in the base year?

Economists calculate the consumer price index each year from prices for a "market basket" of goods and services purchased by a typical family. Economists also calculate a producer price index based on industrial commodities purchased by business firms. The GNP deflator is another price index based on all goods, services, and industrial commodities taken together.

Growth in Real GNP

You can use the following formula to calculate real GNP:

$$real\ GNP = \frac{money\ GNP}{PI}$$

Using this formula, you can set up equations for measuring the growth of GNP over time. Table 7.2 provides data on GNP and its components in selected years since 1929. Data are expressed both in current dollars of each year and in constant dollars, or dollars corrected for inflation.

In the table, 1982 is used as the base year for calculating the price index. Notice that money GNP and real GNP for 1982 are identical at $3166 billion. This is understandable, because the price index for 1982 is

$$PI = \frac{current\ year\ price}{base\ year\ price}$$
$$= \frac{\$1.00}{1.00} = 1.00 = 100\ percent$$

Table 7.2   Gross National Product in Current Dollars (1) and in Constant Dollars of 1982 (3-6).

Year	(1) Money GNP ($ billions)	(2) Price Index	(3) Real GNP ($ billions)	(4) Real Personal Consumption Expenditures ($ billions)	(5) Real Gross Private Domestic Investment ($ billions)	(6) GNP per capita (in 1982 dollars)
1929	103.9	14.6	709.6	471.4	139.2	5557
1933	55.8	11.2	498.5	378.7	22.7	3804
1939	90.8	12.7	716.6	480.5	86.0	5254
1945	212.3	15.7	1354.8	592.7	76.5	8591
1950	286.2	23.9	1203.7	733.2	234.9	8200
1955	399.3	27.2	1494.9	873.8	259.8	8486
1960	506.1	30.9	1665.3	1005.1	260.5	8770
1965	688.1	33.8	2087.6	1236.4	367.0	10,247
1970	982.4	42.0	2416.2	1492.0	381.5	11,286
1975	1528.8	59.3	2695.0	1711.9	383.3	12,105
1980	2627.4	85.7	3187.1	2000.4	509.3	14,292
1981	2937.7	94.0	3248.8	2024.2	545.5	14,062
1982	3166.0	100.0	3166.0	2050.7	447.3	13,677
1983	3309.5	103.8	3277.7	2145.9	503.4	14,090
1984	3774.7	108.1	3492.0	2239.9	661.3	14,754
1985	3992.5	111.7	3573.5	2312.6	650.6	14,963
1986	4208.5	114.5	3676.5	2418.6	659.7	15,225
1987	4524.3	117.4	3853.7	2513.7	674.0	15,798
1988	4880.6	121.3	4024.4	2598.4	715.8	16,337
1989	5233.2	126.3	4142.6	2668.5	724.5	16,652

SOURCE: Economic Report of the President, various years.

The price index for 1929 is only 14.6. This means that prices in 1929 were about one-sixth of prices in 1982. The price index for 1989 is 128.0, indicating that 1989 prices were on the average 28 percent higher than the prices of 1982.

Table 7.2 shows fairly steady growth of real GNP except for the Depression of the 1930s and seven recessions since World War II. Real GNP grew from an estimated $25.8 billion in 1869 to $4142 billion in 1989 (both expressed in dollars of 1982). In per capita terms this represents a real increase from $578 in 1869 to $16,652 in 1989.

PRACTICE MEASURING NET ECONOMIC WELFARE

There are some problems with the use of GNP as a measure of a nation's well-being. GNP measures goods and services produced. It doesn't, however, measure the "bads" that might also be produced! In addition to autos, calculators, and soft drinks, our nation's business firms also produce polluted air and water, scars on the landscape, and junk piles.

When a business firm measures the costs of production, it includes the market prices of all resources purchased in resource markets; that is, the prices of land and buildings, raw materials, machinery, labor, and managerial personnel. However, many kinds of production require the use of resources that are not exchanged in resource markets and therefore have no price: air and water for disposing of waste materials, quiet and pleasant surroundings, and even vacant land for eventual disposal of the product itself. Although such costs are real, they are not paid by the firms that cause them and are, therefore, difficult to measure.

Economists refer to the costs of using these kinds of resources as **external costs** because they are imposed on the community outside the business firm. They are social costs,

as opposed to the **private costs** that appear on a firm's expense statements. The community as a whole pays for a firm's use of these kinds of resources—in the form of air and water pollution, noise, and damaged landscapes.

Because clean air and pleasant surroundings are not exchanged in resource markets, a business firm is not generally required to pay for them. However, as communities become aware of the scarcity of such valuable resources as pure air and water, some are requiring firms to pay for them. They are levying taxes or imposing fines on polluting firms, actions that have the effect of increasing a firm's costs, reducing its output, and reducing its contribution to GNP.

To adjust GNP by the value of external costs would make GNP a better measure of actual levels of well-being. Some economists have defined a new measure, **net economic welfare**, or NEW, that takes into account external costs. Computing NEW requires that the "bads" produced in any year be subtracted from the measured value of GNP. Thus, NEW would more correctly measure improvements in the quality of our lives.

Measuring such things as polluted air and water is a difficult task. Still, efforts are now being made to measure social or external costs and shift them back to the firms that produce them. Coal-burning utilities, for example, are being required to install "scrubbers" in their smokestacks so as to remove impurities from their discharge. Firms guilty of water pollution are being required to clean up their discharge. In some cases, daily fines of thousands of dollars have been imposed, with the revenue to be used by government to operate purification facilities.

Concern for the environment is certainly healthy, and it is healthy to require business firms to assume responsibility for their external costs to the community. Some problems remain, however. If communities impose rigid antipollution laws, some firms will be forced out of business. Others will decide not to locate in communities with such laws. This could mean a loss of jobs and lower incomes. Furthermore, when firms are required to pay for the external resources they use, their costs will rise. They will have to increase their prices to consumers, and their sales will fall. Consumers must be willing to pay the full costs of "cleaner" production if they are to have the goods and services they want.

PRACTICE MEASURING TRENDS IN GOVERNMENT EXPENDITURES

Over the years, several factors have combined to increase the government spending (*G*) component of aggregate demand:

1. The more threatening nature of international relations and the increasing role of the United States in world affairs.

2. Our growing prosperity, which has made us want a better quality of public services.
3. Social and technical changes in ways of life that require collective action. (Our population has shifted from rural areas to crowded cities. We are living longer and are dependent for more years after retirement. Modern industry is more complex and requires a longer period of technical education for the young.)

As a result of all these factors, by 1989, tax receipts and government outlays had grown to almost a third of GNP. This fraction has drifted upward over the last 50 years, showing the greatest increase in years of unstable international conditions or economic crisis. Table 7.3 shows the percentages going to various purposes for selected years.

The percentages in Table 7.3 may overstate the actual shift in resources toward the

Table 7.3 Percentages of GNP used for Public Purposes.

Year	*(1) Government Purchases of Goods and Services Percentage of GNP*	*(2) Total Taxes State, Local, and Federal as Percentage of GNP*	*(3) Government Transfer Payments as Percentage of GNP*
1929	8.3	11.0	1.0
1933	14.3	16.6	2.7
1939	14.3	16.9	2.7
1945	38.7	25.1	2.7
1950	13.3	23.5	5.0
1955	18.6	25.2	4.0
1960	19.8	27.8	5.3
1965	20.0	27.6	5.4
1970	22.5	31.0	7.6
1975	21.9	31.4	12.4
1980	20.3	31.7	11.2
1981	20.3	32.6	11.0
1982	21.2	31.7	11.6
1983	20.9	31.4	12.2
1984	19.5	31.0	14.2
1985	20.4	31.6	14.6
1986	20.7	32.0	12.1
1987	20.5	32.4	11.8
1988	19.9	32.0	11.7
1989	19.8	32.0	11.7

SOURCE: Economic Report of the President, various years.

public sector. Much of government spending goes for services, the costs of which have risen faster than the costs of consumer goods. Also, in earlier years, resources may have been used for public services without having a price tag attached.*

Column (1) lists federal, state, and local government purchases of goods and services as a percentage of GNP. The data show the greatest increase in expenditures between 1939 and 1945. The great increase was due to military spending for World War II. Not shown in Column (1) is the distribution of expenditures between federal and state and local governments. In 1989 state and local government spending constituted 12 percent of GNP, and the federal government's spending only 8 percent.

Column (2) shows the percentages of GNP that governments have collected in business and personal taxes. Taxes at the state, local, and federal level include personal income taxes, corporate profits taxes, indirect business taxes, and contributions to Social Security. Total taxes claimed almost one-third of GNP in 1989. Again, the greatest increase was in 1945.

Column (3) lists transfer payments as percentages of GNP. Transfer payments have grown from only a small part of GNP during the 1930s to almost 12 percent in 1989. The higher percentages in the mid 1980s were partly a result of a severe business recession. In general, when GNP growth slows and workers lose their jobs, government outlays for welfare and unemployment compensation increase.

* In another way, the percentages understate the shift of resources toward the public sector, because they fail to account for the cost to private firms of complying with government regulations.

PRACTICE FORECASTING SPENDING TRENDS

Crystal balls grow cloudy when it comes to predicting consumer behavior in the future. Who in the 1960s could have predicted the popularity of home computers or the disappointing sales of luxury automobiles in the 1980s? Consumers are influenced by such a wide range of circumstances that it is impossible to know for certain what products will sell in the 1990s, what businesses will be profitable, and what training will earn you the highest income.

It is possible, however, to note some long-range trends that have been affecting markets since World War II. Increased productivity in agriculture and manufacturing has given Americans more income to spend and more leisure time to enjoy the things we buy. Nowadays we are spending a smaller share of our earnings for the ordinary necessities of life. Whereas nondurable consumer goods like food, clothing, gasoline, home heating oil, and so forth comprised more than half of consumer spending in 1946, by 1989 the typical family spent less than a third of its budget on such necessary items. While real spending for all goods grew about three percent annually, consumer spending for nondurable goods grew much more slowly. The only exception was spending for gasoline and oil, which grew at the rate of almost 14 percent a year in real terms. These changes have meant decreasing job opportunities for workers producing food, textiles, shoes, and other nondurable goods.

While spending for nondurable goods has been growing relatively slowly, consumers have been spending a larger share of their budgets for durable consumer goods. Spending for such durable goods as automobiles, furniture, and household appliances rose from 11 percent of consumer purchases in 1940 to 15 percent in the mid 1980s. For this reason, workers employed in factories producing dishwashers, stereos, and pleasure boats, for example, enjoyed better job opportunities and higher wages. (In 1989 spending for durable goods was down to 13 percent of consumer spending.)

The greatest change in consumer spending habits has been the spectacular increase in spending for services. In 1989, services absorbed 55 percent of the typical family budget compared with only 31.5 percent in 1946. The greatest gain occurred in spending for housing and household services, which increased more than 9 percent a year in real terms.

Another reason for the increase in services has been spending for health care, in part a result of government programs like Medicare and Medicaid. Because supplies of health care resources are limited, this field offers good job opportunities for workers and even provides some government support for education and training.

Recreation, including travel and entertainment, is also a fast-growing service industry. Hotel and restaurant chains are taking advantage of rising consumer incomes and increased leisure time. The effects of early retirement and an increasing elderly population have also been favorable for recreation services. The outlook is less favorable for education. Slower population growth has reduced the demand for primary and secondary education, but community colleges and adult education programs are continuing to grow.

The tremendous growth of service industries has important consequences for the nation's economy. Probably most important is the fact that services are relatively labor-intensive. In contrast to manufacturing, many services require a greater use of labor resources relative to capital equipment. When machines cannot be used to supplement human labor, there are fewer opportunities to increase productivity. This means that production costs cannot be reduced very much; increasing demand for services is likely to mean rising prices.

Slow productivity growth in service industries will mean slow growth in real incomes. During the years of fast growth in manufacturing, U.S. workers became accustomed to rapidly rising incomes. Workers' families increased their spending, which, in turn, contributed to further growth in manufacturing. The shift to service industries may mean slower economic growth.

There is a positive side to the growth of service industries. To provide certain services requires a higher level of skills than many manufacturing jobs, so that service jobs may be more challenging. This may help workers develop their creative skills and enjoy increased job satisfaction.

Finally, production of many services is relatively nonpolluting. Services involve few smokestacks, result in little chemical discharge, and are generally free of industrial blight.

SUMMARY

1. An economic system can be described in terms of flows of spending and income: spending flows paid from *households* to purchase consumer goods and services, from *businesses* to purchase capital investments, and from *governments* to purchase goods and services; and flows of income received in the form of wages, rent, interest, and profit.

2. The gross national product (GNP) is the final value of all goods and services produced for the market. GNP can be measured as total spending for output or as total income received from resource employment.

3. When consumer, business, or government spending increases, the flow of production and income expands. When spending decreases, the flow of production and income contracts.

4. An increase in spending can be seen as an increase of new spending inflows into the circular flow; inflows are investment spending and government purchases. A decrease in spending can be seen as an increase of outflows from the circular flow; outflows are savings and taxes.

5. Measures of GNP must be corrected by the use of a price index to take account of price changes. The result is real GNP, a value that reflects the real quantities of goods and services produced.

6. GNP is not a perfect measure. It does not include production carried on outside the market, and it does not reflect negative environmental changes that may accompany increases in production.

7. Over recent years government expenditures have risen as a fraction of total spending. This is partly a result of our rising demand for public services and partly a result of the prominence of the United States in world affairs. Consumer spending has shifted toward increased purchases of consumer services.

TERMS TO REMEMBER

macroeconomics: the study of the economy in the aggregate, or total sense; all markets taken together

investment: business spending for plants, productive equipment, and inventories

transfer payments: government income-support payments to individuals, including welfare benefits, veterans' pensions, food stamps, social security benefits, and unemployment compensation

national income: income *earned* by productive resources after business taxes are paid and after a portion of income is set aside in the form of business saving and allowances for depreciation of capital equipment

personal income: income, including transfer payments, that is actually *received* by people

disposable income: personal income minus personal taxes

gross national product (GNP): the final value of all goods and services produced for sale during the year

aggregate demand: the total of all planned spending for newly produced goods and services by consumers, business, and government

aggregate supply: the value of output produced by all business firms during the year

recession: two quarters during which GNP declines

inflation: a general rise in prices

TOPICS FOR DISCUSSION

1. What would be the effect on GNP of each of the following? Would *C*, *I*, or *G* be affected? Discuss the changes in spending and production that would follow each.
   a. Population growth increases so that the average age of the population falls from roughly 33 to 28. There are more young marriages and more teenagers.
   b. An inventor develops a process for converting cottonseed into a milk-like drink, high in nutritional value.
   c. The U.S. government signs nonaggression pacts with other nations and promises to limit production of offensive weapons.
   d. The public becomes convinced that the American way of life is too materialistic. People return to a simpler life-style and cut down on the use of modern conveniences.
   e. Stricter eligibility requirements reduce the number of families receiving transfer payments from government.

2. Distinguish clearly between each of the following pairs of terms:
   Money GNP and real GNP
   Microeconomics and macroeconomics
   Inflows into and outflows from the spending flow

3. Explain how each of the following terms is related to the others:
   GNP
   National income
   Personal income

4. Use the information below to compute real GNP for the years shown (figures are in billions of dollars):

Year	Money GNP (Current $s)	Price Index (1982 = 100)	Real GNP (1982 $s)
1929	103.9	14.6	_____
1940	100.4	13.0	_____
1958	456.8	29.7	_____
1972	1212.8	46.5	_____
1982	3166.0	100.0	_____
1989	5337.0	128.0	_____

5. Explain the concept of social or external costs. Who should pay the social costs of production? (Careful!) How is it possible to shift social costs to the proper party?

    There is a parallel concept of social benefits. It refers to benefits received from production, for which the community doesn't have to pay. Some examples of social benefits are higher skill levels of workers and the movement of new supplying firms into an area, resulting in higher levels of employment. Does your community benefit from the production of some business firms? How can firms be encouraged to provide more social benefits?

6. Do you know of polluting business firms? Have antipollution regulations been imposed on them? In what circumstances might a community reduce its pollution standards?

ANSWERS TO PRACTICE MEASURING GNP

1. $3540 + 780 + 1017 = 5337$
2. $3230 + 5 + 478 + 630 + 570 + 424 = 5337$
3. $3230 + 5 + 478 + 630 = 4343$
4. $4343 + 616 = 4959$
5. $3540/5337 = 0.66$
   $1017/5337 = 0.19$
   $3230/4343 = 0.74$
   $630/4343 = 0.15$
6. $206/4959 = 0.04$
7. $424 + 570 + 1675 + 206 = 2875$
   $780 + 1017 + 616 = 2413$

ANSWER TO TEST YOURSELF

(p. 158) $12,000/90 percent = $12,000/.90 = $13,333.33; .90 × $12,000 = $10,800

Chapter

8

Cycles in Economic Activity

or What Goes Up Must Come Down

As we saw in Chapter 7, GNP reaches equilibrium at the level of production at which planned spending for goods and services is just equal to the value of goods and services produced during the year:

$$AD = \text{aggregate demand} = \text{GNP}$$
$$= \text{aggregate supply} = AS$$

If planned spending increases during the year, business firms are encouraged to increase production; thus, increasing aggregate demand means an increase in aggregate supply and GNP. If planned spending decreases during the year, business firms will cut back production to avoid losses on unsold goods; thus, decreasing aggregate demand means a decrease in aggregate supply and GNP. Only if planned spending is just equal to production for the year will GNP remain stable at the current level of production and income.

Business firms learn about changes in aggregate demand through unplanned changes in inventories. An increase in aggregate demand causes inventories to shrink and encourages business firms to increase production so as to rebuild their inventory stocks. A decrease in aggregate demand causes inventories to build up and encourages firms to cut production until inventories come down to their desired level. If aggregate demand is equal to aggregate supply, there is no unplanned change in inventories, and GNP remains stable.

A perfectly stable, unchanging GNP is not always desirable. It is better if GNP grows steadily in line with the nation's growing productive capacity. Unfortunately, things do not generally work out that way. More often, the

Contemporary Thinking about Economic Issues

TAMING THE BUSINESS CYCLE

Economists who serve in government are accustomed to worrying about business cycles. Charles L. Schultze has served four presidents, most recently President Carter as chairman of the President's Council of Economic Advisors. In this capacity, he frequently gave advice regarding taxes and government spending, with the objective of ensuring stable economic growth without business cycles.

Schultze has studied business cycles of the 1800s and compared their severity with those since World War II. Between 1871 and 1914, he says, the U.S. economy spent half its time on the downside of business cycles and half on the upside. Since 1945 the economy has spent only one-fifth its time on the downside and four-fifths on the upside. Moreover, business cycles in the earlier period were about twice as severe as those in the later period. As a result, the shape of cycles was like "a deep symmetrical V" in the earlier period and "a shallow check mark" in the later period.

How can this difference be explained?

According to Charles Schultze, investment spending was particularly variable during the earlier period, and banks provided credit at low interest rates to accommodate changes in investment spending. Then a large multiplier effect aggravated the effect of changes in investment, so that income fluctuated widely over the cycle. Since World War II, interest rates have moved up or down more strongly to moderate tendencies toward variability in investment spending. Moreover, the multiplier effect has been smaller, so that changes in investment spending have meant smaller changes in income.

A smaller multiplier effect today is the result of changes in consumer behavior, in particular, changes in the marginal propensity to consume. Since World War II, U.S. consumers have had a larger pool of savings and greater access to credit than in the earlier period. With these advantages, consumers are less dependent on disposable income for their consumption spending. They can spend at roughly the same rate regardless of the level of current income. Spending at roughly the same rate helps stabilize total spending and moderates tendencies toward business cycles. Another stabilizing factor is government taxes and transfer payments, which keep consumer spending from rising or falling very much in business cycles.

If all these tendencies continue (or improve), Charles Schultze believes the nation can enjoy relative freedom from business cycles in the future.

Charles L. Schultze, *Other Times, Other Places,* The Brookings Institution, Washington, D.C., 1986.

nation experiences fluctuations in economic activity, with periods of too rapid growth followed by periods of slower growth.

Irregular growth creates either of two kinds of problems. If aggregate demand and GNP grow too fast, the result can be inflation. If aggregate demand and GNP grow too slowly, the result can be business failures, with lost job opportunities and hardships for unemployed workers.

Alternating starts and stops in economic activity are called **business cycles**. In this chapter we will study the Keynesian explanation of business cycles, developed by John M. Keynes (1883–1945). In the two chapters that follow we will learn about economic policies designed to deal with the problems of too fast or too slow growth of GNP.

CONSUMER SPENDING (C)

Many economists explain fluctuations in GNP growth in terms of changes in demand, and they explain changes in demand through use of the Keynesian model of income determination. The Keynesian model focuses first on consumer spending and then on total spending in the economy as a whole. Economists refer to consumer spending as **consumption (C)**.

The Marginal Propensity to Consume

The largest part of total spending comes from the household sector. Consumers plan their spending in relation to their incomes. In fact, a typical U.S. consumer spends about $.96 of each dollar of his or her take-home pay for consumer goods and services.

Because business cycles are caused by *changes* in spending, economists are particularly concerned with the amount a consumer spends from *changes* in disposable income. The amount a consumer spends from a change

in income is called the **marginal propensity to consume (MPC)**. To illustrate, suppose a consumer's income rises from $10,000 to $12,000 a year, and he or she increases spending from $9500 to $11,000. Out of the additional $2000, this consumer would have increased spending by $1500. On the average, this consumer's spending would have increased by

$$\frac{\text{change in consumer spending}}{\text{change in income}} = \frac{\$1500}{\$2000}$$
$$= \frac{3}{4} \text{ of each additional dollar.}$$

Thus, the consumer's marginal propensity to consume is:

$$MPC = \frac{\Delta \text{ consumer spending}}{\Delta \text{ income}} = \frac{\Delta C}{\Delta DI} = \frac{3}{4}$$

where Δ stands for "change in."

The MPCs of different consumers vary. A wealthy consumer probably spends a smaller portion of each additional dollar of income than a poorer consumer. Thus, the wealthy consumer may have an MPC of, say,

$$MPC = \frac{\Delta C}{\Delta DI} = \frac{\$10,000}{\$20,000} = \frac{1}{2}$$

and a poorer person

$$MPC = \frac{\Delta C}{\Delta DI} = \frac{\$100}{\$100} = 1$$

Some consumers have an MPC greater than one, which is made possible by borrowing or by using accumulated savings.

TEST YOURSELF
How do you think your own *MPC* differs from your professor's? From your parents'? Why?

The Consumption Function

The consumption plans of all households in the economy can be combined to describe the

Table 8.1 **Expenditures and Aggregate Demand (billions of dollars).**

(1) Income = GNP	(2) Consumption (C)	(3) Investment (I)	(4) Government Expenditures (G)	(5) Aggregate Demand (C + I + G)
0	125	200	300	625
500	500	200	300	1000
1000	875	200	300	1375
1500	1250	200	300	1750
2000	1625	200	300	2125
2500	2000	200	300	2500
3000	2375	200	300	2875
3500	2750	200	300	3250
4000	3125	200	300	3625

consumption plans of the nation as a whole. Table 8.1 shows what spending might be for the nation as a whole at various levels of GNP. The change in consumer spending associated with each $100 billion change in hypothetical GNP is $75 billion. Thus, the *MPC* for the nation shown in Table 8.1 is

$$MPC = \frac{\Delta C}{\Delta DI} = \frac{75}{100} = \frac{3}{4}$$

Column (2) shows hypothetical consumption $C > GNP$ if GNP is very low, $C = GNP$ at some middle value of GNP, and $C < GNP$ if GNP is very high.

Figure 8.1 is a graph of the hypothetical data shown in the table. GNP = income is measured on the horizontal axis, and consumption (C) on the vertical axis. The line labeled C represents consumer spending and is called the **consumption function**. The consumption function in Figure 8.1 is drawn to show that consumers would spend on the average three-quarters of each additional dollar of current income.

Now look at Figure 8.2. The 45° line drawn from the origin in Figure 8.2 connects points with equal values on both axes, so that $C = GNP = $ income all along the line. Combining the 45° line with the consumption func-

tion allows us to compare consumer spending with GNP (or income) at all levels of income. This has been done in Figure 8.3, in which we see that $C > GNP$ if GNP is low, and $C <$

Figure 8.1 The Consumption Function.

Consumer spending depends on income. This consumption function is drawn on the assumption that all consumers taken together spend three-quarters of each additional dollar in disposable income: $MPC = \frac{3}{4}$.

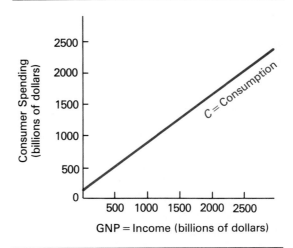

Figure 8.2   The 45° Line.

A 45° line connects all points where quantities on
the vertical axis are equal to quantities on the
horizontal axis.

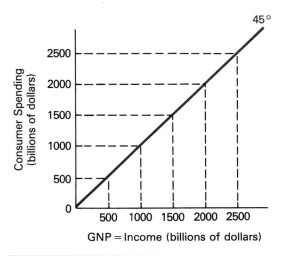

GNP = Income (billions of dollars)

Figure 8.3   C = GNP = $500 billion.

Consumption is equal to GNP = income at income of $500 billion.

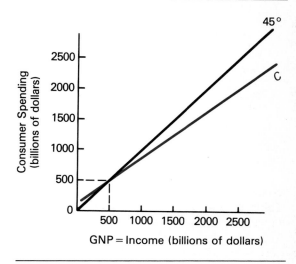

GNP = Income (billions of dollars)

GNP if GNP is high. The point where the
consumption function crosses the 45° line
identifies the level of income at which consumer spending is equal to GNP (and income).
At that point, consumer spending alone is just
equal to the total value of all new goods and
services produced. In Figure 8.3 consumer
spending is equal to income at GNP of $500
billion. Refer to Table 8.1 and verify that $C =$
GNP at GNP = $500 billion.

TOTAL SPENDING (C + I + G)

Now let us combine our hypothetical consumer spending data with the spending plans
of business firms and government. Economists refer to planned business investment
spending as (I) and government spending as
(G). Current investment spending is not
strongly related to income in the current period. This is because investments depend on

expectations of profit and may or may not be
related to the current level of income. Moreover, investment plans take months or even
years to complete and do not rise or fall
quickly in response to changes in current income. Table 8.1 shows planned investment
spending of $I =$ $200 billion. Planned invest-
ment spending of $200 billion is shown in Fig-
ure 8.4 by adding a parallel line $200 billion
above the consumption function.

Government spending is also independent
of income in the current period. Government
spending is based on our nation's need for
public services and defense and does not depend on changes in current income. Thus,
government spending is listed in Table 8.1 as
$G =$ $300 billion, regardless of the level of
income, and shown by the addition of another
parallel line above the consumption function
in Figure 8.5.

Adding business planned investment (I)
and government spending (G) to the consumption function (C) produces an aggregate de-

Figure 8.4 *C + I.*

Adding planned investment to consumer spending is shown by drawing a parallel line above the consumption function.

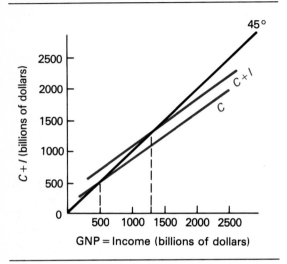

mand function (*AD*). The aggregate demand function shows total spending associated with every level of current income:

$$AD = C + I + G$$

as measured on the vertical axis. The next section will show how the interaction between aggregate demand and aggregate supply determines the equilibrium level of GNP.

EQUILIBRIUM GNP (*AD = AS*)

Figure 8.5 represents the Keynesian model of income determination. The model allows us to measure the components of aggregate demand and illustrate their effects on aggregate supply and GNP. We have said that the actual level of GNP for any year tends toward the level at which aggregate demand equals aggregate supply:

$$AD = AS$$

With aggregate demand equal to aggregate supply, planned spending for new goods and services is just enough to purchase total production for the year. We call the level of GNP at which aggregate demand is equal to aggregate supply equilibrium GNP.

Look again at the 45° line drawn from the origin in Figure 8.5. The 45° line marks all points where aggregate demand (measured on the vertical axis) is equal to aggregate supply (measured on the horizontal axis). Compare the graph of *C + I + G* with the 45° line to locate the level of GNP at which *AD = AS*. Aggregate demand is equal to aggregate supply where *C + I + G* crosses the 45° line. At income of $2500 billion, aggregate demand = *C + I + G* = $2000 + $200 + $300 = $2500 = aggregate supply. Business firms are encouraged to produce goods and services worth a total of $2500 billion = GNP.

For all levels of income less than $2500 billion, planned spending is greater than the

Figure 8.5 *C + I + G* = 2500 billion.

Adding government spending to *C + I* completes the aggregate demand curve.

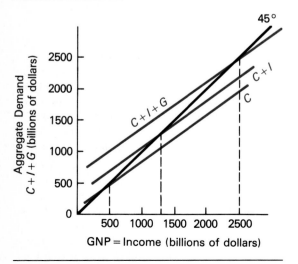

output of goods and services. We know this because $C + I + G$ lies above the 45° line. With aggregate demand greater than aggregate supply, business firms would have to make sales from inventories. In order to fill the higher demand and maintain their inventory stocks, business firms will increase their orders and expand production, so that GNP expands toward $2500 billion.

For all levels of income greater than $2500 billion, planned spending is less than total production: $C + I + G$ lies below the 45° line. With aggregate demand less than aggregate supply, unplanned inventories begin to accumulate. In order to avoid losses on unsold inventories, business firms will cut back their orders and reduce production. GNP will contract toward $2500 billion.

Only at income of $2500 billion are the combined spending plans of all buyers equal to the production plans of all business firms. With $AD = AS$, GNP is in equilibrium.

These results are easy to read from Table 8.1. For all levels of income less than $2500 billion, $AD = C + I + G > AS$, and GNP tends to expand. For income greater than $2500 billion, $AD = C + I + G < AS$, and GNP tends to contract. At income of $2500 billion, $AD = C + I + G = AS$, and GNP is stable. The economy is in equilibrium.

What can we learn from the Keynesian model of income determination? The model helps us locate the equilibrium level of spending, production, and income. It does not tell us whether the equilibrium level of GNP = income is a technically efficient level of income. To determine whether the equilibrium level of GNP is technically efficient, we must answer the following questions:

1. Is the equilibrium level of GNP too low to employ all available resources? Too low a level of spending, production, and income means that we are failing to use our scarce resources productively, and we are sacri-

ficing the goods and services we might have had. This cannot be considered an efficient equilibrium level of GNP.
2. Is the equilibrium level so high that we are pushing against the limits of our resource capability? Too high a level of spending, production, and income could mean rising prices, as rising demand creates shortages in the markets for goods and resources. This cannot be considered an efficient level of GNP.
3. Only if equilibrium GNP is neither so low as to cause unemployment nor so high as to cause inflation can we say that the economy is technically efficient.

Changes are constantly taking place in spending, changing the position of the consumption function (C) and increasing or decreasing planned business investment spending (I) and government spending (G). All these changes move the economy to new equilibrium levels of GNP. Economic analysis helps project and evaluate future equilibrium levels of GNP. If the projected equilibrium level is not technically efficient, macroeconomic policy may be designed to change it. Macroeconomic policy to correct business cycles is the subject of Chapters 9 and 10.

CHANGES IN EQUILIBRIUM GNP

What lies behind changes in aggregate demand that move the economy to new equilibrium levels? Remember that changes in spending plans can come from any of the three groups of spenders: consumers, business firms, or government.

Changes in Total Spending

Consumers may decide to spend more for household appliances, recreation equipment,

Contemporary Thinking about Economic Issues

MULTIPLE PROBLEMS!

Until the mid 1970s, Silt, Colorado, was a sleepy town in the Piceance Creek Basin. Then the oil crisis hit the nation, and the fact that Piceance Creek Basin contains 500 billion barrels of oil in shale rock changed the town forever. In fact, throughout the American West major oil companies set up operations to extract the oil.

Billions of dollars were invested and more than a million people were moved in to dig colossal strip mines. The multiplier worked to increase incomes, and property values soared. Tax revenues increased, too, making it possible to build new schools and sewers and adding even more spending power to the local economy.

In due course, the oil crisis faded away. Oil supplies increased, prices fell, and imports rose to half the nation's annual oil needs. In 1982 the big oil companies announced they were discontinuing their Colorado oil shale projects, cutting investment, and wiping out jobs. Unemployment rose to double-digits in the Piceance Creek Basin, and small-business bankruptcies skyrocketed.

Silt, Colorado, understands only too well how the multiplier works in reverse.

Andrew Gulliford, *Boomtown Blues: Colorado Oil Shale, 1885–1985,* University Press of Colorado, Boulder, 1990.

---

or personal services. They may save less from their current incomes, spend from past savings, or borrow against future earnings. An increase in consumer spending shifts the *C* component of aggregate demand upward. Total spending increases, and business firms expand production and employment.

The same result follows an increase in the investment plans of business firms. The development of new manufacturing processes, for example, requires new investment spending and shifts the *I* component of aggregate demand upward. Figure 8.6 shows new investment spending of $250 billion, causing an increase in equilibrium GNP from $2500 billion to $3500 billion.

Figure 8.7 shows the effect of a decrease in government spending. Suppose government spending (*G*) falls, perhaps in response to the

end to a military threat from abroad or to voters' insistence on the elimination of public spending programs. If government spending falls from $300 billion to $50 billion, equilibrium GNP will fall to $1500 billion, as shown on Figure 8.7.

The Multiplier Effect

Have you noticed that the $250 billion in new investment spending in Figure 8.6 caused equilibrium GNP to increase by $1000 billion and that the $250 billion reduction in government spending in Figure 8.7 caused equilibrium GNP to fall by $1000? In both cases, the change in equilibrium GNP was greater than the initial change in spending. The greater change in equilibrium GNP was a re-

Figure 8.6   An Increase in Investment Spending.

An increase in *I* causes a greater increase in income. Compare the increase in *I* with the increase in GNP.

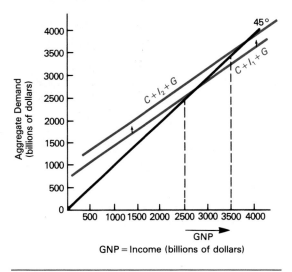

GNP = Income (billions of dollars)

Figure 8.7   A Decrease in Government Spending.

A decrease in *G* causes a greater decrease in income. Compare the decrease in *G* with the decrease in GNP.

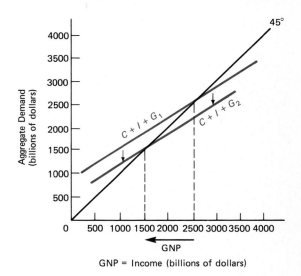

GNP = Income (billions of dollars)

sult of what economists call the multiplier effect.

The multiplier effect results from the fact that people who receive as income the increase in business investment tend to respend a portion of their own increase in income. Then people who receive their respending enjoy an increase in income, too, which they also spend. Finally, many people will have received additions to income, such that the total of all new income will be greater than the initial increase in spending.

An illustration may be helpful. Remember that the tendency to spend changes in income is called the marginal propensity to consume and that the *MPC* in our example is $MPC = \frac{3}{4}$. With $250 billion in new investment spending, income earners around the country receive increases in income totalling $250 billion. Then with $MPC = \frac{3}{4}$, these income earners

tend to increase their spending by $MPC \times \Delta I = \frac{3}{4}(250) = \$187.50$ billion. The $187.50 billion is paid to other income earners who increase their spending by MCP ($MPC \times \Delta I$) = $\frac{3}{4}(187.50) = \$140.63$. This means that still other income earners receive additional income totaling $140.63 billion and increase their spending by $MPC [MPC(MPC \times \Delta I)] = \$105.47$ billion.

The process of spending and respending continues until the total of all increases in income is a multiple of the initial change in spending. The value of the multiplier for measuring the change in income is determined by the following formula:

$$\text{multiplier} = k = \frac{1}{1 - MPC}$$

or in our example

$$k = \frac{1}{1 - \frac{3}{4}} = \frac{1}{\frac{1}{4}} = 4$$

The total change in income or GNP is

$$\Delta GNP\ k \times \Delta I = \frac{1}{1 - MPC} \times \Delta I$$

Substitute the values from our examples into the formula and verify the results.

The important consequence of the multiplier is that changes in C, I, or G have substantially greater effects on the equilibrium level of GNP than the initial change in spending. Does this result make our economy more or less efficient?

The answer depends on the current level of resource use. If there are unemployed resources available to be drawn into production, it is technically efficient to use them. The multiple effect of new spending would be welcome. On the other hand, if the economy is already producing at full employment, any further increase in GNP makes the economy less efficient. This is because increases in C, I, or G will only aggravate the problem of scarce resources and tend to cause inflation.

Inflationary Gap

In this section we will use the Keynesian model of income determination to show how increases or decreases in equilibrium GNP may make the economy less technically efficient. In Figure 8.8, $C + I + G$ shifts upward by $250 billion, as before, and the increase in spending causes equilibrium GNP to increase from $2500 billion to $2500 + 4(250) = $3500 billion. However, suppose the nation's productive resources can produce only $2500 billion worth of goods and services when fully employed; that is, maximum production possibilities are $2500 billion. The full-employment level of output is shown in Figure 8.8 by a dashed line drawn at GNP = $2500 billion.

Figure 8.8 Inflationary Gap.

Aggregate demand is greater than aggregate supply at full employment. Follow the dashed line up from the full-employment level of $2500 billion. The portion of the dashed line above the 45° line and below $C + I + G$ measures the inflationary gap.

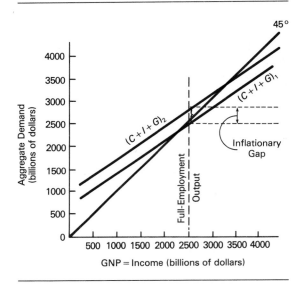

If aggregate demand is $3500 billion, total spending is greater than the full employment output of the economy. The nation's business firms will produce $2500 billion worth of goods and services for which $3500 billion will be spent. Result: inflation!

The difference between total spending and the full employment level of production is a measure of excess spending. The excess is measured by the difference between aggregate demand and the 45° line at full employment. We call the difference between AD and the 45° line at full employment the **inflationary gap**. Spending greater than the productive capacity of our economy is not a technically efficient use of the nation's scarce resources.

How Things Have Changed

INTERNATIONAL COMPARISONS OF ECONOMIC PERFORMANCE

Country	Real Gross Domestic Product per Capita (1988)	Inflation (1989) (%)	Unemployment (1989) (%)
Canada	$16,951	5.1	7.6
France	12,490	3.6	10.1
West Germany	13,204	3.0	5.6
Italy	11,955	6.5	7.7
Japan	13,204	2.3	2.3
United Kingdom	12,312	7.7	5.9
United States	17,843	4.6	5.3

SOURCE: Economic Report of the President, 1990.

Deflationary Gap

Figure 8.6 illustrated an increase in investment spending that caused a multiple increase in equilibrium GNP. Figure 8.7 showed a downward change in government spending and a multiple decrease in income. In fact, if any of the components of planned spending falls, there will be a multiple decrease in GNP. Spending not received as income is not spent and not respent!

If consumers become worried about the future, for example, and decide to increase their saving, the C component of aggregate demand will fall. Unsold inventories will pile up, and manufacturers will reduce production. Likewise, if business firms decide to invest less, the I component will fall. Equipment orders will be canceled, and construction workers will be laid off. Finally, if public projects are completed or abandoned, the G component of aggregate demand will fall.

TEST YOURSELF
What kinds of workers are likely to lose their jobs as a result of the end of a public construction project?

Figure 8.9 illustrates a multiple downward shift in income. If planned investment or government spending falls from $300 billion to $50 billion, the equilibrium level of GNP in Figure 8.9 will fall from $2500 billion to only $1500 billion.

Compare the lower equilibrium GNP in Figure 8.9 with the full-employment output of $2500 billion. Then look at the aggregate demand line at the full-employment level. The difference between aggregate demand and the 45° line at full employment is a measure of the deficiency of spending. The difference between total production and total spending at full employment is called a **deflationary gap.** As long as aggregate demand is less than aggregate supply at the full-employment level of

Figure 8.9 Deflationary Gap.

A decrease in *I* or *G* causes a greater decrease in spending, production, and income. Compare the drop in *C* + *I* + *G* with the drop in GNP. Follow the dashed line up from the full-employment level of $2500 billion. The portion of the dashed line from *C* + *I* + *G* to the 45° line measures the deflationary gap.

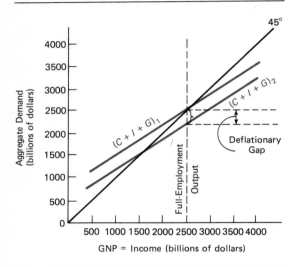

CUMULATIVE UPSWINGS AND DOWNSWINGS

Even small changes in any of the components of aggregate demand can produce much larger changes in equilibrium GNP. A small increase in *C*, *I*, or *G* can send the economy into a strong upward spiral of employment, production, and income, with increasing tendencies toward price inflation. A small decrease in *C*, *I*, or *G* can start the economy into a deep slide of worsening unemployment, falling incomes, and declining production.

The United States experienced many swings in production and income over its first 100 years as a nation. Many economists finally came to believe that some forms of government intervention might be necessary to help correct business cycles, with their alternating periods of inflation and unemployment. They recommended frequent small changes in government tax and spending policies to push aggregate demand toward a full-employment, noninflationary level of GNP.

In the remainder of this chapter we will describe the actual performance of the U.S. economy in recent years. Then, in Chapters 9 and 10, we will examine the federal government's two instruments for influencing aggregate demand: fiscal policy and monetary policy. Fiscal policy involves the use of government spending and taxing powers to affect total spending. Monetary policy involves control of the supply of money to affect consumer and business spending.

output, resources will be idle and workers unemployed.

Too little spending relative to the productive capacity of the economy is not a technically efficient use of our nation's scarce resources.

Viewpoint

ANOTHER EXPLANATION FOR BUSINESS CYCLES?

Some early economists blamed business cycles on sunspots! According to their theory, sunspot activity produced a favorable climate and good crops, increasing the incomes of farmers and encouraging spending for the products of manufacturing industries. Greater spending would then encourage business firms to increase productive capacity, raising the number of jobs in industry and generally stimulating expenditures throughout the economy. As sunspot activity slowed, the process would go into reverse. Incomes and spending would decline, followed by bankruptcies, general pessimism, and lower rates of economic growth.

Indeed, in years past, there did seem to be some correlation between the highs and lows of economic activity and the 11-year cycles of sunspots. Circumstances may be different today, however. Today the farming sector is such a small part of the U.S. economy, it can hardly be blamed for wide changes in total spending. (Still, the severe worldwide recession of 1974–1975 was certainly worsened by climatic changes and crop failures in many of the world's farming regions.)

Self-Check

1. **An individual's marginal propensity to consume may depend on all but which of the following?**
   a. The quantity of goods already owned.
   b. The level of consumer debt outstanding.
   c. Plans for future spending.
   d. The portion of total income spent.
   e. The backlog of saving already accumulated.

2. **Equilibrium GNP:**
   a. Is determined where aggregate demand is equal to aggregate supply.
   b. May leave workers unemployed and factories idle.
   c. May exceed the nation's productive capacity.
   d. May change if $C + I + G$ changes.
   e. All of the above.

3. **You carry mail for Uncle Sam during the Christmas season and use your earnings for a skin-diving trip to Florida. This is an example of:**
   a. Noneconomic behavior.
   b. Recession.
   c. The multiplier effect.
   d. A business cycle.
   e. The sunspot theory of economic activity.

4. **Enrollment increases at your college and a hamburger chain enlarges its restaurant nearby. This is an example of:**
   a. Technological advance.
   b. Inflation.
   c. The multiplier effect.
   d. An increase in investment expenditures.
   e. Excess saving.

5. **In 1975 Queen Elizabeth II decided that, "in view of the economic situation," she would postpone redecorating her vacation home. The queen must have believed there was:**
   a. Excess saving in the British economy.
   b. An inflationary gap.
   c. A deflationary gap.
   d. A high level of unemployment
   e. Excess capacity in industry.

6. **In 1975 Congress voted to send taxpayers a rebate on their 1974 income taxes. Congress must have believed there was:**
   a. Too much business investment spending.
   b. An inflationary gap.
   c. A deflationary gap.
   d. Too much demand in relation to our productive capacity.
   e. A cumulative upswing in GNP and income.

Theory in Practice

PRACTICE EVALUATING
THE U.S. ECONOMY

Since World War II ended in 1945, the United States has experienced seven recessions. A **recession** is a period in which real GNP (GNP corrected for inflation) fails to grow for at least two quarters. Figure 8.10 is a time-series graph showing real GNP for each of the years since 1945. (Money GNP has been corrected for inflation through the use of a price index with base year 1982.) The seven postwar recessions are marked by shaded bars.

The first postwar recession followed World War II by about three years. Civilian industries were unable to employ the large numbers of returning members of the armed

Figure 8.10   Growth of Real GNP Interrupted by Seven Recessions.

The usual definition of recession is two consecutive quarters of negative real growth of GNP.

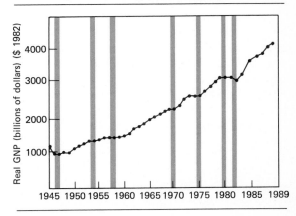

Viewpoint

PROJECTING ECONOMIC ACTIVITY

Some economists specialize in forecasting the size and direction of GNP. Forecasts are of particular value to business firms (for planning capital investments) and governments (for estimating tax revenues and public spending requirements).

One way to forecast economic trends is to analyze the data on the major components of aggregate demand: consumer spending, planned business investment spending, and government spending. Forecasters project consumer purchases of autos and other durable goods; food, fuel, and other nondurable goods; and services, such as housing, transportation, and medical care. They estimate business investment spending for homes and other structures, producers' durable equipment, and inventories. Finally, they look at information on state and local government purchases and federal spending for de-

fense and nondefense purposes. Combining projections of all the major components of aggregate demand yields an estimate of GNP for the coming period. From projections of GNP it is possible to estimate the behavior of other variables, like wages and salaries, profits, personal tax payments, savings, and prices.

In 1990 forecasters of aggregate demand were projecting GNP growth of about 6.5 percent for 1991, of which about 4.5 percent would reflect price increases, for real GNP growth of about 2 percent.

Another way to forecast economic trends is to look at particular activities that bear significantly on economic activity as a whole. For example, the number of housing permits conveys information about future trends in homebuilding—along with all the accompanying activity in firms producing plumbing equipment, elec-

forces, and unemployment rose from 3.8 percent in 1948 to 5.9 percent in 1949.

There were two recessions in the 1950s, one immediately following the Korean War in 1954 and one in 1958. A contributing factor was too optimistic production of consumer goods, which could not be sold and piled up in business inventories. Many firms were forced to cut back production and lay off workers. In the recessions of the 1950s, unemployment rose to 5.5 percent in 1954 and 6.8 percent in 1958.

Unemployment remained high until 1961 when increases in government spending began to be effective in stimulating total spending

and production. Vietnam War spending picked up in 1965 and absorbed much of the slack in the labor force. Unemployment dropped to 3.5 percent in 1969. Still, in the recession of 1971 unemployment again reached 5.9 percent, almost 5 million workers.

Unemployment reached more than 9 percent during the "OPEC" recession of 1974–1975. The oil embargo and a tripling of oil prices caused total production to fall by 2 percent in real terms.

Three years of strong growth followed the OPEC recession. The expansion weakened in 1979 when OPEC announced another quadrupling of oil prices, and a new recession

trical appliances, furniture, draperies, and so forth. Combining information on activities that signal economic trends yields a value called the **index of leading indicators**. Some other leading indicators are the average workweek for production workers in manufacturing, net business formations, and contracts and orders for plant and equipment. In general, a change in the direction of the leading index that persists for two or three months is considered an indication of underlying strength or weakness in the economy as a whole.

Activities that tend to change along with changes in economic activity comprise the index of coincident indicators; activities that change after changes in economic activity yield the **index of lagging indicators**.

In February 1990 the index of leading indicators fell by 1 percent, largely because of a decline in building permits. Other indicators showing a decrease were deliveries to factories by suppliers, stock prices, plant and equipment orders, material prices, factory backlogs, and consumer expectations. Indicators showing an increase were growth in the money supply, a decrease in unemployment claims, and growth in new orders for consumer goods. The average workweek was unchanged. Economists interpreted the behavior of the leading index as suggesting some weakness in the economy, with slow growth for the year ahead.

No forecasting technique is perfect. And in fact, forecasters are constantly changing their methods to accord more closely with actual economic conditions.

Explain why each of the leading indicators named above is a valid "indicator" of future economic activity.

---

seemed imminent. A single quarter of negative real growth in 1979 failed to satisfy the usual definition of recession, however. A similar pattern occurred again in 1980, and analysts finally declared a brief recession. In early 1981, the economy seemed to be floundering again, and by 1982 the economy was suffering the worst of the post-war recessions. Real GNP fell 0.6 percent during the year, and unemployment climbed to 10 percent. Recovery began early in 1983, and the last half of the year was marked by a substantial expansion of economic activity. Strong growth continued for two years, but growth leveled off as the 1980s ended, and in 1990 economists were worried about the possibility of another recession.

What are the common factors in all these recessions? Each followed a period of heavy new spending: for military equipment, increased inventory investment, or new government programs. Increases in spending raised incomes and encouraged increased consumer spending, which further stimulated factory construction and employment. All good things must come to an end, however, and eventually new spending slackened. Incomes failed to rise further, new factories were not needed, and unemployment spread.

Investment spending fluctuated widely

during those years. Real investment spending declined by about 20 percent during the OPEC recession in 1975, but grew by almost 10 percent in the recovery of 1976, 14 percent in 1977, and 10 percent in 1978. Investment spending grew by only 4 percent in 1979, and between 1980 and 1982 real investment spending declined by almost 12 percent. Real investment spending grew by 8 percent in the recovery of 1983 and 17 percent in 1984 and then leveled off at about 3 percent annual growth for the rest of the decade.

Wide swings in investment spending put strains on the nation's productive resources. Increases in investment spending create shortages and push up the prices of food and industrial commodities. When costs rise too high, firms are forced to cut back investment spending and lay off workers.

Once a decrease in spending occurs, other changes take place that reduce chances for recovery. In the 1980s, for example, much consumer spending was financed by borrowing. Both mortgage and consumer debt grew more than 10 percent a year on the average. Unemployment (or the fear of unemployment) makes large debt especially burdensome. Consumers cut back on new spending to pay off old bills. This is particularly true in the market for "big ticket" items: durable goods like autos, appliances, and furniture, whose purchase can be postponed.

When spending falls, inventories pile up, and firms cut back on their new orders. Manufacturers postpone plans for building new capacity. All of this aggravates the problem of declining total spending and worsens unemployment.

PRACTICE USING THE MULTIPLIER

Many large U.S. cities are planning mass-transit systems to reduce the use of private automobiles in urban areas. One southern city decided on a plan for mass transit with an estimated cost of $2.1 billion. The U.S. Urban Mass Transportation Agency agreed to contribute part of the cost, perhaps as much as 80 percent. The remainder was to come from local tax revenues.

Local economists predicted that as a result of the construction project, personal income across the entire state would increase an average of $475 million a year over the ten years required for construction. An estimated 35,300 new jobs would be created, and tax collections would go up by an average of $16.2 million per year.

Construction projects like this illustrate the multiple effect new spending can have on GNP. Contracts are signed with designers, landowners, earth-moving companies, equipment manufacturers, electricians, and builders. Firms hire new workers, order steel and cement, and install new machinery. Incomes grow throughout the area. Rising incomes allow consumers to increase their spending for homes, furnishings, and recreation. All these expenditures add a further push to incomes and GNP.

Occasionally, things don't turn out so well. For years Britain and France dreamed of a connecting tunnel under the English Channel. The project finally got under way in the 1970s and was nicknamed the "Chunnel." For several years many millions of British pounds were spent for planning and construction costs. Nevertheless, in 1975 British planners decided the project was impractical and too costly, and the Chunnel was abandoned. Work on the Chunnel resumed in 1988, and the project is expected to be completed late in 1993.

Remember that the multiplier works in reverse when spending falls. What were the probable effects for the British and French economies when the Chunnel was abandoned? What were the effects of orders not made, income not spent, workers not hired? Trace through the chain of events when work was resumed and their effects on economic activity in Britain and France.

MORE PRACTICE WITH AGGREGATE DEMAND AND AGGREGATE SUPPLY

Throughout this text we have been concerned with supply and demand. Demand reflects the willingness of people and organizations to spend their dollars for certain goods and services. A demand curve for a particular good is drawn in relation to its price. Typically, quantity demanded is greater at low prices, so that a demand curve slopes downward from left to right. The demand curves in Chapters 2 through 6 were drawn according to this fundamental law of demand.

In this chapter we have been concerned with *aggregate* demand—the total of spending for all goods and services taken together. We expressed aggregate demand in relation not to price but to income; that is, we assumed that consumer spending as a whole depends on the nation's income. Thus, the aggregate demand curves in this chapter were drawn in relation to income.

Aggregate demand may also be thought of in relation to price, however. In this case, we would assume that real purchases of goods and services depend on the general price level. An aggregate demand curve drawn in relation to price would look very much like a single demand curve, sloping downward from left to right according to the law of demand.

In Figure 8.11 the horizontal axis measures real output of goods and services. The vertical axis measures prices in terms of a current price index that varies from zero to 150. The line labeled *AD* is drawn by dividing the current equilibrium level of GNP by various price indexes. Thus, the *AD* line represents the real quantity of output, whatever the level of prices. At prices higher than a price

Figure 8.11   Aggregate Demand.

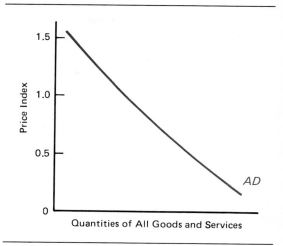

index of 100, current real output is less than the money value of GNP. At prices lower than a price index of 100, current real output is greater than money GNP.

Aggregate supply can also be drawn in relation to a price index. Aggregate supply represents the sum of all production plans in business firms. Remember that for a single firm, supply obeys the law of supply; that is, larger quantities are supplied only at higher prices. We drew individual firms' supply curves to slope upward from left to right because of rising marginal costs in the short run.

Aggregate supply may behave differently. When all firms are considered together, larger quantities may be produced with no increase in price. This is because new firms are constantly entering the market, adding their output to that of existing firms. Over a wide range of output, quantity supplied may increase without putting upward pressure on the price index. Aggregate supply may actually be drawn as a horizontal line, as shown in Figure 8.12.

A horizontal aggregate supply curve is an

Figure 8.12   Aggregate Supply.

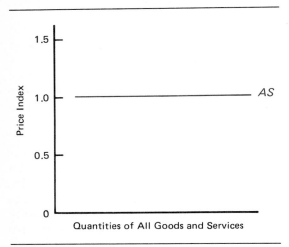

Figure 8.13   Aggregate Supply and Aggregate Demand at Full Employment.

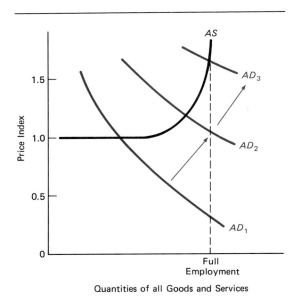

advantage to all of us. It makes it possible for us to consume larger quantities of goods and services without having to pay higher prices. In fact, as our population grows and as demand for goods and services increases, we would expect the nation's aggregate demand curve to shift to the right. With a horizontal aggregate supply curve, larger quantities can be purchased at constant prices. (Pencil in a series of aggregate demand curves on Figure 8.12 and show the effect on prices when the aggregate supply curve is horizontal.)

Of course, the picture is not yet complete. We know that the total supply of goods and services cannot increase indefinitely at constant prices. New firms cannot continue to enter the market producing additional output without eventually experiencing rising costs. As resources become fully employed, their prices will rise, and firms must raise their prices for finished goods. The aggregate supply curve will begin to slope upward. At the absolute limit of the nation's productive capacity, aggregate supply will become very steep. No additional quantity is possible, but sharply rising prices are indeed possible.

Figure 8.13 combines a shifting *AD* curve with an *AS* curve that becomes steeper as production approaches full employment. Increases in consumer spending, business investment spending, and government purchases are not inflationary as long as there are unemployed resources ready to be drawn into production at constant prices. As resource markets tighten, however, the price index rises. Aggregate demand may continue to increase, but the actual quantity of goods and services produced cannot increase. The result is an inflationary gap.

Fortunately, there is still more to this story. Aggregate supply may also change with time. Improvements in the quantity and quality of resources are constantly working to increase our nation's productive capabilities. The full-employment limit to aggregate supply has moved to the right fairly steadily from year to year. We may hope that it continues to do so in the future. (Pencil in a new aggregate supply curve and comment on the implications.)

PRACTICE WITH PRODUCTIVITY

The average worker's share of total output is measured by productivity:

$$\text{worker productivity} = \frac{\text{total output or GNP}}{\text{hours of work}}.$$

If output grows faster than hours worked, we say that worker productivity has increased and, likewise, workers' share of output can grow. Through much of the 1960s and 1970s, worker productivity did increase, but by the end of the decade the reverse was true. During 1979, 1980, and 1982 GNP grew more slowly than hours worked, so that worker productivity fell.

Many reasons are suggested for the decrease in worker productivity. Some attribute the decrease in productivity to the quantity and quality of new capital investment in manufacturing. Rising energy costs have reduced business profits and discouraged investment in new capital equipment. Also, new environmental and safety regulations have reduced the measured efficiency and increased the risks of new capital investment. Worsening recessions in the 1970s and 1980s have shattered business confidence and worsened the outlook for investment still further.

Other factors have reduced the savings available for investment. Members of the "baby boom" generation (born in the years 1948–1961) required a high level of consumer spending as youngsters in the 1970s. An exceptionally high marginal propensity to consume during those years left less savings for investment and helped keep interest rates high. Also, persistent inflation moved many households into higher income tax brackets, increasing their tax bills and further discouraging saving for investment.

Changes in the work force may also have reduced productivity. During the 1970s many new entrants to the work force were young and inexperienced. In particular, the increase in female employment increased the fraction of workers with relatively less experience in modern industrial jobs. Much of the earlier gains in productivity had come as a result of the movement of labor out of agriculture (where worker productivity was relatively low) to mechanized industry (where worker productivity was relatively high). Lately, this process has slowed and will contribute less to productivity gains in the future. The same may be true of productivity gains that resulted from improved worker health and education.

What is the outlook for worker productivity in the future? In turn, what is the likely course of aggregate supply for the nation?

High energy costs will continue to challenge business firms to develop new, less costly technical processes. New government regulation is being adjusted to focus on only the most critical environmental and safety problems and to emphasize the least costly solutions to these problems. The baby boom generation has matured and become more productive; many baby boomers have reached an age when saving is possible. Finally, changes in tax laws are being considered to encourage saving and investment for increasing productivity.

In terms of aggregate supply, all these changes should increase our nation's capacity to produce goods and services.* The result may be a horizontal aggregate supply curve over a longer range of output. If more goods and services can be produced per hour of work, then aggregate demand can grow without causing prices to rise.

* On the other hand, the general shift toward a service-oriented economy may reduce opportunities for increasing productivity.

TEST YOURSELF
Might increased worker productivity cause the aggregate supply curve to shift downward? (Pencil in the effect of increased worker productivity on the aggregate supply curve in Figure 8.13.)

SUMMARY

1. A rising GNP means more goods and services for the population, but if spending for GNP rises faster than the nation's capacity to produce goods and services, the result may be inflation. A falling GNP, or one that rises too slowly, may mean unemployment and low production. Alternating periods of rising and falling GNP are called business cycles.
2. Consumer spending at various levels of income is shown graphically by the consumption function. Consumer spending depends on the marginal propensity to consume (*MPC*). *MPC* measures the fraction of additional income that consumers will spend.
3. The economy will tend to stabilize at an equilibrium level of GNP at which aggregate demand is equal to aggregate supply. At equilibrium there is no tendency for production to expand or contract.
4. If aggregate demand is greater than aggregate supply at the full-employment level of GNP, there will be an inflationary gap. If aggregate demand is less than aggregate supply at the full-employment level of GNP, there will be a deflationary gap.
5. Small changes in aggregate demand produce cumulative changes in income because of the multiplier effect. Changes in total spending have been a result partly of irregular changes in business investment spending.
6. Increases in aggregate demand may be satisfied by increases in aggregate supply at constant prices. However, as resources become fully employed, increases in aggregate supply will be associated with rising prices.
7. Slow growth in worker productivity in recent years has been attributed to factors affecting capital investment and to the quality of the work force. Current developments may reverse the trend, so that worker productivity increases and the aggregate supply curve remains flat over a longer range of output. The hoped-for result is that aggregate demand can increase without price increases.

TERMS TO REMEMBER

business cycles: recurring upswings and downswings in the level of economic activity
marginal propensity to consume (*MPC*): the fraction of each additional dollar of income that consumers will spend
consumption function: the graph showing consumer expenditures for every level of GNP (income)
equilibrium GNP: the level of GNP at which aggregate demand is equal to aggregate supply; total spending is equal to total output
multiplier effect: the multiple change in income that results when an initial change in spending is spent and respent many times
recession: a period of two or more quarters during which real GNP fails to grow
inflationary gap: an excess of aggregate demand over aggregate supply at full employment
deflationary gap: a deficiency of aggregate demand below aggregate supply at full employment

TOPICS FOR DISCUSSION

1. Explain and illustrate each of the following pairs of terms:

   Aggregate demand and aggregate supply
   Inflationary gap and deflationary gap

2. During a recent recession, trash collectors in a large U.S. city were interviewed. They reported a noticeable drop in the appearance of usable items in trash collections, even from wealthy neighborhoods: fewer pairs of shoes, pieces of furniture, and repairable small appliances. Does this suggest anything about the rate of consumer saving in hard times? What does this imply about the chances of recovery from a recession?

3. Producers of most goods suffer declining demand during recessions, but others may enjoy *rising* demand. How would you explain the increasing sales of the following goods during a recent recession?

    white bread   sewing machines
    beer   movie tickets
    home freezers   dehydrated foods

4. During the same recession, economists were worried about the high level of inventory accumulation in business firms. What signals does a business firm receive from an exceptionally high level of inventory stock relative to monthly sales? Discuss this situation in terms of flows of spending and income. What implications do you foresee for the levels of employment, production, investment, and prices?

5. Droughts in the 1980s reminded many meteorologists of the historical pattern of dry spells that have often damaged U.S. agriculture. The dustbowl days of the 1930s and the long dry spell of the 1940s are examples. There were fears that recent droughts signal a new prolonged period of reduced output from U.S. farms. Some believed the droughts were related to sunspot activity.

    Discuss the implications of prolonged drought for the U.S. economy. How would prolonged drought affect production in other sectors of the economy, real income of workers, the federal government's budget, and technological progress?

6. Explain the origins of inflation and recession as summarized in Chapters 7 and 8. What are the characteristics of each? How is each related to the rate of growth of GNP? What rate of growth of GNP would be most efficient for the nation?

7. Using the multiplier developed in this chapter, compute the effect on GNP of a $20 billion drop in government expenditures. Explain why the marginal propensity to consume is incorporated in the formula for the multiplier.

8. In mid 1990 economists were concerned about a decrease in "consumer confidence." The source of the problem seemed to be a high level of consumer debt. What is the basis for concern regarding consumer confidence? Explain the relationship between a high level of debt and (a) economic growth, (b) interest rates, (c) inflation.

ANSWERS TO TEST YOURSELF

(p. 169) The MPCs of young people tend to be greater than those of older (wealthier) people because young people have greater unsatisfied material needs.

(p. 177) Surveyors, designers, engineers, draftsmen, equipment operators, carpenters, technicians.

(p. 188) Yes, because current output can be produced at lower prices.

Chapter

Government Finance and Fiscal Policy

or How to Spend Money When You Don't Have Any

LEARNING OBJECTIVES

After reading this chapter, you will be able to:

1. Describe three ways governments finance their expenditures.

2. Define three kinds of taxes.

3. Explain how the federal government's fiscal policy helps stabilize economic activity for the nation as a whole.

4. Discuss some advantages and disadvantages of fiscal policy.

5. Explain the origin, composition, advantages, and disadvantages of the national debt.

CURRENT ISSUES FOR DISCUSSION

How well has fiscal policy worked?

What were the major points of President Reagan's fiscal program?

What is the fiscal outlook for the 1990s?

Nobody loves the tax collector. The story is told of how Saint Peter stood at the "pearly gates" checking the qualifications of all who wanted to enter Paradise.

First, a politician convinces Saint Peter of his good intentions during his life. Still, he is told he must pass a test before entering Paradise. "Spell 'God'," he is told, and upon answering correctly he is ushered in.

Next a police officer tells of her sufferings in life, carrying out her duties as preserver of the peace while she is ridiculed and spat upon by lawbreakers. Likewise, she must be tested. "Spell, 'God'," she is told, and likewise, she passes through the pearly gates.

Finally, a tax collector tells of his tribulations in a thankless and friendless job. Saint Peter agrees that he is also worthy. He, too, must pass a test. "Spell 'asafoetida'," he is told.

ALLOCATION OF RESOURCES: PUBLIC OR PRIVATE?

In our nation's early years, settlers willingly combined their energies and talents to construct public projects: roads, meeting houses, fortresses, and even stockades. Later, as the nation grew, citizens continued to contribute a few days each month to maintain the community's property. In those days, there was a direct and visible relationship between citizen participation, on the one hand, and the growth and security of the community, on the other hand.

Direct citizen involvement created bonds of satisfaction often lacking today. Today a taxpayer merely completes a "form 1040" and thus assigns a part of his or her production to the U.S. Treasury. The citizen often feels not a part of government, but a victim, struggling to escape its clutches!

Taxes represent a major form of government intervention in the market system. Through taxes, government takes purchasing power away from spending for private purposes and spends it instead for public purposes—for producing goods and services to be used by the community as a whole. When you pay your dollars for sales and property taxes and income and social security taxes, you have fewer dollars to spend for autos, appliances, clothing, and trips to the shore. Government casts some of your "dollar votes" for you—for schools, highways, and national defense.

Purchase of some goods and services is clearly an individual's responsibility; other goods and services can be provided best by group action. In the United States, the first group includes consumer goods, like food, clothing, and automobiles. The second group includes defense and international relations, highway systems, and regulation of interstate and foreign commerce. In a gray area, where public and private responsibilities mingle, are education, health and nutrition, housing, and the arts.

As a nation, we try to achieve the most efficient combination of production of goods and services for private enjoyment and goods and services for the use of the entire community. Given our limited productive resources, we try to achieve the allocation of resources that will best serve the objectives of the community and its citizens.

Our choice of private goods and public goods can be shown on a production possibilities curve like the one in Figure 9.1. The two axes represent private goods—for the consumer's own use—and public goods—for

Figure 9.1 Private Goods and Public Goods.

The Government channels some of our resources into the production of public goods.

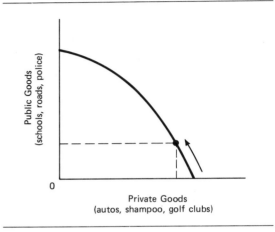

the use of the community as a whole. Our willingness to give up part of our income in taxes permits us to use some of our nation's scarce resources for producing goods and services to be enjoyed by the community as a whole.

SPENDING FOR PUBLIC GOODS AND SERVICES

In the fiscal year 1989, the federal government's outlays in the United States were more than $1.1 trillion. Shares of the annual budget allocated to specific purposes are shown in Figure 9.2.

National defense and defense-related expenditures comprised the largest part of the federal budget. National defense consumed more than $303 billion, or about 28 percent of the total. Defense-related expenditures—international affairs, space research and technology, interest on the public debt, and

Figure 9.2   Allocative Shares of the Federal Budget for 1986 (dollar figures in billions).

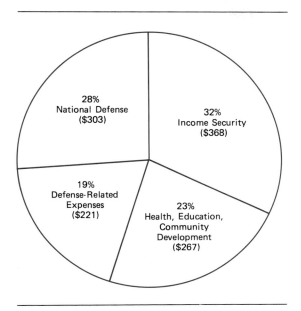

28%
National Defense
($303)

32%
Income Security
($368)

19%
Defense-Related
Expenses
($221)

23%
Health, Education,
Community
Development
($267)

as expressed in voting trends and in public opinion polls.

State and local government expenditures focus primarily on community services. Education is highest on the list of local government expenditures, with highways an important second. Fire and police protection, water and sewage, and parks and recreation are other local government responsibilities.

GETTING THE MONEY

How does government obtain the money it needs to finance its programs? Government outlays can be financed in three ways:

1.   By printing new money.
2.   By borrowing from the public.
3.   By taxing the public.

Let us look at each of these methods in more detail.

veterans' benefits and services—consumed an additional $221 billion (19 percent). Health, energy, education, housing, commerce and transportation, agriculture, and rural and natural resource development took about $267 billion (23 percent). Income-support payments to individuals (such as social security benefits, welfare, and unemployment compensation) were about $368 billion (32 percent). Note that the total percentage adds up to 102, a result of rounding.

Shares of federal expenditures spent for various purposes have remained fairly constant over the years. An exception has been the greater emphasis on military expenditures in wartime. The emphasis on public services such as education and health has varied also, depending on the priorities of the administration in power and on the mood of the public,

Printing Money

Printing new money sounds like a relatively safe and easy way for the federal government to finance its expenditures. In fact, it is the poorest way to obtain funds and is not now used by the U.S. Treasury. The reason has to do with its effect on total spending. If the government were to print money for its own spending without taking money away from consumers, consumer spending would continue at the same level. Then individuals would be competing with government for the limited supplies of goods and services. As government and individuals bargained and bid for the things they wanted, prices would rise and all money would be worth less. The result of printing new money could be inflation.

After World War I the German government needed money to make its reparations payments to the victorious powers. Many of those debts were paid by printing new money. The German money supply increased by almost 10 billion times in four years! The result of money growth was inflation so severe that workers had to be given time off during each day to spend their pay before prices could rise again.

Borrowing from the Public

A better way to raise money is to borrow from the public. Government can sell bonds to individual consumers and business firms. (When you buy a government bond, you are, in effect, lending your savings to government.) If consumers and business firms buy bonds with money they otherwise would have spent, their own spending will fall by the amount government wants to spend. If buyers of bonds use money they otherwise would have loaned to banks or other businesses, investment spending will fall by the amount government wants to spend. Thus, the sale of bonds to consumers and business firms withdraws from spending enough money to offset the amount government wants to spend.

A disadvantage of this method is that at times it may be difficult to persuade consumers and business firms to buy bonds unless the Treasury agrees to pay higher interest rates. Interest charges on U.S. Treasury bills and bonds rose from around 5 percent in 1972 to more than 14 percent in 1982. Higher interest rates pushed total interest expense on the federal debt from only $20 billion in 1972 to almost $170 billion in 1989!

Taxing the Public

Perhaps the best way to finance government spending is through taxation. Through taxation, other spending is reduced by the amount government wants to spend, and it isn't necessary to persuade taxpayers to cooperate!*

In 1989 total federal tax receipts were $990 billion. Personal and corporate income taxes were the major source of federal tax revenue, making up more than half of the total. The U.S. Treasury ran a deficit of more than $150 billion, which was financed by borrowing.

A CLOSER LOOK AT TAXES

Because taxes make up the major portion of government revenue, we will look at them in more detail. The various taxes levied by government are often classified by comparing the amount paid in taxes with taxpayers' income base:

$$\frac{\text{total taxes paid}}{\text{taxpayers' income}}$$

Regressive Taxes

A tax that takes a larger fraction of income from low-income earners than from high-income earners is a regressive tax. Examples are:

1. Any uniform "head" tax such as the (now outlawed) poll tax, which takes the same dollar amount from every citizen regardless of income.
2. Social security taxes, which take a fraction of an employed person's earnings up to a certain amount, above which earnings are not taxed.
3. Sales taxes.

The regressivity of items 1 and 2 above is easy to see, but why is a sales tax regressive?

* Citizens in some cities and towns have lately begun to resist new tax measures, however. Passage of property-tax limitations in California is an example of what some have called a "taxpayers' revolt."

How Things Have Changed . . .

EFFECTIVE RATES OF FEDERAL, STATE, AND LOCAL TAXATION
(percent of income)

Decile	1966	1980	1988
Lowest	16.8	17.1	16.4
Second	18.9	17.1	15.8
Third	21.7	18.9	18.0
Fourth	22.6	20.8	21.5
Fifth	22.8	22.7	23.9
Sixth	22.7	23.4	24.3
Seventh	22.7	24.4	25.2
Eighth	23.1	25.5	25.6
Ninth	23.3	26.5	26.8
Highest	30.1	28.5	27.7
Top 5%	32.7	28.9	27.4
Top 1%	39.6	28.4	26.8
All taxpayers	25.2	25.3	25.4

SOURCE: *Brookings Review*, Spring 1990.

A decile is a tenth of the population, here ranged from the lowest income earners to the highest. Look down each column to see the level of progressivity of the tax structure as a whole. Look across the lines to see how the level of progressivity has changed over the years shown.

A sales tax is a fixed percentage of expenditures for goods. However, a sales tax is considered regressive because low-income families generally spend a larger fraction of their income on taxed goods than do higher-income families. High-income families generally spend more of their earnings on untaxed services, and they save more. (Excluding such necessary purchases as food and medicine from the sales tax makes it less regressive.)

There is some difference of opinion on the proper classification of the property tax. Most agree that low- and middle-income families are likely to spend a larger fraction of their incomes for housing than are high-income families. This would make the effects of the property tax regressive.

Proportional Taxes

A tax that takes an equal fraction of income from all taxpayers is a proportional tax. An example is the Illinois personal income tax, which is $2\frac{1}{2}$ percent for all income levels. (However, exemptions for dependents have

Contemporary Thinking about Economic Issues

THE PROGRESSIVITY OF THE FEDERAL INCOME TAX

The late Joseph Pechman devoted his entire career to the study of the nation's tax system. One of his last articles reported on the effects of the 1986 Tax Reform Law.

Because of its progressivity, the federal income tax system serves to redistribute income from high-income earners to low-income recipients of government programs. Its effects are small, however. In fact, before the 1986 tax reform, the progressive income tax reduced income in equality by only 3.8 percent (1984). During the period 1966 to 1985, reductions in the top tax rates had the effect of reducing the tax burden of the top 5 percent of income earners by about one-fifth. For the top 1 percent, the reduction was more than one-third. Other factors in the declining tax burden of high-income taxpayers were the decrease in the federal corporate income tax and the increase in personal deductions (for such things as interest payments, individual re-

tirement accounts, and state and local taxes).

The Tax Reform Act of 1986 returned some of the lost progressivity to the federal income tax. By increasing personal exemptions, standard deductions, and the earned income credit, the 1986 law removed about 5 million low-income people from the income tax rolls. It still left the top tax rates below their 1966 levels, however. The effect of the law was to reduce income inequality by a modest 4.4 percent in 1988.

When transfer payments are considered along with taxes, the result is an increase in tax progressivity. The redistribution that results from transfer payments, however, is not from the wealthy to the poor but from the low- and middle-income groups to the poor.

Pechman proposed additional reforms to make the income tax more progressive:

1. Capital gains should be taxed at the

the effect of reducing the proportional effect of the tax.)

Progressive Taxes

A tax that takes a larger fraction of income from high-income earners than from low-income earners is a progressive tax. The personal income tax is the best example. Tax rates increase as the taxpayer moves into higher income brackets. For a typical married

couple with two children, the tax rate on the first $29,750 of taxable income is 15 percent: thus, $0.15(\$29,750) = \$4,462.50$. The tax rate on income between $29,750 and $71,900 is 28 percent: Thus, $0.28(71,900 - 29,750) = \$11,802$. For a family earning precisely $71,900, therefore, the fraction of income paid in tax is $(\$4,462.50 + \$11,802,00)/\$71,900 = 0.23 = 23$ percent. Families earning less than this amount pay a smaller fraction, and families earning more pay a larger fraction. The reason is that tax rates increase with income.

same rate as ordinary income, but gains should be adjusted for inflation. Moreover, capital gains should be taxed at death, whether or not the appreciated asset is sold.

2. Employee fringe benefits should be taxed as part of income. Fringe benefits typically favor high-income workers; paying cash instead of benefits would allow all workers greater choice in the use of their earnings.

3. Recipients of social security benefits should be subject to tax on a larger fraction of benefits (roughly 85 percent versus the current 50 percent).

4. Interest payments should continue to be deductible from taxable income but only to the level of reported investment income. Deductions should also be allowed for medical payments and casualty losses and for state income taxes, but not for property taxes or small charitable contributions.

5. The withholding system should be extended to interest and dividends, and more rates should be added to the schedule (so that it ranges from 4 to 48 percent).

6. The corporate tax rate should be reduced from 34 percent to 15 percent, but interest on corporate borrowing should not be deductible.

7. The earned income credit for low-income families should be increased, and it should be graduated with family size.

Pechman estimated that his plan would increase the effective tax rate of the top 1 percent of family units from 21 percent to 30 percent.

Evaluate each of Pechman's proposals in terms of its effects on saving and investment, GNP growth, efficiency, and equity.

Joseph A. Pechman, "The Future of the Income Tax," *American Economic Review,* March 1990.

(Families earning more than $71,900 pay a surtax of 5 percent above the top rate of 28 percent on income up to about $200,000.)

The Tax Structure as a Whole

State and local taxes, dominated by sales and property taxes, tend to be regressive. Federal taxes, dominated by income taxes, are progressive.

The progressivity of the federal tax struc-
ture is affected also by the existence of **negative taxes,** which are government payments to individuals or groups and are called **transfer payments.** (Transfer payments were discussed in Chapter 7.) Remember that transfer payments are not payments in exchange for goods or services but are additions to the disposable incomes of particular groups. When negative taxes received from government are subtracted from taxes paid to government, the result is net taxes: the net amount government has withdrawn from private income.

The effect of net taxes is to increase the progressivity of the federal tax structure. This is because low-income families who pay a lower tax rate are more likely to receive government transfer payments of some kind. When you subtract negative taxes received from taxes paid, their net tax rate is very low, perhaps even less than zero. High-income families who pay a higher tax rate receive fewer transfer payments. This makes their net tax rate relatively high.

In 1986 Congress and President Reagan decided on a new tax law. One objective of the new law was to reduce tax rates while eliminating certain tax advantages high-income earners enjoyed under the old tax law. Under the old tax law many high-income taxpayers reduced their tax bills by increasing their deductions from taxable income. Allowed deductions under the old law were: losses from side business ventures; interest on consumer loans; fast depreciation of business equipment or facilities; and entertainment and other expenses related to business.

Under the old law many high-income taxpayers arranged to receive a portion of their income in the form of capital gains. A **capital gain** is the difference between the original cost of an asset and the selling price when it is eventually sold by the taxpayer. Before the 1986 tax law, a capital gain was taxed at less than half the rate of the tax on the taxpayer's earned income.* The 1986 tax law eliminated this tax advantage and called for a tax rate on capital gains equal to the tax rate on the taxpayer's other income.

Economists at the Brookings Institution in Washington, D.C., examined the effects of the old tax law at various income levels. Except for the 10 percent of families having the lowest incomes and the 3 percent having the highest, almost all families paid between 25 and 27

*If an asset is sold for less than its purchase price, the seller experiences a capital loss.

percent of their incomes in federal, state, and local taxes. Persons with the lowest incomes actually paid a higher fraction of their income in taxes (mostly state and local sales taxes) than the 87 percent of the population in the middle range. The new law has had the effect of reducing the total tax bills of low-income families and increasing the tax bills of high-income families.

Another effect of the 1986 tax law has been lower taxes for individual taxpayers and higher taxes for business firms. There is some disagreement as to whether this has made the tax structure more or less progressive. The reason for the disagreement has to do with the incidence of the corporate income tax. Corporations pay taxes, but the funds for paying taxes come from charging higher prices for their products, paying lower wages to their workers, or paying lower dividends to their stockholders. Thus, the effect of corporate income taxes is spread across all income classes and may actually be heaviest on low- and middle-income families.

On the basis of these findings, some economists have concluded that our tax structure as a whole is regressive at low levels of income, proportional over a wide range of middle incomes, and slightly progressive for a small group at the top of the income scale. (Can you explain what this means?)

FISCAL POLICY

The U.S. government uses its tax revenue to provide public goods and services. However, government taxing and spending policies also have important consequences for the level of economic activity in the nation as a whole. The use of federal tax and spending programs to affect economic activity is called **fiscal policy.** The word *fiscal* evolved from "fisc," which referred to a money basket carried by tax collectors in the days of the Roman empire.

The Keynesian Revolution

The Great Depression of the 1930s awakened Congress to the damaging effects of wide swings in economic activity. Voters insisted that Congress adopt policies to correct widespread unemployment and to protect against unemployment or inflation in the future. In the late 1930s the British economist, John Maynard Keynes, presented his ideas on economic stabilization policies to President Franklin Roosevelt.

Keynes' basic proposition was simple. Any time total spending was too low, such that there was unemployment and recession, government should increase its spending and reduce taxes and in that way increase aggregate demand. On the other hand, if total spending were to be too high, with worsening shortages and inflation, government should reduce its spending and raise taxes. Changes in government spending and taxes would offset unwanted changes in private spending, and the nation would avoid the damaging effects of unemployment or inflation.

Keynes declared that there is no necessary relationship between government expenditures and tax revenues. This was a rather startling pronouncement, because it meant that government would not be required to balance its budget. According to Keynes, in times of too little private spending, government spending should exceed tax revenues. Higher government spending would funnel more spending power back into the circular flow than is taken out through taxes. Operating "in the red" tends to cause a deficit in the government budget:

government expenditures − tax collections
$$= G - T = \text{government deficit}$$

When private spending is too high, tax revenues should exceed government spending, draining out more purchasing power from the circular flow through taxes than is put back through spending. Collecting more taxes than it pays out yields a surplus in the government budget:

tax collections − government expenditures
$$= T - G = \text{government surplus}$$

In deficit years, government spending greater than tax receipts would be financed through the sale of bonds. Then in surplus years, tax revenues greater than spending would make it possible to redeem bonds for cash. If by some (unlikely) coincidence government borrowing during deficit years is precisely offset by loan repayments in surplus years, there is no permanent increase in total federal debt. In any case, according to Keynes, small increases in government debt are a small price to pay for maintaining an efficient level of economic activity.

Keynes's ideas were considered revolutionary. For several decades, policymakers hesitated to recommend that government spend more than it collected in taxes. During recessions the budget tended to show a deficit anyway, because incomes (and income tax receipts) tended to fall. It was not until the 1960s that the federal government actually planned a budget deficit. (The first planned government deficit is discussed in more detail in the second part of this chapter.)

Some features of fiscal policy are automatic, with built-in tax and spending changes that take effect automatically when private spending changes. Other features are discretionary. They require an act of Congress before they can be put into effect.

Automatic Fiscal Policy

Automatic fiscal policy has two parts: the progressive tax structure, including tax rates that rise with income; and negative taxes, like farm subsidies, unemployment compensation, welfare benefits, veterans' benefits, and other payments that tend to fall with income.

With progressive tax rates, when incomes rise, taxpayers move into higher tax brackets. They pay higher taxes, and they cut their spending to a smaller fraction of income. On the other hand, when incomes fall, taxpayers pay lower tax rates, so that their spending does not fall as fast as income.

Negative taxes have a similar effect. When incomes rise, welfare benefits, subsidies, food stamp allotments, and unemployment compensation tend to fall. Smaller transfer payments tend to slow the rise in personal income and slow the rise in spending. On the other hand, when incomes fall, negative tax payments add more to incomes and keep spending from falling too far.

Fiscal policy to increase the level of spending and maintain high employment is called **expansionary fiscal policy.** Fiscal policy to contract spending and reduce inflationary pressure is called **contractionary fiscal policy.** Together, expansionary and contractionary fiscal policy work to increase the efficiency with which the nation employs its scarce resources. In the next section we will consider in detail the automatic features of the net tax structure that can avoid either too rapid expansion or contraction.

Expansionary Fiscal Policy

Much of expansionary fiscal policy works automatically to maintain spending and full employment. It works this way. If spending should fall, unemployment would tend to increase, and the economy could spiral downward into recession. In this case, the following automatic changes go to work to cushion the effects of a drop in spending:

1. Lower incomes are taxed at lower tax rates.
2. Transfer payments increase as more families move down the income scale.

The result is to pump purchasing power into the pockets of low-income families particularly likely to spend it. The increased purchasing power cushions the downward slide of spending and helps keep employment and production from falling as far as they might otherwise. It also tends to produce an automatic deficit in the federal budget.

Contractionary Fiscal Policy

Other automatic features take effect when spending is increasing too fast. If spending increases too fast, employment and production increase, and prices tend to rise. This time, the automatic changes noted above go into reverse, helping to hold down the increase in spending:

1. As families move into higher income brackets, they are taxed at higher rates.
2. They are entitled to fewer government transfer payments.

The result is to drain purchasing power from the spending stream. The reduced purchasing power slows down the increase in spending and helps hold prices down. It also tends to create an automatic surplus in the federal budget.

Discretionary Fiscal Policy

We have seen that automatic fiscal policy works without the intervention of public officials. (This may be seen as an advantage or a disadvantage, depending on one's confidence in public officials!) Occasionally, however, automatic fiscal policy is not enough to keep spending at a full-employment, noninflationary level. In such times it may be necessary to make fundamental changes in the tax structure and government spending programs. Changes in the entire tax structure and in government spending plans are called **discretionary fiscal policy.** Discretionary fiscal policy can be either expansionary or contractionary.

Discretionary Policy to Increase Employment

In times of high unemployment, more expansionary fiscal policy may be needed to increase aggregate demand. As a part of expansionary fiscal policy, Congress might decide to reduce tax rates for individuals and corporations. Lower personal tax rates will leave households with more money to spend for consumer goods and services, and lower corporate income taxes will leave business firms with more money for making new investments. Or, Congress might decide to increase funds distributed as transfer payments. Increasing transfer payments reduces net taxes, increases disposable income, and increases the level of private spending.

Finally, Congress might decide to increase government expenditures. Expenditures might be increased for public projects like dams and highways, education and health services, or scientific research and resource development. Increasing government spending increases aggregate demand and causes employment, production, and income to rise.

Discretionary Policy to Reduce Inflation

In times of inflation, more strongly contractionary policy may be needed to reduce aggregate demand and hold down the level of resource use. Congress might decide to raise tax rates or impose a temporary surtax on tax bills. (A surtax is an extra tax—a tax on a tax.) Higher taxes will leave families with less money for consumer spending and leave business firms with less money for investment spending. (If families and business firms cut back on their savings in order to pay their higher taxes, however, they can offset at least part of the higher taxes and continue to spend at roughly the same rate.)

Congress might also decide to reduce government expenditures. Reducing expenditures may be difficult if essential public projects are under way and must be continued. Congress may hesitate to cut transfer payments, too, since transfer payments generally go to low-income families who suffer severely from inflation.

The best remedy for unemployment or inflation is probably some combination of discretionary policies that avoid the disadvantages of a single policy. For example, during the recession of 1974–1975, President Ford recommended that Congress:

1. Reduce personal and corporate tax rates.
2. Increase unemployment compensation.
3. Appropriate funds for public-service jobs in highway maintenance, library and hospital services, and other public projects.

During the inflation of 1979, President Carter recommended that Congress:

1. Allow taxes to increase automatically.
2. Reduce the growth rate of federal outlays.
3. Encourage labor-management cooperation in a voluntary program of wage and price restraint.

Some Disadvantages

One disadvantage of discretionary fiscal policy is the lack of well-planned and needed public projects for which to spend government funds. A major energy research and development program or a space program may come up only once in a generation—make that a century! Moreover, massive government spending programs are difficult to administer without waste and duplication. Occasionally, projects completely fail to achieve their intended aims.

They are also slow to put in place. Ideally, policymakers would maintain a backlog of desired projects, engineered and ready to go. The plans could be begun quickly when needed and in spending amounts ranging from very small to rather large. Better long-range planning and flexibility in the injection of new spending would improve the efficiency of discretionary fiscal policy.

Another disadvantage of discretionary fiscal policy is the lack of current economic information. Economic forecasting and planning is not as exact a science as, perhaps, horticulture. The story is told of a New York apartment dweller who owned a collection of cactus plants and wanted a precise indicator to tell her when they should be watered. She solved her problem by subscribing to an Arizona newspaper. Whenever the paper reported rain, she watered her plants!

Unfortunately, Congress has no equally precise indicator that signals when to inject or hold back new spending, and there are no foolproof ways to accomplish the desired results. Proposals must be debated and compromised, voters must be informed and persuaded and, finally, administrative procedures must be designed and put into effect. All in all, it is a frustratingly difficult and time-consuming process. By the time any decision is put into effect the problem may be much worse (or it may have disappeared altogether).

The most serious disadvantage of discretionary fiscal policy stems from political considerations. Tax and spending proposals often depend more on election-year politics than on what is best for the nation's long-range economic health. Spending for rural development or for supersonic transport affects different groups of voters differently. Each legislator tends to support tax and spending proposals that provide the most help for his or her own constituents. It is very difficult to separate economics from politics!

Political considerations give an inflationary bias to discretionary fiscal policy. Congress finds it easy to turn on the faucet and allow more government spending to flow into the spending stream. New spending bills and tax reductions receive little objection from voters and maintain a legislator's popularity in his or her district.

The reverse is not so agreeable. Closing off spending through reductions in government outlays and increases in taxes doesn't secure a legislator's seat in the next Congress! The result is that expansionary fiscal policy to fight unemployment is generally favored at the expense of contractionary fiscal policy to fight inflation.

THEN THERE'S THE NATIONAL DEBT . . .

According to Keynesian economic policy, it is acceptable for the federal government to spend more than it collects in taxes. If consumer spending and business investment spending fall short of the full employment level of spending, more government spending and lower taxes can make up the difference. A balanced federal budget is desirable only if a balanced budget plus private spending will achieve full employment.

Spending more than tax revenue requires that government borrow. Deficits in the federal budget are financed by the sale of bonds to individuals, business firms, financial institutions, and state and local governments. Fortunately, many savers look upon government bonds as a safe way to store their money assets. Bonds generally pay enough interest income to offset the effects of inflation, and they provide financial security for the holder's retirement years.

The first major increase in government debt occurred in World War II, when total debt soared from $45 billion to more than $250 billion. In 1946 the government's total debt amounted to 125 percent of GNP. Obviously the increase in debt was not a result of govern-

Contemporary Thinking About Economic Issues

HOW BAD IS THE DEBT?

Robert Heilbroner and Peter Bernstein have tried to dispel some of the myths they believe distort public concerns regarding the national debt and instead focus attention on the nation's more serious problems. They make the following points:

1. The tight money policy intended to fight inflation has had three damaging effects: It has increased the interest expense of financing government debt, activated cost-of-living adjustments in government transfer payments, and precipitated a recession that reduced government tax revenues.
2. Rather than a national liability, the national debt is the total of Treasury obligations backed by the nation's productive power and its real human and physical assets.
3. At 43 percent of GNP our present debt is about the same proportion as it was in 1940 and comparable to the debts of other industrialized nations.
4. The burden of the debt falls on the generation that enjoys its benefits: The taxes they pay to service the debt return to current holders of the debt.
5. The debt increases our well-being by stimulating the economy when needed and financing major capital projects.
6. The real size of the debt is reduced each year by inflation; moreover, between 5 and 20 percent of the debt

represents public investment.
7. Better understanding of the debt would require separating from the normal operating budget expenditures for capital improvements, including education.
8. Government borrowing may not force up interest rates, and government expenditures may yield more productive assets for the nation than some private investment expenditures.

According to Heilbroner and Bernstein, we should not be distracted by concerns regarding the debt but rather focus our attention on improving the nation's competitiveness in the world economy, controlling the inflationary threat, correcting urban blight and environmental decay, and revitalizing our education system. Failure to solve these problems would more severely damage our nation's future than failure to reduce the debt. Solving these problems will require government finance, but, more importantly, it will require the adaptation of our institutions to modern challenges.

The chief problem with the debt would occur if debt rises faster than GNP, if interest rates rise significantly, or if foreigners substantially increase their holdings of debt.

Robert Heilbroner and Peter Bernstein, *The Debt and the Deficit: False Alarms/Real Possibilities,* Norton, New York, 1989.

ment spending to achieve full employment. In fact, the great increase in the debt was necessary to finance spending for defense.

Between World War II and the beginning of the 1970s, the federal debt grew at an annual rate of less than $5 billion. During the 1980s it grew at an average annual rate of $200 billion. At the end of 1989 total federal debt amounted to almost $3 trillion. This was 56 percent of GNP for the year, up from 33 percent in 1980.

Who Holds the Debt?

To focus on total federal debt is somewhat misleading. Much of the debt has been borrowed from agencies within the federal government itself. Many government agencies receive payments for special purposes and use their funds to buy government securities temporarily as interest-earning assets. For example, the U.S. highway trust fund receives gasoline tax revenues, which it spends for interstate highway construction. The social security trust fund receives employee and employer contributions, from which disability and pension payments are made. In all, about $1 trillion of the federal debt was held by such agencies of the government in 1989.

The largest single holder of government debt is the Federal Reserve System, with more than $227 billion. Federal Reserve banks receive interest on their holdings of government bonds, but by law they are required to return part of the interest to the U.S. Treasury. Private commercial banks, money market funds, and insurance companies together hold about $330 billion in government debt. Other corporations hold about $90 billion, and state and local governments about $325 billion.

Another $595 billion of federal debt is held by miscellaneous creditors such as nonprofit institutions and pension funds. Foreigners hold an increasing amount of the debt: $395 billion, or 13 percent of total debt in 1989—up from $20.6 billion in December 1970. As foreigners earn more U.S. dollars from their export sales to the United States, they often use their dollars to buy government securities.

When all these holders of federal debt are considered, the amount remaining in the hands of individual investors in the United States is about $200 billion.

Some Advantages

An advantage of the federal debt is that it provides the government a way to stabilize economic activity through variations in taxes and spending. Furthermore, the purchase and sale of government securities is a way to change the quantity of money in circulation, as the Federal Reserve buys and sells securities from its own holdings. (We will discuss this subject more fully in Chapter 10.)

Government securities provide financial security to many small investors. Many individuals and institutions regard U.S. government securities as a convenient and safe way to store their savings for their future needs.

Because the U.S. government is a continuing operation, it is never necessary to repay the debt entirely. While retired people are cashing in their securities for cash, young people are buying securities for their long-range security. Only when foreigners cash in their securities is it necessary to send dollars outside the country.

Some Potential Disadvantages

The disadvantages associated with the federal debt have very little to do with the need to repay it. In fact, to repay the debt entirely would require only that taxes be raised by the amount of the debt in order to pay cash to bondholders. The result would be a redistribution of wealth away from taxpayers toward holders of the debt. Because bondholders would likely be from higher-income groups, they would tend to spend a smaller fraction of their receipts. So another result might be a decrease in total spending and a decline in economic activity. Nevertheless, to repay the debt would not significantly affect the nation's total wealth.

Similar reasoning applies to the collection of taxes for paying interest on the debt. All income earners are taxed to pay interest charges to bondholders—almost $170 billion in 1989. Interest payments amount to about 15 percent of all federal outlays and about 3 percent of GNP. Holders of debt gain from their interest earnings, of course, but most gainers are also taxpayers, whose tax payments offset their interest earnings. The extent to which some groups gain and others lose from the effects of the federal debt has never been precisely measured.

Some people argue that a large federal debt places a burden on future generations, who must tax themselves to pay interest charges or to repay the debt itself. We have seen that total repayment is not necessary or desirable. Interest charges are necessary, of course, and are passed on to future generations. The interest income, as well as the securities themselves, are also passed down to these future generations by their parents and grandparents.

The chief disadvantage of the debt has to do with the fact that, at any point in time, there is a limited quantity of savings for lending. Thus, government borrowing absorbs savings that might have been borrowed for new investment. Whether government borrowing helps or hurts the economy depends on whether borrowed funds spent by government help achieve a more productive economy than would have resulted from the private use of the same funds.

Supply-Side Economics

The Keynesian model of income determination dominated economic theory for a quarter of a century. Economic policymakers tended to follow Keynesian recommendations, in particular, increases in government spending to increase aggregate demand and correct tendencies toward recession.

Through the 1970s and into the 1980s, however, a new group of economists began to question the effectiveness of Keynesian policies. Keynesian policies concentrated too much on the demand side of the circular flow, they said, in the expectation that increases in spending would encourage the investment necessary to produce more goods and services. These economists argued that high taxes to finance government spending programs had, in fact, reduced taxpayers' ability to save. Lower saving had the effect of pushing borrowing costs up and driving investment down. They worried that without adequate investment, increases in aggregate demand would lead to accelerating inflation.

This new group of economists rejected what they called **demand-side** economic policies and called for policies they called **supply-side policies.** Supply-side policies included tax cuts to increase saving and investment and stimulate the production of goods and services.

Ronald Reagan campaigned in 1980 on a platform that emphasized supply-side solutions to the nation's economic problems. Tax cuts and cuts in civilian spending programs were put in place late in 1981, but the results were not as expected. In fact, in 1982 the economy moved into the most severe reces-

Viewpoint

THE POLITICS OF ECONOMICS

Our democratic political system guarantees a voice for the interests of many citizen groups, no matter how small. There are some disadvantages to this. Decision making in a democracy requires a consensus from many groups before action can be taken. Problem solving cannot proceed smoothly from description to analysis to policy. The interests of affected groups must first be considered, and compromises must be made. The result of consensus politics may be economic policies that are too little or too late—or just plain wrong.

Voters disagree about the appropriate types and amounts of government spending programs. In general, people tend to favor spending programs that increase their own income, whether or not those programs promote the nation's economic welfare. This is especially true of spending for national defense. Spending for defense increases the incomes of some groups and increases the tax bills of many others. Particular regions or occupations often use their legislative power to benefit proportionally more from defense spending. (A distinguished senator from Georgia was for many years chairman of the Senate Armed Services Committee. It was sometimes said that if his state received one more defense installation, it would sink into the Atlantic Ocean.)

What is politically desirable for a particular interest group may turn out to be undesirable for the economy as a whole. For example, when resources are diverted to military production instead of long-range economic development, the result may be slower economic growth. Moreover, when defense spending is eventually cut off, affected areas may suffer severely from the loss of jobs and income. (Remember that the multiplier works in reverse!)

The farming sector is another that is strongly affected by government economic policy. Farmers generally favor free markets, and they oppose price fixing for the farm equipment they must buy. At the same time, farmers sometimes insist on government price supports for the farm commodities they sell. In the end, farm price supports increase the prices consumers have to pay for many other goods. Strong farm lobbies in Congress can exert political pressure (and contribute campaign funds) in support of policies that benefit farmers.

Economic decisions must be made in the light of political realities. What is politically popular may at times outweigh what is economically efficient. It is little wonder, therefore, that the study of economics was originally known as political economy.

sion since World War II, with record unemployment and business failures.

After the recession, the nation experienced a strong expansion, with growth averaging 3.8 percent over the next four years. Saving actually fell as a fraction of income, however, and investment grew by less than ½ percent as a fraction of income. Some economists began to worry that slower growth in tax collections and increased need for government borrowing was depriving private investors of the funds they needed for investment.

In the remainder of this chapter, we will focus in detail on the record of fiscal policy over the past several decades.

Self-Check

1. **The largest single federal outlays go for:**
   a. Health, education, and welfare.
   b. Revenue-sharing to states.
   c. National defense and defense-related expenditures.
   d. Interest on the national debt.
   e. Highway construction.

2. **When negative taxes are considered, the federal net tax structure:**
   a. Is generally regressive.
   b. Includes primarily sales and excise taxes.
   c. Is considered roughly proportional.
   d. Requires low-percentage tax rates on high incomes.
   e. Becomes more progressive.

3. **Automatic fiscal policy depends on:**
   a. Changes in net taxes as incomes change.   e. The consent of voters.
   b. Lower tax payments during inflation.
   c. Lower transfer payments during recession.
   d. Congressional action to change tax rates.

4. **Discretionary fiscal policy:**
   a. Will never create a government deficit.   d. Is easiest to accomplish
   b. Is a foolproof instrument of economic policy.   during inflation.
   c. Requires congressional action.   e. Focuses on welfare
                                            payments and subsidies.

5. **As a result of national debt:**
   a. The United States is heavily indebted to foreign banks.
   b. Many private investors are dependent on risky assets.
   c. We must tax ourselves heavily to pay bondholders as bonds mature.
   d. There is some redistribution of spending power.
   e. We have placed an unfair burden on our grandchildren.

6. **The federal government provides funds for industrial development in areas of high unemployment. This is an example of:**
   a. Automatic fiscal policy.   d. Contractionary fiscal policy.
   b. Discretionary fiscal policy.   e. Both (b) and (c).
   c. Expansionary fiscal policy.

7. **Which of the following would be an appropriate way to deal with inflation?**
   a. Build a dam.   d. Run a deficit in the federal budget.
   b. Increase farm subsidies.   e. Run a surplus in the federal budget.
   c. Reduce social security taxes.

Theory in Practice

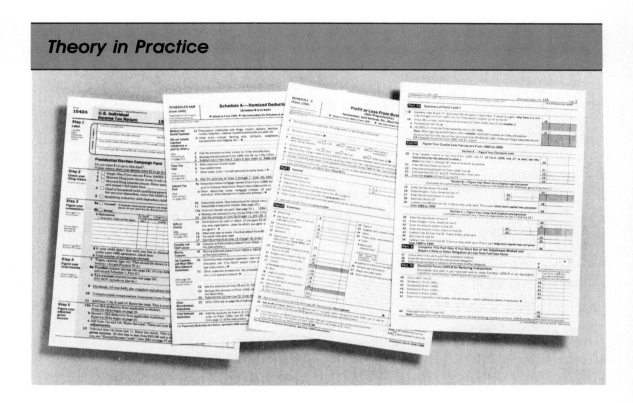

EVALUATING KEYNESIAN POLICIES

During the Great Depression of the 1930s, Keynesian policy was still a new and untried idea. Expansionary fiscal policy was not used vigorously enough to offset the decrease in private spending. Keynes himself joked that it might be a good idea to bury jars of money around the countryside and encourage people to dig them up. In that way, consumers would obtain the spending power which, when spent, would increase someone else's income and spending. Ultimately there would be a multiple increase in spending and income and, finally, increased employment.

Such schemes were not carried out, of course, but government did sponsor public works projects under the Works Progress Administration, Civilian Conservation Corps, and Public Works Administration. Through these agencies, unemployed workers were hired to construct public roads, bridges, parks, and so forth. Still, the level of government spending was rather small.

Total federal, state, and local government spending did not rise substantially during the Depression. Tax revenues fell, however, so that by 1940 the federal government had incurred automatic deficits averaging almost $4 billion a year for seven years. Fear of increasing debt drove policymakers to cut spending. In 1940 there were still 10 million people unemployed.

During the recessions of the Eisenhower years (1954–1955 and 1958–1959), the balanced budget philosophy dominated policy-

Viewpoint

LETTING GOVERNMENT DO IT

If you are ever in Beaver Creek, Minnesota, on Saturday night, don't miss the big dance at the community recreation center just outside town. Just about everyone in town will be there, for in many ways this is the center of the town's social, economic, and political life.

It also illustrates an important relationship between citizens and their government. The voters of this small, isolated community agreed to combine their resources for construction of a community recreation center. In effect, they agreed to "tax" themselves a small amount each week, and in return they enjoy the recreation services at the hall.

That is the way it has always been in the United States. Citizens have perceived needs for community services and have elected representatives to plan programs to fill the needs. In the beginning, most services were provided by local government—usually on a small scale. Since the Great Depression, however, the federal and state governments have been providing more services for their citizens.

How well does the system work? The answer depends in part on the level of government involved. Some needs can be perceived and filled most effectively at the local level. Public education and local law enforcement are examples. Other needs, like dam construction, agricultural research, and forest conservation, are more complex and extend over larger areas. Plans must be made and carried out at the level of the state or even federal government.

In terms of overall productivity, the government sector is probably far behind the private sector. One reason is mechanization. Gains in productivity are generally the result of mechanization, but government services are not easily mechanized. The high labor-intensity of government services makes it difficult to cut costs. Moreover, at the local level especially, it is difficult for governments to

making. It was not until the early 1960s that Keynesian economic policy was actively applied. At that time a conscious decision was made to unbalance the budget in order to stimulate spending and increase employment. Walter Heller, chairperson of President John F. Kennedy's Council of Economic Advisors, persuaded the president to ask Congress for a tax cut at a time when the federal budget was already in deficit.

Heller argued that the deficit was a result of high tax rates. High tax rates kept consumer and business spending low. This meant low levels of employment and income and, hence, low tax revenues. He believed that a reduction in tax rates would leave consumers and business firms with more income for spending. The result would be more job opportunities and higher incomes, with higher tax revenues for the Treasury.

establish clear goals and to use scientific management to carry out programs.

How can government be helped to perform better? Critics have offered some suggestions:

1. Local governments might be combined into metropolitan or regional units. Larger units could use professional management techniques for a more systematic approach to broad, area-wide problems.
2. Another way to improve government performance might be to hire private firms to produce some public services. Garbage collection, school lunch programs, data processing, fire protection, and even law enforcement are examples of services that might be provided more efficiently by private firms.
3. Finally, if public services are to be produced efficiently, they must be performed at the level of government that

can do the job at the lowest cost. This may mean that taxes should be collected by one level of government and revenues spent by another level. The federal government appears to be better at collecting taxes than state and local governments. This is partly a result of the progressive income tax, which yields more revenues as national income grows. On the other hand, state or local governments may be better able to tailor spending programs to their particular needs.

In the United States, we ask government to do for us what we cannot do for ourselves. Unfortunately, some jobs may be too complex even for government. When government programs fail to accomplish their objectives, it is unfair to compare the failed results with some ideal standard. A truer test would be to compare results with results at another level of government—or with no government at all.

The tax cut was finally implemented in 1964 under President Lyndon Johnson, and Dr. Heller's prediction proved correct. The federal budget went from a $3 billion deficit in 1964 to a $1.2 billion surplus in 1965. Tax revenues for 1965 were nearly $10 billion higher than revenues in 1964 before the tax cut!

The success of expansionary fiscal policy (along with increases in the money supply, a topic to be considered in Chapter 10) added to the confidence of economic policymakers and strengthened their commitment to Keynesian economic philosophy. Toward the end of the 1960s, however, economic conditions changed from recession to inflation. Inflation called for contractionary fiscal policy.

The problem of inflation illustrates the principal weakness of Keynesian fiscal policy, a weakness that results from political realities.

When spending for the Vietnam War began to overheat the U.S. economy in the late 1960s, inflationary pressures began to build up. Keynesian fiscal policy called for increased taxes to channel spending away from private purposes and move resources into military production. However, the unpopular war and the insecure political positions of the president and Congress precluded a tax increase until 1968. By that time inflation had accelerated beyond the point where simple policy tools would have had a substantial effect.

The end of the war and the slowing of government spending in the early 1970s brought rising unemployment, while inflation continued at abnormally high levels. The problem of unemployment called for expansionary fiscal policy, with lower taxes and higher government spending. Throughout the 1970s, federal budget deficits averaged $37 billion per year. This was in sharp contrast to the preceding 20 years, when the average deficit had been only $4.3 billion.

In spite of large budget deficits, there was no significant reduction in unemployment. In fact, unemployment rose to 9.2 percent in 1975 and exceeded 7 percent through much of 1980. Continuing inflation was also a disturbing problem. Keynesian remedies for unemployment seemed only to aggravate inflation, which exceeded 13 percent in 1981.

Some economists belive it is impossible to control both unemployment and inflation at the same time. For policymakers in the 1970s it seemed impossible to control either!

PRESIDENT REAGAN'S FISCAL POLICY

President Reagan came to office sharply critical of Keynesian economic policies. High inflation and unemployment, the nation's weakening status in world affairs, and faltering economic growth seemed to call for a change in economic policies. Congress was willing to cooperate in the new administration's efforts to correct long-standing economic problems.

We have referred to President Reagan's economic program as **supply-side economics.** Supply-side economists argued that **demand-side economics** focused too much on consumer spending, expecting that a high level of consumer spending would create incentives for investment and growth. Instead, they said, high taxes to pay for government social programs had absorbed so much spending power that investment had suffered. Without new investment, productivity growth had slowed and inflation had accelerated.

Policy Changes

The new administration adopted a package of programs to change the fiscal policies that it believed contributed to the crisis:

1. *A reduction of government's role in the economy.* Throughout the 1970s total federal government outlays (including government spending and transfer payments) grew from about 17 percent to about 21 percent of GNP, and taxes to 19 percent. Fearing increasing dominance by government in the allocation of scarce resources, the administration promised significant cuts in taxes and government spending.

2. *Personal tax cuts.* Personal income taxes were cut substantially, with the greatest savings going to high-income families who pay proportionally higher taxes. Tax cuts were expected to increase work incentives, thus increasing incomes and ultimately increasing tax revenues. Higher disposable incomes were expected to increase current saving, thus increasing funds for investment. Beginning in 1985,

tax rates were to be **indexed,** or adjusted downward to offset inflation. Indexing would prevent automatic increases in tax rates when wages and prices were rising.

3. *Business tax cuts.* Business firms were allowed larger tax deductions, leaving greater retained profits to finance expansion and modernization.

4. *Government spending cuts.* Tax cuts would reduce government revenues and create a larger deficit, at least at the beginning. Government spending programs that were judged wasteful or not essential would have to be cut or eliminated.

5. *Increased defense spending.* A perception of military weakness relative to the Soviet Union and a fear of increasing world tensions led to a significant increase in defense spending.

6. *Decreased government regulation.* Environmental, health, and safety regulations of the 1970s were believed to have increased the risks of investment and stifled innovation. Therefore, regulatory agencies were asked to reduce the level of new regulatory activity and consider carefully the impact of existing regulations.

The Results

The gravity of the economic situation ensured substantial public support for the president's proposals. Unfortunately, the actual results differed sharply from expectations:

1. Although supply-side economic policies were expected to reduce the role of government, the recession so reduced the growth of GNP that federal outlays increased to 24 percent of GNP in 1982 and federal tax revenues to more than 20 percent. Personal taxes rose as a share of personal income, and median family in-

come fell in real terms. Gross investment, industrial production, housing construction, and corporate profits fell, and the level of plant utilization fell to less than 70 percent. The business failure rate jumped to 61.3 per 10,000 enterprises (from 24 per 10,000 in 1978), the highest rate in 20 years.

2. Personal income tax cuts favored high-income taxpayers, whose incentives were already high, at the expense of low-income taxpayers, who were forced to reduce their savings to maintain a reasonably satisfactory standard of living. Indexing was expected to reduce future tax revenues, and in fact the federal deficit continued in the three-digit range throughout the 1980s.

3. Business income tax reductions were of little use to firms with slowing sales growth and falling income. Moreover, record federal deficits forced the government to compete against private business borrowers for the limited stock of savings, causing interest rates to rise and real investment spending to fall.

4. Cuts in government spending reduced the incomes of many families and business firms, who cut their own spending and made the recession worse.

5. Increases in defense spending required the Department of Defense to spend vast sums quickly, and there was evidence of waste and inefficiency. Also, increased defense production put upward pressure on the wages of skilled workers and on the prices of basic commodities essential in manufacturing.

6. Efforts to reduce government regulation met with mixed success. Deregulation of certain industries did allow competition to increase, but at the cost of a record number of business failures. The public opposed proposals to cut environmental and safety regulations very much.

Contemporary Thinking about Economic Issues

WHEN PEACE BRINGS A "DIVIDEND"

Since the Cold War began in 1945, the United States has allocated more than three-fourths of federal spending to defense. When Soviet President Mikhail Gorbachev moved to reduce Cold War pressures, U.S. taxpayers began to recommend a cut in defense spending. They expected that lower defense spending would leave an excess of government revenues they called a "peace dividend."

There has been no shortage of suggestions for putting the peace dividend to use. A popular suggestion is to eliminate it entirely by cutting taxes. Another is to spend it to improve the nation's deteriorating infrastructure: roads, bridges, transport facilities, and (especially!) public schools. Some economists say that no new spending should be undertaken until we have reduced the national debt. They would use the peace dividend to redeem existing government securities and allow private investors to use the funds as they see fit.

Economists caution against too optimistic expectations with respect to the peace dividend. The national defense bill runs about $300 billion per year, or about $1200 per person. Cuts in troop deployments in Europe might reduce that by $3 billion to $10 billion, but the cuts would show up gradually over several years. U.S. taxpayers often resist closing down military bases in local areas, and contracts for new military technology and equipment continue over many years.

It is probably a good thing that the peace dividend will appear gradually. This will give policymakers time to allocate government spending wisely to achieve the most efficient results.

Alan Blinder, "Uncle Herman and the Peace Dividend," *Business Week,* March 16, 1990.

In 1982 President Reagan bowed to political pressure and agreed to a tax increase to reduce the federal deficit. Congress began considering new policies to deal with high unemployment, and in 1983 the nation began to recover from recession. Real economic growth continued throughout the 1980s, and in 1988 President Bush was elected in a climate of prosperity. Although the budget deficit remained high, candidate Bush promised voters "no new taxes." He hoped that continued growth would provide the increased tax revenues to balance the budget without an increase in tax rates. By 1990, increased deficit projections made that hope appear unrealistic, and the President indicated that tax increases would be considered.

THE GRAMM-RUDMAN-HOLLINGS LAW

The 1980s saw budget deficits on a scale never before experienced, rising above 6 percent of GNP in 1983 and remaining above 5 percent for the next several years. Financing budget deficits requires federal borrowing, which pushes up interest rates and discourages new investments.

Reducing deficits is difficult, because many voters oppose tax increases and cuts in government spending programs. In an attempt to force these essential changes, in 1985 Congress passed the Balanced Budget and Emergency Deficit Control Act, known more commonly as the Gramm-Rudman-Hollings Law, or G-R-H. G-R-H set targets for lower deficits each year until 1993, when the federal budget is to be balanced. If the projected deficit in any year is as much as $10 billion more than the G-R-H target, the law requires automatic cuts in most spending programs to bring the deficit in line with the target.

G-R-H has not been 100 percent successful, because Congress has ways of manipulating projected revenues and outlays to appear to meet deficit targets without actually accomplishing that objective. Moreover, G-R-H has no way to deal with a difference between the projected deficit and the actual deficit. Still, the threat of automatic spending cuts may have forced Congress and the President to move toward budget balance.

THE FISCAL OUTLOOK

The federal budget is closely tied to changes in the level of economic activity. Certain classes of federal outlays rise automatically with increases in total spending and incomes. For instance, social security benefits are tied to consumer price increases, Medicare and Medicaid payments are tied to the price of medical services, and interest on the debt is influenced by other interest rates in the economy. Also, tax revenues are particularly sensitive to changes in incomes when taxpayers move into higher or lower tax brackets.

Table 9.1 shows federal spending and tax revenues for selected years. The deficit in 1939 could be attributed to the sharp drop

Table 9.1 Federal Budget (in millions of dollars).

Year	Receipts	Outlays	Surplus or Deficit
1929*	3862	3127	734
1939	4979	8841	− 3862
1943	23,649	78,533	− 54,884
1951	51,646	45,546	6100
1959	79,249	92,104	− 12,855
1968	153,671	178,833	− 25,161
1975	280,997	326,092	− 45,095
1980	520,050	579,613	− 59,563
1981	599,272	657,204	− 57,932
1982	617,766	728,375	− 110,609
1983	600,562	795,969	− 207,764
1984	666,457	851,781	− 185,324
1985	734,057	946,232	− 212,266
1986	769,091	989,815	− 220,725
1987	854,143	1,003,830	− 149,687
1988	908,954	1,064,044	− 155,090
1989	990,691	1,142,643	− 152,951
1990	1,073,451	1,197,236	− 123,785

SOURCE: *Economic Report of the President,* Various years

in tax revenues during the Great Depression; in 1943, to the large World War II defense expenditures. The recession of 1958–1959 again reduced federal tax revenues, and Vietnam expenditures contributed in large part to the deficit in 1968. Deficits in the mid 1970s were primarily a result of lower levels of income and tax revenues during the prolonged recession. In 1980 an inflationary recession again pushed up federal outlays faster than the growth of tax revenues, and President Reagan's tax cuts and increased defense spending produced additional deficits in 1982–1989.

Projections of economic activity for future years permit tentative forecasts about the size of federal expenditures and tax revenues. Many government programs continue over several years, making it possible to predict spending fairly accurately. Projected GNP and budget data for future years are shown in Table 9.2.

Between 1992 and 1995 real GNP is projected to grow about 2.4 percent annually.

Table 9.2 Projected Federal Budget (in billions of dollars).

Year	1991	1992	1993	1994	1995
GNP					
Current $	5893	6279	6688	7121	7579
Constant $ (1982)	4388	4540	4700	4867	5043
Budget					
Tax receipts	1137	1204	1277	1355	1438
Outlays	1275	1339	1418	1484	1555
Surplus or deficit	− 138	− 135	− 141	− 130	− 118

SOURCE: *The Economic and Budget Outlook,* Congressional Budget Office.

Government spending is expected to increase only enough to keep up with inflation, which is expected to continue at about 4 percent a year. Total federal government outlays are projcted to comprise about 21 percent of GNP through 1995.

Personal and corporate tax revenues and social security contributions are projected to increase as a share of federal receipts, and total tax receipts are expected to increase about 6 percent annually. However, tax revenues will constitute about 19.3 percent of GNP in 1995, so the federal government will run a deficit amounting to almost 2 percent of GNP.

SUMMARY

1. Civilized communities have long depended on the cooperative work of their citizens to provide services to be enjoyed collectively by the community as a whole. Nowadays, we provide public services indirectly through payment of taxes, which governments use to finance the services the community wants.
2. Nearly one-third of total spending in the nation goes to satisfy our collective demand for public services and national defense. About 20 percent of national income and output is used by the federal government and about 10 percent is used by state and local governments. The largest single purpose of federal expenditures is defense and defense-related expenditures. State and local governments provide community services.
3. Taxes are classified as regressive, proportional, or progressive, depending on the fraction of income paid at various income levels.
4. A progressive tax structure provides a degree of automatic stability in the level of economic activity. It helps moderate a tendency toward inflation or recession. Stability is accomplished by withdrawing more net taxes from the spending stream when income rises too fast and withdrawing less net taxes when income falls.
5. When the automatic changes in tax payments are not sufficient to prevent unemployment or inflation, discretionary changes in tax rates or government spending may be necessary. Discretionary fiscal policy is difficult because of the time required to plan, debate, and, finally, put new proposals into effect. Furthermore, political pressure may favor types of government projects or tax policies that do not serve the long-range interests of the nation.
6. When government spending exceeds tax revenues, the Treasury borrows by selling bonds. Treasury bonds are held by individuals, businesses, financial institutions, and local gov-

ernments and are considered a safe way to store purchasing power. Because government debt is held largely within the United States, the interest costs on the bonds are paid by U.S. taxpayers to U.S. bondholders. If borrowed funds are used wisely, they can improve quality of life in the nation.

7. Disillusionment with the results of Keynesian economic policy in the 1970s led to the emergence of supply-side economics and the election of President Reagan. Supply-siders recommended cuts in federal taxes and spending and increased incentives to business investment. These programs were implemented late in 1981, but the results differed from the administration's expectations, and taxes were raised in 1982. Recovery from the recession began in 1983 and continued into 1990, when economists began to worry about the possibility of a new recession.

TERMS TO REMEMBER

regressive tax: a tax that takes a larger fraction of income from low-income earners than from high-income earners

proportional tax: a tax that takes the same fraction of income from all taxpayers

progressive tax: a tax that takes a larger fraction of income from high-income earners than from low-income earners

negative taxes: government income-support payments to individuals; transfer payments

net tax: the tax paid by income groups after allowance is made for payments *received* from government

fiscal policy: the use of the federal government's tax and spending powers to promote economic stability

deficit: an excess of spending over revenues

surplus: an excess of revenues over spending

Keynesian economic policy: the use of government tax and spending policies to affect the level of aggregate demand

supply-side economics: policies to stimulate production of goods and services through tax cuts to encourage private investment

TOPICS FOR DISCUSSION

1. Explain the effects of each of the following on national income and expenditures:

    negative taxes and net taxes
    revenue sharing
    federal deficits and surpluses

2. What is meant by the statement that our tax structure is regressive at low income levels, proportional at medium income levels, and progressive at high income levels?

3. Subjects for debate:

    What is the proper allocation of economic responsibility to the public sector and to the private sector?
    What is the proper allocation of economic responsibility to the federal government and to state and local governments?

4. A respected British economist once called for an "international fiscal policy." What do you think she meant by that? How do you suppose her suggestion might be carried out?

5. In contrast with government, private enterprises must attempt to balance their budgets each financial period. Can you envision a time when a large, healthy corporation might spend more than it collects in revenues? How might such a condition come about? Where would the corporation get the extra funds to spend? Would you like to own stock in such a company? Explain your answer.

6. Some analysts view the growth of government debt as less a threat than the growth of consumer installment debt. In what ways is growing consumer debt a threat to economic stability? What policies might be useful in managing the level of consumer debt?

7. The author suggests that lower tax rates may actually *increase* tax revenues collected by the government. Explain this paradox. Is the reverse also possible?

8. British taxpayers took to the streets in 1990 to protest a revolutionary change in taxes. The

change was from a property tax levy on dwellings to a ''head tax'' on each adult living in the dwelling. Explain the economic basis for opposition to this tax. How would such a tax be greeted in the United States?

9. Consult the most recent edition of *The Economic Report of the President* for information regarding the latest government deficit. Calculate the fraction that defines the deficit as a share of GNP. Compare the current deficit share with the share in earlier years. Explain the basis for notable trends in deficit share.

10. The U.S. Office of Management and Budget (OMB) projects the federal budget deficit for

1993 at $194 billion. In the same year the Social Security trust fund is expected to have a surplus of about $100 billion. What are the advantages and disadvantages of using the Social Security surplus to finance the deficit in the general budget? How would this take place? What are the likely consequences with respect to the progressivity of the nation's tax structure, economic growth, interest rates?

11. In 1990 fears of recession made cutting the nation's budget deficit difficult. Explain how fears of recession tended to (a) increase the deficit and (b) make it more difficult to agree on solutions to the deficit problem.

Chapter

Banking and Monetary Policy

or Money Isn't Everything—Most of the Time It Isn't Even Enough

Tools for Study

LEARNING OBJECTIVES

After reading this chapter, you will be able to:

1. Explain how the use of money overcomes the disadvantages of barter.

2. Describe how banking developed and explain how banks create and destroy money.

3. Explain the role of the Federal Reserve System in regulating the nation's money supply.

4. Describe the financial services performed by nonbank financial institutions.

5. Explain how monetary policy works to stabilize economic activity and discuss some of the problems.

CURRENT ISSUES FOR DISCUSSION

What is the debate over the quantity of money?

How successful has monetary policy been?

How do changes in bank lending affect the nation's money?

How do politics affect monetary policy?

Natives of the North Georgia mountains tell about an illiterate country fellow who is particularly ignorant about money matters. According to the tale, this old gentleman is unable to recognize the value of a half-dollar over that of a quarter. When offered his choice between the two coins, he always chooses the quarter. In the fall of the year, when it's "leaf-looking" time in the Blue Ridge, tourists line up before his bench on the courthouse lawn for the opportunity to offer him coins. True to legend, he invariably selects the quarter and drops it into his overalls pocket.

We should all be so "ignorant" in money matters as this mountain gentleman!

MONEY IS AS MONEY DOES

The first use of money was a kind of watershed in the history of economic development. Before money came into use, exchange was possible only through barter. In **barter,** goods are exchanged for other goods. Thus, barter requires a "double coincidence of wants." Traders have to find someone willing to accept their own goods in exchange for the goods they want. (You have a pig and want cloth; I have cloth and want a pig.) Barter makes trade difficult and time consuming.

Payment in the form of tokens or symbols for the goods, rather than the goods themselves, helped overcome the disadvantages of barter. The use of tokens promoted specialization and division of labor. With specialization, each worker could develop a skill for producing a particular good or service and receive some type of token in exchange. Then workers could use their tokens to purchase the products of other workers.

Viewpoint

BARTER: ITS TIME HAS COME

Barter requires a "double coincidence of wants." This requirement makes barter difficult and time consuming—at least it did before the age of computers!

Certain changes in the U.S. economy have had the effect of reviving barter as a means of exchange. In some years, inflation has reduced the value of receipts from a sale faster than the seller could spend them. Barterers receive what they want simultaneously with the sale of what they don't want. High taxes have also discouraged sales for cash and encouraged barter. Barterers are supposed to report their gains as taxable income, but some don't.

How do computers fuel the growing "barter fever"? Computers can be used to identify goods for trade. They help identify people with a double coincidence of wants, and they make barter more convenient.

Around the nation, barter clubs, barter newsletters, and barter exchanges have sprung up. With the information they provide, barterers can trade such things as legal services for recreation equipment, prime beef for dental work, and house plans for stereos. U.S. exporters have even traded Pepsi Cola for Russian vodka and airplanes for Yugoslavian ham.

There is no way to measure precisely the extent of barter in the United States, but one government agency is trying—the Internal Revenue Service!

What do you think about barter? Are there advantages and disadvantages not mentioned here?

These tokens served as the first money. They provided flexible purchasing power that could be used for whatever a worker wanted to buy.

Functions of Money

The preceding section implied that in order for something to serve as money it must perform certain functions. There are, in fact, three necessary functions of money.

First and most important, money is a medium of exchange. It is accepted as payment for goods and services and, in turn, can be used to buy other goods and services.

Second, money is a standard of value. It provides a way to measure the worth of goods and services. As such, it also provides a way to compare values. (For example, in the United States, the standard of value is measured in dollars. A pound of chicken may be worth half a dollar while a pound of beef may be worth two dollars, or four times as much.)

Finally, money serves as a store of value. It can be saved and used to buy goods and services some time in the future.

Bones, Bullion, and Bank Notes

Money can take many shapes and forms. Whatever is generally accepted as money becomes money. Throughout history the functions of money have been carried out by such diverse things as shells, cattle, and bones.

For many years gold and silver served well as money. These precious metals were scarce and durable, they were easily divided into small pieces, and they had few other uses than as money. In ancient times, chunks or flat pieces of gold and silver promoted the free flow of trade in the Near East and Europe.

Occasionally, cheaters would chip away the edges of these early coins to form more pieces. Eventually, it became necessary to make coins round with serrated edges so that any tampering could be detected.

The difficulty of storing and transporting gold and silver led to the development of banking. (Primitive banks may have existed as far back as the seventh century B.C.) The first banks held gold on deposit for their customers and issued certificates or notes promising to pay gold to the bearer on demand. They charged a small fee for the service, and their notes circulated widely as money.

Banks soon discovered they could not earn enough income simply by storing gold for their depositors. By the seventeenth century, they began to make loans for borrowers to invest in new business ventures. Loans took the form of new bank notes, issued to borrowers with the expectation that profits from the business venture would allow the borrower to repay the loan with interest.

Issuing new bank notes meant that the amount of bank notes outstanding would exceed a bank's supply of gold, but this was not considered a problem. Bankers reasoned that not all depositors would want their gold at the same time. On any given day while some depositors might be withdrawing gold, others would be depositing gold. As long as holders of bank notes had faith in the bank and did not all insist on withdrawing their gold at once, lending was reasonably safe.

BANKING IN THE UNITED STATES

Banking developed in the United States during the early 1600s. The first independent banks tended to overissue bank notes. A bank with $1 million in gold might issue several times that much in notes. At first, the notes would be perfectly good as purchasing power. They would circulate freely until holders began to realize that the bank would never be able to redeem all its notes in gold. Many holders would begin demanding gold for their bank notes. With the loss of its gold the bank would vanish and, along with it, the savings of many of the bank's trusting depositors.

Some banks were called **wildcat banks** because they grew up in the wilderness, "out where the wildcats howl." Wildcat banks accepted gold deposits from trappers and miners and went through a brief orgy of lending. Many wildcat banks collapsed when note holders insisted on exchanging their gold certificates for the real McCoy.

A Move Toward Centralized Banking

After the Revolutionary War, Treasury Secretary Alexander Hamilton helped set up a central bank to regulate bank lending and protect depositors' accounts. Many voters distrusted centralized government control, however, particularly control by powerful moneyed interests of the Northeast. Southern and western opposition to the central bank brought on its collapse in 1836 during the administration of President Andrew Jackson.

The problem of overissue of bank notes and frequent bank failures worsened until finally, in 1863, Congress passed the National Banking Act to regulate banks chartered by the federal government. The National Banking Act set up cash reserve requirements for national banks and limited their lending. This brought some stability to the supply of bank notes. However, the states still had power to charter state banks, and state regulations were much more lenient than the regulations of the National Banking System.

Viewpoint

PAUL VOLCKER'S DILEMMA

Paul Volcker was appointed chairperson of the Board of Governors of the Federal Reserve by President Carter in 1979. His job was particularly difficult, in part because of the debate over the proper goal of monetary policy and in part because of the conflict between fiscal and monetary policy over the period.

Debate over the goal of monetary policy involves the proper way to measure the effectiveness of policy. One way is to measure the growth of the money supply, with the goal that money should grow just as fast as the nation's productive capacity grows and no faster. In this view, money growth in line with productive capacity ensures that the general price level neither rises nor falls.

Another way is to monitor interest rates, holding interest rates constant so as to ensure stable credit conditions and steady growth in investment. By this method, rising interest rates send a signal to the Board of Governors that more money is needed to satisfy the needs of borrowers and investors. Falling interest rates send a signal that there is more money than borrowers and investors currently want to borrow. Thus, interest rates indicate whether money growth should be speeded up or slowed down.

Paul Volcker came into office believing that money should grow at a fairly steady rate—in line with fairly steady increases in productive capacity. He believed that speeding up money growth when interest rates rise would fuel excessive spending and lead to inflation. In fact, according to Volcker, speeding up money growth during the 1970s had helped bring

The Federal Reserve System

Around the turn of the century the nation again experienced a series of financial crises, with bank failures and loss of deposits. Following the Panic of 1907, voters finally began to support the idea of a strong national banking system. They hoped that centrally regulated banking would protect the value of their deposits and achieve greater stability in the supply of bank money

In 1913, Congress passed a new National Banking Act setting up the Federal Reserve System, commonly called the Fed. Commercial banks throughout the country are now regulated by the Federal Reserve. The Fed is controlled by a seven-member Board of Governors appointed by the president with Senate approval. Governors serve staggered terms of 14 years. Apppointment by the president removes the governors from political pressure; and their staggered terms make it generally impossible for a president to appoint more than two governors during a four-year term. The president names one member of the Board of Governors to serve as chairperson.

Federal Reserve Banks are situated in 12 Federal Reserve districts. They do not deal with the U.S. public, but rather with the Treasury and with commercial banks. Their

on the high inflation the nation was experiencing when he took office.

For all these reasons, Paul Volcker was determined to slow down money growth and then hold growth to a fairly steady rate. This turned out to be a particularly difficult policy to maintain, for at the same time Congress and President Reagan were putting in place a program of expansionary fiscal policy. They cut taxes substantially and increased defense spending. Lower taxes encouraged individuals and business firms to spend, and higher government spending created an additional multiplier effect on GNP growth.

The problem was that increased consumer, business, and government spending could not take place without speeding up money growth, and this Volcker was reluctant to do. In fact, Volcker was successful in slowing money growth to the average of the previous decade. Slow money growth had the effect of slowing consumer and business spending, so that inflation fell dramatically. Unfortunately, the nation also suffered a severe recession, with rising unemployment and falling productivity growth.

Finally, the Federal Reserve decided to increase money growth, and the economy began to expand. By the mid 1980s money growth was twice the rate of the 1970s, and some economists were worried that inflation would soon return.

What political issue is involved in the Fed's decision whether to stabilize money growth or interest rates? What political interests are likely to favor the different goals?

most important function is to hold deposits, or reserves, for commercial banks. We will see that their holdings of commercial bank reserves provide an important tool for regulating the nation's money supply. Finally, Federal Reserve Banks act as bankers for the U.S. Treasury, holding the government's tax revenues and paying its bills.

Commercial Banks

Most of us are more familiar with commercial banks. Commercial banks deal with individuals and business firms, accepting **demand deposits** (checking accounts) and **time deposits** (savings accounts) and making loans. They may be chartered by the federal government or by a state government. All federally chartered or national banks are required to join the Federal Reserve System. State-chartered banks may also join but may leave the system if they choose. Almost 6000 of the nation's 14,000 commercial banks are members of the Federal Reserve System. While this number is less than half the total, members tend to be among the nation's largest banks, holding on deposit about three-fourths of the nation's money.

In the beginning, only member commercial banks were required to abide by the rules of the Federal Reserve System, and only members received the benefits. In 1980 Congress extended banking regulations to all commercial banks and other bank-like institutions. According to the Monetary Control Act of 1980, all commercial banks must keep a certain fraction of their deposits in reserve accounts in the Fed, and all must submit to regular supervision and examination. Member banks are required to purchase stock in the Federal Reserve Bank in their district.

In return for their compliance with Federal Reserve regulations, all commercial banks receive these benefits:

1. *A central clearinghouse for checks.* Commercial banks receive as deposits checks drawn on other banks. The checks are then sent to the Federal Reserve for return to the issuing bank. This process is called **check clearing.** It allows all banks to record their customers' deposits and withdrawals promptly.
2. *Deposit insurance through the Federal Deposit Insurance Corporation (FDIC).* Banks pay a small fraction of their deposits into an insurance fund for paying off depositors of failed banks.
3. *A source of borrowed reserves.* Commercial banks may borrow from the Fed to keep their reserve accounts at the level required by banking regulations.
4. *Financial information.*
5. *A 6 percent return on their paid-in stock.* This applies only to member banks.

OTHER FINANCIAL INSTITUTIONS

Commercial banks are important financial **intermediaries.** Intermediaries occupy a position in the market between buyers and sellers of a good or service. For financial intermediaries the good or service exchanged is money, and the buyers and sellers are borrowers and lenders.

Most of us are both borrowers and lenders. We deal with many financial intermediaries for our various financial needs. We deal with commercial banks for deposits and short-term loans. In 1990 commercial banks held deposits of $2290 billion and loans of $2225 billion.* Commercial bank deposits include demand and time deposits; loans include real estate loans, loans to business firms and other financial intermediaries, and installment loans to individuals. Until 1981 commercial banks were prohibited from paying interest on demand deposits. Because demand deposits are subject to immediate withdrawal, commercial banks have been obliged to limit their lending to mostly short-term purposes.

Thrift Institutions. Other financial intermediaries perform certain other specialized functions. For instance, savings and loan associations and mutual savings banks engage in longer-term borrowing and lending. In 1990 these so-called thrift institutions held savings deposits of about $1305 billion, making them second only to commercial banks in size. Until 1981 thrift institutions were not normally allowed to provide checking accounts. Because few of their deposits were subject to immediate withdrawal and because they could pay interest on all their deposits, thrift institutions enjoyed a more stable source of funds than commercial banks. This enabled them to make loans for long-term purposes at rather low interest rates. In 1989 about $1295 billion of their funds were invested in home mortgages. You can understand why healthy savings and loan associations and mutual savings banks were important to the nation's housing industry.

---

*Many of the banks' deposits were created in the process of making loans, as we will soon see.

Insurance Companies. Insurance companies are a third type of financial intermediary. Through insurance policies, savers put aside funds to protect against the ordinary risks of life. These funds are loaned out at interest, earning income to help pay insurance claims and to operate the insurance business. In 1990 life insurance companies had accumulated assets of about $1304 billion. Their funds were invested in corporate bonds and stocks and in mortgages for large commercial or industrial projects. Life insurance companies can afford to make long-term loans because they have rather precise estimates of the number of claims that must be paid in any single year. Fire and casualty insurance companies are subject to greater variability in claims. Therefore, their funds are invested in short-term investments, such as U.S. government securities and state and local government bonds.

Credit Unions. In recent years, credit unions have been emerging as a fourth type of financial intermediary. Most credit unions are made up of employees of a particular firm. A credit union collects the savings of members and makes short-term loans and occasionally mortgage loans to other members. Because borrowers are well known to the credit union, there is little risk of default. As a result, interest charges can be kept fairly low. Also, the administrative costs of running a credit union are low, making it possible to pay rather high interest to savers. In 1990 the total assets of credit unions were about $193 billion.

Money Market Funds. In the past decade a new type of financial intermediary has developed: money market mutual funds. A **mutual fund** is an organization of savers who pool their funds to purchase a diversified portfolio of investments. A money market mutual fund purchases only short-term securities and pays its shareholders dividends according to current interest rates. By 1990 money market

mutual funds held assets of $550 billion. They became a threat to other financial intermediaries when money market rates rose above the interest rates commercial banks and thrift institutions were paying on savings. A drain of savings into money market mutual funds reduced banks' lending ability and reduced profits for many other financial intermediaries.

A well-developed system of financial intermediaries has helped promote our nation's economic growth. Safe financial intermediaries have encouraged saving and provided funds for business investment. Although the major intermediaries tend to specialize in particular kinds of borrowing and lending, there is some overlap in services. When services overlap, there is basis for competition among intermediaries, with the expectation that service will improve and costs fall. The Monetary Control Act of 1980 removed many of the legal restrictions on services performed by financial intermediaries so that now they can compete freely. Savings and loan associations and credit unions are free to offer checking accounts, and commercial banks may pay interest on demand deposits. In the future, banks may be allowed to sell stocks and bonds, and insurance companies might issue travelers checks and money orders.

Increasing competition among financial intermediaries should improve efficiency and strengthen our financial system. On the other hand, competition may also force some firms out of business. Many small financial intermediaries will not be able to compete successfully and may be absorbed by larger ones. Still, the final result should be a more efficient financial sector for the nation.

HOW BANKS CREATE (AND DESTROY) MONEY

When banks make loans to consumers or business firms, they are actually creating money.

Newly created money is expected to stimulate new production and generate profits for repaying the loan with interest.

Economists define **money** most narrowly as the sum of cash in the hands of the public and checkable deposits in commercial banks, thrift institutions, and credit unions. All are money because all are acceptable in exchange for goods or in settlement of financial obligations. Cash is a very small part of the money supply, involving only about one-fifth of all transactions.

Savings accounts and securities are not generally counted as money because they are less liquid than cash or checks. Because they are not immediately acceptable as purchasing power, they are often referred to as **near money.** (Some near moneys are included in the broader measures of the money supply, as we will see.)

A Bank's Balance Sheet

Commercial banks must hold a certain fraction of their checking accounts in reserve accounts at the Federal Reserve. A bank is permitted to make loans in the amount by which its actual reserve account exceeds the required fraction of its deposits.

Table 10.1 is a simplified model of a bank's balance sheet. A balance sheet shows the bank's financial position on a certain date.

It is sometimes called a **T-account,** because items are arranged under the bar of a T.

The bank's **assets** are listed on the left side of the balance sheet. Assets are the things the bank owns: its building, cash in the vault, reserve account at the Fed, interest-earning securities, and loans to customers. Loans to customers are assets because they represent promises to pay the bank. They are normally made to credit-worthy individuals or business firms who are expected to repay their loans with interest when they come due.

The bank's **liabilities** and **capital account** are listed on the right side of the balance sheet. Liabilities are the amounts the bank owes. The checking and savings accounts of its depositors and borrowings from businesses and other banks are a bank's chief liabilities.

Notice that the sum of the asset side is equal to the sum on the liabilities side. This is because any excess of the value of assets over liabilities is added to the liabilities side as the capital account. The capital account represents the *net* amount owned by the bank:

$$\text{amounts owned} - \text{amounts owed} = \text{capital account}$$

The bank's capital account is the portion of total assets that would remain if the bank paid off all its liabilities. Equality of total assets on the left side and total liabilities and capital account on the right makes the statement balance. Hence the term **balance sheet.**

Table 10.1   Balance Sheet for Wall Street Bank, December 31, 1990.

Assets		Liabilities	
Cash and Reserve at Fed	$ 250,000	Demand Deposits	$1,000,000
Loans to Customers	750,000	Other Liabilities	150,000
Securities	200,000		
Building	100,000		1,150,000
		Capital Account	150,000
Total Assets	1,300,000	Total Liabilities and Capital	1,300,000

Making Loans

Suppose the Wall Street Bank, shown in Table 10.1, is required to keep 25 percent of its demand deposits in its reserve account. Notice that the bank is complying with Federal Reserve regulations (25 percent of $1,000,000 in demand deposits is $250,000 in its reserve account).

Now suppose the bank receives a new cash deposit of $100. This might be cash from under someone's mattress, proceeds from the sale of a government bond, or cash received from the sale of goods to a foreign buyer. Let us watch what happens to the bank's balance sheet as a result of the cash deposit. For simplicity, we will show only changes in assets and liabilities. Notice that every change on the asset side requires an equal change on the liabilities side (or an offsetting change on the same side) so that the balance sheet will remain in balance:

1. The $100 deposit adds $100 to Wall Street Bank's cash assets and $100 to its checking account liabilities.

Assets	Wall Street Bank		Liabilities
Cash	+ $100	Demand Deposits	+ $100

2. Non-interest earning cash is of little use to the bank, so it sends the cash to its reserve account at the Federal Reserve Bank.

Assets	Wall Street Bank	Liabilities
Cash	− $100	
Reserves	+ $100	

3. Before the new deposit was made, the Wall Street Bank was maintaining its required reserve account at the Fed. However, it is required to hold only 25 percent of its new deposit: 25 percent of $100 = $25. The bank can extend loans in the amount by which its reserve account exceeds required reserves:

$$\text{actual reserves} - \text{required reserves}$$
$$= \text{excess reserves}$$
$$\$100 - \$25 = \$75$$

With $75 in excess reserves, the Wall Street Bank will normally encourage a credit-worthy borrower to take out a loan, possibly at the same time reducing its interest charge to make the loan more attractive. When the bank makes the loan, it issues a check for $75, which the borrower very likely deposits in a checking account in the same bank. On the left side of the balance sheet, the bank adds the $75 loan; the loan is the borrower's promise to pay and therefore is an asset for the bank. On the right side, the bank adds $75 to the borrower's demand deposit.

Assets	Wall Street Bank		Liabilities
Reserves	$100	Demand	$100
Loans	+ $75	Deposits	+ 75
			$175

Now Wall Street Bank is using its excess reserves as an interest-earning loan. It has complied with Federal Reserve regulations and loaned out only the amount by which its reserves exceed the required percentage of its demand deposits.

4. Suppose the borrower now decides to spend the $75 by writing a check in that amount. Whoever receives the check deposits it in his or her own checking account in another bank, say, the Lombard Bank. The Lombard Bank adds the amount to 'its customer's account and sends the check to the Federal Reserve to be cleared. The Federal Reserve clears

the check by subtracting $75 from Wall Street Bank's reserve account and adding $75 to Lombard Bank's reserve account. Then it returns the canceled check to Wall Street Bank for return to the original borrower in his or her monthly bank statement. When Wall Street Bank reduces the borrower's demand deposit and its own reserve account by $75, actual reserves are precisely equal to required reserves: 25 percent of $100 = $25. Notice that the balance sheet remains in balance.

Assets	Lombard Bank		Liabilities
Reserves	+ $75	Demand Deposits	+ $75

Assets	Wall Street Bank		Liabilities
Reserves	$100 − 75 $25	Demand Deposits	$175 − 75 $100
Loans	$75		

5. Now the Lombard Bank has excess reserves. The Lombard Bank is required to keep 25 percent of the new demand deposit in its reserve account: 25 percent of $75 = $19. It can extend loans in the amount by which its reserve account exceeds required reserves:

$$\text{actual reserves} - \text{required reserves}$$
$$= \text{excess reserves}$$
$$\$75 - \$19 = \$56$$

Assets	Lombard Bank		Liabilities
Reserves	$75	Demand Deposits	$ 75
Loans	+ $56		+ 56
			$131

Suppose it does make a new loan, which this new borrower deposits in a checking account in the Lombard Bank.

6. Just as before, this second borrower will probably decide to write a check for $56 to make a purchase. The person who receives the check eventually deposits it in a third bank, say, the Peachtree Bank. Peachtree Bank sends the check to be cleared and deposited in its reserve account. The Federal Reserve adds $56 to the Peachtree Bank's reserve account and subtracts $56 from the Lombard Bank's account. When the Lombard Bank reduces the second borrower's account and its own reserve account by $56, actual reserves are precisely equal to required reserves: 25 percent of $75 = $19.

Assets	Lombard Bank		Liabilities
Reserves	$75 − 56 $19	Demand Deposits	$131 − 56 $75
Loans	$56		

Assets	Peachtree Bank		Liabilities
Reserves	+ $56	Demand Deposits	+ $56

Let us stop here and calculate the amount added to the nation's money supply as these new loans were created. Thus far, the original $100 in new deposits has led to the creation of $75 + $56 = $131 in additional new money. Presumably, the Peachtree Bank will also make a loan in the amount of its excess reserves. When it does, other banks will receive new checks on deposit and use the excess reserves to extend new loans. Finally, the money supply may increase by as much as $400: the original $100 deposit plus $300 in created money.

How do we know this? With a 25 percent reserve requirement, the initial $100 increase in reserves permits the nation's banking system as a whole to increase demand deposits by up to four times the increase in reserves. The banking system will remain in compliance with the regulations of the Federal Reserve because the banking system's new reserves of $100 are equal to 25 percent of $400 in new demand deposits.

The original deposit of $100 constitutes part of the increase in demand deposits. *The remaining $300 is created money*. It is created by extending loans and adding to the checking accounts of borrowers. The banking system as a whole can create money equal to excess reserves times the reciprocal of the required reserve ratio:

$$\text{created money} = \text{excess reserves} \times \frac{1}{\text{reserve ratio}}$$

Thus, in our example:

$$\text{created money} = \$75 \times \frac{1}{\frac{1}{4}}$$
$$= \$75 \times 4 = \$300$$

Reducing Loans

Banks can destroy as well as create money. Banks *must* destroy money when they lose reserves and are failing to maintain the required reserve ratio. The process is the reverse of the process outlined above.

Suppose a bank loses a deposit of $100 in cash. This time it might be a withdrawal of cash to put under someone's mattress, cash to buy a government security, or cash to buy goods from a foreign seller. As the $100 check clears at the Federal Reserve, the issuing bank loses reserves. It may have to reduce its loans in order to maintain its required reserves.

How does a bank reduce its lending?

Every day old borrowers repay loans by writing checks to their banks. Every day new borrowers receive new loan checks. If a bank needs to reduce its total demand deposits to comply with reserve requirements, it will accept loan payment checks and not extend new loans in their place. Loan payment checks will reduce borrowers' checking accounts until demand deposits are the permitted multiple of bank reserves.

In effect, the bank has destroyed money.

TEST YOURSELF
Follow the procedure used to describe money creation to demonstrate how money is destroyed.

MONETARY POLICY

The Federal Reserve System is responsible for planning and carrying out the nation's monetary policy. **Monetary policy** involves changes in the supply of money to meet the nation's changing need for purchasing power. Because about three-fourths of the nation's money supply is held in commercial banks under the regulatory authority of the Federal Reserve, a decision by the Board of Governors can significantly affect the nation's spending power.

The objective of monetary policy is to ensure the appropriate supply of money for achieving an efficient level of economic activity. As our capacity for producing goods and services increases, the supply of money must increase also. Money must be available for spending by consumers and business firms so that our nation's productive capacity will be fully utilized.

On the other hand, if the supply of money increases too fast, spending may exceed our nation's capacity to produce goods and services and may bring on inflation. In such times, the Federal Reserve should hold down the supply of money and limit consumer and business spending.

GREENSPAN AT THE FED

Many economists predicted that former Federal Reserve Chairperson Paul Volcker would be a "tough act to follow." Volcker's tight money policy was largely responsible for reducing inflation from 9 percent to 3 percent in the 1980s. In 1987, however, President Reagan appointed Alan Greenspan to the job. Greenspan was an economic consultant who had served as chairperson of President Ford's Council of Economic Advisers.

Alan Greenspan has proved to be just as strong an inflation fighter as Paul Volcker. In fact, by 1990 some members of President Bush's administration were complaining that Greenspan's tight money policy was stalling economic growth and threatening recession.

Greenspan is worried about an increasing "core" rate of inflation; that is, the inflation that remains after more volatile food and fuel prices have been removed from the price index. He contends that the economy continues to grow too fast, with little risk of recession. With prices rising by around 5 percent a year, Greenspan would like to slow growth gradually and avoid a more vigorous clamp-down later.

Some members of Congress would like to assert more control over the Fed's policies. One group favors a change to include the secretary of the Treasury as a voting member of the Fed's Board of Governors. Another favors mandatory policies to push the inflation rate to zero. (Which group is the administration likely to support? Why?)

The Congressional Budget Office estimates that reducing the inflation rate by 1 percentage point would require two or three "point years" of unemployment: Stated differently, each 1 percentage point reduction in inflation would mean an unemployment rate two to three points higher on the average for one year or 1 percentage point higher for two to three years. This suggests that bringing today's inflation rate of 5 percent down to only 1 percent would require 8 to 12 point-years of unemployment. Accomplishing the job in three years, for example, would increase today's unemployment of about 5.3 percent to between 8 and 9.3 percent for the entire three years.

Either proposal now before the Congress would reduce the independence of the Fed and bring its policies more closely under political control. What are the advantages and disadvantages of political control of the Fed versus independence from political control?

How are changes in the money supply accomplished? It isn't generally practical to fly over cities and towns scattering currency from airplanes!

The Federal Reserve System has three ways to influence the supply of money. All three ways work primarily by changing the level of checking accounts in commercial banks. The Fed changes the level of checking accounts by changing a bank's ability to make loans, that is, by changing its capacity to create new demand deposits.

The Fed changes a bank's lending capacity by:

1. Changing the required fraction of deposits to be held as reserves in the Federal Reserve Bank.
2. Changing the discount rate on borrowed reserves from the Federal Reserve.
3. Conducting open-market operations involving the purchase and sale of U.S. government securities.

We will consider each of these methods in turn.

Changes in Required Reserves

The first tool of monetary policy involves the ratio of required reserves to a commercial bank's holdings of demand deposits. The Federal Reserve establishes a required fraction of demand deposits that a commercial bank must keep in its reserve account. (The actual fraction is currently about 12 percent.) The bank can lend out only the amount by which its reserve account exceeds the required amount.

A bank must be careful not to extend too many loans. Otherwise when its checks are cleared, the bank will lose too much from its reserve account and find that it isn't in compliance with reserve requirements. (How do you like the thought of your bank being "overdrawn"?)

Increasing the Money Supply

Consider a situation in which all banks are maintaining their required reserve accounts. For simplicity, we will assume the required reserve ratio is 25 percent. There are no excess reserves, so no new loans may be made.

Now suppose the Board of Governors wants to increase the nation's money supply, hoping to encourage new spending and increase production and employment. The governors might decide to reduce the required reserve ratio to 20 percent so that all commercial banks would have excess reserves to support new lending. Commercial banks would probably reduce the interest charges on their loans to encourage consumers and business firms to borrow. The new borrowers would deposit their loan checks in their checking accounts.

Eureka! From nothing there is money!

With a required reserve ratio of 20 percent, total demand deposits in the banking system can increase to five times total bank reserves, whereas the limit before the change was four times reserves.

A Numerical Example: "Easy Money"

Imagine the banking system as a whole has demand deposits of $100 billion. If we ignore cash in the hands of the public, we can regard the $100 billion in checking accounts as the nation's money supply. Under the 25 percent reserve requirement the banking system must be holding $25 billion in Federal Reserve accounts.

Now the Board of Governors decides on an "easy money" policy, that is, to expand the money supply. It changes the reserve requirement to 20 percent. Banks are now required to hold only $20 billion; immediately the banking system has excess reserves of $5 billion.

Loans will be made and loan checks deposited in the accounts of borrowers. As demand deposits expand, the banking system as a whole experiences an increase in checking accounts and, therefore, an increase in the money supply.

What will finally be the level of deposits in the banking system? With reserves of $25 billion and a 20 percent reserve requirements, the banking system as a whole can hold total deposits of $125 billion: reserves of $25 billion = 20 percent of $125 billion in demand deposits.

In fact, the money supply may grow by as much as $25 billion:

created money

$$= \text{excess reserves} \times \frac{1}{\text{reserve ratio}}$$

$$= \$5 \text{ billion} \times \frac{1}{\frac{1}{5}} = \$25 \text{ billion}$$

Reducing the Money Supply

Of course, this process works also in reverse. This time suppose the Board of Governors wants to reduce the supply of money to discourage spending and hold down inflation. The governors might decide to increase reserve requirements, perhaps to 33.33 percent. Now all banks must reduce their checking-account balances until total deposits are only three times reserves.

Banks will collect old loans and make fewer new loans. They will raise their interest charges on loans to discourage borrowing. Old borrowers will pay off loans by writing checks, and the level of checking accounts in the country will fall.

A Numerical Example: "Tight Money"

Again, imagine total demand deposits of $100 billion and a 25 percent reserve requirement. The banking system as a whole is holding reserves of $25 billion. The Board of Governors decides on a "tight money" policy, that is, to reduce the money supply. It changes the reserve ratio to 33.33 percent. With deposits of $100 billion, banks are required to hold $33.33 billion in reserves. Thus, under the new reserve requirements banks have negative excess reserves:

actual reserves − required reserves
= excess reserves
$25 − $33.33 = −$8.33

With negative excess reserves, commercial banks must collect old loans, deducting the loan payment checks from borrowers' demand deposits. Throughout the banking system checking accounts will fall, and the money supply will fall as well.

What will finally be the level of demand deposits in the banking system? With reserves of $25 billion and a 33.33 percent reserve requirement, the system as a whole may have total deposits of $75 billion: reserves of $25 billion = 33.33 percent of $75 billion.

The money supply must decline by at least $25 billion:

destroyed money

$$= \text{excess reserves} \times \frac{1}{\text{reserve ratio}}$$

$$= -\$8.33 \times \frac{1}{\frac{1}{3}} = -\$25 \text{ billion}$$

The Discount Rate

Now we will discuss the second way the Federal Reserve can change commercial banks' ability to make loans: through changes in the discount rate.

Just as individuals go their commercial banks for loans, commercial banks can go to their banker, the Federal Reserve Bank, for borrowed reserves. A commercial bank may need to borrow reserves to comply with re-

How Things Have Changed

HOW THE DISCOUNT RATE CORRESPONDS TO OTHER INTEREST RATES

| Year | Discount Rate | Interest Rates | | |
		U.S. Treasury 3-month bills	High-grade Corporate Bonds	New Home Mortgages
1960	3.53	2.93	4.41	NA
1965	4.04	3.95	4.49	5.81
1970	5.95	6.46	8.04	8.45
1975	6.25	5.84	8.83	9.00
1980	11.77	11.51	11.94	12.66
1985	7.69	7.48	11.37	11.55
1986	6.33	5.98	9.02	10.17
1987	5.66	5.82	9.38	9.31
1988	6.20	6.69	9.71	9.19
1989	6.93	8.12	9.26	10.13

Identify the years in which the Federal Reserve was attempting to slow credit creation. Explain the differences in interest rates among Treasury securities, high-grade corporate bonds, and new home mortgages.

SOURCE: Economic Report of the President, 1990.

serve requirements, particularly if reserve requirements have recently been increased.

The Federal Reserve Bank charges an interest rate, called the **discount rate,** on loans to commercial banks. If the Board of Governors wants to encourage bank lending, it can reduce the discount rate, encouraging commercial banks to borrow to maintain their reserve accounts. However, if it wants to discourage new lending, it will raise the discount rate. A higher discount rate will force banks to reduce their demand deposits to avoid the Fed's higher borrowing charges. There will be fewer new loans made and fewer loan checks to deposit in borrowers' checking accounts. The money supply will fall.

Open-Market Operations

The third tool for changing bank lending is **open-market operations.** This is the tool used most often because it can be carried out quietly and without embarrassing headlines to aggravate ulcers on Wall Street!

The Federal Reserve Banks and most

commercial banks, as well as many individuals, hold some of their savings in the form of U.S. government securities. U.S. Treasury bills, notes, and bonds are considered safe investments and provide interest income to their owners. Open-market operations involve the purchase and sale of these securities.

The Federal Reserve Bank of New York is constantly buying and selling securities in the open market. If the New York Fed buys more securities than it sells, it pays for them with new money, which increases the nation's money supply. To illustrate, suppose the Federal Reserve increases its holdings of Treasury securities by $500 million. Individuals, business firms, and banks throughout the country send their securities to the Federal Reserve and receive checks in return. They deposit their checks in checking accounts in commercial banks. Federal Reserve clearinghouses add a total of $500 million to member bank reserve accounts, and the stage is set for the expansion of bank loans.

As you might have expected, the process works also in reverse. If the Federal Reserve sells more securities than it buys, the result is to reduce the money supply. This time suppose the Federal Reserve reduces its holdings of securities by $500 million. Buyers receive securities and send their payment checks to the Federal Reserve banks. Federal Reserve clearinghouses deduct the amounts from commercial bank reserves, and banks reduce their depositor's accounts.

All these changes take place so quietly one scarcely knows whether the Federal Reserve has been expanding or contracting the money supply.

SOME PROBLEMS

Monetary policy can help achieve economic stability. It is not always completely successful, however, and it can create some problems.

If the Board of Governors correctly analyzes the state of the economy, if they quickly prescribe the proper remedy, and if borrowers respond as expected, the Federal Reserve's purpose will be accomplished. The problem is it is sometimes difficult for commercial banks to find creditworthy borrowers to take their loans.

During recessions, for example, when spending, production, and employment are low, an increase in spending would be most welcome. Unfortunately, at those times business firms may very sensibly hesitate to undertake the risks of borrowing to increase their investments. After all, who will buy the newly produced goods and services if income and employment are low? This means that monetary policy is least effective for increasing spending in recession.

Alas, it may be just as difficult to put the brakes on inflation. Once business borrowers come to expect inflation, higher interest costs may not discourage borrowing for new investment. They will expect prices on finished goods to rise faster than the cost of borrowing, so that new investment will still be profitable. Moreover, in inflation, business borrowers know they can repay their loans with dollars that are worth less than the dollars originally borrowed. In fact, some economists believe that higher interest charges make inflation worse, as business borrowers raise their prices to cover the higher cost of borrowing.

Another problem with monetary policy is the lag between deciding on a new policy and waiting for it to take effect. Delays in the effects of policy can cause alternating periods of expanding and contracting the money supply, by turns helping and hurting the situation the policy was designed to correct. An easy money policy may last too long and aggravate a tendency toward rapid growth and inflation.

Then changing to a tight money policy may cause a recession, with worsening unemployment and slowing growth.

Critics of monetary policy worry that certain borrowers are more seriously harmed by high interest rates than others. Small home builders are particularly hurt by a shortage of funds for home mortgages. In contrast, large firms with substantial retained earnings may be able to finance major investment projects without having to borrow. State and local governments are also harmed by high interest rates. High borrowing costs may cause them to neglect local services, which later must be provided by the federal government.

Other critics worry about the effect of monetary policy on economic growth. When the Federal Reserve is fighting recession, it tries to increase the money supply and push interest rates down. However, low interest rates in the United States cause many wealthy individuals, financial institutions, and business firms to lend their savings to foreign borrowers for higher interest earnings. In this case, dollars flow abroad where they are unavailable for fighting the domestic recession.

On the other hand, when the Federal Reserve is fighting inflation, it tries to reduce the money supply and push interest rates up. High interest rates are supposed to hold down business investment spending. However, business investment is the principal means by which we increase the productivity of our economy. Thus, policies to reduce inflation may also reduce the growth of productivity in the nation as a whole.

High interest rates also affect the U.S. Treasury. The Treasury owes total debt of almost $3 trillion, and annual interest charges are considerable. When the U.S. Treasury is pinched, you can expect an eventual yelp from the U.S. taxpayer!

All these problems suggest that rapid or radical changes in monetary policy may not be wise. It may be better to combine rather consistent monetary policy with flexible fiscal policy to ensure a healthy level of economic activity.

In the second part of this chapter we will consider in detail the debate concerning the effectiveness of monetary policy.

Self-Check

1. **Which of the following is not a true description of money?**
   a. It permits specialization in production.
   b. It facilitates trade among producing regions.
   c. It provides a standard of value.
   d. It makes barter necessary.
   e. It permits division of labor in production.

2. **Which of the following is not a characteristic of monetary gold?**
   a. It serves as a medium of exchange, a store of value, and a standard of value.
   b. It is scarce and durable.
   c. It is easily transported and stored.
   d. It has few uses other than as money.
   e. All are characteristic of gold.

3. **Which of the following is not a function of the Federal Reserve System?**
   a. It provides loans to individuals and businesses.
   b. It holds the accounts of the U.S. Treasury.
   c. It provides a system for clearing checks.
   d. It holds reserve accounts for member banks.
   e. It helps stabilize the nation's money supply.

4. **Changes in the money supply:**
   a. Aim at influencing the level of total spending.
   b. Are accomplished primarily by purchases and sales of securities.
   c. Are actually changes in the lending capacity of banks.
   d. All of the above.
   e. None of the above.

5. **An important defect of monetary policy is that:**
   a. Low interest rates retard economic growth.
   b. High interest rates cause loanable funds to flow to other countries.
   c. Business firms may not respond properly to changes in interest rates.
   d. It is removed from political influence.
   e. High interest charges benefit home builders.

6. **Which of the following policy actions is most appropriate for reducing inflation?**
   a. Federal Reserve purchases of U.S. government securities.
   b. An increase in required reserves.
   c. Easy money to hold down interest rates.
   d. Encouragement of banks to borrow from the Fed.
   e. An increase in the growth rate of the money supply.

Theory in Practice

WINDSOR SAVINGS

| MONEY MARKET PLUS | 25,000 AND UP | 1,000 TO 24,999 | |
| ANNUAL EFFECTIVE YIELD | 6.40 | 6.14 | |

TIME DEPOSIT ACCOUNTS	50,000 & UP	10,000 TO 49,999	2,500 TO 9,999
1 YR CD	7.50	7.40	7.25
ANNUAL EFF. YIELD	7.71	7.61	7.45
180 DAYS	7.25	7.15	7.00
ANNUAL EFF. YIELD	7.45	7.34	7.19

PRIME RATE CD AVAILABLE
MPACT 24 HR. 6TH STREET ACCESS
RATES SUBJECT TO CHANGE
MEMBER F

MIND YOUR P'S AND Q'S

Much of monetary theory can be summed up in a simple expression: $MV = PQ$. The left side of the equation measures total spending over a particular period of time: the quantity of money in the system (M) times its velocity (V), or the average number of times each dollar is spent. The right side of the equation measures the value of total production over the same period: the prices of all goods and services (P) times the quantities sold (Q).

This simple equation describes the quantity theory of money. The equation must always balance because total expenditures (MV) will always equal the value of output (PQ).

Surprisingly, the expression $MV = PQ$ is the source of much controversy among economists. The debate concerns the proper conduct of monetary policy. One group of economists, called **monetarists,** believes that the supply of money (M) is the most important factor in determining economic activity. A steady increase in M in line with our nation's growing productive capacity will keep production (PQ) growing at a full employment, noninflationary rate.

The leader of the monetarists is economist Milton Friedman. Friedman favors automatic increases in the money supply of about 4 percent a year. He believes that regular, automatic increases in the money supply will allow

Contemporary Thinking about Economic Issues

REFORMING THE FEDERAL RESERVE

Milton Friedman favors free-market solutions to economic problems and worries about potential mistakes when individuals or groups are given too much power to decide economic policy. His concerns are directed primarily at the power of the Federal Reserve System.

Friedman distinguishes between the tactics used by the Fed to accomplish monetary policy and the strategy and institutions through which monetary policy is carried out. The tactics have to do with the choice of a target for policy (interest rates or the quantity of money), the growth path of the target, and procedures for achieving the target. Friedman believes that the Fed has too much discretion in using these tactics and recommends a change in monetary institutions.

First, Friedman recommends establishing the money base as the Federal Reserve Target. The money base is the sum of commercial bank reserves plus currency in the hands of the public. (Because public holdings of currency shift easily in and out of banks, they are potentially available as bank reserves to support an increase in the money supply.) According to Friedman, Congress should pass legislation limiting the increase in currency and bank reserves to between 3 percent and 5 percent per year.

Following establishment of a money-base rule, Friedman recommends removing responsibility for bank regulation and supervision from the Fed and limiting the Fed to open market operations to achieve the legislated growth of the money base. Then the Fed should be converted from an independent agency to a bureau of the Treasury Department. An advantage of this change is that a single, unified agency of government would be held responsible for the conduct and performance of monetary policy. Another advantage is the resulting political influence over the Fed, which Friedman believes would result in more stable money growth.

Finally, Friedman would freeze the supply of Federal Reserve currency and deposits and allow the increasing variety of money forms to compete with currency issued by the government. Eventually, financial institutions might be given the unlimited right to issue claims against the existing money supply. Furthermore, as output increases in the nation, new financial institutions and instruments would develop to use the fixed supply of money more efficiently, Or, alternatively, prices would fall. According to Friedman, transition to the new financial arrangements could take place over a period of about five years.

The advantages of Friedman's proposals would be the end of the "arbitrary power of the Federal Reserve System to determine the quantity of money . . . to permit a reduction by one-third during the Great Depression or a near doubling from 1970 to 1980."

Milton Friedman, "The Case for Overhauling the Federal Reserve," *Challenge,* July/Agust 1985, pp. 4–12.

spending to increase in line with increases in productive capacity, thereby avoiding either rising prices or falling production. Moreover, automatic increases in the money supply have the advantage that they do not depend on decisions made by the Board of Governors (who sometimes disagree with Professor Friedman).

There is another advantage to regular, automatic money growth. Decisions to change money growth, says Friedman, cannot take effect for a year or more, during which economic conditions can turn completely around, so that current policy decisions are no longer appropriate. Unless policymakers follow clear, unchanging rules for money growth, they are likely to make mistakes.

Another group of economists argues that steady, automatic increases in M will not keep spending steady if V is changing at the same time. In fact, during recessions with high unemployment and low consumer confidence, the rate of turnover (V) of the available money supply could slow. Therefore, in recessions, policymakers should increase M faster than normal so that the growth of M will offset the decline in V. On the other hand, in periods of inflation the rate of spending (V) tends to speed up; in this case policymakers should cut back the growth of M to offset the increase in V.

Measuring Money

Before the proper policy is decided, it is necessary first to measure M. The traditional definition of the money supply is bank checking accounts plus cash in the hands of the public. However, we have seen that today many non-bank financial intermediaries offer deposits to their customers that closely resemble traditional bank checking accounts. Accounts in savings banks and savings and loan associations, for example, can be withdrawn by check. Today, all these new kinds of checkable deposits are included in the most spendable form of money: $M1$. In 1990, $M1$ amounted to almost $800 billion.

In addition to cash and checkable deposits, some near moneys are almost as spendable as $M1$: savings accounts and time deposits and shares in money market mutual funds. Holders of near money probably feel wealthier as a result and probably spend more freely than they would otherwise. Including near moneys in the money definition produces $M2$ money, which amounted to almost $3220 billion in 1990. Other long-term time deposits are added to $M2$ to yield the $M3$ definition of money, $4040 billion in 1990. (See Table 10.2 for a breakdown of money measures.)

Controlling the growth of such diverse forms of money has become increasingly difficult, and the Federal Reserve has come under increasing criticism. Worsening inflation during the 1970s seemed to call for slower money growth, but attempts to reduce bank lending were ineffective or—if effective, as they were in the early 1980s—plunged the economy into recession.

HOW SUCCESSFUL HAS MONETARY POLICY BEEN?

How closely does the reality of monetary policy conform to the theory? How successfully

Table 10.2   Money Forms—December 1989.

$M1$	Cash and checkable deposits in commercial banks, savings and loan associations, credit unions, and mutual savings banks	$ 797.6 billion
$M2$	$M1$ plus savings and short-term time deposits and money market fund shares	3217.0 billion
$M3$	$M2$ plus long-term time deposits in all financial institutions	4039.6 billion

has the Federal Reserve managed the money supply to promote stable prices and steady growth of production?

Fluctuations and Frustrations in the 1970s

As the 1970s began, the economy was experiencing a recession. To deal with the recession, the Fed purchased government securities, increased bank reserves, and allowed the supply of currency and checking accounts to grow about 6 percent annually. By 1972, the recession had ended, and the Fed cut back reserves to hold down the growth of the money supply. Still, the money supply continued to grow, by 9 percent that year, and the Fed began to worry about inflation.

A tight money policy was begun in earnest in 1973, with six increases in discount rates during the year. The interest rate charged by banks to their best customers rose ten times to reach 12 percent in 1974, and rates on short-term business loans rose to almost 14 percent. Reserve requirements were increased also. Still, business firms expected new investment to be profitable; so they continued to borrow, and inflation soared.

Inflation increased to dangerous levels in 1974, and the Federal Reserve cut money growth sharply. Finally, business borrowing fell, the business failure rate jumped, and unemployment spread. By February 1975, the money supply was actually shrinking. Many economists predicted that the drastic reversal in monetary policy would throw the economy into a severe recession, and, in fact, the bottom of the fifth postwar recession was recorded in March.

The Fed was not entirely to blame for the slowdown in money growth. Evidence suggests that by early 1975 the Board of Governors was trying to relax the earlier tight money policy. They were buying U.S. Treasury securities and increasing reserves, but banks were not making new loans. Business firms were just too pessimistic to take on the risks of borrowing.

The situation in 1975 gave economists an opportunity to use one of their old familiar sayings: You can't push on a string. You can pull money out of the economy during inflation; but you can't push money into the economy during recession if banks are unwilling to lend and if creditworthy borrowers are hard to find.

Recovery from the 1975 recession was slow, in part because of high consumer and business debt built up during the previous expansion. Especially stubborn inflation and job uncertainty also reduced consumer confidence and held spending down. The Fed struggled to achieve the appropriate monetary policy for ending the recession without worsening the inflation. For the first time, the Fed announced its target rate of money growth for the year: a range of 5 to $7\frac{1}{2}$ percent growth of currency and checkable deposits. All the tools of monetary policy were put to use to achieve this goal, but cash and checking accounts grew by less than 5 percent.

Money growth speeded up to 6 percent in 1976, but high unemployment and inflation continued. Hoping to avoid a new recession, the Board of Governors decided to reduce money growth slowly until inflation subsided. Consumer, business, and government spending continued to grow in 1977, pushing the economy closer to the limits of productive capacity and pushing money growth higher (8 percent) than the Fed's targets.

Vigorous expansion continued in 1978, and inflation accelerated. Higher food and labor costs and declining worker productivity led to a program of voluntary wage and price restraint under President Carter. Nevertheless, beat-the-price-rise psychology continued to increase consumer spending for goods and housing.

An Experiment with Monetarism

Paul Volcker was appointed chairperson of the Board of Governors in 1979, and the Fed announced a new guide to monetary policy. Throughout the 1970s the goal of policy had been to maintain stable interest rates. Keeping interest rates stable required frequent changes in money growth: to accommodate abnormally high (or low) loan demand without causing interest rates to rise (or fall). By the end of the decade the Fed became convinced that varying money growth had worsened inflationary pressures, and the Board of Governors changed its fundamental goal to maintaining steady money growth. The new policy was more in keeping with recommendations of the monetarists, led by Milton Friedman.

Contractionary monetary policy took hold at the same time fiscal policy was becoming strongly expansionary. At first, President Reagan's tax cuts and increased defense spending were ineffective against the most severe postwar recession yet. Then finally in late 1982 the Fed abandoned its commitment to monetarism and allowed money growth to speed up. A strong expansion began, but budget deficits soared. More and more, the budget deficit was financed through bond sales to foreigners. Real interest rates in the United States were higher than rates aboard, but they were not as high as they might have been without the inflow of funds from foreigners.

Another result of the inflow of foreign funds was increased demand for the U.S. dollar. Demand for dollars kept their value high and enabled U.S. consumers and business firms to buy goods and services cheaply abroad. Cheap imports helped keep U.S. prices down throughout a long business expansion that continued into 1990.

Some fundamental imbalances remain in the U.S. economy today, largely a result of large government deficits and increasing trade deficits. (We will have more to say about international trade in Chapter 15.) Both deficits reflect an increasing tendency to borrow for current consumption: that is, to increase spending at a faster rate than the increase in productivity.

Changes in *V*

Throughout the 1970s and 1980s, *M2* and *M3* grew substantially faster than *M1*. High interest rates encouraged consumers and business firms to ''economize on money balances'': that is, to transfer more of their funds to interest-earning accounts and spend their cash and checking accounts faster. The result has been an increase in the velocity of spending (*V*). The increase in velocity has made the Fed's job of regulating total spending more difficult.

Changes in Interest Rates

Events in recent years have called attention to a peculiar relationship between money growth and interest rates. Economic theory predicts that easy money reduces interest rates and encourages investment; tight money increases interest rates and reduces investment. Indeed, the short-range effects may be as expected. However, the long-range effects of easy money may be higher incomes and inflation, with rising interest rates as lenders insist on protection against inflation. On the other hand, tight money may reduce employment and incomes so that interest rates actually fall.

Gibson's Paradox and Real Interest Rates

A **paradox** is a statement that seems contradictory or absurd but may actually be true. In the early 1900s, a British statistician named Gibson thought he saw a paradox in the behavior of the money supply, prices, and interest rates.

What happens when the money supply increases? First, banks have more money to lend, and, second, people have more money to spend. The first result should cause interest rates to fall, and the second, prices to rise. Thus, falling interest rates would accompany rising prices.

At least this is what we might expect to happen, given our understanding of market supply and demand and the effects of shifts in supply or demand curves on equilibrium price. Gibson's paradox was that events did not turn out that way at all. In fact, over the years Gibson observed, prices and interest rates tended to move together, indicating a "contradictory, absurd" result.

The explanation has to do with nominal and real interest rates. The **nominal interest rate** is the rate paid for borrowing; nominal rates are frequently quoted in the newspaper and always appear on a loan agreement. The **real interest rate** is the real purchasing power the borrower pays for the loan; the real interest rate is determined by subtracting the rate of inflation from the nominal interest rate. If inflation exceeds the nominal rate, the real interest rate is negative. In this case, a lender sacrifices more purchasing power to the borrower than he or she receives in final payment of the loan. In effect, the lender is paying someone else to use his or her money!

Most lenders take steps to avoid this unhappy result. When prices are rising, they build into interest rates a return sufficient to offset inflation. Thus, high prices—and the expectation that prices will continue to rise—prompt a move to higher interest rates. On the other hand, stable prices cause interest rates to fall to the real rate of interest that satisfies most lenders. (Historically, the real rate of interest has been about 2 percent.)

Throughout the 1970s, the U.S. economy suffered abnormally high inflation, along with interest rates reaching as high as 20 percent. Easy money policies, which were intended to keep borrowing costs low and encourage investment spending, instead contributed to inflation and high nominal rates. Maybe Gibson's paradox was not "absurd" after all!

BANK LOANS AND MONETARY POLICY

If monetary policy is to be successful, banks must adjust their deposits to the level of reserves supplied by the Federal Reserve. The level of reserves is intended to limit a bank's ability to create new deposits. Until the 1960s the system worked rather well; but then changes took place in bank lending that loosened the tie between bank reserves and money creation.

Remember that a bank's financial assets are primarily its reserves at the Federal Reserve, loans to customers, and securities. Its securities are short-term, interest-earning debt issued by private business firms, the U.S. Treasury, and state and local governments. The permitted level of bank lending depends on the bank's demand deposits, required reserves, and actual reserves.

In the past, if a bank needed more reserves, it could increase its reserve account by shifting its assets. It could sell some of its securities and add the proceeds of the sale to its reserves. The increase in reserves would allow the bank to increase its lending.

Selling securities turned out to be an unattractive option for many banks. The reason is the effect of Federal Reserve policy on the market price of securities. In practice, a tight money policy withdraws money from the system and makes it difficult for banks to sell securities. If a bank wants to make new loans, it may have to sell securities for less than their purchase price and suffer a loss.* The expectation of a capital loss tends to discourage banks from selling securities and making new loans—in line with Federal Reserve tight money policy.

Banks sought a more attractive way to increase reserves, and during the 1980s they turned to the liabilities side of the balance sheet to finance new lending. To attract new liabilities, many banks offered high interest rates on short-term deposits in savings accounts or certificates of deposit. Then they loaned out these funds, with a comfortable spread between the interest paid to the new depositors and the interest received from business borrowers. Generally, their loans to business firms carried flexible interest rates, to reflect frequent changes in banks' costs of borrowing. Flexible interest charges on loans guaranteed the banks' profits, regardless of the interest rate they had to pay for borrowed funds.

This new process violated a fundamental rule of banking: borrow "long" and lend "short." In other words, make certain you have long-term control over your funds, and avoid the possibility that your depositors will want to withdraw their money before your borrowers are ready to repay their loans.

In years past, most commercial bank loans were short term to finance business firms' inventory. As borrowers sold their inventory, they repaid their loans. More recently, however, commercial banks have made loans for long-term construction projects, like executive parks and high-rise office and apartment buildings. These loans depend

*Whenever an existing security is sold before maturity, its price must be competitive with new securities being issued currently. If new securities are paying higher interest rates than the existing security, their prices will be lower. In general, a tight money policy causes current interest rates to rise and the selling prices of existing securities to fall.

for repayment on the success of the project, with profitable sales and rental income flowing into borrowers' accounts.

As long as the economy is growing, long-term loans are safe. High rentals and inflated property values enable borrowers to pay high interest charges on construction loans. When growth slows, however, half-empty office buildings cannot produce enough rental income to pay off the loans. Borrowers default, and banks become the unhappy owners of a great deal of real estate, much of it worth less than the loans the banks have carried. Loan losses make banks reluctant to extend new loans to anyone other than their most dependable borrowers.

The switch to lending based on bank liabilities (rather than assets) and growing fears of default have led to wide swings in banks' willingness to make new loans. The result may be that banks are less sensitive to Federal Reserve policy than they formerly were. If this is true, banks may be expected to increase their lending during inflationary periods and reduce lending during recessions—contrary to the intentions of the Federal Reserve.

POLITICS AND THE FEDERAL RESERVE

From time to time there are conflicts between the interests of the U.S. Congress and the president, on the one hand, and the interests of the Federal Reserve Board, on the other.

The president and Congress may want to use expansionary fiscal policy to stimulate spending and cause production and income to grow. Toward this objective, they may favor increased government spending and lower taxes. Such programs are popular with voters, but they can cause a deficit in the federal budget that must be financed by borrowing. The Treasury will have to sell bonds to finance

Viewpoint

THE CRISIS IN THE SAVINGS AND LOANS

In the 1990s the U.S. financial sector faces a savings-and-loan (S&L) crisis. The crisis arises from the kinds of loans S&Ls have been allowed to make.

When the financial sector was strictly regulated, S&Ls were required to limit their lending to long-term mortgages. Because the difference between interest received on mortgages and interest paid to S&L depositors was rather small, this limitation reduced S&Ls' profit potential. Moreover, rising inflation led to depositors' demands for even higher interest payments; otherwise they would (and did) withdraw their savings to take advantage of higher paying opportunities elsewhere. At the same time, many S&L mortgages were earning lower interest rates, negotiated many years before when inflation was also lower.

Declining profits led many S&Ls to demand freedom from regulation, and in 1980 the rules governing S&L lending were relaxed. In order to satisfy their depositors' demands for higher interest earnings, many S&Ls made loans to more risky borrowers in agriculture, energy, and even foreign countries. Because of their higher risk, such loans paid higher interest rates than home mortgages. Because of their higher risk, however, they were also more subject to default. Many S&L borrowers did just that.

When S&L assets turned into worthless paper, S&Ls were unable to pay their depositors. Most deposits were insured by the federal government, however, through the Federal Savings and Loan Insurance Corporation (FSLIC). The regulatory authorities were obliged to step in and protect depositors' funds. They did this in either of two ways: by selling the S&Ls' good assets at a bargain price to investors who would assume the responsibility of collecting loans and paying off depositors or by closing the S&L and paying off depositors from FSLIC's insurance fund. (Because FSLIC's resources were insufficient to do the job, a new agency, the Resolution Trust Corporation was set up to handle it and awarded billions of dollars for the work.) In either case, the federal government was left holding rather shaky loans on questionable properties; it would try to collect the loans and/or sell the properties to pay the cost of paying off depositors.

More than 400 S&Ls have been taken over in the S&L crisis, and the problem is expected to cost the government at least $200 billion during the 1990s.

How do S&Ls violate the basic financial rule to borrow long and lend short?

the deficit, and it would prefer to pay low interest rates on its debt.

At the same time, the Federal Reserve may believe spending is increasing too fast. It may worry about increasing inflation and favor a slowdown in the growth of production and income. The Board of Governors may decide on a tight money policy to hold down the level of spending. As a result, there will be less money available for lending, and the Treasury will have to pay higher interest rates if it is to sell its bonds.

Occasionally, the Fed may give in to pressures from the president and Congress and increase money growth. Accusations were made (and denied) that the easy money policy followed in 1972 was in response to political pressure in an election year. Some critics believe that excessive money growth in 1972 contributed significantly to high inflation in the rest of the 1970s.

Conflicts between Congress and the Federal Reserve have generally been settled by compromise. When the Treasury desperately needs funds, as it did during World War II, for instance, the Fed has been willing to supply money at a faster rate. However, it is important that the Board of Governors have the power to restrict all spending—including government spending—when inflation threatens. Likewise, during recession the Board of Governors should provide the additional money for greater government spending. Otherwise fiscal and monetary policy might be pushing the economy in opposite directions.

Some legislators have urged new legislation to bring the Federal Reserve more completely under the control of Congress. The aim is to guarantee a steady increase in money and to ensure that available funds are allocated toward programs to deal with the nation's most pressing needs, housing and productive enterprises, rather than speculative buying and inventory accumulation. Many economists are strongly opposed to Congressional control of the Fed. They see the Federal Reserve as the only way to balance the occasionally excessive spending plans of the president and Congress.

Viewpoint

THE THEORY OF RATIONAL EXPECTATIONS

In this text we have been concerned with the Keynesian model of income determination. Remember that a model is a simplified view of reality. It summarizes economic behavior and projects the results of policy according to certain assumptions about behavior. Whether the model's projections are right or wrong depends on the correctness of its fundamental assumptions.

Certain changes have been taking place in the U.S. economy that have led economists to doubt some of their fundamental assumptions and, therefore, to question some of the policy recommendations that depend on them. Ironically, this new skepticism is the result of more intelligent understanding of economic conditions among the public at large.

Improved communications have made families and business firms more sensitive to trends in production, employment, prices, and interest rates. Even more important, widespread availability of information about Keynesian economic theory has caused people to anticipate government policy before it actually takes place.

All these factors have worked to change behavior, so that many families and business firms now act according to their expectations of future economic conditions.

The theory that explains this new type of behavior is called the **theory of rational expectations.** It states that rational people behave according to what they expect future economic conditions to be. Rational expectations may have changed the results of Keynesian economic policies, reducing their effectiveness and possibly causing more harm than the problems they were designed to correct.

To illustrate the theory of rational expectations, suppose the growth of spending slows and the economy enters a recession. Unemployment increases, and the automatic stabilizers go into effect to push the federal budget toward an automatic deficit. The low level of aggregate demand holds down price and wage increases, so that inflation slows. What would a rational person expect to happen next?

Having studied economics, a rational

SUMMARY

1. The first use of money was a milestone in the process of economic development. Money promoted trade, with specialization and division of labor.

2. The development of banking eased the process of exchange and provided credit for ex-

panding investment. Early unregulated banks often caused alternating periods of overexpansion of money, followed by business bankruptcies and bank failures.

3. In 1913 the Federal Reserve System was established. Through centrally regulated banking, the Fed attempts to influence economic activity by expanding the money supply when

person would probably expect the use of expansionary fiscal and monetary policy to speed recovery from recession. As expansionary policies take effect, all the current measures of economic activity would reverse themselves. Unemployment would fall, and inflation would begin to accelerate.

A general belief that recessions will be short and expansion the normal economic condition affects behavior significantly. There is less fear of unemployment and easier acceptance of inflation. In fact, consumers and business firms tend to behave as if inflation is inevitable and to try to protect themselves against it. Workers insist on cost-of-living wage increases, and business firms insist on price increases that will guarantee profits even when their costs rise. Through these kinds of behavior, workers and business firms bring on the very inflation they expect.

Now suppose that inflation accelerates to the point that contractionary fiscal and monetary policy are put into place to slow the rate of growth. As higher taxes, reduced government spending, and slower

money growth take hold, the expansion slows, and the economy moves toward recession. Rational people, however, understand government's reluctance to let unemployment build up, and they will expect expansionary policies to be resumed fairly quickly. Expecting inflation to resume as well, they fail to adjust their wage demands downward, and the eventual inflation is worse than it might otherwise be.

All of this reduces the effectiveness of traditional economic policies and aggravates tendencies toward inflation. For government policies to change behavior in a certain way, they must be so different from expected policies as to startle people into totally new patterns of behavior.

The theory of rational expectations poses new problems for economic policymakers. The extreme version of the theory implies that no policy can affect behavior for long in the intended direction.

How might the theory of rational expectations be used to support or oppose government intervention in the economy? Discuss.

there are unemployed resources to be brought into production and contracting money growth when spending exceeds the full employment capacity of the nation's resources.

4. Other financial intermediaries now offer a variety of services, including long-term mortgages, loans to state and local governments, and short-term consumer loans. The growth of

lending institutions has helped promote economic growth but may have complicated the Fed's money management role.

5. Monetary policy aims at providing stable increases in purchasing power in line with increases in our nation's productive capacity. Monetary policy is carried out through changes in the required reserve ratio of com-

mercial banks, changes in the discount rate, and Federal Reserve purchase and sale of U.S. Treasury securities (open-market operations).

6. Changes in the level of reserves affect banks' willingness to lend and affect interest rates. Changes in interest rates in turn affect the costs of new business projects, encouraging or discouraging business investment spending.

7. Monetary policy is not always fully effective. If there is a recession, business firms may be too pessimistic to risk borrowing for new investment, even if interest rates are low. If there is inflation, business firms may be willing to pay high interest rates to avoid even higher costs in the future.

8. Contractionary monetary policy may be particularly hard on small business firms, which depend on credit for their investment funds. Contractionary monetary policy also increases the cost of borrowing for state and local governments and for the U.S. Treasury.

9. The quantity theory of money ($MV = PQ$) has been a source of controversy among economists. Part of the controversy stems from the difficulty of defining M. The traditional definition of money, $M1$, is currency and checkable deposits in all bank-like institutions.

10. The results of monetary policy have not been completely satisfactory. Money growth has had paradoxical effects on nominal interest rates; banks have become less sensitive to Federal Reserve policy; and politics continue to affect Fed decisions.

TERMS TO REMEMBER

barter: trade in which goods are exchanged for other goods

demand deposits: deposits in checking accounts that are available on demand

time deposits: deposits in savings accounts, often available only after a stated time period

capital account: the difference between the value of a bank's assets and the value of its liabilities; a bank's net worth

monetary policy: deliberate exercise of the Federal Reserve's power to expand or contract the money supply in order to promote economic stability

required reserve ratio: the percentage of its demand deposits a bank must keep in its reserve account at the Federal Reserve

easy money: policies to increase money growth

tight money: policies to slow money growth

discount rate: the rate of interest a bank pays on funds borrowed from the Federal Reserve

open-market operations: Federal Reserve purchases and sales of government securities

nominal interest rate: the stated charge for borrowing

real interest rate: the charge for borrowing, corrected for inflation

TOPICS FOR DISCUSSION

1. From your reading of the text determine the meaning of the following expressions:

   Clearinghouse for checks
   Automatic monetary policy

2. What is meant by the following statement? "Monetary and fiscal policy may at times be pushing the economy in opposite directions."

3. Distinguish clearly among the Federal Reserve's three instruments for affecting the nation's supply of money.

4. Some critics of monetary policy point out that restricting the supply of money and reducing the growth of production may, over time, *increase* prices. Can you suggest reasons for this result?

5. In late 1974 the Federal Reserve announced a reduction in the reserve requirement on certain large certificates of deposit (CDs). CDs are sold by banks to savers, and the money is loaned to business. The CDs affected by the ruling were those sold for over $100,000, with maturities of more than four months. In 1974 the banks were handling almost $90 billion of these large CDs with a reserve requirement of

8 percent. The new ruling reduced the reserve requirement to 5 percent. Figure the amount of excess reserves this new ruling released for new loans. What results would you expect?

6. The problem of balance between growth in spending and production of new goods and services is complicated by the fact that the existing supply of money is spent several times. An economy that produces $100 billion in GNP annually may need only $20 billion in money, if each dollar is spent five times during the year. Economists refer to the number of times money is spent as its **velocity.** Thus, the quantity of money times its velocity is equal to the value of GNP: MV = GNP. Below are GNP and money supply data for selectead years in the United States. Calculate the velocity for each year. What do you notice about velocity in recent years? What factors may influence the speed with which money is spent?

		MONEY SUPPLY:
		CURRENCY+
YEAR	*GNP**	*DEMAND DEPOSITS**
1947	$ 231	$113
1951	338	123
1955	398	135
1959	484	143
1965	685	171
1969	930	209
1974	1397	284
1978	1890	478
1985	4015	620
1989	5233	798

*In billions

7. Explain why headlines describing Federal Reserve intentions might "aggravate ulcers on Wall Street!"

8. Consult the *Economic Report of the President* for data on money growth, prices, and interest rates over recent years. Comment on your findings.

9. Explain how following Milton Friedman's prescription for steady money growth is expected to reduce inflation. Might it also help relieve unemployment?

10. Because "perestroika" in the USSR is causing significant price inflation, many Soviet consumers are resorting to barter. Discuss the disadvantages associated with barter, particularly in a period when the nation is attempting to establish a market system.

11. In 1990 U.S. Treasury securities were yielding an interest return of about 8.4 percent, compared with 11.3 percent in Great Britain. How are differences in interest rates worldwide likely to affect the Federal Reserve's use of monetary policy? Give examples of the effects on U.S. employment and prices.

ANSWERS TO TEST YOURSELF

(p. 231) When a bank's reserves fall below the required fraction of deposits, it must collect old loans and refuse to issue new loans. Borrowers will pay off their loans by drawing funds from their accounts in other banks. Other banks will lose reserves and be forced to reduce their lending. This process continues until deposit accounts in all banks fall to the permitted multiple of reserves.

Inflation

or Losing Your Assets

After reading this chapter, you will be able to:

1. Define inflation, identify its causes, and explain its effects.
2. Suggest some policy remedies for demand-pull and cost-push inflation.
3. Discuss the difficult problem of structural inflation.
4. Discuss the inflationary effects of economic and social regulation.

CURRENT ISSUES FOR DISCUSSION

Who are the gainers and losers in inflation?

How effective is a wage-price freeze?

How well does price indexing work and what are its disadvantages?

It has been said that if you ask five economists for their opinions on a subject, you will get six opinions—one of them won't be able to make up his or her mind.

This is particularly true of the subject of inflation. Because the sources of inflation are difficult to identify, it is difficult to choose the proper cure. Before a cure can be decided, the problem must be carefully analyzed and the process by which it travels through the economic system clearly understood. If the problem is approached haphazardly, the results of policy may be worse than the problem itself.

Economists define **inflation** as a general rise in the prices of goods and services. Some prices are rising and others falling all the time. If the average price level remains the same, however, there is no inflation. When the average price level rises, we have inflation.

A LOOK AT HISTORY

Primitive economic societies do not have to worry about inflation. Inflation is primarily a problem of growing, industrialized economies.

From Self-Sufficiency to Specialization

Primitive people had to struggle just to stay alive. Because primitive tribes were isolated, they had to be self-sufficient. Each tribe had to produce its entire reserve of game, grain, shelter, and cloth or skins. Later, some tribes began to specialize and trade with neighboring tribes. Specialization made possible greater production so that both tribes could live better. Material gains were accomplished at the expense of self-sufficiency, but that was a small price to pay.

Specialization and trade required the use of money. Primitive tribes used as money whatever tokens they found at hand—special beads and stones and rare shells. As long as the supply of tokens remained in balance with the supply of goods, there was no problem of rising prices. There was just enough money to purchase the available goods at their customary prices.

Money and Prices

As technical knowledge spread, production grew. More money was needed to symbolize the greater quantities of goods and services offered in trade. The need for money created a dilemma: Money had to be scarce enough to retain its value, but it also had to be plentiful enough to exchange for a growing supply of goods. Gold and silver fulfilled both these requirements for many centuries. Eventually, fewer new sources of precious metals (as well as the difficulty of carrying them around in one's pockets) made it necessary to find a substitute. Paper money "tied" to gold or silver was the result.*

Balancing the supply of money with the available supply of goods became more difficult as economic life became more complex. When the supply of money increased faster than the supply of goods, more buyers would bid for relatively fewer goods. Prices tended to rise, and the economy experienced infla-

---

*Our money is no longer tied to gold or silver. Most of our currency is issued by Federal Reserve banks, so that the supply is not limited by our holdings of precious metals.

tion. When the supply of money increased more slowly than the supply of goods, sellers would compete for buyers' money. Prices tended to fall, and the economy experienced deflation.

Automatic Balance Through Trade

Eighteenth-century economists believed that imbalances between spending and goods would correct themselves automatically through free trade. More money than goods in one nation would bring on inflation, and buyers would look elsewhere for cheaper goods. They would spend their money in nations with less money than goods, since prices would be lower there. Money would flow from high-priced nations to low-priced nations until the supply of money and goods would be in perfect balance in all nations. Then prices would stabilize.

This happy result might have come to pass if there had been no barriers to the free flow of spending and goods among nations. In fact, in addition to the barriers of distance, there were political and economic boundaries, each nation having its own monetary system, quotas, tariffs, and other limits to free trade. (International trade is the subject of Chapter 15.)

Another problem arose with the growth of democracy. When democratic governments face domestic problems like unemployment, poverty, illiteracy, and homelessness, voters insist on new government programs to correct them. (Less frequently do they insist on new taxes to pay for the new programs.) Increases in government spending (without increases in taxes) call for the creation of new money and increase total spending for the available supplies of goods and services. Unless government programs succeed in increasing production as fast as the growth of money, there will be inflation.

WHY ALL THE FUSS ABOUT INFLATION?

Why should inflation concern us? A $1 bill and a $10 bill look pretty much the same. Why should it matter whether a day's welding, a truckload of soybeans, a college course, or a suit of clothes is counted as $50 or $500?

It matters if a day's welding today at $50 is to be exchanged in ten years for a suit of clothes. By that time the value of the $50 may have shrunk and a suit might cost as much as ten days' welding. Inflation is especially hard on people who depend on money as a store of value: savers, the elderly, pensioners. (We'll all be there one day!)

If matters, too, if the price of a college course, for example, rises more slowly than the price of a truckload of soybeans. Workers who depend on income from the sale of college courses may be unfairly penalized by uneven price changes. Inflation brings a lower standard of living to people whose occupations or incomes are relatively fixed, including teachers, government workers, and families who receive government transfer payments.

The most unpleasant effects of inflation pertain only to unexpected inflation, however. If inflation is predicted correctly, welders, retired persons, and college teachers may be able to build into their wage agreements and retirement funds a cost-of-living adjustment to compensate for inflation. (This process creates other problems, as we will soon see.)

Unexpected inflation interferes especially with our ability to plan for the future. Most of us were taught to save part of our income to provide financial security for our retirement years. Our savings may earn interest of up to, say, 7 percent a year. However, suppose inflation is reducing the value of our money at the rate of 10 percent a year. The unsuspecting saver will actually lose 3 percent in purchasing power every year. The saver may be worse off

then the profligate who squanders his or her earnings on riotous living!

What is even more disturbing is the fact that the saver's interest earnings of 7 percent are taxed as part of his or her personal income. In effect, savers are taxed twice for being virtuous—once through inflation and again by the Internal Revenue Service.

Those who lend money (creditors) or borrow money (debtors) are affected differently by unexpected inflation. In fact, borrowers are helped by unexpected inflation, since they pay back less in purchasing power than they originally borrowed. Unless interest rates compensate fully for inflation, unexpected inflation hurts lenders, who may become reluctant to lock themselves into long-term loans.

TEST YOURSELF
Calculate the return to the lender and the cost to the borrower of a loan at 10 percent when inflation is 8 percent and both lender and borrower pay taxes at the rate of 25 percent.

Rampant inflation is often followed by recession or depression.* During inflation, there is feverish spending for capital resources, so as to satisfy the increased demand for goods and services. When all firms are fully stocked with new capital equipment and inventories, the level of investment and production falls back. The result may be increasing unemployment and economic distress.

Regrettably, even the expectation of inflation worsens the tendency toward inflation. If speculators expect prices to rise, they will buy and hold goods or raw materials to sell later at higher prices. When speculators hold goods and raw materials off the market, the im-

---

*Recession or depression may in fact be caused by government's contractionary fiscal and monetary policy put in place to correct inflation.

balance between spending and goods becomes even worse. Prices rise faster, and speculators are rewarded with windfall gains. More damaging still, when money is spent for speculation, less is available for investment in factories, machines, and vocational training for new workers. These are the investments that enable our nation to produce more goods and services in the years to come. With fewer resources for increasing production, our economic system is less able to avoid inflation in the future.

Some economists worry that continuing inflation brings on social and political problems. Strikes, shortages of goods and services, and loss of confidence in government have been linked to inflation in the past and have been a source of public concern. Uncontrolled inflation may even make a country ripe for a change in political philosophy. In times of inflation in the past, nations have turned to demagogues or dictators who promised "painless" solutions to the problems of inflation.

Other economists contend that creeping inflation of about 2 percent a year may be good for the economy. Rising prices mean higher profits for business firms. Higher profits stimulate increased production, which in turn encourages investment in new manufacturing capacity and creates more jobs. The problem with this theory is the difficulty of making sure inflation continues only to "creep." If business and labor unions, for example, use 2 percent inflation as a base on which to add further price and wage demands, the creep may accelerate into a headlong lurch!

ANALYZING AND CORRECTING INFLATION

If we agree that inflation is indeed a serious problem, the next step is analysis. What are the forces producing inflationary pressures in a modern nation? How is inflation transmitted through the economic system? Finally, what policies may be effective for dealing with inflation?

There are basically four kinds of inflation.

Demand-Pull Inflation

The demand-pull explanation for inflation focuses on the demand side of markets. Economists worry that "too much money is chasing too few goods."

If buyers want more goods and services than the nation can produce, they tend to push total spending beyond the production possibilities curve. When finally there are no more unemployed resources to be drawn into production, output cannot increase. Excess spending starts an upward spiral of bidding for the limited supply of goods, raising the prices of finished goods and the costs of the labor and material resources needed to produce them.

Demand-pull inflation is most common during wars or during periods of heavy social spending or rapid economic development.

Policies for Demand-Pull Inflation

Cutting Total Spending and Raising Taxes. If excess spending is, in fact, the cause of inflation, what policy would be appropriate for correcting the problem?

When excessive spending heats up inflation, Keynesian economists recommend raising taxes and cutting nonessential government spending. Needless to say, this is very unpopular medicine. Few policymakers campaign on a platform promising to raise taxes and cut popular spending programs.

Political considerations were a factor in the inflation of the 1960s and 1970s. The federal government was spending heavily to finance the

How Things Have Changed

CORRECTING INFLATION

Brazil's new president is fighting inflation, but the task is difficult. Layoffs have spread, concerts and flights have been canceled, and grocers accused of violating a price freeze have been arrested. There are plans to trim the government bureaucracy and sell state enterprises. The majority of Brazilians seem to support tough measures.

Argentina's President Carlos Menem has imposed similar measures to slow inflation in his country. Today several Latin American nations are exploring the possibility of freer trade between their nations. They expect that lower inflation and increased international competition will help make their economies more prosperous.

war in Vietnam, but tax increases and cuts in other government programs would have been political suicide for many legislators. Consequently, the high levels of spending were allowed to continue. Rising government spending for defense and urban and rural development programs, and consumer spending for civilian goods quickly translated into ever-rising price levels.

Stabilizing Money Growth.   Another anti-inflation plan is favored by the monetarists, led by Milton Friedman. The monetarists' proposal would avoid the political problems associated with increasing taxes and reducing government spending.

Friedman argues that if we are to control inflation, we must keep the quantity of money in balance with the nation's growing capacity to produce goods and services. Our productive capacity has grown an average of almost 4 percent each year through increases in the quantity and quality of our resources and through improvements in technology. Therefore, according to Friedman, the Federal Reserve should allow the money supply to increase each year only as much as the average expected growth in productive capacity: about 4 percent.*

Under Friedman's proposal, if growth is actually greater than 4 percent, inflation will tend to accelerate. The inflation would be only temporary, however. If the Federal Reserve continues to supply new money at the rate of only 4 percent, the constant addition of new money will not be enough to pay the higher prices. The result will be a tendency for some prices to fall, which in turn will reduce production and decrease economic growth. Furthermore, the smaller than necessary quantity of money will push interest rates up and discourage borrowing for new investment. Without any need for government intervention, production will fall, bringing annual growth of production back down to 4 percent and bringing prices back to normal.

Actual growth in production less than 4 percent could not be sustained either. At

---

*The 4 percent rate of money growth could be altered if growth in productive capacity were to change.

Viewpoint

HOW TO FINANCE A WAR

It is said that there are three ways to finance a war. (This might be a war on poverty, a war on drugs, or a war on AIDS, as well as a conventional war.) The methods are difficult and desirable in the same order:

1. The most desirable and the most difficult is through taxation. If citizens are prevented from spending the amount government wants to spend, resources can be moved from production of consumer goods to production of goods for fighting the war.
2. The second most desirable and difficult method is through bond sales to the public. If individuals can be persuaded to lend their money to government, they will not spend it for consumer goods.
3. The least desirable and least difficult (and therefore most often resorted to) method is through creating new money. A government can avoid prevention and persuasion to reduce private spending and simply create new money to pay for necessary government programs. In the preceding chapter we learned how the Federal Reserve banks can enable commer-

cial banks to create new money for lending to government.

Regardless of the means used to finance a war, a government must channel resources away from the production of consumer goods and toward production of military goods. Taxes and borrowing are obvious ways to reduce the use of resources for producing consumer goods. Creating new money, however, gives government the dollars it needs without taking money away from consumers. Thus, creating money can cause inflation.

It is the inflation that causes resources to be channeled away from production of consumer goods and toward production of goods to fight the war. It works this way. When inflation reduces the purchasing power of consumers' incomes, their spending power falls. Then resources are used to produce the goods and services the government needs to fight the war.

In the end, consumers get fewer goods for their money. Indeed, inflation amounts to a kind of tax, but the tax is hidden, less easily measured, and probably less equitable than a tax that has been agreed to by the voters.

growth rates less than 4 percent, some resources will be unemployed, and there will be a temporary drop in prices. If the Federal Reserve continues to supply new money at the rate of 4 percent, the constant addition of new money will be greater than needed for the current price level. Too much money will encourage consumer spending and push prices back up. Furthermore, the surplus of money for lending will push interest rates down and encourage borrowing for new investment. This time the result will be an increase in production, bringing annual growth in production back up to 4 percent and bringing prices back to normal.

Thus, according to Milton Friedman, a steady increase in the money supply will serve as an automatic regulator of spending and an automatic stabilizer of prices. Without any sort of government intervention, economic growth will tend to stabilize at roughly 4 percent per year, and prices will remain stable as well.

Cost-Push Inflation

A second explanation for inflation focuses on the supply side of markets. This explanation bears a somewhat "chicken-and-egg" relationship to the first, but it may be a better explanation for the inflation of the 1970s.

Cost-push (or wage-push) **inflation** places the blame for inflation on rising costs of production. Resource owners (generally owners of labor) demand larger shares of income from production. As resource prices rise, business costs of production rise (particularly wage costs), and prices rise for finished goods and services. Rising prices for goods and services, in turn, create even higher wage demands (or activate cost-of-living clauses in wage contracts).

Rising wages do not necessarily cause inflation. Wages may increase every year with no price increases as long as productivity increases at the same rate as wages. If productivity increases by 3 percent a year, for example, wages can increase by an average of 3 percent without causing cost-push inflation.

On the other hand, if wages rise faster than productivity, labor cost per unit of output increases. To make up for higher labor costs, business firms must raise prices on finished goods. Consumers must then, in effect, pay a bonus to labor for every unit bought. When consumers see their own buying power shrinking, they insist upon receiving higher incomes, too, thus adding another loop to the upward spiral of wages and costs and prices.

The whole problem is complicated because wage costs bear more heavily in certain industries. Wage costs are a small part of production costs in modern, automated manufacturing plants. However, the service industries are less easily automated, generally requiring more labor input per unit of output. Unfortunately, these are precisely the things we affluent Americans want most after our basic material needs are satisfied—services like health and beauty services, educational and environmental services, recreational and travel services, processed foods and custom designs. Rising wage costs are especially inflationary when consumers spend more of their incomes in the service industries.

Policies for Cost-Push Inflation

Stabilizing Income Shares. If we accept the cost-push explanation for inflation, we should look for ways to balance the income demands of the owners of labor, land, capital, and entrepreneurial resources. One such effort was the wage guideposts of the Kennedy administration. The Kennedy guideposts were used to hold down wage demands and preserve the existing relationships among income shares. Wages were allowed to rise only as much as average gains in productivity (3.2

percent). Price increases were allowed only in industries where productivity had grown more slowly than the national average. In industries where productivity had grown faster than the national average, it was expected that prices would fall.

Attempts to control inflation through guideposts were moderately successful. This was partly because there was plenty of excess capacity in the economy from an earlier recession. Hefty productivity gains in certain key industries made up for price increases in others. Also, organized labor was willing to cooperate with the wage guideposts as long as the cost of living remained stable. Unhappily, prices continued to rise in those sectors where the guideposts were not applied: agriculture and services.

Policymakers experimented with wage and price controls again during President Nixon's administration in the early 1970s. Price inflation moderated somewhat during the period of wage-price controls, but there was a "bulge" in prices after controls were lifted. Then in 1973 and 1979, OPEC raised the price of oil exports, causing the worst cost-push inflation our nation has experienced in recent decades. Presidents Ford and Carter introduced voluntary wage-price controls in an attempt to deal with the inflation that resulted from oil price increases.

Increasing Productivity. During the Kennedy administration, programs were also put in place to hold down business firms' costs of production and encourage them to expand and modernize productive capacity. Business firms were allowed a tax credit to help pay for new capital investment, and they were allowed to deduct larger amounts from taxable income for depreciation of old equipment. The Economic Development Act encouraged the use of modern equipment and new technologies in regions of low productivity. Govern-ment loans, public works projects, and technical assistance programs were concentrated in depressed areas.

Efforts were also made to increase the productivity of labor. The Manpower Development and Training Act, Job Corps, Neighborhood Youth Corps, and Adult Work Programs provided funds for programs to increase labor skills. Many disadvantaged and unskilled persons were retrained. Such programs are costly, however. In later government programs, on-the-job training in private business firms received greater emphasis.

Stagflation and Structural Inflation

Throughout the 1970s and into the 1980s a new problem appeared in the wage-cost-price relationship. The new problem was christened **stagflation**—price inflation accompanied by stagnation, or slower growth of production in industry.

We have discussed two traditional explanations for inflation: **demand-pull,** too much spending over and above the productive capacity of the economic system, and **cost-push,** the attempts of resource owners to increase their own incomes faster than the increase in productivity. Demand-pull inflation can only occur at full employment, and cost-push inflation is most often associated with high employment.

Recently, however, inflation has been associated with high unemployment. In the early 1980s, unemployment was more than 7 percent and the utilization rate of manufacturing capacity was less than 80 percent. Still, inflation averaged almost 10 percent a year. (This contrasts with what might be called the "good old days" of the 1960s, when the average unemployment rate was only 4.8 percent and inflation was only 2.5 percent.) When there is a lot of unused industrial capacity, it is difficult to accept the demand-pull explanation for inflation.

Some economists suspected the problem was a new form of cost-push inflation—one that depends on the structure of resource markets. **Market structure** refers to the number and size of firms, the types of raw materials used in production, the types of labor required by modern technology, and the skills of the available labor pool. Thus, the third explanation for inflation was labeled **structural inflation.**

Administered Prices

Many economists blamed structural inflation on administered prices in highly concentrated industries. **Administered prices** are prices set by the largest firms in a concentrated industry. Smaller firms in a concentrated industry tend to go along with the large firms, worsening the resulting inflation.

In certain industries, price-fixing agreements may seem necessary because of the large capital investments required and the technical complexity of production. Costly plants and equipment must be operated fairly continuously and the output sold at profitable prices. Large-scale manufacturers cannot afford price wars. Therefore, they set prices high enough to maintain a target rate of return: a certain percentage return on their invested capital.

The paradoxical result of target pricing is that when demand falls and plant operation must be cut back, each unit of the smaller output must bear a larger share of the target return. Thus, falling sales may force firms to increase price in order to pay their full costs.

Suppliers of certain industrial materials have the power to set higher prices even when spending is low and unemployment high. The only requirement is that the material be a necessary component of manufacture, for which

there are few substitutes: steel, aluminum, zinc, copper, and processing machinery are examples. Alternate suppliers often do not exist, and buyers of these materials know they can pass on their higher costs to final consumers anyway.

Often, highly concentrated industries are associated with powerful labor unions. Unions can insist on higher wage contracts, knowing that large firms can pass on their higher wage costs to the unfortunate consumer. Thus, the combination of market power and union power leads to higher wages and prices, with lower utilization rates and increased unemployment.

Policy for Structural Inflation

Breaking Up Market Power.   This rather gloomy conclusion leaves the policymaker in a dilemma. If structural inflation results from excessive market power, a policy to reduce or restrain that power is needed. Manufacturers whose pricing policies add to inflation would have to be separated into smaller enterprises, or their pricing policies would have to be regulated by a public commission. Neither approach is very satisfactory.

Breaking up large firms might mean sacrificing large-scale, low-cost production. Also, large firms may be better equipped than small firms to conduct research and develop new technologies. Finally, regulatory commissions are costly and often poorly prepared for making policy decisions in a complex manufacturing environment.

Nevertheless, the Antitrust Division of the Justice Department, the Federal Trade Commission, and the federal courts in various states have been looking into the pricing policies of some highly concentrated markets: sugar, bread, coffee, beer, aluminum, breakfast cereals, pharmaceuticals, and petroleum. If administered pricing can be brought under control, perhaps inflationary pressures can be moderated.

Regulation Inflation

Government frequently gets the blame for causing inflation. Sometimes government is not entirely at fault, but there is one instance in which government must certainly accept the blame. That is the area of regulation.

In general, government regulation of business has one of two objectives: economic or social. The economic objective is primarily to protect competition in particular industries. The social objective is to protect workers and consumers. In both cases the result of regulation may be higher prices.

Regulation for economic purposes is generally directed toward a particular sector of the economy: agriculture, air transportation, communication, banking, or energy. In such capital-intensive industries, industrial concentration is fairly common. (In fact, we have referred to some of these markets as **natural monopolies.**) The goal of regulation is to retain a degree of competition so as to avoid the harmful effects of monopoly. Even when larger enterprises might be more efficient, regulation can protect small competitors by setting prices above the minimum costs of production for large firms.

Regulation for social purposes is a more recent form. The objective of social regulation is to require firms to include external costs in their costs of production. External costs are costs generally borne by others outside the business firm that creates them. Some examples of external costs are environmental pollution and the costs of employee health and safety on the job.

Free markets cannot handle external costs well. This is because the benefits of money spent to correct the problems don't necessarily come back to the firm. Like the costs, the benefits of improved health and living conditions are distributed over the entire community. Social regulation forces firms to "internalize" their external costs. Ultimately, the "internalized" costs are paid by consumers of the products involved, in the form of higher prices for finished goods.

Regulation of any kind has another inflationary effect. To administer rules requires a staff of lawyers, inspectors, accountants, and specialists of all types. Government employees must be paid salaries comparable to those they could earn in private industry, but they produce no marketable good or service. Again, the result is to raise prices.

Policies for Regulation Inflation

Deregulating Industry. In the early days of economic regulation, it seemed necessary to protect small competitors so that a monopoly could not achieve total control over output and prices. More recently, however, technological changes and economic growth have weakened the market power of monopolies, so that regulation may no longer be necessary. In some regulated industries, firms have offered to reduce prices and introduce new technologies if the regulatory authorities would let them.

In 1978 Congress and the Civil Aeronautics Board began deregulating the airline industry. Airline firms were allowed to cut prices and cancel unprofitable routes. Small airlines sprang up to take advantage of markets abandoned by the giant airlines. By the end of the 1980s competition had reduced airline profits substantially, and several major firms had declare bankruptcy. Still, many analysts believed that the industry has become more efficient without regulation.

Deregulation continued when Congress and the Interstate Commerce Commission began deregulating the trucking industry in 1980. New banking laws in the 1980s removed re-

Contemporary Thinking about Economic Issues

CURING INFLATION

Martin Spechler believes there are two ways to cure big inflations—neither of them very pleasant.

In Latin America and Eastern Europe, big inflations have been cured by authoritarian means, with a strengthened police force to suppress unions and compel workers to accept painful cuts in living standards. In Western Europe and the United States, curing inflation has required similar pain, but individual liberties have generally not been threatened.

The most dramatic inflations of Western Europe have been associated with recovery from war. War destroys production and transportation facilities, depletes the labor force, and breaks apart traditional social and economic ties. Thus, war leads to shortages, hoarding, and loss of confidence in national currencies. Prices rise so fast that people return to barter, with all the inconveniences barter brings.

After World War I, inflation in Germany reduced the value of the German mark to 4.2 trillion marks to the dollar; in Austria the crown fell to 71,060 crowns per dollar; in France the franc fell to 200 per dollar. In all these countries, curing inflation required high interest rates and tight controls on credit, tax increases and reduced government subsidies, high unemployment and numerous bankruptcies. After World War II, curing inflation in Germany and Italy was helped by foreign loans, which enabled these countries to import needed materials for rebuilding their war-torn industries. In both these countries, fears of a Communist takeover contributed to strong citizen support of government measures to cut spending. What are the lessons from these experiences?

Big inflations cannot be stopped by half-hearted means. In fact, programs to slow spending *gradually* may make inflation worse, since failure to accomplish their objectives reduces their credibility and forfeits public support. Strong measures are needed, even though the effect of strong measures is to hold living standards down for a period of several years. Moreover, the necessary result of strong measures is to increase the share of profits at the expense of wages. The transfer of wealth to the capitalists makes possible new investment, which will ultimately increase productive capacity and restore economic growth.

Our democratic society depends on citizen involvement and cooperation to achieve results that benefit the nation as a whole. Citizen support of painful policies to reduce inflation has helped us avoid the authoritarian measures that have been necessary in other nations.

Martin C. Spechler, "Big Inflations Need Potent Cures," *Challenge*, November/December 1986.

strictions on competition among banks and other financial intermediaries. In both these cases, Congress hoped that competition would encourage individual firms to adapt their service and adjust their pricing policies to serve particular markets and operate more efficiently.

Cost-Benefit Analysis of Social Regulation.   Some economists worry that social regulation has not only raised the costs of production for business firms but has also increased the risks of business, discouraged new capital investment, and slowed productivity growth for the nation as a whole. Aside from these harmful effects, however, regulation also yields benefits that our society values and for which citizens are willing to pay; some

obvious examples are healthy working conditions and clean air and water. Still, it is important to compare these and other benefits with their costs and impose social regulations only to the point that the benefits gained clearly justify the costs paid.

In order to do this, Congress has mandated a new benefit-cost approach to social regulation. Social regulatory agencies are now required to estimate the benefits of a proposed new regulation and compare the benefits with all the costs: the enforcement costs for government, the compliance costs for business, and the long-term economic costs for our economic system. Making such calculations is difficult and imprecise, but considering benefits along with costs should increase the efficiency of social regulation.

Self-Check

1. **Trade will adjust the balance between money and goods:**
   a. If nations restrict the flow of money over their borders.
   b. As money flows into nations experiencing inflation.
   c. If democratic governments carry on large spending programs.
   d. Helping to achieve price stability.
   e. If consumers buy from high-price producers.

2. **Inflation is hardest on:**
   a. Those who borrow money to be repaid in future years.
   b. Speculators who hoard basic commodities.
   c. Fixed-income recipients and retired persons.
   d. Workers with escalator clauses in wage contracts.
   e. The federal government, whose tax revenues must decline.

3. **The main cause of demand-pull inflation is:**
   a. Excessive production of goods and services.
   b. Heavy sale of government bonds to the public.
   c. Excessive saving by consumers.
   d. A high level of total spending relative to available goods and services.
   e. A substantial increase in the productivity of resources.

4. **According to the monetarists, a steady increase in the supply of money should:**
   a. Give politicians more control over monetary policy.
   b. Be in line with the average growth in production.
   c. Increase spending during inflation.
   d. Reduce spending during recession.
   e. None of the above.

5. **In order to avoid inflation, wages must:**
   a. Rise only as much as productivity.
   b. Be distributed equally among wage earners.
   c. Rise faster than the return to owners of capital.
   d. Be taxed at lower rates.
   e. Be controlled by the government.

6. **Concentration in industry:**
   a. Allows monopolistic industries and labor unions to maintain high prices.
   b. May cause high prices even when employment drops.
   c. Permits firms to establish a target rate of return.
   d. Has no simple policy remedy.
   e. All of the above.

Theory in Practice

WINNERS AND LOSERS IN INFLATION—MOSTLY LOSERS!

Inflation shrinks your income and erodes the value of your savings. A 7 percent annual rate of inflation will halve the value of your dollars in ten years. (Divide the rate of inflation into 70. The answer is the number of years before the value of money is cut in half if inflation continues at the same rate. Thus, for a 2 percent annual rate of inflation: $\frac{70}{2} = 35$ years. This is known as the **rule of 70.**)

TEST YOURSELF

If your income increases in value at the rate of 5 percent a year, calculate the number of years before your income will double in value.

In 1982, average per capita income in the United States was $9724 after taxes; in 1989 it was $15,191, an impressive increase. When the 1989 figure is corrected for inflation and translated into 1982 dollars, however, it is worth only $11,681. More than one-third of the apparent gain reflected only higher prices.

Inflation is especially hard on production workers. Weekly earnings averaged $220 in 1979. By 1989 earnings had risen to $335. In real terms weekly earnings had actually fallen by almost $20. Without cost-of-living clauses in wage contracts, a worker is relatively helpless against inflation.

Savers and owners of financial assets didn't fare much better in inflation. High-grade, low-risk corporate bonds earned between 7 and 10 percent during the 1970s. Short-term commercial loans earned somewhat less. Tax-exempt municipal bonds earned between 5 and 7 percent. The safest U.S. government securities earned less than 7 percent. Thus, on the average, owners of financial assets increased their dollar value somewhat more than 7 percent annually over the period.

How much were those additional dollars worth?

During the decade of the 1970s consumer prices rose 120 percent, reducing the value of the dollar by more than 10 percent per year. This means that many owners of America's financial assets saw their incomes eroded by inflation. To make matters worse, they had to pay income taxes on their interest earnings in addition to their losses to inflation.

Who does gain from inflation? The biggest gainer is government! The federal government's income tax revenues increase with inflation, as taxpayers move into higher tax brackets and pay higher tax rates.* Inflation awards the U.S. government an increasing share of the nation's income to use for social programs, public works, and defense. Thus, inflation channels more and more resources into production for public purposes and away from private purposes.

Is this what we want? Whatever we decide, we may discover that controlling inflation requires some political decisions as well as economic ones.

WAGE-PRICE CONTROLS

A politically acceptable and widely debated anti-inflationary tactic has been wage-price

*Government's gains from inflation are reduced when income tax brackets are "indexed" for inflation. We will have more to say about indexing later.

controls. (The popular expectation is that your wages are controlled but not necessarily mine; prices I pay are controlled but not necessarily those I receive.) Most economists oppose price controls except occasionally as a means of affecting inflationary psychology and ending inflationary expectations. Recent experience with wage-price controls illustrates some of their advantages and disadvantages.

The Vietnam War created major distortions in the U.S. economy. Increased government spending for the military brought on inflation. Without contractionary fiscal policy to hold down civilian spending, the Federal Reserve was obliged to use strongly contractionary monetary policy to slow the inflation.

By 1971, the shortage of money had pushed the economy into recession. Unemployment was more than 5 percent, and real GNP was declining. It began to appear that expansionary fiscal policy should be used, but fears of again setting off inflation stood in the way. Finally, in August 1971, President Nixon and the Federal Reserve Board agreed on a package of policies that included expansionary fiscal and monetary policies and temporary wage-price controls.

Most nonfarm wages and prices were frozen for 90 days. Then in December 1971, a Pay Board was set up to monitor wage increases, which were generally limited to 5.5 percent. A Price Commission was set up to review price increases, which were limited to "pass throughs," that is, firms would be allowed to "pass through" higher production costs in the form of higher prices. Profit margins were held to the average of previous years.

Except for farm prices, which were not controlled, wage and price inflation slowed considerably under controls; the consumer price index rose only 1.9 percent and wages 3.1 percent. After controls were lifted, there was a slight "bulge" in prices, but then the indexes of wages and prices settled down to a rate of increase that was lower than before

Viewpoint

THE POLITICS OF INFLATION

In the late 1970s and early 1980s the United States suffered high inflation along with high unemployment. Policymakers seemed unable to correct the problem. To cure inflation through contractionary monetary and fiscal policy would mean severe recession, stalled economic growth, and impaired technological progress. Policymakers wanted to avoid a new program of wage-price controls because of the price distortions controls cause and the scarcities they create.

Most economists blame the inflationary spiral on the food and fuel price increases of the 1970s. Because higher domestic food costs were partly a result of increased exports of U.S. grains to pay for imported oil, we might identify higher energy costs as the principal source of the inflation.

Higher energy costs had two important results for the world economy: First, the economic pie did not grow as fast as when energy was plentiful and cheap; and second, the distribution of the pie changed as energy producers demanded a relatively larger share of the world's output of goods and services. These two developments seriously affected the U.S. economy. Most of us were harmed by the first result, and we resisted the second. We were harmed by the fact that material standards of living did not improve as fast

as we would have liked; we resisted a reduction in our real purchasing power that would have reduced our own relative shares of the economic pie. Instead, we demanded wage increases to compensate fully for each increase in our living costs. We continued to claim our "fair share" of the pie.

Of course, all our increased claims did not increase the size of the pie at all. The result of higher claims was only to raise prices all around. In 1990 energy producers demanded another increase in their share of the pie, and the price of energy rose again. Some economists worried that the experience of the 1970s will soon be repeated—one worsening spiral after another.

The problem doesn't have a simple solution. In fact, there may be many partial solutions, each of which helps in only a small way. The most obvious efforts might be toward increased productivity in all industries, reduction of unnecessary government claims on GNP, conservation and development of new energy sources, and persuasion to avoid excessive claims against total output. All these measures require the willing cooperation of every one of us. Curing inflation may be the test that determines the survival of a democratic market system!

controls. In January 1973, a Cost of Living Council was set up to review price increases, with special emphasis on prices of food and medical care, areas of greatest inflationary pressure.

In late summer of 1973 inflation heated up again. Increased exports and shortages of food, energy, and industrial commodities pushed up prices. During the last half of 1973, prices of food rose 10 percent, services 5.4 percent, and industrial commodities 6.1 percent. New price controls were put into effect for 60 days, but for the next decade annual price increases averaged 8 percent.

How successful were wage-price controls? Probably the greatest success of controls came at the very beginning of the program when there was excess productive capacity available in the economy. With excess capacity, expansionary monetary and fiscal policy could be used vigorously with little fear of price increases. Furthermore, in the beginning expectations of lower inflation probably reduced the rate of inflation that actually occurred.

Why was this? Expectations of future price increases often prompt labor to demand higher wage contracts; likewise, expectations of future cost increases prompt business firms to increase their prices on finished goods. When inflation is not expected, wages and prices will not rise as fast.

The main problem with controls comes when they are lifted. After controls, business firms worry about another price freeze and hurry to increase their prices. Likewise, labor unions demand catch-up wage increases. Another problem is the potential for worsening scarcities. When controlled prices fail to cover rising costs and yield an acceptable profit, firms tend to cut production, particularly of low-profit goods and services. (Many Americans remember the slaughter of thousands of baby chicks during the period of price controls.) The result of shortages may be black markets, with the further problem that the reduced supplies may be allocated unfairly.

Wage-price controls can bring on other long-range effects. Remember that free markets depend on flexible prices to send out signals of changes in resource supplies and consumer demand. Price signals force buyers and sellers to adjust to changing market conditions. For example, high prices for beef should stimulate increased production and help bring prices down. High wages for auto mechanics should encourage more workers to learn these skills and help bring wages down. Price controls interfere with the adjustment process, prolong shortages of goods and resources, and make the ultimate price increases even greater. Furthermore, under a free-market system, improved resource availability and new technology may be expected to reduce costs of production in many industries. But when firms are afraid of price controls, they will hesitate to pass these kinds of cost savings on to consumers.

Price controls may help control inflation in highly concentrated industries, but there may be other undesirable side effects. In steel production, for example, President Kennedy used the power of his office to hold down price increases in the 1960s. Low steel prices held down production costs in the many industries using steel, moderating price increases for automobiles, appliances, and building materials. But low steel prices also reduced profits in the steel industry and discouraged new investment. One result of low profits was a failure to modernize steel production and, finally, even higher prices for steel.

INDEXING

We have attributed many of the harmful effects of inflation to expectations of future inflation. Business firms and workers demand price and wage increases at least as great as expected inflation; lenders demand interest rates at least as great as expected inflation. Their expectations help bring about the inflation they expect.

Economist Milton Friedman has proposed to correct the problem of inflationary expectations through a process called **indexing.** Indexing would establish a cost-of-living correction, to be added to all incomes. With indexing, all wages, rent, and interest payments are adjusted upward in line with changes in the general price level. Thus, indexing keeps real incomes from falling with inflation. Milton Friedman believes that ensuring all groups against a loss of purchasing power through inflation would help hold down their wage and price demands.

With indexing, cost-of-living escalator clauses would be written into all labor contracts, guaranteeing wage earners a fair increase in incomes. Interest rates on loans would vary with the rate of inflation, too. Lenders would be more willing to make loans to home builders and other businesses if they were assured a return high enough to offset inflation. The hope is that indexing would correct the distortions that inflation sometimes creates in the distribution of income.

There are disadvantages, of course. Perhaps the most serious disadvantage of Friedman's proposal would be its effect on the government budget. Indexing adjusts tax brackets, tax credits, and tax rates so that income tax revenues do not increase automatically with inflation. At the same time, however, indexing adjusts government's transfer payments upward, worsening a tendency toward budget deficits.

By maintaining stable income shares, indexing reduces the ability of the price system to allocate resources efficiently and to reward increased productivity. Finally, protecting all income earners against inflation probably reduces their will to fight against inflation. The result could be wildly accelerating prices, with

harmful national and international consequences.

SUMMARY

1. Inflation is an increase in the general price level. The difficulty of keeping spending in balance with total output of goods and services may lead to changing prices, usually in the upward direction.
2. An excess of money in one region will tend to cause the price level to rise. If there is free trade, consumers will spend in other, lower-priced regions, causing money to flow out and eventually bringing the supply of money into balance with the supply of goods. However, modern nations have erected international barriers and established domestic economic programs that interfere with automatic adjustment processes.
3. Demand-pull inflation results from an excess of spending by consumers, business firms, and/or government. Spending over and above the nation's capacity to produce goods may be curtailed by increasing taxes on consumers and business firms, reducing government spending, or restricting the supply of money for loans.
4. Cost-push inflation results from increases in the costs of productive resources. Higher costs are passed on to consumers in the form of higher prices for finished goods. To avoid inflation, wages must not rise faster than labor's productivity. Likewise, returns to owners of capital must not rise faster than productivity.
5. Structural inflation is blamed on highly concentrated industries in which firms agree among themselves not to reduce prices. The result has been stagflation—high prices even when unemployment is high. The problem may worsen in the coming years because of the technical requirements of modern manufacturing and the difficulty of maintaining price competition among large firms.
6. Government regulatory policies may add to costs of production and keep many prices higher than free-market prices; however, there are some benefits associated with regulation.

7. Inflation imposes particular burdens on savers, the aged, and people on fixed incomes. It creates distortions that may be damaging to the entire society. Some recent programs to deal with inflation are wage-price controls and indexing.

TERMS TO REMEMBER

inflation: an increase in the general price level

demand-pull inflation: inflation that results from excess demand, over and above the capacity to produce goods and services

cost-push inflation: inflation that results from increasing costs of production

stagflation: inflation and unemployment at the same time

structural inflation: inflation that results from the concentration of industry into large firms

administered prices: prices established by tacit agreement among large firms in concentrated industries

indexing: automatic changes in incomes and tax rates to compensate for changes in the general price level

TOPICS FOR DISCUSSION

1. Explain the following expressions and discuss the implications of each for price stability:

    Speculative buying
    Cost-of-living clauses
    Administered prices
    Indexing

2. Is it correct to say that inflation is the cruelest tax? Explain.

3. What does the author mean by the statement that there is a "chicken-and-egg" relationship between the demand-pull and cost-push explanations of inflation?

4. A successful U.S. businessperson once said, "The best way to prevent higher prices is high prices." Explain.

5. The 1978–1979 inflation was worsened by lagging productivity throughout the U.S. economy. Over the two years the United States experienced a 0.6 percent decrease in output per labor hour. Over the same period, wages rose 18.3 percent. Price increases of 16.2 percent eroded the value of the higher wages and complicated the fight against inflation. Workers claimed their pay was worth less, and employers pointed to falling labor productivity. What are the political implications of this problem for policymakers? Do you see any ways to resolve the impasse? What ultimate results would you predict?

6. Federal Reserve Chairperson Alan Greenspan was once quoted as saying that inflation is primarily a political, not an economic, problem. According to Greenspan, a policymaker's dilemma results from the emphasis of short-term gains at the expense of long-term costs. Comment on Greenspan's assessment of the problem of inflation. Do you agree with his conclusion? What sugggestions would you make to correct the problem?

7. A letter to the editor of a local newspaper stated: "Let's put all congressional salaries on a 'reverse' cost-of-living basis. Whenever the cost-of-living index goes up, our senators and representatives would have to take a cut in pay." What does the writer believe about the causes of inflation? Evaluate his or her policy prescription.

8. Discuss the major advantages and disadvantages of government regulation.

ANSWERS TO TEST YOURSELF

(p.255) Return to lender = $(1 - 0.25)(0.10) - 0.08 = -0.005 = -\frac{1}{2}$ percent = cost to borrower.

(p.266) $70 \div 5 = 14$ yrs. before your income doubles.

Unemployment

or What Good Is a Raise If You Don't Have a Job?

Tools for Study

LEARNING OBJECTIVES

After reading this chapter, you will be able to:

1. Explain the GNP gap.
2. Define frictional, cyclical, and structural unemployment and discuss some remedies.
3. Discuss the relationship between unemployment and inflation.
4. List the various programs that have been adopted to deal with unemployment.

CURRENT ISSUES FOR DISCUSSION

How can a minimum wage actually harm those it is intended to help?

What groups in the population are most subject to unemployment?

What are the most favorable job opportunities for the future?

The classical economists believed that unemployment would not be a serious problem in a free-market system. They thought that markets for resources would operate smoothly and competitively just like markets for goods and services. Many business firms would enter the market to demand labor resources, and many individuals would offer to supply labor to business firms. The result would be an equilibrium price, or wage, and a quantity of employment that would clear the market.

The classical theory of labor markets is shown graphically on Figure 12.1. With the demand for labor shown by D_1, the equilibrium wage rate is \$3.50 per hour, and employment is 200,000 workers.

Now suppose total spending in the economy falls and the demand for workers falls. The labor demand curve shifts to the left, shown as D_2 in the figure. At the old wage of \$3.50 per hour, the quantity of workers demanded is now only about 125,000, while the quantity supplied is still 200,000. There is a surplus in the labor market. In a free market, surplus workers compete for jobs, causing the wage rate to fall to a new lower equilibrium wage of \$3.25. Again, the market is cleared. At \$3.25 per hour, 150,000 workers supply labor and 150,000 workers are demanded by business firms. All workers who want to work for the going wage are employed. Thus, when wages are flexible, there is no unemployment.

The classical economists went a step further. They concluded that the lower wage would not necessarily mean a lower standard of living for workers. Because goods and services would be produced at lower labor costs, they would sell for lower prices. Thus, a

Figure 12.1   Wage and Employment Adjustments in a Free Labor Market.

In a free market a decrease in demand for labor would cause the equilibrum wage to fall.

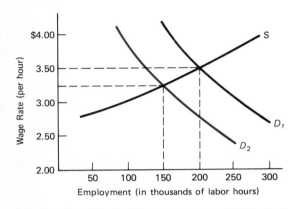

worker's lower money wage might actually yield roughly the same real purchasing power.

Classical labor market theory depended on competition for these smooth adjustments to take place. Wages would have to be flexible enough to rise or fall in response to changes in the demand for labor. In periods of slack demand, surplus workers would have to compete for jobs by offering to work for lower wages. In periods of excess demand, employers would have to compete for workers by offering higher wages. Unemployment would be only temporary. Wages and prices would rise and fall together, and real wages would depend on the productivity of the economic system as a whole.

Classical theory may have been more relevant in years past than in a modern economy. Modern economic development has brought changes that interfere with the automatic adjustments of free markets. Employers and workers have organized into groups to gain market power and to fix wages and prices. Wages have lost their flexibility, and today a

drop in demand creates unemployment rather than a lower equilibrium wage. In addition, structural changes have taken place in the labor market, producing prolonged unemployment for particular groups of workers.

MEASURING UNEMPLOYMENT

Failing to employ resources productively has long-range and short-range effects—economic, social, and perhaps even political. It is impossible to measure all the harmful effects of unemployment, but some of the material costs can be measured.

The GNP Gap

Do you remember our discussion of the economic problem? The economic problem involves the scarcity of productive resources and the vastness of wants. Unless available resources are used efficiently, fewer of our unlimited wants will be satisfied. Fewer homes will be built, dental services performed, or consumer goods produced.

When resources are unemployed, we say there is a **GNP gap**. The GNP gap is the difference between potential GNP and actual GNP. It represents the sacrifice of goods and services we might have had if all resources had been fully employed. During the recessions of 1980–1982, the estimated GNP gap was more than $200 billion worth of goods and services not produced! The saddest aspect of unemployment is that the loss of production can never be recovered. Coal not produced this year may be mined in the next. Trees not cut remain for cutting some time in the future. However, hours of work not used today are gone forever.

Aside from these material sacrifices borne by the entire economic system, unemployment causes particular hardships for particular regions of the country.* Regions with substantial unemployment often suffer social unrest, high crime rates, and environmental decay. For individuals, unemployment often means lower material standards of living, emotional distress, and, even more damaging, the loss of skills and motivation that comes with idleness.

The Unemployment Rate

Another, more direct measure of unemployment is the unemployment rate. The **unemployment rate** is estimated by the Department of Labor and expressed as the percentage of the labor force not currently employed.

The **labor force** is defined as all people 16 years of age or older, not in school or other institutions, who are employed or who are unemployed but actively seeking work. People are counted as employed if they did any work for pay or profit during a given week, regardless of the amount. People who worked in a family business for 15 or more hours in the week are also counted as employed, whether or not they received pay. People are counted as unemployed if they were laid off from their latest job or actively sought work within the past 30 days. (Actively seeking work means filling out applications and answering want ads, going to job interviews, or registering with an employment agency.)

Thus, the unemployment rate is the percentage of the total labor force that was classified as unemployed during the week.

The estimated unemployment rate tends to be understated, however, particularly during periods of rising unemployment. A person who would like a full-time job but can find a job working only ten hours per week is counted as employed, as is a person who is working at a job that is beneath his or her full

capacity. These workers are considered to be employed, but more correctly they should be considered "underemployed" and included in the unemployment rate. Finally, workers who have stopped looking for work out of discouragement or failure to find a job are not included among the unemployed.*

How can these factors affect the unemployment rate? Between November and December of 1980 the unemployment rate dropped from 7.5 to 7.4 percent. Over the same period, total employment also dropped by 57,000 workers. Apparently, large numbers of workers left the labor force and were not counted as unemployed, so that what seemed to be a gain in employment was really a decrease in the supply of labor.

ANALYZING THE PROBLEM OF UNEMPLOYMENT

The Employment Act of 1946 gave the U.S. government the responsibility to establish policies for achieving the maximum practical level of employment in the nation.

Deciding on policy for full employment requires a correct analysis of the sources of unemployment. Then policymakers can design effective programs to correct each type. Economists classify unemployment into three categories: frictional, cyclical, and structural.

Frictional Unemployment

Many economists define full employment as that condition when approximately 97 percent of the civilian labor force is employed. The remaining 3 percent are unemployed because of "frictions" in the movement of workers

---

*Examples are Appalachia in the 1960s and Detroit in the 1980s.

*Discouraged workers constitute what is sometimes called **hidden unemployment.**

from job to job or among workers entering the labor force for the first time.

Frictional unemployment is necessary and even desirable in a dynamic economy. It is a reflection of the healthy growth and decline of different sectors of the economy. Markets and production techniques are constantly changing to reflect changes in consumer demand. Workers must move out of declining industries and into expanding industries. If there were no frictional unemployment, expanding industries would have to bid up the wages of employed workers, aggravating tendencies toward inflation.

In recent years, frictional unemployment has come to constitute a larger portion of total employment. This is primarily because of the growing numbers of married women and teenagers in the job market, with typically higher rates of entry and re-entry into the labor force than adult male workers.

Frictional unemployment is, by definition, temporary. Its effects may be relieved by better job information and aids to worker mobility. For example, workers can be provided job counseling, or they can be helped to move to a new location where jobs are more plentiful.

Cyclical Unemployment

The term **mass unemployment** brings to mind the more serious problem of **cyclical unemployment**—unemployment associated with cycles of economic activity. The Great Depression provides the best example of cyclical unemployment. During the Great Depression, the unemployment rate reached as high as 25 percent of the labor force.

Typically, economic activity grows in spurts. Periods of great optimism and growth are followed by slower growth or decline. Once homes are equipped with video recorders, microwave ovens, and personal computers, demand for consumer goods diminishes. Retailers cut back on inventories and cancel orders to wholesalers. The whole economic system seems to pause before the next round of innovations brings on a new outpouring of gadgets, and the cycle begins again.

Cyclical swings in employment are most severe in industries producing durable goods. Purchase of an auto, refrigerator, or machine can be postponed if consumers are worried about their jobs. Cyclical swings are less severe in the production of nondurable goods and services. Purchase of food, clothing, and health services, for instance, cannot generally be postponed.

When consumer demand declines, blue-collar production workers are more likely to suffer unemployment than professional or supervisory workers. One reason is the specialized functions of these latter workers, which the firm cannot afford to lose to other firms. Another is the fact that many professional workers are covered by contracts that protect their jobs.

Expansionary fiscal and monetary policy make cyclical unemployment less a threat to our economic system today than it was in former years.

Structural Unemployment

More threatening to our prosperity and social health is the growing problem of **structural unemployment.** Structural unemployment is caused by an imbalance between the structure of the labor force, on the one hand, and the requirements of modern industry, on the other. Unless available labor skills correspond to the needs of industry, there will be unemployment. Substantial unemployment may persist even when there are job vacancies. Structural unemployment is worsened by the entry of untrained workers (such as teenagers) into the labor force.

The greatest needs in business today are for skilled workers and for workers in the growing service sector. For example, there are extreme shortages of workers in machine trades, engineering, nursing, and transportation.

Federal and state programs to train workers in new skills, better job information and counseling, and private on-the-job training can help relieve structural unemployment.

AIDS TO UNEMPLOYED WORKERS

The U.S. government has established a number of programs to aid unemployed workers. One such program is the national unemployment insurance system, a part of the Social Security Act of 1935. The states administer this program, within federal guidelines. Private nonfarm workers and certain state employees are covered. (Separate programs cover most workers not covered under this plan.)

Unemployment insurance is financed by a tax on employers and is available to persons who have lost their jobs and are actively seeking employment. These unemployed persons are normally paid benefits up to a maximum of 26 weeks. During periods of high unemployment, emergency legislation may provide additional benefits for up to 25 weeks in some states. Funds for additional benefits come from general revenues of the federal government.

Benefits under the unemployment insurance program range from one-half to two-thirds of a worker's average weekly wage. Some states also provide allowances for children or for a nonworking spouse. Weekly benefits in 1989 averaged about $150.

Some union contracts now provide additional unemployment compensation. United Auto Workers' contracts provide for Supplemental Unemployment Benefits (SUBs) financed by employers. Under combined state and private programs, total compensation for unemployed auto workers amounts to approximately 95 percent of regular earnings. Be-

cause these benefits are not taxed, however, the actual purchasing power of unemployment benefits is greater than the numbers suggest.

In addition to income-maintenance programs, public-service employment programs developed by the federal government provide many jobs for the unemployed. The first major program of this kind was the Works Progress Administration (WPA) of the 1930s. During the 1960s, the Neighborhood Youth Corps and Operation Mainstream provided jobs for youths and the elderly, respectively. In the 1970s, the Comprehensive Employment and Training Act (CETA) established training programs, public-service jobs, summer youth programs, and on-the-job training in areas where unemployment was greater than 6.5 percent. In the 1980s, the Reagan administration established the Job Training Partnership program, but it provided limited funds to run the program.

Public-service jobs produce useful goods and services while helping workers maintain or improve their skills. However, when public-service jobs begin to compete with employment opportunities in the private sector, they should be stopped. Otherwise, excess demand for labor will push all wages up and add to inflation.

UNEMPLOYMENT AND INFLATION

In years past, the levels of unemployment and inflation have tended to move in opposite directions. Rising unemployment has been associated with falling price inflation; falling unemployment has meant rising price inflation.

Why has this been so? The answer has to do with the availability of productive resources. As the economy approaches its full capacity, resources become scarcer and their prices rise. With zero unemployment, employers have to bid resources away from their current employment by offering higher pay. Then

Contemporary Thinking about Economic Issues

A CURE FOR STAGFLATION

Martin Weitzman believes he has a cure for the combination of unemployment and inflation that economists call **stagflation**. According to Weitzman, stagflation is a result of the common practice of tying wages to conditions outside the firm: the general level of wages or changes in wages and prices. A better plan would be to tie wages to conditions inside the firm: specifically, the firm's own revenues or profits. Tying wages to revenues or profits within the firm would provide the appropriate incentives to resist unemployment and inflation, and it would do so automatically.

To illustrate his proposal, Weitzman poses an example of General Motors, which hires, say, 500,000 workers at an hourly wage of $24. The $24 wage is the wage rate at which the value of the output of the last worker hired is equal to the wage. Total wages are 500,000 × $24 = $12,000,000, which represents two-thirds of GM's total revenue of $18,000,000. Under these conditions, GM's remaining revenue after paying all labor costs is $6,000,000. Under these conditions also, there is no incentive to hire additional labor, because additional workers would add less to total revenue than the wage rate and reduce GM's profit.

Suppose instead of paying a flat hourly wage GM paid workers two-thirds of the revenue contributed by workers to GM's total revenue: thus,

[$\frac{2}{3}$ × $18,000,000]/500,000 = $12,000,000/500,000 = $24. The wage is the same as before; but under these conditions, GM has incentives to increase employment. To understand this, assume GM hires one additional worker and that total revenue rises to $18,000,024. Paying workers two-thirds of total revenue yields an average wage of [$\frac{2}{3}$($18,000,024] / 500,001 = $23.999984. The total wage bill increases to $12,000,016, and GM's profit increases to $18,000,024 − 12,000,016 = $6,000,008.

Under these conditions, GM would be encouraged to add workers until all qualified workers have jobs. Adding workers would also have the effect of increasing output at constant prices. In fact, GM would have no incentive to increase prices, because only one-third of any price increase would be added to profit. (Two-thirds would go to labor.)

Weitzman proposes a more realistic arrangement in which workers would be paid a base wage plus a percentage of the firm's total revenue. He concludes that paying workers according to production would enable the nation to overcome its persistent unemployment problem and hold down inflation, too.

Martin L. Weitzman, *The Share Economy: Conquering Stagflation*, Harvard University Press, Cambridge, Mass., 1984.

higher resource costs are built into the prices of finished goods, increasing inflation. On the other hand, when resources are unemployed, surplus resources compete for employment and their prices tend to fall. Accordingly, the prices of finished goods fall (or at least fail to rise).

The Phillips Curve

The typical inverse relationship between unemployment and inflation is illustrated by a **Phillips curve**. The curve was developed by a British economist, A. W. Phillips, to illustrate unemployment and inflation in Britain. A Phillips curve slopes downward, in keeping with the usual inverse relationship between the variables. The Phillips curve in Figure 12.2 is drawn to show unemployment and inflation in the United States for the years 1950–1989. Note that for the years 1950–1969, the relationship between unemployment and inflation was inverse, as expected.

When unemployment and inflation move in opposite directions, an economy may lie within either of the following ranges on the curve:

1. Excessive inflation with low levels of unemployment (e.g., 1951).
2. Excessive unemployment with virtual price stability, i.e., almost zero inflation (e.g., 1961).
3. Moderate inflation with moderate unemployment (e.g., 1957).

Our democratic society has tended to favor the third alternative, which imposes fewer hardships on the population as a whole. As a result, most of the points on Figure 12.2 cluster around the center of the Phillips curve. Whenever economic conditions began to move toward either of the extremes, (1) or (2),

Figure 12.2 A Phillips Curve.

The Phillips curve shows the historical relationship between inflation and unemployment. In the past, as unemployment increased, price inflation tended to fall. In the 1970s and early 1980s, high levels of unemployment were associated with high levels of inflation.

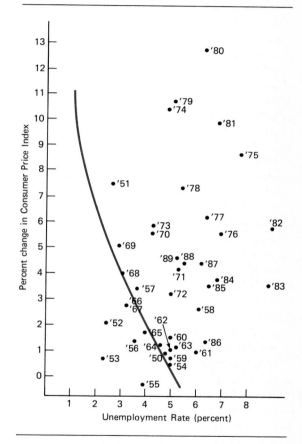

monetary and fiscal policy have been used to push the economy back toward the center.

TEST YOURSELF
In what range of the curve is it appropriate to use expansionary policies? In what range are contractionary policies appropriate?

A Shift of the Phillips Curve

More recently, the U.S. economy has experienced a fourth alternative:

4. Excessive inflation and excessive levels of unemployment.

This situation is represented by a point off the historic Phillips curve and is shown by points for the years 1970–1989 on Figure 12.2.

Look at the points for the years 1970–1989. With extremely high values of both variables, it was impossible to select appropriate monetary and fiscal policies for correcting both problems. Expansionary policies to reduce unemployment worsened the problem of inflation, and contractionary policies to correct inflation worsened the problem of unemployment.

The existence of both excessive inflation and excessive unemployment led some economists to conclude that the Phillips curve itself had shifted to the right. A rightward shift meant higher levels of inflation for every level of unemployment.

Three explanations were offered for the shift in the Phillips curve.

Expectations

Many problems of adjustment in economics can be blamed on expectations. If employed workers expect continued inflation, they demand excessive wage increases; higher wage costs, in turn, are reflected in price increases even without an accompanying increase in employment. Likewise, if manufacturers expect continued increases in their costs of production, they mark up the prices of finished goods in order to stay ahead of cost increases. Either way, excessive inflation can continue even when there is substantial unemployment.

Structural Changes

Another explanation blamed the shift in the Phillips curve on structural changes in the U.S. economy. Advancing technology has changed the type of labor needed in production, but our labor force has been slow to adapt its skills to these changing needs. The result is substantial unemployment at the same time that many jobs remain unfilled.

Some economists believe that there is some "natural rate" of unemployment that will always exist regardless of government's monetary and fiscal policies. They estimate the natural rate at between 5 and 6 percent; the natural rate of unemployment includes workers whose skills are inappropriate for filling the available jobs, as well as those workers who are classified as frictionally unemployed. If this explanation is correct, the Phillips curve would become roughly vertical at about 6 percent unemployment. (Note that many of the recent points on Figure 12.2 do lie on a roughly vertical line between 5 and 6 percent.)

Other Factors

Financial conditions may also have affected the location of the Phillips curve: the availability of unemployment insurance and other income-support programs; the increased wealth of the labor force; and the availability of consumer credit. All these factors allow workers to maintain their standards of living even while unemployed. Their job search may not be as vigorous as in years past, so that periods of unemployment tend to last longer. Also, because these financial factors allow consumer spending to remain fairly stable, demand for goods and services remains strong and adds to inflationary pressures.

Some economists blame the shift in the Phillips curve on **rational expectations**. Remember that the rational expectations of workers and employers can cause them to expect expansionary fiscal and monetary policies that stimulate employment and increase inflationary pressures. With these kinds of expectations, wages and prices can continue to rise even when employment and production are falling.

Self-Check

1. **The classical economists believed that:**
   a. Wages would fall when the demand for labor falls.
   b. At lower wages, labor would be fully employed.
   c. Competition would make wages and prices flexible.
   d. Lower wage rates would not necessarily mean lower real wages.
   e. All of the above.

2. **Which of the following is not generally a result of unemployment?**
   a. Development of new skills during leisure hours.
   b. High crime rates and social unrest.
   c. Loss of material production.
   d. Lower standards of living.
   e. Emotional distress.

3. **Which of the following types of unemployment seems most difficult to correct?**
   a. Frictional unemployment.
   b. Cyclical unemployment.
   c. Structural unemployment.
   d. Phillips unemployment.
   e. All can be corrected with expansionary fiscal and monetary policy.

4. **Public-service employment has all but which of the following advantages?**
   a. Producing generally useful output.
   b. Helping maintain worker skills.
   c. Not competing with the private demand for workers.
   d. Providing on-the-job training for youths.
   e. Providing spending power for workers who would otherwise be unemployed.

5. **Expectations can affect unemployment by:**
   a. Increasing hiring when wages are expected to rise.
   b. Increasing wage demands when prices are expected to rise.
   c. Increasing prices when wages are expected to rise.
   d. Reducing hiring when wages are expected to rise.
   e. (b), (c), and (d).

6. **A Phillips curve shows the relationship between:**
   a. Employment and prices.
   b. Labor force and unemployment.
   c. Labor force and prices.
   d. Unemployment and prices.
   e. Economic growth and prices.

Theory in Practice

THE DILEMMA OVER
THE MINIMUM WAGE

The purpose of a minimum wage law is to increase the incomes of low-income workers. A legally enforced minimum wage acts like a price floor to keep wages from falling below the legal minimum.

The first legal minimum wage was established in 1938, with a minimum of 25 cents per hour for certain employees. In 1990, the minimum wage increased from the 1981 level of $3.35 to $3.80 (with a further increase to $4.25 scheduled for 1991). Small businesses are exempt from the minimum wage law.

The result of the minimum-wage law of 1989 was expected to be:

1. Pay raises totaling several billion dollars to workers getting less than the minimum and additional pay increases to other workers so as to preserve customary wage differentials.
2. Higher prices, particularly in labor-intensive retail and service industries.
3. Higher property taxes, a result of local governments' attempt to finance the rising cost of hiring public employees.

Although the goal of the minimum wage is

to increase incomes, the frequent result is to increase unemployment. Remember that firms hire workers only up to the point at which the value of the output of the last worker is equal to the cost of hiring him or her. When wages are set higher than the equilibrium wage, employers move up their labor demand curves and hire fewer workers.

Figure 12.3 shows the market for a certain type of unskilled labor. In a free market, the equilibrium wage is $1.80 per hour, at which 750,000 hours of labor are demanded and supplied. How many hours are demanded and supplied at a government-imposed minimum of $3.80?

The employment effects of the minimum wage are probably hardest on workers who are least able to find other jobs. To understand this, consider the market for unskilled work-

ers and teenagers. Because employers can generally find substitutes for such workers, demand is relatively price elastic. When wages rise, employment falls sharply for such workers.

Policymakers face a difficult dilemma. Should there be a minimum wage law if it means fewer job opportunities for low-skilled workers, higher production costs for labor-intensive industries, and price inflation for many consumer goods? Or should labor markets be free, even though the result might be low earnings for some workers?

WHO ARE THE UNEMPLOYED?

Levels of unemployment differ widely among different groups in the labor force. Unemployment is higher among teenagers than other age groups, among blacks than whites, and among women than men. Table 12.1 shows unemployment rates broken down into these three categories.

Some groups enter and leave the labor force frequently. Their high job turnover gives them a higher unemployment rate than the

Figure 12.3   Effects of a Minimum Wage.

A minimum wage has the effect of a price floor. With quantity supplied greater than quantity demanded, there is a surplus of labor at the minimum wage rate. A minimum wage may work against those it is intended to help by reducing the level of employment.

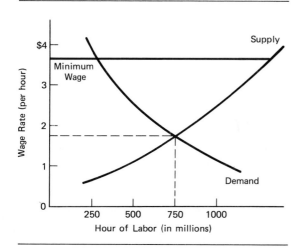

Table 12.1   Unemployment Rates by Age, Race, Sex (1989).

	Unemployment Rate
Whites	4.6
Men, 20 years and over	3.9
Women, 20 years and over	4.1
Teenagers (male)	14.0
Teenagers (female)	11.9
Blacks and other minorities	11.8
Men, 20 years and over	10.8
Women, 20 years and over	10.0
Teenagers (male)	30.1
Teenagers (female)	31.4
Total unemployment rate	5.3

Source: *Economic Report of the President*, 1990.

How Things Have Changed

HIGH SCHOOL DROPOUT RATES

Dropout rates have fallen among blacks to 18 percent but are still high among Hispanics: 43 percent. Across the population, the 15 percent of young adults who are high school dropouts face low earnings and high unemployment. Many high school students lack basic skills and perform below students in Japan, South Korea, the United Kingdom, and Spain, a situation that threatens future U.S. competiveness in the world economy.

national average. Many teenagers and some women, for example, are counted as unemployed if they are seeking a job while working as a student or housewife. Experienced women who regard employment as permanent have about the same unemployment rate as men. Similarly, teenagers who expect employment to be permanent have lower unemployment rates than students.

High turnover rates for teenagers may reflect the fact that they are changing jobs to achieve work experience and job advancement. They are more likely to go directly from one job to another without ever being unemployed. White-collar workers in clerical or supervisory jobs are less subject to cyclical fluctuations in employment than blue-collar workers.

Unemployment among blacks has been about twice that of whites for many years. However, when only experienced adult workers are considered, unemployment rates are almost the same for both races. Some of the difference that remains may be explained by job discrimination, although fair-employment

laws in the states and the Civil Rights Act of 1964 have helped reduce differences resulting from overt discrimination.

A SURPLUS OF LABOR? OR A SHORTAGE OF CAPITAL?

A careful reader of this chapter might think that once and for all we have solved the "economic problem"! Remember we began this text by pointing out that every nation faces the problem of scarce resources and unlimited wants. If there is substantial unemployment, might we conclude that we have too many resources?

A more correct conclusion would be that our supply of labor doesn't always match up with other available resources. Remember that labor resources must be used along with capital resources: improved land, buildings, equipment, and inventories. In fact, the average production worker in manufacturing works with invested capital worth more than $50,000. In some manufacturing industries, average invested capital per production worker is even higher: petroleum, $345,000; chemicals, $150,000; tobacco, $115,000. Non-manufacturing industries like transportation, utilities, finance, real estate, insurance, and mining require still higher levels of capital investment per worker.

The United States has been fortunate in the richness of our resource base. Production and incomes have been high, permitting high levels of saving for investing in capital resources. In the past half-century, real wealth has grown about 2.5 percent a year. Growth in capital resources has been slightly greater than growth in the labor force, providing more capital for each worker every year.

Nevertheless, our need for capital is increasing. New health, safety, and environmental regulations call for more costly capital equipment. Technological change has made some existing plant and equipment obsolete. If we are to employ our expanding work force in productive jobs, new investments must provide the necessary tools and equipment.

Over the years, investment spending in the United States has been fairly stable at 16 to 17 percent of GNP. (In the recession of 1982 the percentage dropped to 14 percent.) The level of new investment each year depends on business firms' expectations of profit opportunities. Conditions of recent years have made many business firms more pessimistic with respect to future profits:

1. Recessions and slow growth have left firms with unsold goods and increased the rate of business failures.
2. Inflated costs of materials and labor and the persistent threat of government price controls have reduced profit expectations.
3. Tax bills have risen faster than inflation and reduced savings available for investment.

4. New environmental and health regulations threaten to make new equipment obsolete in only a few years.

At the same time that profit expectations have been falling, the cost of borrowing has remained high. Interest charges have risen to compensate lenders for expected inflation. Government has been competing with business borrowers for a limited quantity of funds, driving interest rates up still further. Finally, many holders of funds prefer to use their savings to purchase safe, secure assets like raw land, jewels, works of arts, and gold. These purchases are not investments in the economic sense; that is, they are not capital resources capable of producing goods and services. Still, purchases like these reduce the savings available for true investment and keep interest rates on business loans high.

There is no single solution to the problem of insufficient growth of capital resources. An improved economic climate would probably improve business profit expectations. Greater confidence in government tax and regulatory policies would help, too. Without a substantial revival of private investment spending, the problem of unemployment becomes increasingly a govenment problem. Unfortunately, government may not have the answer!

EMPLOYMENT OPPORTUNITIES FOR THE FUTURE

Where are the greatest employment opportunities for young people entering the labor force in the 1990s? The demand for workers with particular skills or aptitudes will be high: professionals, technicians, managers, and clerical workers. Openings will grow more slowly in blue-collar fields.

Viewpoint

A FOUR-DAY WORKWEEK?

We have characterized our most severe unemployment problems as cyclical or structural. In practice, it may be difficult to separate these types of unemployed persons precisely. On the down side of the business cycle when production starts to fall, the first workers to lose their jobs are often blacks, teenagers, and women. Whereas this kind of unemployment would be described as cyclical, these are the workers who are also most subject to structural unemployment.

What is the best way to help these cyclically/structurally unemployed workers?

Some labor unions believe they have the answer. A new proposal being tested in some firms is a four-day workweek. A shorter workweek spreads the available work over more employees and reduces layoffs. In general, the proposed shorter workweek involves no cut in wages.

A five-day, 40-hour workweek has been the standard in manufacturing since the Fair Labor Standards Act was passed in the 1930s. In recent years, some firms have been experimenting with four ten-hour days as a means of reducing employee transportation costs. Other firms have cut hours to 32, with the hope that improved employee morale would bring on increased productivity. In many cases, this has not happened. In fact, labor costs have risen and forced up the prices of finished goods. Higher labor costs are the most serious disadvantage of the shorter workweek.

The United Auto Workers union was the first to sign a contract that comes close to a four-day workweek. Because spending for autos drops sharply in a business recession, auto workers are often the victims of cyclical/structural unemployment. In 1977 the United Auto Workers' contract provided for more than 40 paid vacation days a year, a major step toward the four-day week.

In general, business firms resist such a change. To establish the four-day standard throughout the economy would require a new labor law, not likely in the near future.

Some service fields such as state and local government, trade, and financial services will also be expanding. Shortages will appear for health personnel, general salespeople, and accountants.

Listed in Table 12.2 are some job categories with expected annual job openings in the 1990s. The projections are taken from a survey by the U.S. Department of Labor.

Table 12.2   Projected Annual Job Openings 1986–2000

Job	Number of Openings
Retail, trade, salespeople	85,786
Waiters, waitresses	53,714
Registered nurses	43,714
Building custodians	43,143
General managers and top executives	41,571
Cashiers	41,071
Truck drivers	37,500
General office clerks	33,071
Nurses' aides, orderlies	31,000
Stenographers, secretaries	30,286
Guards	27,357
Accountants	26,929
Computer programmers	23,857
Food preparation workers	23,143
Financial managers	21,560
Elementary-school teachers	21,357
Receptionists	20,143
Computer systems analysts	17,929
Cooks, chefs	17,071
Practical nurses	17,000
Maintenance repairers	16,500
First-line supervisors and managers	14,643
Electrical and electronic engineers	13,643
Lawyers	13,643
Carpenters	13,000
Secondary-school teachers	10,857
Computer operators	8,857
Social workers	8,571
Medical assistants	8,500
Radiologic technologists and technicians	5,357
Welders	−1,000
Private household workers	−2,714
Sewing machine operators	−6,571
Typists	−10,000
Farm workers	−13,571

SOURCE: *Statistical Abstract*, 1989.

SUMMARY

1. According to the classical economists, in a competitive market system unemployment would be only temporary. Wages would rise and fall with changes in the demand for and supply of labor, and all those willing to work at the equilibrium wage would be hired. Prices would fluctuate, too, so that real wages would not change as much as money wages.

2. Organized groups of employers and workers can interfere with the smooth adjustments under the market system. The result has been periods of unemployment with the sacrifice of goods and services that might have been produced. The loss of production from unemployment is called the GNP gap.

3. Frictional unemployment is a normal result of temporary idleness while changing jobs. Frictional unemployment may be relieved by policies to provide job information and to ease mobility into new types of employment.

4. Cyclical unemployment is associated with a decline in total spending. It is especially severe in industries producing durable goods, whose purchase can be postponed. Cyclical unemployment is treated by expansionary monetary and fiscal policies to stimulate total spending.

5. Structural unemployment results from an imbalance between the skills of the labor force and the jobs available in modern industry. This type of unemployment may be relieved by job counseling and training.

6. In recent years the problem of unemployment has worsened and has often been accompanied by inflation. The usual inverse relationship between unemployment and inflation is shown by the Phillips curve. Changing conditions within the economic system may have increased the levels of unemployment associated with every level of inflation.

7. Unemployment rates differ among different groups of workers. In general, however, experienced workers in their peak years of productivity have about the same rate of unemployment. Women and teenagers may enter and leave the labor force more often and

thus experience higher rates of unemployment. Blacks may suffer higher unemployment as a result of past discrimination.

8. Unemployment insurance helps workers maintain a moderate standard of living even while unemployed. Public-service employment provides jobs for the unemployed through the federal government. The nation's capital stock must grow if it is to provide jobs for an expanding labor force.

TERMS TO REMEMBER

GNP gap: the difference between actual production of goods and services and those that would have been produced at full employment

labor force: all people aged 16 and over who are currently employed or who are unemployed but actively seeking employment

frictional unemployment: unemployment caused by the movement of labor from job to job or the movement of new workers into the labor force; frictional unemployment is considered normal and desirable

cyclical unemployment: unemployment caused by a decline in economic activity with a drop in total spending; it is treated with expansionary fiscal and monetary policy

structural unemployment: unemployment caused by an imbalance between the structure of the labor force and the requirements of modern industry; it is treated with job training and counseling

Phillips curve: a graph showing the inverse relationship between price inflation and unemployment in years past

TOPICS FOR DISCUSSION

1. Define the following terms and discuss how each is involved in the problem of unemployment:

   GNP gap
   Phillips curve
   "natural rate" of unemployment

2. Distinguish clearly among the three types of unemployment and describe the types of policies designed to remedy each.

3. Under the Comprehensive Employment and Training Act of 1974, the federal government pumped millions of dollars into state and local programs for public-service employment. Thousands of new jobs were created for unemployed workers, veterans, and welfare recipients. Jobs were in public schools, libraries, parks, hospitals, and fire and police departments. Workers were given on-the-job training in skills that would help them eventually move into employment in the private sector.

   How does this program fit into our discussion of unemployment? What are the problems associated with programs of this kind?

4. Recessions typically create a conflict within the labor force over seniority rules. Labor union contracts protect the jobs of experienced members by a ''last hired, first fired'' rule. In many firms the last workers hired are the minorities who have recently won job opportunities under the Equal Employment Opportunity Act. The result is that women and blacks are more subject to layoffs and are less able to weather a long period of unemployment. This dilemma has sharply divided the labor movement, producing problems for labor leaders. How would you resolve the problem?

5. In the 1980s, large numbers of workers were added to the labor force as a result of the post-World War II ''baby boom.'' A substantial number of new jobs were created to absorb these workers and the many women and minority workers who were competing for employment opportunities. Today, many more college-trained workers are competing for the limited number of job openings requiring higher education. What are the social aspects of this problem? How might the new conditions change all our outlooks about what constitutes a successful life?

6. The classical economists believed that wage reductions would increase hiring. However, unions generally resist wage reductions. As a result, much of the government's employment

policy in recent decades has brought on higher *prices* rather than more jobs. How has this policy affected *real* wages? How has it affected profits? How might it stimulate employment? If unions refuse to allow wage gains to lag behind price increases, what will be the result?

7. Use the data below to calculate the real value of the minimum wage in the years shown.

YEAR	MINIMUM WAGE	PRICE INDEX ($1982)	REAL VALUE
1974	$2.00	54.0	_____
1977	$2.30	67.3	_____
1981	$3.35	94.0	_____
1989	$3.40	126.3	_____

8. Congress has been debating a day-care law that would provide low-cost, dependable child care for working mothers. How would you expect such a law to affect:

the labor force
the unemployment rate
the GNP gap.

9. Explain how the unemployment rate can fall at the same time that new job creation is slowing.

10. By the early 1990s, growth in the civilian labor force was slowing, with fewer teenagers and women entering the labor force. What effect will these changes have on the Phillips curve? What effect will an increase in "discouraged workers" have on the curve?

ANSWERS TO TEST YOURSELF
(p.279) Expansionary policies are appropriate in range 2, where unemployment is high and inflation low. Contrationary policies are appropriate in range 1, where inflation is high and unemployment low.

Chapter

Poverty and Income Distribution

or Poor Is a Four-Letter Word

Tools for Study

LEARNING OBJECTIVES

After reading this chapter, you will be able to:

1. Discuss the origins of our attitudes toward poverty.
2. Describe the extent and characteristics of the problem.
3. Define three kinds of poverty and discuss some remedies for each.
4. Discuss the advantages and disadvantages of direct financial assistance to the poor.

CURRENT ISSUES FOR DISCUSSION

Can the scientific method be applied to economic problems like poverty?

How successful have antipoverty programs been?

What's ahead for social security?

What are the causes and consequences of urban poverty?

There's a story told of a little Spanish town whose only distinction was its annual poetry contest. Eager contestants came from miles around to compete for recognition. For the winners, three prizes were awarded: Third prize was an artfully crafted silver rose; second prize, a dazzling golden rose; and first prize (can you guess it?) was a real rose.

Aside from its pleasing quaintness, the story allows us to compare value structures in different societies. First of all, a poetry contest would probably not receive much attention in our materialistic society. Also, most of us would certainly demand a different arrangement of awards!

We may conclude that standards of performance and reward differ sharply among people. The incidence of poverty depends to a large extent on these standards. Whatever the performance/reward structure that emerges in a particular society, it virtually ensures a poor status for people at the bottom.

THE SIZE AND SHAPE OF THE PROBLEM

In addition to cultural differences among nations, there are differences in the way poverty is defined. A family with a yearly income of $10,000 may be quite wealthy in a nation such as India but below the poverty line in the United States. In primitive societies, one's wealth may be based on the number of pigs or cattle one owns. (High social status has at various times and places been based on quality of penmanship, length of earlobes, skill in directing a javelin, and even the ability to detect a pea through a stack of mattresses!)

In the United States, a definition of poverty is established by the federal government, based on the estimated cost of a nutritionally sound diet. By the government's definition, a family is poor if its annual income is less than three times the amount necessary to purchase such a diet. The poverty level is adjusted each year for price changes, and it differs according to family size, sex of family head, and type of residence (farm or nonfarm). In 1990, the average poverty threshold for a nonfarm family of four was $12,700.

Table 13.1 gives a breakdown of persons below the government's poverty threshold in selected years. As the table shows, only about 11 percent of all persons in the nation were classified as poor in 1973, compared with 22 percent in 1959. In 1983, however, the poverty rate had risen above 15 percent. By 1988 it had fallen to 13 percent. Government "in-kind" benefits such as food stamps, public housing, and health care are not included in income when calculating the number of persons in poverty.

The decline in poverty in the United States is largely a result of economic growth. Improved labor skills and productivity and greater participation of wives in the labor force have increased earnings for many families. The greatest gains have been for nonwhite families with a male head. Regrettably, a large percentage of female-headed families continue to be classified as poor, particularly among nonwhite families.

When all low-income families are considered together, female-headed families constitute about half of poor families, even though the percentage of female-headed families in the population as a whole is only about 30 percent. Their higher poverty rate is probably because female heads of families often are not properly trained for employment or are prevented from seeking employment by the responsibility of caring for young children. Rural families and the aged also constitute a larger percentage of the poor than their percentage of the population as a whole.

More than one-fourth of heads of poor families work, but their wages are not enough to move them above the poverty level.* Lack of education and skills limits their employment opportunities to the shrinking number of unskilled jobs. Most of the poor are children, old people, or women—only a small percentage of the poor are able-bodied men.

CLASSIFICATIONS OF POVERTY

Poor families may be classified according to the reasons for their poverty. Then, appropriate remedies can be suggested to aid families in the various classifications.

*Working full time at the minimum wage would yield annual income of $7600, well below the poverty line for a nonfarm family of four in 1990.

Table 13.1   Families Below the Low-Income Level.

	1970	1975	1980	1985	1988
Percentage of all white families	8.0	7.7	8.0	9.1	7.9
Percentage of all nonwhite families	29.5	27.1	28.9	28.7	28.2
Percentage of all families with female head	32.5	32.5	32.7	34.0	33.5
Total number of persons (in millions)	25.4	25.9	29.3	33.1	31.9
Percentage of all persons in the nation	12.6	12.3	13.0	14.0	13.1

SOURCE: *Economic Report of the President,* February 1990

Contemporary Thinking about Economic Issues

CHANGES IN THE POVERTY POPULATION

From average annual growth of nearly 4 percent in the three decades following World War II, since 1973 median family income in the United States has experienced about a $\frac{1}{2}$ percent a year decline. (Median family income is the income of the middle family in the income scale and is distinguished from average family income, which may be distorted upward by the high incomes of a small fraction of families.) In real terms, the loss of income per family has been more than $150 per year and has been most severe for families with children. The loss occurred in spite of the fact that many women entered the work force during the period and the number of two-earner families with children increased.

Working for the Joint Economic Committee of the Congress, economists Sheldon Danziger and Peter Gottschalk conducted research into the incidence of poverty in the United States and changes in the poverty population over recent decades. They attributed the decrease in median family income to the poor performance of the economy as a whole. From an average annual growth of 3.4 percent between World War II and 1972, GNP growth has slowed to less than 3 percent.

Real wages and salaries per worker have fallen by almost 1 percent a year. Moreover, many second wage earners work less than full time at less than the median wage. Even after the economy's strong recovery from the 1981–1982 recession, average family income in 1984 was still below the 1973 level, making unlikely any tendencies toward redistribution to families at the lower end of the income scale. Both poverty and unemployment rates remain well above those of 1979. (Note: By 1988 the poverty rate had risen to 13.1 percent, from 11.7 percent, but unemployment had fallen to 5.3 percent, from 5.8 percent.)

The authors are concerned over the economic and social implications of the trend. It may call for an increase in the allocation of resources for the care and support of the nation's children. It may mean a dramatic change in the ability of families to achieve a middle-class lifestyle. It may also affect decisions to have children and to purchase homes.

Sheldon Danziger and Peter Gottschalk, "How Have Families with Children Been Faring?" Institute for Research on Poverty, The University of Wisconsin, January 1986. Paper prepared for the Joint Economic Committee of the Congress.

Business Cycle Poverty

Some families are temporarily poor because of cycles in the national economy. **Business cycle poverty** is the result of a low level of total spending for goods and services. When total spending drops, the demand for labor falls, throwing many unskilled and semiskilled workers out of work. The Great Depression of the 1930s and the long recessions of 1981–1983 pushed many families over the poverty line when the family wage earner was laid off.

Business cycle poverty may be helped by the use of expansionary fiscal and monetary policy to keep total spending high. Thus, whenever private spending falls short of the full employment level of aggregate demand, government might cut personal and corporate tax rates, increase spending for local or national projects, or expand the money supply to encourage business investment and increase employment.

Insular Poverty

Some families are trapped in islands of poverty when a particular industry or craft collapses and leaves workers with no other source of income. The most familiar examples of insular poverty have resulted from the decline of the coal-mining industry in Appalachia and the cutbacks in the auto industry in Detroit.

Insular poverty results from human immobilities—the difficulty of leaving familiar surroundings or abandoning a familiar trade to begin a new way of life. (For many families, five people to a room in a rural shack among family and friends is preferable to five people to a room in an urban slum, even if employment opportunities are somewhat greater in the city.)

Geographic pockets of poverty present a particularly difficult question, that is, whether to move new factories to the poverty areas or to move unemployed labor out to other industrialized areas. The first solution may be impractical from an economic standpoint. The second may run into human and social barriers.

One solution for workers whose jobs have become technically obsolete is retraining for jobs in growing sectors of the economy. The cost of retraining may be looked upon as an investment in worker productivity. (However, this too may run into human barriers, with many workers being reluctant to take on unfamiliar jobs.)

The Economic Development Act of 1965 and the Appalachian Regional Development Act of 1966 focused on area redevelopment in an effort to create new jobs. In 1974, the Comprehensive Employment and Training Act (CETA) began providing on-the-job training and work experience to Indians, migrants, and Job Corps participants. Efforts like these aim to correct insular poverty, but real gains have been slow. In 1981, the Reagan administration cut government job training programs as a means of reducing federal expenditures and slowing inflation.

Categorical Poverty

Some people are locked into poverty because of personal inadequacies that prevent them from functioning within our economic system. These poor people are classified according to categories including the physically and mentally handicapped, the emotionally unstable, the chronically ill or aged, and children.

Victims of **categorical poverty** require regular, dependable public assistance. Social workers must be trained to locate people in the various categories, inform them of the available aid, and administer special-purpose programs.

The categorical approach to public assistance originated with the Social Security Act of 1935. The social security program has

Viewpoint

DIFFERENT VIEWS OF POVERTY

In 1859, Charles Darwin published a revolutionary book on evolution called *On The Origin of Species*. The book explained Darwin's theory of *natural selection*, or survival of the fittest. According to the theory, nature "selects" the life forms that are best suited for carrying on the stream of life. Life forms that are weak and unable to adapt to the environment die out, so that only the strongest survive and reproduce.

Eventually some philosophers applied Darwin's theories about plants and lower animals to human society, creating a kind of "social Darwinism." Social Darwinism allowed its followers to oppose government aid to weak or incompetent persons. For government to sustain persons who cannot care for themselves, they said, is to interfere with the laws of nature.

Followers of social Darwinism found support for such cold-blooded ideas in their religious and political principles. The Puritan ethic supported the idea of self-sufficiency, independence, and individualism. Religious sects like the Calvinists felt little responsibility for the well-being of others, and they rejected the idea of a paternalistic government. Personal wealth came to be seen as a sign that the wealthy person was leading a life pleasing to God.

Democratic political theory also supported the idea of each individual's responsibility for his or her own life. A perfectly free and democratic society places no restrictions on economic or social gain.

In a democratic society everyone has unlimited opportunity to succeed (or to fail) according to his or her own abilities and effort.

With scientific and religious support, revolutions have been fought in the name of freedom and equality. Yet a disturbing contradiction has arisen: Individual freedom often creates a difference between equality of opportunity and equality of results. In fact, with individual freedom, equality of opportunity virtually guarantees inequality of results!

If all people have absolute freedom to pursue individual gain, the inevitable result is misery for the people who are least able to succeed. On the other hand, ensuring all people equal standards of living tends to destroy incentives to succeed and undermines the drive for achievement.

The Eastern European countries that are struggling to reform their economies are facing this contradiction. Their former Communist governments ensured them equal (but low) standards of living. Today the people are demanding freedom to achieve a better life. This very freedom, however, will impose a cost in terms of job losses and lower standards of living for those least able to succeed. The fear of poverty is causing some workers to oppose reform.

Citizens of Eastern European nations must ask themselves the following questions: Is it better to be equal and backward? Or is it better to be unequal and free?

two parts, an insurance part and a welfare part. The insurance part of the Social Security Act is the Old Age, Survivors, Disability, and Hospital Insurance (OASDHI) program. Regular contributions from workers and employers finance benefits provided under the workers' insurance program. Employers and employees each contribute 7.65 percent of earnings up to a certain level of income ($51,300 in 1990). For workers who have contributed to the program, benefits are based on past contributions rather than need.

The noninsurance or welfare part of social security makes payments to the needy whether or not they have paid in contributions to the social security program. One noninsurance program that is shared with state and local governments is Aid to Families with Dependent Children (AFDC). Other noninsurance aid is provided to the elderly, the blind, and the disabled under the Supplemental Security Income program (SSI).

In 1961, the federal food stamp program was put in place to provide further aid to needy families. Under the food stamp program, a family of four with no income receives about $200 in food stamps each month. Other poor families receive various amounts of food stamps, depending on their income during the month. Until 1977 recipients of food stamps paid a portion of their value. About 20 million people use food stamps annually at a cost to the government of more than $10 billion.

Total outlay of all public assistance programs in 1989 was more than $630 billion, more than half of which represented insured benefits under OASDHI.

A disadvantage of the categorical approach to poverty is the vast and costly bureaucracy it requires. Furthermore, there may be undesirable side effects for families receiving aid. The most serious side effect is the break-up of families, because AFDC is generally provided only to families without a father. Moreover, many poor people may not fit into any of the established categories. About half the nation's poor receive no public assistance of any kind. On the other hand, many nonpoor people may qualify for several categories and receive more than their fair share. Finally, the poor themselves object to categorical aid because they feel it is demeaning.

AID PROPOSALS

Objections to current aid programs have come from business leaders, sociologists, and economists from both extremes of the ideological spectrum. For example, Milton Friedman generally opposes government intervention in free markets. He has recommended eliminating all aid categories and providing grants to poor people solely on the basis of need.

Direct Grants

To raise the incomes of all poor families above the poverty threshold in 1989 would have required income transfers of less than $80 billion. This is only about 2 percent of GNP and less than the normal annual growth of GNP. (The $225 billion actually spent on public-assistance programs in 1989 could have been divided among the nation's 7 million poor families for a direct income grant of more than $32,000 for each family.)

Direct grants could be administered without establishing a new bureaucracy, perhaps through the existing Internal Revenue Service. Grants would be made in cash so that recipients could pay for food, housing, and health and social services in the open market. In this way, grants would provide economic incentives to business firms in the private sector. Direct grants would strengthen an individual's sense of responsibility to budget family income wisely. On the other hand, a disadvantage of direct financial assistance would be the social stigma often attached to the ''dole.''

With the exception of the United States and Japan, every industrialized nation now pays an allowance to all families, regardless of income. Under a progressive tax structure, some fraction of the total earned income plus family allowance is returned to the government in income taxes. Thus, at very low levels of income, a family keeps the entire family allowance. At some level of income the family allowance is just offset by income taxes; and at higher incomes, taxes exceed the family allowance.

The Negative Income Tax

Another remedy for poverty proposed by Milton Friedman is the negative income tax.* Friedman's proposal is based on the fact that a low-income family is unable to use certain tax advantages that are available to high income families.

Our tax schedule allows tax advantages in the form of exemptions amounting to $2000 per person and a standard deduction from taxable income of roughly $4550 per family. However, families whose income is too low to pay taxes are unable to use these tax advantages. Under a **negative income tax**, families earning less than the established level of tax exemptions and deductions would pay no tax. Instead, they would receive a negative tax or grant amounting to some percentage of the short-fall between their earned income and the agreed-on income floor.

For instance, a family of four would be entitled to total tax deductions and exemptions of roughly $12,550: (4 × $2000) + $4550 = $12,550. Families with incomes of less than $12,550 would receive some fraction

of the difference between their earned income and the $12,550 income floor. A family earning $4000, for instance, would pay no tax but receive a payment of, say, 50 percent of the family's unused tax deductions and exemptions: 0.5 ($12,550 − 4000) = 0.5(8550) = $4275. Thus, total family income would be $8275. The family's earnings could rise as high as $12,550 before aid would be cut off.

Both direct grants and a negative income tax would eliminate the need for the welfare bureaucracies that administer categorical aid. Experiments with direct income grants have been conducted in communities in New Jersey, Iowa, and North Carolina. Policymakers hope that the results will help them predict the likely effects of direct grants nationwide.

The Problem of Economic Incentives

The major disadvantage of public assistance programs is that they tend to destroy the incentive to make one's own way in life. Because we depend on human labor for a large portion of production, particularly in the growing service sector of our economy, the loss of incentives can be a real problem. The disincentive effect may be greatest under plans providing either direct grants or a negative income tax.

The reason is that if government makes up the entire difference between earned income and some income floor, there is little incentive for people to strive to increase their earnings. On the other hand, if government reduces aid dollar for dollar as earned income increases, it destroys incentives to increase earnings. In this case, government is, in effect, collecting a 100 percent tax on additional income.

The disincentive effect of the negative income tax can be reduced by reducing the tax rate on the earned portion of income. A low tax rate would allow a worker to earn addi-

*The current earned income tax credit for poor families is a kind of negative income tax.

tional income without losing an equal amount of government aid. Total income could rise above the guaranteed floor before financial assistance would be cut off. A low tax rate would increase the cost of the program, at least in the short run. However, it might also strengthen economic incentives and help relieve critical shortages of low-skilled workers.

Another, less substantial, objection to direct financial assistance is that simply making payments to poor families does nothing to correct the basic causes of poverty. This criticism implies that we can identify and deal directly with the specific characteristics that make people poor. It is not clear that this is true. Furthermore, it was our attempt to deal with the specific characteristics of poor people that led to the costly welfare bureaucracy we now employ.

The Problem of Inflation

Direct financial assistance may lead to a problem more difficult to handle than poverty—the problem of inflation. Unless funds paid to poor families come from tax revenues, there will be a net increase in disposable income. A net increase in disposable income means increased demand for goods and services. If total production fails to increase, there will be inflation, as larger amounts of consumer spending compete for a constant quantity of goods and services.

The threat of inflation makes it important to build incentives into financial assistance programs so as to encourage increased worker productivity. Research and training programs and investment tax credits may also be a way to encourage increased productivity.

WHAT CAN WE CONCLUDE?

The fact is that we really don't know enough about poverty and its causes to simply solve the problem. Without a simple solution, we must fall back on a combination of partial solutions: programs to improve health and nutrition for children and expectant mothers, educational and vocational training for disadvantaged workers, income-support payments and child-care programs, and emergency relief for unemployed workers. To be successful, these programs must be carried on within a climate of increasing production and equality of opportunity.

A chief disadvantage of any program is its initial cost. Also, it is unlikely that there will be measurable results in any short period of time. One of the characteristics of the American approach to problems is excessive optimism at the start of a new program. Often, highly publicized expectations fail to come true immediately, and disillusionment sets in. As a result, many programs are abandoned prematurely, before a legitimate trial period has elapsed.

Viewpoint

DISCRIMINATION

A major cause of poverty is discrimination: discrimination in access to education or housing and discrimination in employment. Discrimination arises when people are treated differently on some basis other than their individual merit. Discrimination frequently affects blacks and women. One result of discrimination is low-status jobs of low productivity with low earnings and few opportunities for advancement.

Sometimes discrimination is the result of prejudice on the part of an employer, landlord, or school administrator. Although laws prohibit these forms of discrimination, the laws are not fully enforced. Sometimes what appears to be discrimination in employment is really only the result of discrimination in educational opportunities, which makes some workers more productive than others. Sometimes discrimination is actually self-imposed, when blacks or women unconsciously place limits on their own aspirations.

During the 1960s strong federal laws were passed forbidding discrimination on the basis of race, color, religion, sex, national origin, or age. In response to the new laws, many schools and business firms established "affirmative action" programs, seeking members of groups formerly subject to discrimination. In many cases, institutions have reevaluated their admission or hiring standards and eliminated requirements that do not directly affect a potential employee's qualifications for a job.

In spite of such efforts, significant evidence of discrimination remains. Women and blacks are poorly represented in highly paid occupations like business management and production, and they are overrepresented in low-paid occupations like clerical and service work. In every occupation the median income of women is barely half the median income of male workers in the same occupation. One result of low earnings is that one-third of female-headed families and one-third of black families have incomes below the poverty level. For black female-headed families the fraction is more than one-half. Women and blacks experience substantially higher unemployment than average—up to two or three times unemployment rates for white male workers.

Discrimination harms us all, whether or not we are ourselves targets of discrimination. When workers are unable to compete freely in the labor market, labor costs are kept artificially high. Higher labor costs raise the prices of many things we buy. When workers are deprived of educational or job opportunities, our economy fails to develop its human resource capabilities to the fullest. Total output is less than it might be. When workers' incomes are held artificially low, they cannot buy the goods and services our business firms produce. Profits and economic growth are lower as a result.

Can you cite specific examples of the harmful effects of discrimination?

Self-Check

1. **Poor people in the United States:**
   a. Constitute about 25 percent of the population.
   b. Consist mainly of able-bodied men.
   c. Include only unemployed people.
   d. Are concentrated in industrial areas.
   e. None of the above.

2. **Which of the following is treated primarily by categorical aid programs?**
   a. Cyclical poverty.
   b. Insular poverty.
   a. The aged poor.
   d. All of the above.
   e. None of the above.

3. **Which of the following is a disadvantage of a program of direct grants?**
   a. Direct grants reduce the need for a large bureaucracy.
   b. Direct grants give the poor money to spend as they see fit.
   c. Taxes take the entire grant away as earnings rise.
   d. Direct grants do not deal with the real causes of poverty.
   e. Direct grants abolish categorical types of aid.

4. **Which of the following is not a danger of direct grants or the negative income tax?**
   a. There is a possibility of reducing incentives.
   b. Increased incomes may contribute to inflation.
   c. Some poor people would not receive aid.
   d. There may be a social stigma attached to aid.
   e. Many social workers may become unemployed.

5. **Which of the following terms is paired incorrectly?**
   a. Insular poverty—Appalachian Redevelopment Act.
   b. Cyclical poverty—expansionary fiscal policy.
   c. Categorical poverty—Aid to Families with Dependent Children.
   d. Cyclical poverty—contractionary monetary policy.
   e. Categorical poverty—Social Security Act.

Theory in Practice

PROBLEMS IN APPLYING THE SCIENTIFIC METHOD

The scientific method of investigation requires that any problem be examined in systematic steps:

1. First define the problem. One of the most baffling problems in economics is the problem of poverty.
2. Second, gather data describing and measuring the problem.
3. Organize the data and pose an hypothesis, or a theory that explains the behavior of the data.

4. Test the hypothesis by changing certain data within the problem (while holding the other data constant) and noting whether the results of the change support the hypothesis.
5. Continue to alter the hypothesis until the results of changing certain data do in fact support the hypothesis. The hypothesis is finally accepted if it can be used to predict the actual results of a change in the data. Finally, the hypothesis can be stated as a scientific law or principle that explains the problem under investigation.

   In economic analysis, we would add another step to the scientific method. The practical goal of economic analysis is to prescribe policy to correct the problem under investigation.

Problems of Designing Policy

Economic analysis suffers from a disadvantage not encountered in scientific analysis. It is much more difficult to test hypotheses in an economic system than in a scientific laboratory. To test an economic hypothesis, for instance, may require changes in government tax and spending policies (all the while holding other things in the economic environment constant). Needless to say, such changes are more difficult to accomplish than merely changing the temperature in a chemistry laboratory. For this reason, many economic theories (or hypotheses) cannot be tested to produce definite results and clear policy remedies.

This is especially true of the problem of poverty. There is no scientific law or principle to explain the problem. Consequently, there is no single policy that is clearly acceptable as a cure.

Over the past several decades a variety of government programs have been put in place to deal with poverty. Their objectives have been humanitarian as well as economic. Evaluating the results of these programs may be considered a form of hypothesis testing. Thus, a successful program may be assumed to have been based on a correct explanation of the causes of poverty. Lack of success would suggest an incorrect explanation of the roots of the problem.

Unfortunately, it is difficult to evaluate results even when a program appears successful. Many forces other than the particular government program may be operating on the problem at one time. A decrease in poverty may be the result not of government policies but of increased economic growth or better education and health care. Thus, even if a program appears successful, it is impossible to prove whether success is the result of the program alone or of some other outside influence.

An Example

Aid to Families with Dependent Children (AFDC) illustrates the difficulty of designing a program when scientific analysis and control are not possible. The original purpose of AFDC was to assist families when the father was unable to support them because of death or disability. In the beginning, about 75 percent of the families involved fit this classification. The remainder had fathers who were absent through divorce, separation, or desertion.

The availability of benefits under AFDC, however, had the unintended effect of encouraging fathers to desert their families. As a result, the number of families receiving AFDC is now five times the number receiving aid in 1950. The 3 million families now receiving aid under AFDC constitute almost 6 percent of the nation's population.

How can we deal with the problem of desertion and nonsupport by the fathers of these families? Extending benefits to families with an unemployed father is the approach used by about half the states. However, this approach increases the cost of the program considerably.

Another problem with AFDC involves the work status of the mother. Originally, the program's intent was to enable mothers to care for their children without having to work outside the home. Because benefits were reduced dollar for dollar with outside income, the result was to reduce the mother's incentive to find outside employment. Work incentives were added to the program in 1967. Now a working mother loses less in AFDC benefits for each dollar earned. She is also eligible for

How Things Have Changed.

SHARES OF INCOME (%) GOING TO THE WEALTHIEST TAX UNITS

Year	Top 1%	Top 5%	Top 10%	Top 15%	
1948	9.8	20.2	27.9	34.3	Look down the columns to
1952	8.7	18.7	26.7	33.4	understand changes in the
1963	8.8	19.4	28.2	35.5	distribution of before-tax
1967	8.8	19.6	28.3	35.5	income in recent years.
1972	8.0	18.7	27.8	35.4	
1977	7.8	18.9	28.3	36.1	
1981	8.1	19.0	28.6	36.5	
1986	14.7	26.6	36.8	45.1	

SOURCE: *Brookings Review, Spring* 1990.

job training and counseling and publicly supported child care under the Work Incentive Program. Still, only about one-sixth of the mothers receiving AFDC are employed.

Without controlled experiments to test the results of various aid programs, it is not possible to predict all the effects. When results are unfavorable, new approaches must be tried. However, new programs are costly and frequently require new or expanded bureaucracies. All of this suggests that the problem of poverty may remain with us, despite our sincere efforts to correct it.

WHAT HAS BEEN ACCOMPLISHED?

Average levels of living in the Western world have improved regularly since the Industrial Revolution. For the last several centuries, real purchasing power per capita has doubled about every 40 years.

Absolute and Relative Poverty

Absolute poverty is a condition below a certain income level described as the poverty level. In the United States, the percentage of families subject to absolute poverty has fallen by about half since 1959.

While absolute poverty has fallen, there has been little change in relative poverty. **Relative poverty** refers to the proportional shares of income going to various income groups. Relative income shares have remained roughly stable, suggesting that there has been no significant trend toward equality of incomes over at least the last 30 years.

In fact, when all U.S. families are ranked according to income and divided into fifths, we discover that the shares of total income going to each fifth have remained roughly the same in recent decades. Table 13.2 shows the shares of income before taxes for families in selected years since 1947.

Table 13.2   Shares of Aggregate Income (%) Before Taxes Received by Each Fifth of Families, Ranked by Income.

	1947	1950	1960	1966	1972	1981	1984	1987
Lowest fifth	5.1	4.5	4.8	5.6	5.4	5.0	4.7	5.1
Second fifth	11.8	11.9	12.2	12.4	11.9	11.3	11.0	11.6
Third fifth	16.7	17.4	17.8	17.8	17.5	17.4	17.0	17.5
Fourth fifth	23.2	23.6	24.0	23.8	23.9	24.4	24.4	24.3
Highest fifth	43.3	42.7	41.3	40.5	41.4	41.9	42.9	41.6
Top 5%	17.5	17.3	15.9	15.6	15.9	15.4	16.0	15.3

SOURCES: *Economic Report of the President*, February 1974, *A Guide to Consumer Markets, 1977/78*, and *Statistical Abstract of the U.S.*, 1979, 1980, 1985, 1986 and 1989.

The lowest fifth of families still receive about 5 percent of total income and the highest fifth, more than 40 percent. (The share of the top 5 percent has fallen slightly.) Translated into dollar amounts, in 1987 this meant that the lowest fifth were those families with incomes of less than $14,450; the second fifth had incomes of $14,450 to $25,100; the third fifth, $25,100 to $36,600; the fourth fifth, $36,600 to $52,910; and the top fifth, more than $52,910. The top 5 percent had incomes of more than $86,300.*

The Lorenz Curve

A useful tool for comparing income shares is the **Lorenz curve.** The Lorenz curve is drawn in a square as in Figure 13.1. The horizontal axis measures percentage of families, ranked according to income. The vertical axis measures percentage of income before taxes. As you move from 0 to 100 percent along either axis, percentages are cumulative. That is, values are associated with the lowest 20 percent, the lowest 40 percent, the lowest 60 percent, and so forth.

The diagonal line across the square is a reference line. It associates equal percentages

of the values along the axes and represents perfect equality of income distribution. For example, point *A* on the diagonal represents the condition where the lowest 20 percent of families receives 20 percent of income; point *B* represents the condition where the lowest 80 percent of families receives 80 percent; and so forth.

If the actual graph of income shares corresponds to the diagonal, then income is distributed precisely equally. To the extent

Figure 13.1   A Lorenz Curve Showing Distribution of Income (1947).

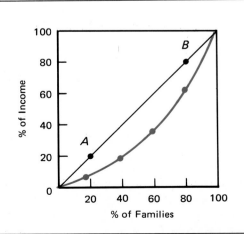

*The disparity of income is aggravated by the fact that the distribution of wealth is also uneven.

Figure 13.2   Relative Income Shares in the United States.

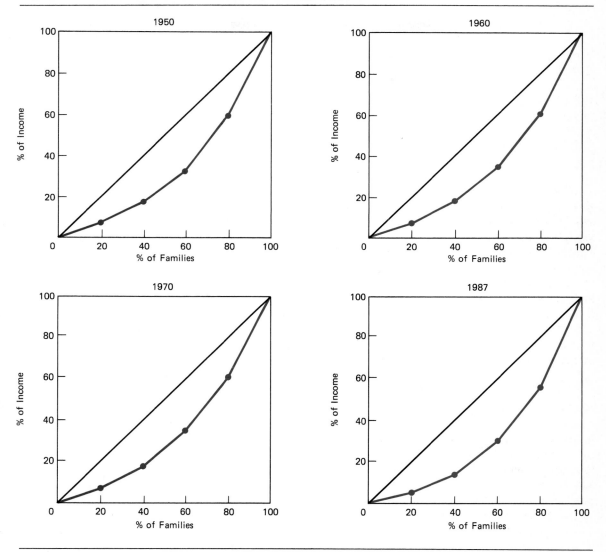

that the actual graph deviates from the diagonal, income is distributed unequally.

The Lorenz curve in Figure 13.1 tells us that the lowest fifth of incomes received about 5 percent of income. The lowest 80 percent received slightly more than 50 percent. This means that the top fifth of families received

more than 40 percent. Put another way, the top fifth of families received more than eight times as much income as the bottom fifth.

Figure 13.1 illustrates income distribution in the United States in 1947. Lorenz curves for the years 1950, 1960, 1970, and 1987 are shown in Figure 13.2. As you can see, the curves have moved somewhat closer to the reference line over the years, but there has been no significant reduction in inequality.

Some Conclusions

We may conclude that absolute poverty has fallen in the United States, along with advancing technology and increased productivity. Still, there has been no significant decrease in relative poverty in recent years.

The greatest reductions in relative poverty probably took place in the early decades of this century. Antitrust laws, the growth of the labor movement, and greater opportunities for education and training in new expanding industries had the effect of reducing the relative advantages of the upper fifth of families. The trend toward equality has slowed in recent decades, although antidiscrimination laws are now helping resume the trend.

WHAT'S AHEAD FOR SOCIAL SECURITY?

Social security has been the mainstay of public assistance programs in the United States since 1935. Social security trust funds receive tax payments from workers and employers, and each month the Social Security Administration sends checks to about 36 million retired persons, orphans, widows, and disabled persons.

In the 1980's, contributions to social security fell below benefits paid, and the Social Security Administration had to dip into its emergency trust fund. There are several reasons for the shortfall. Retired persons are living longer these days and drawing larger benefits, and Congress has adjusted benefits upward to correct for the effects of inflation.

To correct the shortfall, Congress legislated an increase in the social security tax rate and an increase in the income base to which the tax is applied. The result was to increase social security tax revenues substantially above annual benefits paid. Thus, in 1989 the surplus added to the social security trust fund amounted to more than $50 billion.

By law, the social security trust fund must be invested in U.S. government securities, so the social security surplus was used to finance the deficit of the federal government as a whole. Some time in the future when the securities are redeemed to pay benefits, the federal government must replace the funds either by increasing taxes, reducing spending, or increasing borrowing.

Probably the major reason for concern about social security is a change in the composition of the U.S. population. Families are having fewer children, so that in the future fewer new workers will enter the labor force each year relative to the numbers of dependent persons who will begin receiving income-support payments. The current ratio is about three taxpaying workers for every dependent person receiving benefits, but the ratio is expected to fall to about 2 to 1 by the year 2030.

If the Social Security Administration has difficulty meeting its obligations to beneficiaries, some changes may be necessary. One possibility would be to reduce the benefits paid. The trend, however, has been to increase benefits in order to offset the effects of inflation, to add new beneficiaries, and to include health benefits in the program. Many recipients of social security are totally dependent on their monthly check. At present the average monthly benefit is about $550 for a worker retiring at age sixty-five. It is difficult to imagine cutting these meager benefits.

Another way would be to increase taxes on employed workers. The current rate is 7.65 percent of earnings up to an income of $51,300 (as of 1990), for a maximum tax per worker of $3924.45 each year. (An equal amount is collected from each worker's employer.)

A problem with raising the tax rate is that social security taxes are regressive. Remember that a regressive tax takes a higher percentage of low incomes than high incomes. Therefore, many lawmakers oppose making the tax more regressive by raising the tax rate without also raising the income level on which the tax is paid.

Some economists have proposed doing away with the social security tax altogether and paying benefits from federal income tax revenues. This plan would require an increase in income tax rates, but the change would be toward greater progressivity in the tax structure as a whole. An alternative plan would be to move only hospital benefits out of the social security program and into the general revenue portion of the federal budget. This would leave all social security funds for payment to social security beneficiaries.

There is still another possibility. Raising the retirement age would enable many healthy workers to continue to pay into the trust fund and might reduce the benefit payments ultimately required. The problem with this is that younger workers frequently urge older workers to retire and open up job opportunities to new workers on the way up.

More changes in the social security program will undoubtedly come soon. Social security touches almost every one of us: either through taxes paid, benefits received, or benefits provided to our dependents. This makes it especially important to develop the best solution to its funding problems, preferably before they become a crisis.

LIVING POOR IN THE CITY

It used to be that poverty was mostly a rural problem. Tarpaper shacks dotted the rural landscape on farms hardly productive enough to supply minimum family needs. Today poverty is increasingly an urban problem. The evidence is aging and overcrowded tenement buildings, crime and decay in urban neighborhoods. Frustration with urban poverty has probably contributed to the problem of drug abuse among idle and bitter urban youths.

The trend began half a century ago. New technology and scientific farming forced small, inefficient farmers off the land and replaced them with modern machinery. A steady flow of new job seekers moved into the cities. Often these displaced farm workers were poorly educated and ill prepared for work in industry. Unable to find jobs, they were unable to provide their children the attitudes and skills needed for success in a modern economic system. New generations of poor people have continued to develop in a worsening spiral.

Other causes were also significant. In the past, factories processed goods through the **gravity-flow method:** raw materials were first processed on the top floor of a tall building and then dropped through a chute for successive stages of processing on lower floors. In contrast, modern factories use the **assembly-line method** of production, which requires them to be spread out over large continuous spaces. Whereas the older factories could be built in cities, urban land is too costly for the new assembly-line factories. Therefore, manufacturing plants have moved to the outskirts of the cities, far from the homes of urban dwellers. The urban poor frequently lack the transportation facilities for traveling to jobs far from the central city.

The increasing population of poor people has imposed a severe financial burden on city governments. Poor people need more police and fire protection, more emergency medical care, more specialized educational facilities—all costly to local governments. To make matters worse, the inflow of poor people has been accompanied by an outflow of middle-income taxpayers in search of more pleasant and less costly living in the suburbs. The out-migration of its middle-income tax base has been a severe problem for many cities.

Some policies of the federal government have worsened the problem of urban poverty. Since the 1930s, the federal government has subsidized mortgage loans for middle-income home buyers. It has subsidized the building of highways for low-cost commuting into the city. It has neglected some projects like mass transportation that would benefit the poor. Finally, a large part of federal grant funds is paid to state governments. Central city residents tend to be underrepresented in state governments, which tend to be more strongly influenced by voters in affluent towns and suburbs. The result is a tendency to use federal money for projects that do not directly help the urban poor.

The problem is complex. Current poverty programs tend to focus on particular poor people but do little to correct the problem as a whole. Some new ideas have been proposed to deal with the problem of urban poverty: Examples are subsidized housing for the poor in suburban neighborhoods; compensatory education and skill development programs for urban youths; increased federal aid to city governments; and rigorous enforcement of antidiscrimination laws in hiring.

Michael Harrington has concluded that American society is becoming two separate societies, with poor people increasingly set apart from the mainstream of American life. The division of society is destructive to the principles on which our nation was founded. It is also wasteful of the potential output the poor could be producing and consuming as full participants in our economic system.

SUMMARY

1. A society's standards of performance and value will determine priorities of rewards in which some groups will have low status. The value structure of any society virtually ensures that those at the bottom will be poor.
2. Poverty is classified as business cycle poverty, insular poverty, or categorical poverty. Business cycle poverty is best remedied by policies to stabilize total spending. Insular poverty is associated with isolated, depressed industries or regions. It may be treated by job training and relocation of workers. Categorical poverty requires public assistance to persons who are unable to function in our economic system.
3. The Social Security Act of 1935 provides for insurance payments to the aged, dependent, disabled, and unemployed and relief payments to the needy. A large portion of public relief goes to Aid to Families with Dependent Children (AFDC).
4. Administration of public assistance is costly, involves undesirable side effects, and may fail to achieve its intended objectives. Some proposed alternatives to current public assistance programs include direct grants to all families and the negative income tax. However, the problem of reduced incentives among recipients plagues all public assistance programs.
5. It is difficult to apply the scientific method to economic problems. This means we have no precise explanation for poverty and no clear policy remedies. Also, because many factors affect the economic environment, it is difficult to evaluate a program's success in relieving poverty.
6. Although absolute levels of living have advanced fairly regularly since the Industrial Revolution, there is still marked inequality of income in the United States. Relative shares of

income have remained roughly the same since 1947.

7. Social security legislation must be amended soon to deal with the problem of an increasing dependent population. Proposed changes include cutting benefits and raising taxes.

8. The increase in urban poverty has strained the resources of local governments and calls for new policy approaches.

TERMS TO REMEMBER

business cycle poverty: poverty that results from the lack of jobs during a business recession or depression

insular poverty: poverty that results when islands of depressed economic activity appear following the collapse of a particular craft or industry

categorical poverty: poverty among particular groups who are unable to function in our economic system

direct grants: cash payments to increase the incomes of families

negative income tax: a payment to families whose earned income is less than the level of allowed income tax credits

Lorenz curve: a graph showing a nation's income distribution

TOPICS FOR DISCUSSION

1. Distinguish clearly between each of the following pairs of terms:

Equality of opportunity and equality of results
Categorical aid and direct grants
Absolute poverty and relative poverty

2. Explain the basis of the three major classifications of poverty. What policy recommendations would you propose for dealing with each? Give specific instances of each kind of poverty and specific programs that have been used to remedy them.

3. What are the similarities and differences between scientific analysis and economic analysis?

4. Minimum-wage legislation is usually defended as a means of relieving the plight of the poor. However, it may actually work against the poor. Explain.

5. Consider the dilemma of a low-skilled worker. If the legal minimum wage is kept low, he or she may find it more beneficial not to work and to draw welfare payments. If the legal minimum wage is raised, the worker may be unemployable because his or her skills do not justify paying the higher wage. Keeping welfare benefits low increases the misery of the poor, but raising them reduces economic incentives and raises the burden to the taxpayer. Do you see any hope for resolving this problem in the future? Can you design a statistical study for evaluating the effects on incentives of various changes in welfare payments and the minimum wage?

Chapter

Economic Growth

or Those Who Ride the Tiger Dare Not Dismount

LEARNING OBJECTIVES

After reading this chapter, you will be able to:

1. Discuss the origins of our attitudes toward economic growth.
2. Describe growth trends in GNP and explain how growth takes place.
3. Discuss the problems that face a mature economic system and some possible problems resulting from growth.
4. Explain the sectoral and export-base theories of growth and describe how they affect the choice of growth policy.

CURRENT ISSUES FOR DISCUSSION

What are we doing to promote growth of production possibilities?

How can we make sure the advantages of growth outweigh the disadvantages?

What can be done about the world food shortage?

John Stuart Mill, a leading economist of the nineteenth century, is said to have read Greek literature by the age of eight. I blush to admit that one of the most memorable literary experiences of my own childhood was a little book called *Pigs Is Pigs*.

The story concerned a controversy between a clerk at the post office and the recipient of a package through the mail. The package contained a pair of guinea pigs, and the controversy centered on the amount of postage due, which the recipient refused to pay. During the course of the dispute, the family of guinea pigs grew and grew—and *grew* and *grew*. The postal clerk became the guardian of a flock ballooning out of control.

The story suggests the conflicting feelings with which we might view economic growth. Are we sure we want economic growth? Do the benefits of growth outweigh the potential costs? What are the sources of growth and what are the consequences? Finally, can we manage growth so as to enjoy its benefits and reduce its costs?

GROWTH AND GNP

In the United States, the drive toward growth has always been strong and has been fed by seemingly endless supplies of land and material resources for our exploitation. Together these influences made our efforts toward growth a success. Seeking a simple and direct way to measure our success, the United States developed the measure known as GNP. (We named the wild cards after we had seen our hand!)

Growth Trends

GNP provides a relatively simple way to measure trends in material production. Over the period for which comparable data are available, both total and per capita GNP have risen fairly steadily. Since 1929, growth has averaged about 4 percent a year, slowing during periods of recession and speeding up in recovery. (You may want to refer back to Table 7-2 for actual data on GNP.)

GNP will tend naturally to grow as more and more production is carried on for exchange in the market. GNP grows as Grandpa's vegetable garden, the neighborhood sewing circle, and the live-in maiden aunt (whose value cannot be determined and, therefore, is not included in GNP) are replaced by the commercial farm, the clothing factory, and the nursery school.

In recent years, the decline of the traditional male-headed household has pushed many females into jobs outside the home. This has also had the effect of raising the level of GNP by the value of female workers' production.

Some Limitations on the Use of GNP

In spite of regular increases in the market value of GNP, it is not clear that it reflects how much better we live than in earlier times. GNP measures the quantity, but not always the quality, of our production. A popular journalist once complained that the strawberries available at the supermarket (included in GNP) are not nearly as tasty as those his grandmother used to raise in her garden (not included in GNP). However, that same journalist showed no inclination to plow up his own yard and spend hours bent over a strawberry patch. Apparently he was willing to give up a little home-grown flavor so that he could work in his chosen profession by day and enjoy professional sports in the evening (included in GNP, by the way).

GNP leaves out some valuable goods—and some unpleasant "bads"—that our economic system produces. Adding all the goods and subtracting the "bads" would make the measure more correct. The "bads" include the change in the environment (such as water pollution) that are not deducted from the value of goods produced but that certainly reduce the quality of our lives. (The discussion of net economic welfare in Chapter 7 treats this topic in more detail.)

Some Predictions

The National Bureau of Economic Research in Cambridge, Massachusetts, has studied recent growth trends in the United States and made some projections of future growth. After World War II, and especially in the 1960s, the United States experienced a tremendous growth in production. Growth was partly a result of the "baby boom," which increased labor resources about 2 percent annually. Technological progress added another 2 percent to production, bringing on an average increase in real output of almost 4 percent a year.

Since the 1960s, population growth has slowed and was closer to 1 percent per year in the 1980s. As a result of slower population growth, we may notice a significant decrease in demand for such goods as autos, furniture, household appliances, and clothing during the 1990s. Along with the decrease in consumer demand, we may expect production to grow more slowly and unemployment in certain industries to rise.

HOW DOES GROWTH TAKE PLACE?

What determines the growth rate of GNP? Any economic system, whether primitive or advanced, has potential GNP limited by:

Viewpoint

WHY GROWTH?

Why has the drive toward higher and higher levels of growth been so strong in the United States? Why have we promoted growth so enthusiastically?

Some say the drive for material wealth originated with the inferior status of our ancestors in the Old World. People who were denied social status because they were born into the lower classes often looked for other routes to advancement: first commerce, then industry and finance. The New World offered plentiful resources for new settlers to use in overcoming the challenges of the environment, and it promised rewards in the form of rising social status.

Historian Arnold Toynbee believed that civilizations grow through challenge and reward. The correct balance between challenge and reward produces the incentives necessary for achievement. According to Toynbee, individuals are frustrated by insurmountable challenges, and they are weakened by excessive re-

wards. However, the appropriate challenge and reward will encourage work and effort. Fortunately, in the United States an appropriate balance between challenge and reward has helped us achieve rising levels of living.

Others say our philosophy of growth originated with the Protestant religion. The Catholic church of the Middle Ages regarded material greed as sinful, but the Protestant church thought idleness was a worse sin. It encouraged Protestants to work hard and save their money. The result was fairly steady growth in the production of material goods. In Protestantism, personal wealth became associated with righteousness.

Perhaps the best reason we have stressed economic growth has been our rapidly increasing population. Unless our people are satisfied with smaller shares of food, clothing, and the comforts of life, production must grow at least as fast as population.

1. The quantity and quality of its human and material resources.
2. Its level of technology.
3. The system through which it organizes its resources for production.

The Importance of Saving and Investment

To understand the relationship between growth and resources, consider a simple par-

able. Imagine a South Pacific island whose workers can produce a certain quantity of fish to feed their families. Total production on the island will grow as the number of workers grows, but per capita GNP may not grow at all.

At some point, assume that some of the island's workers agree to give up fishing for the day in order to build a boat for trips to richer fishing grounds. In effect, these workers have agreed to save a day's labor in order to invest in a capital resource. They have

saved by not consuming a day's production, and they have **invested** by building capital equipment that will enable them to be more productive in the future.

This parable illustrates the simple truth that saving and investment require sacrifice. Sacrifice is possible, however, only if the necessary food for sustaining life is easily obtained. It is possible only if the community is living beyond the bare, subsistence level.

More Capital Resources

With its new capital resource, our island community can expand its output of fish more rapidly. With fewer workers needed to catch fish, the rest will be free to develop still more capital resources, and the community will experience even greater economic growth. New goods and services can be produced to enhance the quality of life. Ultimately, surplus labor may be diverted to less essential work—such as the production of leisure goods and recreation.

Human and material resource supplies may continue to grow under these favorable conditions, and technical knowledge may continue to advance. Producing essential goods will continue to require fewer workers, and still more workers will be released for other activities.

PROBLEMS OF
THE MATURE ECONOMY

In his *Stages of Economic Growth* Walt Whitman Rostow described how a primitive economy grows. First the community must develop the necessary *preconditions* for growth: basic health and education and a general sense of striving among workers to improve their status in life. With these preconditions the economy may experience a takeoff

into industrial development. New investments in transportation facilities and electric power will make possible the growth of manufacturing industries. New manufacturing industries will call for the development of supplying industries, and higher incomes will call for the development of consumer goods industries. Healthy growth will continue until finally the economic system reaches maturity.

Having successfully reached maturity, it would seem that an economic system would be "home free." Regrettably, more perplexing problems remain for the mature economy—in particular, the problem of ensuring the fullest possible employment of available human resources. Full employment depends on sufficient demand for the goods and services a fully employed labor force can produce.

In a mature economy, each family will already own all the durable goods necessary for ensuring a comfortable life. When their desire for new goods and services stops growing, the growth of new jobs will slow as well. Rostow warned that a fully mature eonomic system might have to choose one of three courses if it is to employ all its human and materials resources:

1. The nation may encourage population growth so that it will need more baby carriages, schools, houses, and so forth.
2. It may engage in aggression so that it will need military vehicles, food and supplies for military personnel, and explosives for destroying buildings and equipment (which will then require replacement, relieving the nation's unemployment problems far into the future).
3. Or the nation may use idle human resources to produce public goods (instead of more private goods): things like universities, public parks, hospitals, cultural centers, and urban services.

Vance Packard, a popular critic of the American scene, once jokingly suggested another plan for dealing with the problem of unemployment in a mature economic system. He proposed that factories be designed so that the ends of assembly lines could be swung either to loading platforms in the front or to the rear doors overhanging deep ravines. The output of assembly lines could then be either loaded on trucks for delivery to consumers or pushed into the gorge! (Reckless waste already approaches this ideal in some manufacturing operations.)

Packard also suggested (as far back as 1960) that rockets might be constructed periodically and equipped with specialized equipment to be shot out into space. The announced objective might be to acquire scientific information about the back side of Neptune's moon. Vast quantities of human resources could be employed and there would be no need to sell their output to anyone!

Lacking sufficient high-employment/low-output projects of this type, American industry has turned to the task of persuading consumers to want more and more things. Through advertising, consumers are persuaded to change their fashions and habits of life often and, in this way, to keep the factory wheels turning.* Some goods are designed specifically to break down or go out of style, so that they must be replaced.

One unfortunate result is the decline of tasteful design. The only way to ensure that consumers will become dissatisfied with this year's model is to design it with built-in crudities of some kind. Next year's model will feature crudities of the opposite extreme, making this year's model obsolete.

---

*Not all advertising has this objective, of course. Advertising is often necessary to inform consumers of the characteristics of available goods and services.

AN END TO GROWTH?

An eighteenth-century economist, Thomas Malthus, earned for economics its nickname as the "dismal science." (It is a nickname some of us have been trying to live down ever since.) Malthus agreed with the other economists of his day that the economic system would be self-regulating, but in a most pessimistic way. He predicted that growth must eventually come to an end.

Malthus argued that if production were to be greater than the amount necessary for life, material standards of living would improve. Increased prosperity would encourage high rates of population growth. The larger population would then absorb the entire production until all the people would be living barely above starvation. On the other hand, if production were to become insufficient even for bare survival, population growth would be halted through disease, famine, and war. The death rate would increase until the remaining population was living again at the level of starvation.

Pretty dismal, that Malthus!

The Limits to Growth

A report published in the 1970s revived concerns regarding Malthus's predictions about the consequences of growth. The report, published by the Club of Rome, was entitled *The Limits to Growth*. The Club of Rome was an informal organization that grew out of a 1968 meeting of scientists, educators, economists, industrialists, and government officials. The purpose of the organization was to increase understanding of the various economic, political, natural, and social forces that affect the way we live. Club of Rome researchers used computer models to project the cause-and-effect results of growth for the world environment. Briefly, this is what they concluded:

1. High birth rates and falling death rates increase population growth.
2. Population growth increases food requirements and presses against limited supplies of farm land.
3. Dwindling food supplies require increased agricultural and industrial production, which, in turn, affects environmental quality by polluting air and streams.
4. Environmental decay and depletion of productive resources eventually restricts population growth through disease and famine.

The researchers studied feedbacks within and among all these relationships and made projections of the effects of unrestrained growth. All of the tests predicted catastrophic population and resource problems within the lifetimes of many people alive today. The authors of the study later modified their conclusions and predictions, but the issues they raised cannot be ignored.

Exponential Changes

The frightening point made by the *Limits to Growth* was that environmental changes (such as levels of air and water pollution) are taking place exponentially (like the guinea pigs) rather than linearly. (An example of exponential growth is world fuel consumption. A graph describing annual fuel consumption rises more and more steeply, not only because larger numbers of people consume energy but also because each person's energy consumption is increasing.)

Linear growth involves changes of the same amount every time period so that a graph describing the change rises (or falls) in a straight line: 1, 2, 3, 4, 5. **Exponential growth** involves a percentage change so that the amount of the change increases (or decreases) every time period: 1, 2, 4, 8, 16. Thus, the graph describing an exponential change curves upward (or downward).

Environmental Ceilings and Floors

The effect of exponential change is that the graphs describing environmental changes will reach their limits, whether ceilings or floors, very abruptly. We may bump into the global limits of air, water, and other resources only shortly after we notice the limits are there. When we reach the limits, our entire economic system will collapse. Linear and exponential growth and decline are shown graphically in Figure 14.1.

Figure 14.1   Environmental Ceilings and Floors.

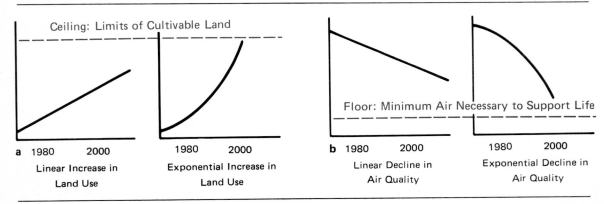

Ceiling: Limits of Cultivable Land

| a | 1980 | 2000 |
| Linear Increase in Land Use |

1980   2000
Exponential Increase in Land Use

Floor: Minimum Air Necessary to Support Life

| b | 1980 | 2000 |
| Linear Decline in Air Quality |

1980   2000
Exponential Decline in Air Quality

Contemporary Thinking about Economic Issues

ESCAPING THE MALTHUSIAN TRAP

The biologists are being attacked by the economists, and victory is still up for grabs.

The basis for the debate is population growth and whether or not population growth is a good thing. The biologists, in the person of author Paul Ehrlich, say that population growth is outstripping the resources of the planet. The economists, in the person of professor Julian Simon, say that every gloomy prediction of the biologists has turned out to be wrong and that, in fact, population growth has brought technical progress and better lives for more people.

Human ingenuity has led to the creation of new resources and the invention of ways to use them more efficiently. While Simon sees the tremendous increases in the earth's productivity, Ehrlich warns that increased productivity has come at the expense of fertile land and groundwater, and thus threatens future productivity.

Can you illustrate each of these positions through the model of production possibilities?

David Berreby, "The Numbers Game," *Discover,* April 1990.

In the past, we in Western nations have paid little attention to the side effects of our commitment to growth. If we are to avoid the catastrophes projected by The *Limits to Growth,* however, we may have to concentrate on living within the limits of our environment. This may require a decrease in population growth, a lower level of resource use, more efficient investments, and possibly lower material standards of living as well.

The Other Side

Perhaps the reader will agree that the drive for growth can lead to some pretty frightening consequences. If so, then we should consider the other side of the argument.

Citizens of less fortunate nations and some of our own citizens who now live in poverty will certainly object to an end to growth: "Now that you have yours, you want to conserve," they might say, or "The party's over just before we arrive."

Modern communications and transportation have exposed the wide gap between the living standards of the world's haves and the have-nots. The result has been a "revolution of rising expectations" among the have-nots in our nation and abroad. The have-nots are beginning to demand a better way of life for themselves. Therefore, it may be that the only acceptable course is not stopping growth entirely but regulating growth and distributing its benefits more equally.

THEORIES OF GROWTH

Why do some nations enjoy strong growth trends and others continue to stagnate at primitive levels of production? Even more puzzling, what explains the difference in growth trends among regions within a single nation?

There are two major theories to explain how and why economic growth takes place. One theory emphasizes the internal circumstances within the nation or region. It focuses on strategic sectors of the economy and is known as the **sectoral theory of growth.** Another theory focuses on the external relationships between the nation or region and the rest of the world and is known as the **export-base theory of growth.**

The Sectoral Theory of Growth

The **sectoral theory of growth** is based on studies of growth in the past. Studies show that the process of growth among sectors of an economy followed similar patterns worldwide.

Typically, the first sector to experience growth has been the *agricultural sector*. This is because agriculture provides the basic necessities of life: food, clothing, medicine. Specialization in agriculture encourages the development of farm equipment and technology for increasing farm productivity. When farm productivity increases faster than the need for basic necessities, human resources can be released for work in other sectors.

The second sector to experience growth is normally the *manufacturing sector*. After basic needs are satisfied, the people begin to want other material goods. Manufacture of consumer goods develops, and support industries spring up to supply raw materials and parts. An important support industry is transportation. Transportation facilities unite small communities into larger, interdependent markets. Larger markets permit greater specialization and division of labor and provide opportunities for large-scale, low-cost production. The effects of increased production and rising incomes spread throughout the eco-

nomic system, as many different kinds of manufacturing mature and prosper.

The third sector to experience growth is the *service sector*. Once basic necessities and material goods are plentiful, consumers begin to want services that will improve the quality of their lives. Business firms are established to produce personal and household services and business services. In the first group are health and education, recreation and the arts, home decorating, and fashion. In the second are financial and consulting services, communications, marketing, and economic forecasting.

Export-Base Theory of Growth

The **export-base theory of growth** focuses on the relationship between the nation or region and the rest of the world. Under the export-base theory a region must produce exportable commodities that are in substantial demand elsewhere. Sales of the export commodity bring income into the nation or region. Income from export sales is invested, first in facilities for producing the export commodity itself and eventually in industries that supply or support the export-base industry.

As rising incomes spread throughout the export and support industries, workers become more prosperous. They use their increased earnings to improve their living standards. Spending for consumer goods and services stimulates production in these industries, and growth gradually extends throughout the entire economic system.

MANAGING GROWTH

Understanding the sources of growth should lead to effective policies for managing growth. Designing proper policies is particularly important for poor nations, as well as for those regions within developed nations where growth has stalled behind the rest of the nation. Ideally, we should be able to manage growth in such a way that we obtain its greatest benefits and avoid its more costly side effects. What policies should we undertake?

Designing Policy

If we accept the *sectoral theory of growth,* we would recommend government programs to aid the agricultural sector. Such programs might include research and development programs in agricultural techniques and investment in agricultural education for increasing productivity. There might also be government-guaranteed loans to farmers for investment in agricultural equipment.

According to the sectoral theory, greater productivity in agriculture causes resources to move into other sectors of the economy. Development will then follow automatically in the manufacturing sector and, finally, in the service sector.

On the other hand, if we accept the *export-base theory of growth,* we would recommend government programs to promote production of materials and goods for sale abroad. These might include programs to develop a domestic mineral resource. Gold, diamonds, petroleum, and tin, for example, have been important export commodities for some nations. Or the export base for development might be an agricultural commodity such as cotton, coffee, rubber, sugar, cheese, or wine. In a more highly industrialized economic system, the export base might be precision instruments, electronic equipment, or computers.

According to the export-base theory, increasing prosperity in the export-base industry will cause growth to spread to other industries. Rising incomes in the export-related industries will lead automatically to growth in the production of consumer goods and services.

Policy Conflicts

Note that these two growth theories produce opposite policy recommendations. The sectoral approach calls for higher agricultural investment. Would this be practical in, say, the depressed regions of Appalachia in the United States or in the new nations of Africa? Why or why not?

In contrast, the export-base approach calls for investment in the production of export commodities. Would it be practical to invest in cotton production in the southern United States or in rubber plantations in Southeast Asia? Why or why not?

A single approach to development has certain disadvantages. If the favored sector or industry suffers a decline in demand, growth in the entire nation or region may slow to a halt. If world food production outstrips demand, for example, the agricultural sector may collapse. Too great a dependence on one crop might also be disastrous. A bumper crop one year could mean falling prices and falling income for the exporting nation. Even worse, a technological change may make an export commodity worthless in world markets. Or an interruption in transportation during a war may bring on economic collapse.

In the past, substantial investment in agriculture or in a particular export industry has not always led to development in other sectors. Sometimes incomes earned in the favored sector are not reinvested in the less developed sectors. Instead savings are sent to other regions or nations that promise a higher return on investment. If this happens, profits from the first stages of development cannot be used to stimulate further stages of growth, and the region or nation may continue to stagnate

Contemporary Thinking about Economic Issues

HAS THE UNITED STATES BECOME A ZERO-SUM SOCIETY?

Lester Thurow of Massachusetts Institute of Technology (MIT) is worried that the United States may have become a **zero-sum society.** A zero-sum society is one in which a gain for one person or group is possible only if another person or group suffers a loss: The sum of a positive gain and an equal negative loss is zero.

In a democratic society like ours, gains and losses are difficult to share. This is because groups whose living standards are threatened with losses will fight vigorously to avoid them. Whereas once upon a time powerful groups in society may have been able to enforce losses on weak groups, a democratic society allows even the weakest minority groups a strong voice in avoiding losses.

Another problem is that as our economic system has grown more complex, we have become more interdependent. In an interdependent society, decisions made to affect one group may affect others indi-rectly, imposing gains or losses on groups that may not deserve them. Our interdependence has made each of us more concerned about our own security and more determined to hold onto it.

Still, economic growth requires change, and change necessarily brings losses to some of us. Unless we are willing to face up to the fact of losses, Professor Thurow worries that economic growth may grind to a halt. We will reach a kind of paralysis, in which each of us works steadfastly to keep what he or she already has, and no one can hope for anything better.

According to Professor Thurow, an example of our paralysis is our response to the energy crisis. From plentiful energy at low prices in the 1950s, we moved to scarce energy with the threat of severe shortages in the 1970s. To allow prices to rise high enough to compensate for new energy exploration and development

at low levels of production and low material living standards.

The lack of a provable theoretical explanation of growth makes policy decisions difficult. The result of bad policy may be foiled expectations, wasted resources, and con-tinued low standards of living for people in many areas of the world. Humanitarian concerns, as well as economic ones, compel a continued search for effective policies to manage growth.

would have reduced the living standards of large groups of people. So we refused to do it. We imposed ceilings on energy prices, and we placed **windfall profits taxes** on energy producers. Recessions in the 1980s kept energy prices from rising and postponed the time when we would have to accept the costs of developing new energy sources. Eventually we will have to pay prices that truly reflect the long-term cost of producing energy. Price increases will be welcomed by groups that expect to gain and resisted by those that expect to lose.

Another example of the nation's paralysis involves our slowing economic growth and the slowing growth of worker productivity. As citizens of the wealthiest nation on earth, we have become accustomed to enjoying living standards that rise with each generation. Our nation's rapid economic growth has yielded a surplus of income for making investments. Invest-

ments, in turn, have created the capacity for still more growth. If growth slows, investment will be possible only through a cut in current living standards. Frequent recessions to curb inflation further act to slow growth by creating excess capacity and stifling incentives to invest.

Solving all these problems will require political decisions regarding the equity of the allocation of gains and losses. Voters have different ideas as to what is equitable, making allocative decisions difficult. To make these decisions, Thurow recommends that leaders acknowledge the necessary costs of growth, inform voters of the costs, and propose ways to share the costs fairly.

Lester C. Thurow, *The Zero-Sum Society,* Basic Books, New York, 1980, and *The Zero-Sum Solution,* Simon & Schuster, Inc., New York, 1985.

Self-Check

1. **Which of the following illustrates the most likely sequence of growth?**
   a. Saving, plentiful resources, capital equipment, investment.
   b. Plentiful resources, saving, investment, capital equipment.
   c. Investment, capital equipment, saving, plentiful resources.
   d. Plentiful resources, investment, capital equipment, saving.
   e. Saving, investment, capital equipment, plentiful resources.

2. **When total resources reach high levels of productivity:**
   a. There is danger of unemployment.
   b. They may produce nonmaterial services to enrich the quality of life.
   c. Production may focus on military equipment.
   d. There may be emphasis on wasteful production.
   e. All of the above.

3. **Which of the following is not a limit to growth?**
   a. Pollution caused by increasing agricultural and industrial production.
   b. Rising birth rates relative to death rates.
   c. Limited supplies of farmland.
   d. Exponential trends in resource use.
   e. All are limits to growth.

4. **The sectoral theory of growth:**
   a. Is based on growing productivity in export industries.
   b. Depends on inflows of spending from other nations.
   c. Emphasizes the development of agriculture, manufacturing, and then services.
   d. Would call for policy to increase agricultural investment in order to encourage growth.
   e. Both (c) and (d).

5. **Under the export-base theory of growth:**
   a. A region must produce commodities that are in demand elsewhere.
   b. Sales of an export good will cause outflows of spending from the producing region.
   c. Growth would be encouraged by investment in the production of export commodities.
   d. All of the above.
   e. Both (a) and (c).

Theory in Practice

GRAPHING GROWTH IN PRODUCTION POSSIBILITIES

Economic growth depends on increases in the quality and quantity of resources and improvements in technology. In the United States, labor resources have increased substantially over the years. Our population grew from 5.3 million in 1800 to 250 million in 1990. The quality of labor has improved, too, through better health and education and longer years of productive life. Improvements in technology have come about through scientific and engineering advances and through better organizational and managerial techniques.

Growth in the stock of capital has also added to our productive resources. Substantial investments in transportation and communication facilities, power plants, and manufacturing plants and equipment have made possible even greater growth.

Remember that investment in capital resources is possible only if individuals refrain from consuming a portion of their incomes. They must save and make their savings available to business for investment in productive facilities. Since 1929, Americans have saved an average of about 6 percent of their disposable income (personal income after taxes).

To be able to save, a nation or region must own resources capable of producing more goods and services than the minimum necessary for life. Surplus production makes it possible to shift resources from the production of life's necessities into the production of new capital resources. Fortunately, the North American continent has provided our nation with plentiful resources. As a result, we have been able to increase our savings and investment fairly regularly throughout our history. In 1989, total investment expenditures amounted to almost $780 billion. Almost one-third of this amount represented net additions to capital stock; that is, additions over and above replacement of depreciated buildings and equipment.

Economic growth can be illustrated as a steady shift to the right of a nation's production possibilities curve. The production possibilities curves in Figure 14.2 illustrate the production capabilities of two countries, one rich in resources and technology and one poor. Suppose a minimum production of 10 units of goods and services is necessary to sustain life in each nation. The rich nation can produce the goods and services necessary for

life and also 20 units of capital resources. The poor nation is able to produce the necessary goods and services and only 5 units of capital.

TEST YOURSELF
How will the ability to invest in capital affect future production possibilities for the rich nation? Pencil in the appropriate changes in production possibilities on the figure.

THE EXTERNALITIES OF GROWTH

We humans are the only animals on earth who significantly change the environment. We have used our superior intelligence to produce a growing variety and quantity of goods and services. In the process of production, however, we have produced some unwanted materials that have changed our environment in unintended ways.

Economists call the side effects of production **externalities.** Many externalities are useful and desirable, as when growth in manufacturing increases the skills of workers and

Figure 14.2   Production Possibilities Curves for Two Nations.

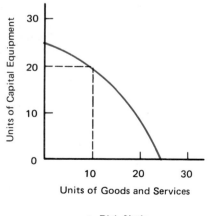

a. Rich Nation

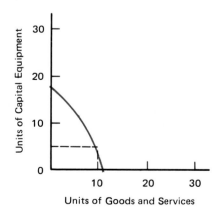

b. Poor Nation

How Things Have Changed

THE COST OF ENVIRONMENTAL PROTECTION

Programs to improve the environment impose a cost today for the sake of benefits to be enjoyed far in the future. When planning such programs, it is important to ensure that the ratio of future benefits to current costs is at least as great as it is for other uses of the nation's resources.

Consider a $1 investment today that yields a real return of 5 percent, which is reinvested in the project itself. By the year 2050 the original dollar will return $18.68 in real purchasing power. Under these conditions, it makes no sense to use a dollar for environmental protection unless the dollar yields at least $18.68 in improved environmental conditions.

enables them to produce a wider range of goods and services. We call externalities that improve the quality of life **positive externalities.** Some other examples of positive externalities are: improved technology of agriculture, which enables more people to live healthy, productive lives and frees labor for other types of work; better housing, which improves our landscape and makes our neighborhoods more stable; immunization against diseases, which halts their spread and limits exposure even for people who have not been immunized.

Other less favorable side effects of production are called **negative externalities.** Negative externalities also extend throughout the society, imposing costs on members of the community as a whole. Most of us are familiar with negative externalities: air pollution, which worsens our health and dirties our homes and clothing; water pollution, which destroys recreation areas and increases the cost of pure water; noise pollution, which damages our hearing and rattles our nerves; discarded junk, which breeds vermin and disease. No doubt, you can add more examples from your own personal experience.

The significant fact about externalities is that they are received by people who did not request them. Positive externalities are enjoyed by everyone within reach of the benefits; negative externalities are suffered by everyone in reach of the social costs . . . whether we want them or not!

This fact makes externalities different from goods and services traded in the market. The market is very careful to extend the benefits of production only to those people who want them and are willing to pay the cost. We say the market is **efficient** because participants in the market evaluate the benefits they expect to receive from a purchase and pay a cost that is just high enough to compensate for those benefits. Stated algebraically,

$$\frac{\text{benefits}}{\text{costs}} \geq 1$$

means an efficient market decision. In market transactions there is little danger that the costs paid for any good or service will exceed the benefits received:

$$\frac{\text{benefits}}{\text{costs}} < 1$$

means an inefficient market decision. Efficiency in many individual markets means efficiency for the economic system as a whole. Throughout our market system, scarce resources are used only to the extent that the benefits received are at least as great as the costs paid.

This result is not necessarily true when there are externalities. When there are externalities, the costs of production are paid for by two groups: those who receive the benefits and pay for them and those who receive no benefits but pay the social costs (or negative externalities) nevertheless.

There is another problem associated with externalities. The problem involves a principle called **equity,** a word that is difficult to define precisely but involves fairness.*

By most definitions, the market system is fair. That is, it gives people what they pay for. People who want the benefits pay the cost. Those who don't, don't. The presence of externalities changes all this, and the result is often not fair.

How can understanding externalities help our nation plan for growth? First, we must recognize that the market system does not account for externalities. Therefore, some decisions about production must be made outside the market, by the nation as a whole through our democratically elected representatives. Making decisions democratically enables us to estimate the ''social benefits'' of production; that is, the benefits received by people who use the good or service directly plus the positive externalities it brings the community as a whole. It also helps us evaluate production's ''social costs'': the costs paid by private users of a particular good or service plus the negative externalities its production imposes on the community as a whole. Stated algebraically;

*What is ''fair'' may mean different things to different people.

$$\frac{\text{total benefits}}{\text{total costs}}$$

$$= \frac{\text{private benefits} + \text{positive externalities}}{\text{private costs} + \text{negative externalities}}$$

$$= \frac{\text{social benefits}}{\text{social cost}} \geq 1$$

Needless to say, the possible side effects of production are difficult to identify and impossible to measure precisely. However, some effort must be made to make sure that resources are used only for projects that provide social benefits at least as great as their social costs.

Once production is judged to be efficient in the economic sense, it should be evaluated in terms of equity. Are the benefits and costs distributed fairly? Do those who enjoy the benefits also pay the costs? How much equity are we willing to sacrifice for production that is efficient but whose benefits and costs are distributed to different groups?

TEST YOURSELF

The economics of the environment can be summarized in three E's: efficiency, externalities, and equity. Make sure you understand these terms and how they contribute to an understanding of economic choice. Then evaluate each of the following projects in terms of the three E's.

1. A proposed highway would transport commuters quickly from the suburbs to their jobs in the city. However, it would also disrupt an established inner-city neighborhood, cut off local business firms from their regular customers, and remove much urban property from the city's tax base. Ninety percent of the cost of construction would be paid by the federal government, and 10 percent by the state.
2. A proposed dam would provide electric power, flood control, and recreational facilities over a large area. It would stimulate industrial and commercial de-

velopment and increase the incomes of poor rural families. However, it would forever change the landscape, destroying valuable farm and timber land, eliminating white-water canoeing streams, and destroying the habitat of a unique species of fish.

3. A chemical process restructures the molecules of petroleum to produce a fiber for weaving into cloth. The cloth never wrinkles or needs ironing, enabling many homemakers to spend their time in other more creative ways. Although the miracle fiber increases the variety and durability of our clothing, production requires vast quantities of imported oil and natural gas and expels heat, chemicals, and nondegradable pollutants into our air and water.

4. Fast-food restaurants package their food in containers that keep hot food hot and cold food cold. Busy people come to depend on quick and nutritious meals stored in such containers. Producing the containers expels a gas that destroys ozone in the earth's atmosphere and increases the risk of skin cancer. Because discarded containers do not quickly biodegrade, they occupy space in landfills for years to come.

ECONOMIC GROWTH AND THE WORLD FOOD CRISIS

Advances in technology have helped more of the world's people live better and longer—and that's part of the problem!

Better health standards have kept more people alive, such that the world's population is now almost 4 billion—and expected to double in only 25 years. Growing population and slowly rising living standards have increased our need for food at the rate of 30 million tons per year. As a result, the world's stockpile of food is declining by about 10 million tons per year.

The Rise and Fall of the Green Revolution

From the early 1950s until 1972, world food production increased dramatically. The "green revolution" extended scientific techniques to agriculture in the form of hybrid seed and livestock, chemical fertilizers and pesticides, and improved irrigation systems. Strains of corn, grain sorghum, soybeans, wheat, and rice were developed to thrive in particular climate and soil conditions around the world.

The green revolution was especially successful in the United States. Corn production per acre quadrupled over the early 1900s. Milk production rose to 10,000 pounds per cow per year, compared to only 600 pounds per cow in India. Chickens were bred to eat less, to grow to maturity in a shorter time, and to produce more eggs. As a result of such scientific advances, our 12 Midwestern states alone now feed one-fourth of the world's people.

Worldwide crop disasters in the mid 1970s brought a halt to the dramatic increase in agricultural production. Much of the increased yields had come from the use of chemical fertilizers, primarily petroleum-based and in increasingly short supply. The drop in world supplies of petroleum- based fertilizers is expected to cause a drop in crop yields of 10 tons for each 1-ton decline in fertilizer applied.

Rising costs of fertilizer present a particular problem for the newly developing nations that often lack the necessary foreign exchange for importing fertilizer. The problem is so serious that Philip Handler, former president of the National Academy of Sciences, has predicted 1 million child deaths per month in newly developing nations by the year 2025.

Proposals and Problems

What can be done? At present the world's farmers are cultivating only about half of the

---

Contemporary Thinking about Economic Issues

PRESERVING THE ENVIRONMENT

Accounting for externalities and making efficient decisions is not easy. Rules prohibiting production of negative externalities tend to increase costs of production without yielding measurable benefits. Economists recommend replacing the hard-and-fast rules of the past with economic incentives to minimize negative externalities while continuing to increase production.

Consider the following examples:

1. When too many fishing boats are depleting fishing grounds, a rule that limits every boat's catch would mean higher average fixed costs and higher average total costs for all fishermen. A better solution to the problem of overfishing would be annual fishing fees and transferable quotas. Revenue from the fees would be used to buy out fishermen who would agree to get out of the business. Those who remained in the industry would look on the annual fee as an investment in increased fish populations.

2. When an area suffers from environmental pollution, a rule that prohibits the entry of new firms may actually keep out firms with more effective pollution-control techniques than existing firms. A better solution to the pollution problem would be to award **emission reduction credits** to existing firms that voluntarily reduce their emissions below prevailing regulations. Then the emission reduction credit would be sold to new firms at prices that reflect the emissions added by their entry to the area. The result is that firms that

---

world's arable land. The most favorable lands are already in use, however, and the additional costs of clearing, transportation, and irrigation associated with developing new farmland would run in the billions of dollars. Adding only 10 percent to the amount of cultivated acreage could cost as much as $1 trillion.

Land reform might help increase productivity in some nations. New foods from the sea are also a possibility, but the potential gain is limited by pollution and by too intensive fishing in past years. New varieties of seeds are still being developed, but the process is slow and costly. Fertilizer production may also be

expanded, particularly in the less developed countries.

Reduction of waste would also help relieve the food shortage. Decreased consumption in the developed nations could increase the quantities available for needy nations. The United States uses the equivalent of 7 pounds of grain in the production of each 1 pound of meat. Reducing meat consumption would free this grain for shipment abroad. It is estimated that the average person in poor countries consumes 400 pounds of grain per year, compared to the citizen of North America who consumes a ton (about 100 pounds of which is in the form of beer or whiskey).

can control their emissions cheaply would create and sell credits to firms whose emission-control costs are prohibitive.

3. The world as a whole is threatened by the greenhouse effect, which occurs when gases are trapped in the earth's atmosphere so that the sun's radiant heat cannot escape. Instead of shutting down emitters of greenhouse gases, a more effective solution to the problem would be to require new sources of greenhouse gases to offset their emissions by conservation, recycling, tree plantations, or closing of older, heavily polluting plants. These higher costs would encourage emitters of greenhouse gases to search for ways to reduce their emissions.

The expected effect of programs like these is to place the cost of negative externalities on the firms that cause them. Profit-seeking firms would then look for ways to reduce their costs. Firms that are unable to reduce their negative externalities will then pass the costs on to consumers, who may be expected to demand smaller quantities of the offending product at the higher price.

Explain how each of the programs above would work to protect the environment more efficiently than rigid rules and regulations. How does pollution affect GNP? How does pollution control affect GNP?

T.H. Tietenberg, "Using Economic Incentives to Maintain Our Environment," *Challenge,* March/April 1990

Lifeboat Ethics

Policy involving food production must eventually deal with the problem of population growth. Some analysts are beginning to recommend what is called **lifeboat ethics:** In the ocean of life we are all adrift, as if in a boat. We would like to bring all others into our boat, but that would exceed its capacity and we would sink. We must choose to help only those nations that are able and willing to make a tremendous effort to help themselves.

The decision to help only selected nations is similar to the principle of **triage** in classifying battlefield casualties. Victims of war are divided into three groups: those who will probably survive without aid, those who will probably survive with moderate aid, and those who will not survive without substantial aid. Limited medical resources are then concentrated on the second group. By implication, the third is left to perish, an ethically difficult decision to make. We may not like it but, in the words of ecologist-biologist Garrett Hardin, it is a little like the law of gravity: "Once you know it's true, you don't sit down and cry about it. That's the way the world is."

In human terms, this conclusion may apply to the one-third of the world's people who live in the hungry nations—nations unable to feed themselves or to produce sufficient goods for export to pay for food imports. These nations are centered in Asia and Africa below the Sahara: Bangladesh and Ethiopia are pitiful examples. It is estimated that one-fourth of the populations of these areas lives on a diet of less than 1000 calories per day.

We continue to hope for a more acceptable alternative than slow starvation for these people. Policy to relieve the crisis in food production will require the best efforts of scientists, sociologists, economists, and humanitarians for many years to come.

AN INTERNATIONAL PLAN FOR GROWTH

By now you are probably convinced that economic growth is:

(a)   Desirable.
(b)   Undesirable.
(c)   Possible.
(d)   Impossible.
(e)   All of the above!

Of course, the problem of growth is much too complex to summarize in a single answer. Even so, it is an important question, and in the 1970s the United Nations established the United Nations Environment Program to study and plan for an International Development Strategy. Guiding the study was Wassily Leontief, a Russian-born economist who is now a professor of economics at New York University.

Professor Leontief is well qualified to conduct such a study. In the 1940s he was responsible for developing a revolutionary new economic model. Leontief's economic model measures the necessary growth in inputs for producing larger outputs from many U.S. industries. The result of his early work was an **input-output table** for the United States, showing all the various inputs required for producing all the outputs demanded by American consumers and business firms.

Measuring inputs and outputs is complicated because many of the inputs to one industry are actually outputs of another. Without the table it would be difficult to measure the necessary growth in inputs (which are also outputs) needed to produce more of any single good.

An example may be helpful. Consider the industry that produces motor vehicles—automobiles, trucks, and moving equipment. On the average, to produce $1's worth of motor vehicles requires the following inputs:

Textile produces	1 cent
Paint	$\frac{1}{2}$ cent
Rubber and plastics	2 cents
Glass	1 cent
Metals	10 cents
Metal products	7 cents
Machinery and equipment	2 cents
Electrical products	$1\frac{1}{2}$ cents
Motor vehicle parts	33 cents
Retail trade and services	3 cents

To increase production of motor vehicles requires that output in all these other industries increase first. To increase production of any one of these inputs, however, requires additional production in still other industries—and those other industries include motor vehicles. Motor vehicles are themselves necessary inputs in the industries producing inputs used in the motor vehicle industry.

Interrelationships among industries create a kind of chain reaction, such that the necessary total change in inputs is greater than the change required for an increase in output in a single industry. Making such complicated computations was not possible before Leontief developed his input-output table.

Leontief saw that his input-output model could be expanded to include all the nations in the world. A global input-output table would enable planners to measure the necessary production of, say, chemical fertilizers in Venezuela for increasing rice production in Southeast Asia. The global input-output table is summarized in 2625 equations, each one describing the interrelationships between production and consumption of a particular good in a particular part of the world. Happily, computers are available for solving the equations!

Using his equations, Leontief was able to predict the necessary growth in all inputs for increasing living standards in any part of the world economy and for promoting more balanced growth worldwide. Where input supplies are scarce, Leontief's model can identify bottlenecks. Where new technology is applied, the model can predict the resulting increase in productivity. A flow of loans or grants from developed to less developed nations shows up as increased investment for increasing global production possibilities. Even pollution is included in Leontief's model, as the net result of new industrial emissions minus the effects of pollution-abatement equipment.

After comparing the expected growth in worldwide demand with potential growth in supply, Leontief came to these conclusions:

1. Under present growth projections, the gap in per capita income between developed and less developed nations will remain about 12 to 1 at least until the year 2000.
2. However, technological and institutional changes in the less developed countries could enable them to double their food production.
3. A general scarcity of mineral resources is not yet a serious problem, but gains in production will become more and more costly in the future.
4. Less developed nations must increase their investment to as much as 40 percent of their GNP. Increased investment will require cutbacks in personal consumption, increased taxes and government development programs, and more investment funds from developed nations.

If Leontief's model is to become a basis for a global growth strategy, there must first be a new willingness to cooperate toward shared goals. Nations must agree to set aside purely national goals and fit their own growth plans into a world context. The prospects for such cooperation become better as more nations come to see the potential gains of cooperation relative to the costs of going it alone.

SUMMARY

1. Economic growth has long been an accepted national goal. Abundant resources in the United States have helped us achieve rising standards of living.
2. GNP is a way of measuring production and growth. Growth in GNP requires saving so that investment can be made in capital equipment. However, an increasing GNP depends also on increasing demand for goods and services.
3. The potential size of GNP depends on the quantity and quality of resources, the level of technology, and the system of organizing resources.
4. A fully mature society may suffer from unemployment as a result of declining demand for goods and services. To offset declining demand, a society may choose to use its resources to provide for a rising population, for military operations, or for public goods. Or it may choose to waste the output of its resources.
5. Some researchers predict that continued economic growth will eventually bring on environmental crises. They recommend planning for environmentally sound growth. More balanced growth may require more equal distribution of output, with lower standards of living for some.
6. Growth may proceed through sectors of the economy or may depend on the development of

an export commodity. A correct analysis of growth should lead to a correct policy to stimulate and manage growth.

7. The production possibilities curve is a useful tool for illustrating growth. A nation or region with large production possibilities is better able to save and invest for future growth.

8. Attempts are being made to improve agricultural techniques and increase productivity in order to deal with the world food crisis. However, dealing with severe shortages in some nations may require difficult choices on the part of more prosperous nations.

TERMS TO REMEMBER

saving: refraining from consumption

investing: using resources to construct capital equipment

linear growth: growth of the same amount each time period

exponential growth: growth at a constant percentage rate, which adds greater amounts each time period

sectoral theory of growth: the theory that growth takes place systematically, first in agriculture, then in manufacturing, and finally in services

export-base theory of growth: the theory that growth takes place through the development of a major export industry

input-output table: a chart showing all resource inputs needed for producing various types of output

TOPICS FOR DISCUSSION

1. Most of us have heard the old saying, "Necessity is the mother of invention." A commentator on the American scene once observed that today it would be more appropriate to say, "Invention is the mother of necessity." What do you think he meant by that? How is the statement related to our discussion of eco-

nomic growth? Discuss the advantages and disadvantages of this philosophy.

2. Nations differ with respect to the quantity of personal savings. The *Wall Street Journal* once reported that Swiss citizens were saving annually the equivalent of $5000 per capita, the highest in the world. The British were second with $4000, and Americans were third with $3300. Last on the list of 29 countries was Ethiopia, with annual per capita savings of $4.36. What factors influence the different rates of savings? How do you think savings might be put to use in each of the countries mentioned?

3. Each year in the United States, labor resources increase at the rate of about 2 percent. Productivity per worker also increases. The potential growth in output is more than 3 percent per year. If new labor is to be employed and higher production to take place, there must be rising demand. Demand must be backed up by spending power. Someone must be willing and able to buy! What problems, if any, can you see in our rising productive potential? What solutions would you propose? Are there other long-range problems that might affect your answer?

4. Walt Rostow has suggested that a mature society may have trouble employing all its labor resources unless it encourages population growth, engages in military aggression, or invests in public goods and services. Vance Packard has pointed out that a mature society often wastes its resources or produces frivolous goods. Is this result consistent with the problem of scarce resources, described in Chapter 1? Is it possible to have unlimited wants and unemployed resources at the same time? Why?

5. How do most Americans save and invest? Are you now saving and investing? Explain how your experience in school is an example of the process of saving and investment.

6. Many state legislatures are considering the following proposals to regulate disposable diapers: disposable-diaper taxes or all-out bans on disposable diapers. How would economists regard these proposals? How would economists define the efficient solution to the environmental problems associated with disposable diapers?

ANSWERS TO TEST YOURSELF

(p. 324) Cause it to shift to the right and make possible even greater production of capital goods.

(p. 326) 1. The highway may provide commuters more efficient employment and higher incomes, but displaced city dwellers and taxpayers across the country will pay the cost.

(p. 326) 2. Some families will enjoy the benefits of irrigation, electric power, jobs, and recreation. Future generations would pay the cost of fewer woodlands and diminished wild life.

(p. 327) 3. Many people enjoy more carefree clothing, but we may damage the atmosphere and the world's climate.

(p. 327) 4. People who eat fast food enjoy the convenience, but others suffer skin cancer.

Chapter

International Trade and Finance

or How Everything King Midas Touched Turned to a Floating Exchange Rate

Tools for Study

One historian has identified the beginning of trade as a significant turning point in human progress. In his account, trade began to flourish about 2000 B.C., when the Egyptians discovered how to make bronze by combining tin and copper. Bronze was a stronger and more useful metal than either tin or copper used alone. However, sufficient quantities of the two metals were found only in distant regions: tin in England and copper in India and parts of the Middle East. Trade was necessary to bring the metals together.

Trade opened many other opportunities for production within trading nations and opportunities for other forms of communication as well. It helped bring together the cultural, intellectual, and technical accomplishments of many scattered peoples.

FREE TRADE

Throughout this text, we have associated economic progress with specialization and exchange. We have suggested that groups can increase their productivity if they specialize in producing a particular good or service that they can exchange for goods or services produced by other groups.

Why Specialization?

There are many reasons why specialization is desirable. Some regions are better suited geographically for certain types of production. Agriculture provides the most obvious examples. Coffee beans grow well in tropical climates; wheat and corn do best in dry, sunny climates; livestock require grassy plains for grazing.

Other geographic features are favorable for other types of production. A sheltered harbor provides protection for shipbuilding; rushing mountain streams provide power for operating machinery; mountainous terrain exposes layers of minerals for use in manufacturing.

Such geographical features are not easily mobile. They can be used to best advantage by local workers. Among local workers, special skills will develop, and new processes and techniques will be designed to improve productivity and make larger quantities available at lower costs.

With specialization, it is likely that the region will produce more of a particular good or service than it needs. Its surplus production can then be exchanged for the specialities of other regions. Throughout the trading area, nations will benefit from the large-scale, low-cost production of their neighbors.

Interdependence

There is one small fly in the ointment, however. Remember that specialization replaces self-sufficiency. Regions that specialize become dependent on other regions for certain goods and services essential for a good life. Interdependent regions must be assured a free flow of goods and services. Otherwise, they will be reluctant to give up their self-sufficiency in production for specialization.

In the United States we have enjoyed the benefits of a large market area. We have many different regions with varied climates, resources, and geographical features. Also, we have one single national government, with laws prohibiting restrictions on the free flow of goods and services. The ability to trade freely has enabled regions of the United States to specialize and enjoy the benefits of specialization without the fears that would otherwise accompany the loss of self-sufficiency.

In recent years, 12 European nations have entered into agreements that encourage free trade. The nations of the European Economic Community—the Common Market—have agreed to allow goods, services, and productive resources to flow more freely across their national borders than was the case when each nation acted independently. The result has been increasing productivity and lower costs, with rising standards of living for their populations. In December 1992 members of the European Economic Community will put in place laws that will combine their economies even more closely, with the further possibility that they may one day adopt a common European currency.

The nations of Eastern Europe and Latin America have also formed free trade blocs, known, respectively, as the **Council for Mutual Economic Assistance** (Comecon) and the **Latin American Free Trade Association** (LAFTA).

ABSOLUTE AND COMPARATIVE ADVANTAGE

To see how specialization and exchange can increase total output, let us look at two imaginary nations, Kant and Troy. Each nation produces food and machinery for its home market. If they decide to specialize and trade, how will each nation determine its speciality?

Absolute Advantage

Each nation's production possibilities are shown in Table 15.1 The table shows the number of units that can be produced in each nation per labor day.* Thus, Kant can pro-

---

*A labor day is a unit of labor resources. It is the use of one laborer for one day. One hundred labor days may be the use of 100 laborers for one day, one laborer for 100 days, ten laborers for ten days, and so forth.

Table 15.1   Production Possibilities in Kant and Troy.

	Number of Units that Can Be Produced per Labor Day	
	Food	*Machinery*
Kant	5 or	2
Troy	3 or	4

duce either five units of food or two units of machinery per labor day. Troy can produce either three units of food or four units of machinery per labor day.

Apparently, Kant's resources are better suited for food production and Troy's for machinery. Because Kant can produce more food per labor day than Troy, we say that Kant has **absolute advantage** in the production of food. Because Troy can produce more machinery per labor day than Kant, Troy has absolute advantage in the production of machinery. If each nation specializes in the production for which it has absolute advantage, both will be better off.

Can we prove this?

Self-Sufficient Production

Suppose both nations have 100 labor days to use in production, and no trade is taking place between them. Both nations decide to use 50 labor days to produce food and 50 labor days to produce machinery. What is the total combined output of food and machinery?

Remember that Kant can produce five units of food per labor day, for a total of 250 units. Troy can produce three units per labor day, for a total of 150 units. Total combined food production is 400 units:

	FOOD	
Kant	5 × 50	= 250
Troy	3 × 50	= 150
		400

Kant can produce two units of machinery per labor day, for a total of 100 units. Troy can produce four units per labor day, for 200 units. Total combined machinery production is 300 units:

	MACHINERY	
Kant	2 × 50	= 100
Troy	4 × 50	= 200
		300

Thus, self-sufficiency in production yields total production of 400 units of food and 300 units of machinery.

Production with Specialization and Trade

Now let us see what happens if both countries decide to specialize and trade. If Kant devotes all 100 labor days to food production, total output is 5 × 100 = 500 units. If Troy uses all 100 labor days to produce machinery, total production is 4 × 100 = 400 units:

	FOOD	*MACHINERY*
Kant	5 × 100	
Troy		4 × 100
	500	400

Specialization and trade have increased total production to 500 units of food and 400 units of machinery, for a gain of 100 units of each kind of output.

Comparative Advantage

So far, so good. Remember that Troy has absolute advantage in production of machinery. Then suppose Troy discovers a new process that allows it to produce more food than before with each unit of labor resources. Its new production possibilities are shown in Table 15.2.

Table 15.2   Production Possibilities with Technological Advance.

| | *Number of Units That Can Be Produced per Labor Day* | | |
	Food		*Machinery*
Kant	5	or	2
Troy	5	or	4

Table 15.3   Cost of Production.

| | *Cost of Producing* | |
	1 Unit of Food	*1 Unit of Machinery*
Kant	$\frac{2}{5}$ units of machinery	$2\frac{1}{2}$ units of food
Troy	$\frac{4}{5}$ units of machinery	$1\frac{1}{4}$ units of food

Troy still has absolute advantage in the production of machinery, but now its resources are as productive as Kant's in food. Will specialization and trade still increase total production?

In order to determine this, we must compare the costs of production in Kant and Troy in terms of goods not produced. (This is another example of our familiar opportunity costs.) Note that Kant can produce either five units of food or two units of machinery per labor day. If Kant decides to produce food, it must give up two units of machinery for every five units of food it produces; if Kant decides to produce machinery, it must give up five units of food for every two units of machinery.

To determine the opportunity cost of one unit of food in Kant, we divide units of machinery by units of food. (Can you explain why?*) Units of machinery/units of food = $\frac{2}{5}$. This ratio tells us that for every unit of food produced, Kant must give up $\frac{2}{5}$ units of machinery. To find the opportunity cost of one unit of machinery in Kant, we divide units of food by units of machinery: $\frac{5}{2}$, or $2\frac{1}{2}$. Kant must give up $2\frac{1}{2}$ units of food for every unit of machinery it produces.

Now look at production possibilities for Troy. Troy must give up $\frac{4}{5}$ units of machinery

for one unit of food, and $\frac{5}{4} = 1\frac{1}{4}$ units of food for one unit of machinery. Opportunity costs for both countries are shown in Table 15.3.

Compare opportunity costs in the two nations, using Table 15.3 as a guide. One unit of machinery costs Troy $1\frac{1}{4}$ units of food and costs Kant $2\frac{1}{2}$ units of food. Kant must give up more food than Troy in order to produce machinery. Because Troy's opportunity costs are lower, it would certainly make sense for Troy to produce machinery. We can say that Troy has comparative advantage in the production of machinery: In terms of food not produced, the cost of one unit of machinery is less for Troy than for Kant.

What about the production of food? As we saw, neither country has absolute advantage in food production. Does this mean that trade will not be worthwhile?

Look again at Table 15.3. One unit of food costs Troy $\frac{4}{5}$ units of machinery. However, a unit of food costs Kant only $\frac{2}{5}$ units of machinery. Kant gives up less machinery than Troy when it produces one unit of food. Thus, Kant has **comparative advantage** in the production of food. Because Kant's opportunity costs are lower, it would make sense for Kant rather than Troy to produce food.

If each nation produces the good for which it has lower opportunity costs, the result is greater total production.

Can we prove this?

Self-Sufficient Production

Again, suppose both countries have 100 labor days to use in production and that no trade is

---

*The formula for computing opportunity costs is a simple algebraic equation. To illustrate, in Kant equivalent production possibilities are shown by: $2m = 5f$. To find the cost of $1f$ (food), we divide both sides of the equation by 5. To find the cost of $1m$ (machinery), we divide both sides of the equation by 2.

taking place. Both decide to use 50 labor days to produce food and 50 labor days to produce machinery. What is the total combined output of food and machinery? (Use Table 15.2 to calculate total output.)

Without trade, Kant can produce five units of food per labor day, or a total of 250 units. Troy can also produce five units per labor day, or 250 in 50 labor days. Total combined food output is 500 units. Kant can produce a total of 100 units of machinery and Troy can produce 200 units. Total combined machinery output is 300 units:

	FOOD	MACHINERY
Kant	5 × 50 = 250	2 × 50 = 100
Troy	5 × 50 = 250	4 × 50 = 200
	500	300

Production with Specialization and Trade

What happens if both nations decide to specialize and trade? If Kant devotes all 100 labor days to food production, total output is 500 units. If Troy uses all 100 labor days to produce machinery, total production is 400 units:

	FOOD	MACHINERY
Kant	5 x 100 = 500	
Troy		4 × 100 = 400

Again specialization and trade have increased total production. Output of machinery has increased by 100 units without sacrificing any quantity of food.

The benefits of trade may be illustrated on a production possibilities curve like the one shown on Figure 15.1. The production pos-

Figure 15.1   Production Possibilities Without Trade (with 100 labor days).

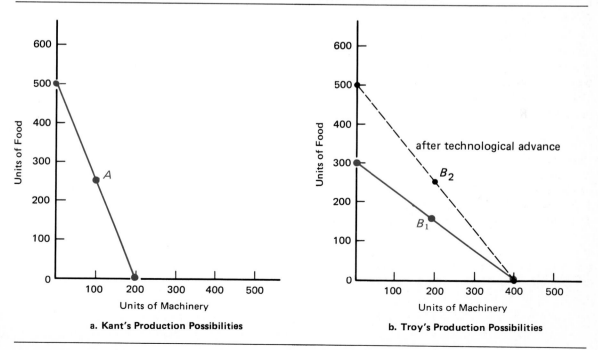

a. Kant's Production Possibilities

b. Troy's Production Possibilities

sibilities curves in this example have been drawn as straight lines because, for simplicity, we have assumed constant production costs. This means that each nation must give up constant (rather than increasing) amounts of one good in order to obtain additional units of the other good. Thus, cost ratios at every point along the production possibilities curves are the same.

TEST YOURSELF

Calculate the cost of producing 50 additional units of machinery in Kant at point A. Must Kant give up $2\frac{1}{2}$ units of food for each unit of machinery?

Without trade, each nation can produce at some point on its own production possibilities curve: Kant may decide to produce at point A; Troy may have produced at B_1 before its technological advance and may decide to produce at B_2 after its technological advance.

If Kant and Troy combine their economies into a large, free-trade area, their combined production possibilities can be shown by Figure 15.2. Total production possibilities are greater with specialization and trade.

TEST YOURSELF

Compare total production at A and B_2 with total production at C.

The Basis for Trade

Nations engage in international trade on the basis of comparative advantage. Each nation benefits from trade by producing and selling goods and services in which it has comparative advantage and buying goods and services in which other nations have comparative advantage. The entire trading area benefits because total production is greater with specialization than it would be if each nation were

Figure 15.2 Combined Production Possibilities with Specialization and Trade.

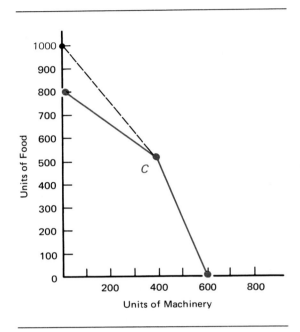

self-sufficient. Each nation is producing and exchanging goods and services at the lowest possible opportunity cost. Of course, this is only true if trade is free; that is, if there are no barriers or restrictions to trade. As we will see later in this chapter, trade is not always free.

Who engages in international trade? You engage in international trade when you purchase a Japanese car or German beer, just as the U.S. government does when it sells surplus military equipment to Israel or grain to India. Business firms engage in international trade when they buy Jamaican bauxite and sell American-made aluminum. Many materials essential for U.S. manufacture are not found in this country, making international trade necessary.

How Things Have Changed

CHANGES IN THE WAY WE FINANCE INVESTMENTS (% of GNP)

	1950–1979	1980–1988
Gross private domestic investment	16.0	15.8
National savings	16.3	14.1
Private:		
Household	5.0	3.8
Business	11.8	12.9
Government:		
Federal	−.6	−3.9
State and local	.2	1.3
Net foreign capital investment	−.3	1.6

Foreign investors have taken advantage of high-yielding investments in the United States, investing $220 billion in 1988, versus $82 billion invested by the United States in other countries.

SOURCE: *Economic Report of the President*, 1990.

THE BALANCE OF PAYMENTS

A nation, just like a business, must keep an account of all financial transactions that take place between it and other nations. It must keep a record of the value of inflows and outflows of spending. This record is known as a nation's **balance of payments**.

All inflows are added together to determine the flow of spending into a nation. All outflows are added together to determine the flow of spending from that nation to other nations. The difference between the two sums is the net flow of spending, or the net balance of international payments.

A positive difference represents a net inflow of spending. It leaves the nation with unspent claims against the wealth of other nations. A negative difference represents a net outflow. It means that foreign nations are holding unspent claims against the wealth of that nation.

Spending Flows

There are three kinds of transactions among nations, listed under three accounts in the balance of payments:

1. The *current account* records the flows of spending for exchange of goods and services.

2. The *long-term capital account* records

flows of spending for long-term investments and U.S. government spending abroad.

3. The *short-term capital account* records the flows of funds for short-term lending.

Table 15.4 lists various types of transactions in the United States falling under each heading and indicates whether the transactions are normally inflows (+) or outflows (−).

Net Flows for the United States

The net flow of spending for goods and services is represented by the balance on current account. Until the mid 1970s, the United States sold more goods abroad than we bought, and this balance was positive; that is, inflows (+'s) exceeded outflows (−'s). Since the mid 1970s, the balance has generally been negative, chiefly the result of the rising cost of petroleum imports into the United States, the rise of consumer goods production in other western nations, and certain barriers to U.S. exports in some nations.

The net flow of long-term investment and government spending is represented by the balance on capital account. Beginning with the Marshall Plan following World War II, more long-term investment and U.S. government spending flowed abroad than foreigners invested in this country. Dollars from private investors and from the U.S. government helped provide raw materials and capital equipment for rebuilding Europe after the war. Until the mid 1980s the balance on capital account was generally negative. However, the outflow of investment funds meant increasing U.S. ownership of productive facilities in other countries, with a potential inflow of investment income.

Table 15.4   Inflows and Outflows in the U.S. Balance-of-Payments Account.

	Inflow or Outflow
Current account (trade)	
1. Exports	
a. Goods sold abroad (e,g,. computers, aircraft, soybeans)	+
b. Services sold abroad (e.g., financial services, insurance, tourism)	+
2. Imports	
a. Goods bought abroad (e.g., petroleum, bauxite, autos, bananas, perfume)	−
b. Services bought abroad (e.g., shipping services, tourism)	−
3. Income	
a. From U.S. investments abroad	+
b. To foreigners from their investments in the United States	−
4. U.S. government military expenditures	−
Capital account (investments or long-term loans)	
1. Long-term capital investments	
a. U.S. investment abroad (e.g., long-term bonds or stocks, factories, hotels, banks, mines)	−
b. Foreign investment in the United States (e.g., long-term bonds or stocks, factories, mines)	+
2. U.S. government grants and aid to foreign governments	−
Short-term capital account (short-term loans)	
1. U.S. lending abroad (e.g., short-term notes, bank accounts)	−
2. Foreign lending in the United States (e.g., short-term notes, bank accounts)	+

In the mid 1980s the U.S. balance on capital account turned positive, indicating a net flow of long-term capital into the United States. Today, foreigners who have earned dollars from sales to U.S. consumers are using their dollar holdings to purchase investments in the United States. In fact, foreign holdings of U.S. investments (net of U.S. holdings of investments abroad) increased from zero in 1984 to almost $600 billion in 1989.

Similar changes have been occurring in the short-term capital account.

In most of the years since World War II, savers in the United States loaned more short-term funds abroad than foreigners loaned in the United States. The result was a negative balance on short-term capital account. In the 1980s this trend reversed, and we are now borrowing more from foreigners than we are leading abroad. The chief reason for international borrowing has been the increase in U.S. imports relative to exports and the massive increase in U.S. government borrowing. Foreigners have loaned funds to finance U.S. imports and to purchase U.S. government securities. For all this short-term borrowing, the United States must pay substantial interest returns to foreign lenders.

When the balance on current account, balance on long-term capital account, and balance on short-term capital account are added together, the result is the net flow of funds between the United States and other nations. Values of each account and the net flow of funds for selected recent years are shown in Table 15.5.

As the table shows, the net flow of dollars has been negative for most of the period. A negative flow means that we are experiencing a deficit in our balance of payments. We are spending more dollars abroad than we are bringing back into the country. A negative balance of payments means that there remain unspent claims against the wealth of the United States in the hands of foreigners.

Foreigners with claims against the United States may settle their claims in any of the following ways.

Short-Term Capital Account

Foreigners can lend dollars on short term to U.S. individuals, banks, and other businesses or to the U.S. Treasury. They do this by buying bank certificates of deposit or other securities or by simply depositing their dollars in banks. Foreigners use their dollars for short-term lending if the interest earnings on short-term loans in the United States are at least as great as the interest earnings on short-term loans elsewhere.

Long-Term Capital Account

Foreigners may use their dollars to make long-term capital investments in U.S. business firms. They do this by buying stocks or bonds or by investing directly in productive facilities in the United States. Foreigners will use their dollars for long-term investments if the expected earnings on U.S. investments are at least as great as the expected earnings on investments elsewhere.

Some Problems

Before we look at the third way foreigners can spend their dollar claims against the United States, let us look at some of the problems associated with short-term and long-term capital inflows. Short-term capital seeks the highest interest return possible. If interest rates in the United States should fall, foreigners will quickly move their dollars out of the United States into other more profitable nations of the world.

The risk of losing short-term capital means that the Federal Reserve has less freedom to use expansionary monetary policy and that, if expansionary monetary policy is used, it may have little effect.

Table 15.5 U.S. Balance of Payments (in millions of dollars).[a]

	1960	1964	1969	1974	1977	1982	1985	1988
Current account								
Exports	+20,282	+26,589	+38,448	+98,533	+122,932	+216,946	+214,424	+319,251
Imports								
Goods	−14,758	−18,700	−35,807	−100,379	−151,713	−247,606	−338,863	−446,466
Services and transfers	− 964	− 1,149	− 1,763	− 2,355	− 2,008	− 2,621	− 4,311	+ 13,423
Income (net)								
Difference between								
investment from U.S.								
investments abroad								
and foreign								
investments in the								
United States	+ 2,287	+ 3,935	+ 3,811	+ 9,516	+ 11,935	+ 27,304	+ 25,187	+ 61,974
U.S government								
transactions	− 2,753	− 2,133	− 3,344	− 2,150	− 1,355	− 5,234	− 14,113	− 14,983
Capital account								
Long term								
U.S. government	− 884	− 1,353	− 1,933	− 2,571	+ 31,237	− 1,793	− 8,006	+ 38,316
Private	− 2,100	− 4,511	− 70	− 3,287	− 6,384	+ 22,428	+ 62,487	+ 40,902
Short term								
Net short-term capital								
flows	− 1,405	− 1,643	− 640	− 14,751	− 4,564	− 45,083	+ 38,524	+ 57,971
Net flow of funds	− 3,677	− 2,696	− 6,081	− 15,655	+ 80	− 35,659	− 24,671	+ 70,388

SOURCE: *Report of the President*, and *Federal Reserve Bulletins*
[a]Values may not total because of minor omissions.

Why is this so?

Remember that the goal of expansionary monetary policy is to reduce interest rates in the United States in order to stimulate spending and speed recovery from a recession. However, lower interest rates will cause more U.S. dollars to flow abroad to nations where interest rates are higher on short-term loans. If U.S. dollars flow abroad, they will not be available for spending at home and cannot stimulate domestic investment.

TEST YOURSELF

The example above describes problems associated with the use of expansionary monetary policy. Can you describe how the possibility of short-term capital flows interferes with the Federal Reserve's use of contractionary monetary policy?

Long-term capital investments have additional disadvantages in that they imply a degree of foreign control of U.S. businesses. Foreigners already own more than 1 percent of the nation's total of almost $15 trillion in assets, including an increasing share of U.S. government securities. Foreign investment has been growing at the rate of almost 10 percent per year. There is always the lurking fear that foreign owners of U.S. productive capital might someday use their economic power to influence U.S. politics.

Having explored the disadvantages of the first two uses foreigners might make of their U.S. dollars, now let us look at the way that is generally preferred by the United States.

Current Account

From the U.S. point of view, the best use of dollars by foreigners is to purchase American-made goods and services. Foreign purchases would add enough spending inflows to the current account to offset spending outflows in the capital accounts. It would also stimulate production in U.S. factories and provide jobs for U.S. workers. Finally, it would increase incomes in the United States and permit our citizens to buy more goods and services from other nations.

If foreigners are to be persuaded to spend their dollars for U.S. goods and services, they must be convinced of their high quality and low price. A goal of U.S. industries must be to make our products attractive to foreign buyers, so that enough of the dollars spent abroad flow back into U.S. markets.

THE FOREIGN EXCHANGE MARKET

Some foreign holders of U.S. dollars may decide not to spend their dollars for goods and services, for long-term investments, or for short-term lending. Instead, they may want to exchange their dollars for other currencies for spending in other nations. For this purpose, they must use the foreign exchange market.

International trade requires the use of many national currencies: francs, marks, dollars, yen, and so forth. The foreign exchange market provides a means for trading national currencies and, like other markets, operates according to the laws of supply and demand. The price of a currency is called its **exchange rate.**

Fixed and Floating Exchange Rates

When currency exchange rates are **fixed**, the price of a currency remains an established amount; the market cannot adjust to changes in supply and demand. For most of the years since World War II, currency prices were fixed: The price of a German mark was fixed at about $.25; the price of a British pound was fixed at about $2.80. Currency values were agreed on by the financial ministers of major nations and were maintained by their Central Banks. A currency's price was maintained by

Contemporary Thinking about Economic Issues

THE BENEFITS OF BEING A "TRADING STATE"

Richard Rosecrance of Cornell University has developed an interesting way of thinking about national goals and the relationship between national goals and economic prosperity. He divided nations into two groups according to their national goals: territorial nations and trading nations.

Because territory means resources and resources mean wealth, territorial nations are concerned with maintaining their territory. A nation with a wealth of territory can impose taxes to support a strong army and gain even more territory. There is another route to prosperity, however, the route followed by trading nations. Trading nations can cooperate and, through trade, produce more than they could have gained through military conquest. The significant thing about trade is that profitable trade depends on markets, and markets exist only where people are prosperous. Thus, to emphasize trade as a national goal brings together the interests of all nations in a mutual drive to achieve prosperity.

Professor Rosecrance believes that territorial goals dominated international politics until fairly recently. Until this century, nations tended to want to get bigger and more self-sufficient. Then after World War II, there began to be a division of the world between the territorial nations and the nations that concentrate instead on trade. The United States and the Soviet Union, he says, continue to place more emphasis on land and the resources and internal markets that keep them self-sufficient. Japan and European nations, on the other hand, now use international trade to acquire the resources they once acquired through military force.

World War II persuaded the world that the benefits of war were no longer sufficient to offset the costs. To gain power through trade would yield more enduring and more widespread benefits, without imposing the costs of war. Because trading nations achieve power through specialization, they value diversity and interdependence. Industrial and population growth strengthen interdependence, says Professor Rosecrance, and make it harder to achieve national goals independently. Moreover, a trading system sets free the productive and trading energies of people, who look for markets and create wealth without any direction from government at all. Trading nations can improve national welfare and the allocation of resources through internal development and trade, without preventing other nations from achieving similar goals.

Richard Rosecrance, *The Rise of the Trading State*, Basic Books, New York, 1985.

Central Bank purchases or sales of currencies, adding to the supply or demand of private consumers or business firms to push the currency's equilibrium price up or down.

In 1971, western nations agreed to stop fixing their exchange rates and allow their currencies to **float**. When exchange rates are allowed to float, prices of currencies rise and fall according to supply and demand among private consumers and business firms only. An increase in private demand for marks, for example, causes their price to rise. An increase in the supply of dollars, on the other hand, causes their price to fall. Floating exchange rates were expected to influence trade and help correct balance-of-payments deficits.

Exchange Rates and Balance-of-Payments Deficits

When balance of payments deficits cause dollars to pile up in the hands of foreigners, the dollar's price in terms of foreign currency tends to fall. This is because the equilibrium price of anything falls if its supply increases faster than its demand. A fall in the price of a currency as a result of market forces is called **depreciation**.*

We have said that the value of the dollar depreciates as it accumulates in foreign hands. How will the depreciation of the dollar affect sales of U.S. goods and services?

Suppose dollars have been exchanging for German marks at an exchange rate of 1 mark = $0.25 or, stated differently, $1.00 = 4 marks. If the supply of dollars held by foreigners increases faster than demand, the dollar's exchange rate will tend to fall relative to the mark. Under floating exchange rates, the

---

*Depreciation is distinguished from **devaluation**, which results from a conscious act of government. A government devalues a currency when it sets a lower value on it in terms of other currencies.

new exchange rate may be 1 mark = $0.50 or, stated differently, $1.00 = 2 marks.

At the lower dollar exchange rate, a German consumer must give up only 2 (rather than 4) marks for every dollar. He or she can buy the same quantity of U.S. goods for fewer marks. Thus, depreciation of the dollar makes U.S. goods cheaper to foreign buyers. The German consumer is likely to want to acquire more dollars for spending in the United States, and our dollars will flow back. All of this tends to reduce our balance of payments deficit and to reduce accumulated holdings of dollars abroad.

At the same time, a U.S. consumer will receive only 2 marks for each dollar rather than 4; purchasing German goods will require twice as many dollars as before. The U.S. consumer is less likely to exchange dollars for marks to buy the more expensive German goods, and more of our dollars will stay at home. In both cases, the result is to correct the unequal flow of currencies that results from balance-of-payments deficits.

> **TEST YOURSELF**
> Can you think of any disadvantages of depreciation of the dollar?

BARRIERS TO TRADE

In the past, nations have often tried to correct balance of payments deficits by setting up barriers to trade. The most common trade barrier is a **tariff**, a tax on imports that makes foreign goods more expensive than goods produced at home. A tariff discourages imports and thus reduces the outflow of domestic currency.

The imposition of a tariff causes a sacrifice of specialization and the loss of the benefits of free trade. Tariffs mean that consumers cannot buy from the lowest-cost producer. Moreover, when one nation imposes a tariff to reduce its own imports, other nations often impose tariffs in retaliation. International trade declines as a result, and producers and consumers in many nations have to accept lower standards of living.

During the years preceding the Great Depression, many nations sought to protect their local manufacturers by imposing high tariffs on imports. In the United States, the Hawley-Smoot Tariff of 1930 imposed tariffs as high as 60 percent on the value of many imports. Tariffs reduced international sales of goods and services, causing production and incomes to fall around the world. Lower incomes meant still fewer purchases. Thus, the decline in international trade aggravated the problem of low production and high unemployment during the Great Depression.

In 1934, President Franklin Roosevelt embarked on a program of Reciprocal Trade Agreements with other nations to reduce tariff barriers. All cooperating nations agreed to reduce certain tariffs so that trade could flow more freely. After World War II, the General Agreement on Tariffs and Trade (GATT) continued to improve trading relations. The United States and other members of GATT meet regularly in negotiations to reduce tariffs and other barriers to trade.

Trade agreements in recent years have often granted "most favored nation" status to particular nations. This means that any tariff reduction given to a favored nation will immediately be extended to all other nations that are parties to the agreement.

Other Barriers to Trade

Other negotiations have aimed at reducing nontariff barriers to free trade:

1. *Import quotas* that limit quantities of particular imports.
2. *Product standards* that restrict certain imports.

3. *Export subsidies* that enable producers to sell abroad at lower prices than at home.

An **import quota** is an absolute limit on the quantity of a foreign good or service allowed in domestic markets. Quotas are generally illegal under the rules of GATT. The United States, however, has been able to negotiate Voluntary Restraint Agreements (VRAs) with foreign producers of steel and other manufactured goods.

A quota is similar to a tariff in that it raises the price of the good in domestic markets. The reason is that it places a limit on the addition to domestic supply from foreign sources. A quota has another disadvantage relative to a tariff. Because a quota places an absolute limit on imports, it reduces the ability of markets to respond to increases in consumer demand.

Product standards also work to restrict trade without actually violating the rules of GATT. Standards covering emissions control, size of tomatoes, and other product features are aimed at particular nations' exports, with the goal of protecting domestic producers of competing products.

Export subsidies are payments to producers of export goods that have the effect of reducing the cost of producing the export item. European nations rebate tax payments to exporters when goods are sent abroad, thus reducing their cost. Export subsidies enable a firm to sell its products more cheaply abroad than in domestic markets and improve its competitiveness relative to foreign producers.

Import quotas, product standards, and export subsidies distort comparative advantage and reduce the efficiency of international trade.

In the remainder of this chapter, we will consider some of the recent controversies regarding free trade.

Self-Check

Use the following table to answer questions 1-3:

	Number of Units That Can Be Be Produced per Labor Day		
	Watches		Cameras
Albia	2	or	3
Verda	3	or	4

1. **Which of the following statements is incorrect?**
   a. Verda has absolute advantage in the production of both watches and cameras.
   b. Verda has comparative advantage in the production of watches.
   c. Verda must give up 4 cameras to produce 3 watches, or $1\frac{1}{3}$ cameras for each watch.
   d. Albia must give up 3 cameras to produce 2 watches, or $1\frac{1}{2}$ cameras for each watch.
   e. All answers are correct.

2. **Assume each nation has 50 labor days to use in production. If each specializes in the product in which it has a comparative advantage, total output will be:**
   a. 100 watches and 200 cameras.
   b. 150 watches and 150 cameras.
   c. 100 watches and 150 cameras.
   d. 150 watches and 200 cameras.
   e. None of the above.

3. **In Verda, the cost of producing each camera is:**
   a. $\frac{3}{4}$ watch.
   b. $2\frac{2}{3}$ watches.
   c. 3 watches.

d. $1\frac{1}{3}$ watches.

e. 4 watches.

4. **Which of the following will cause an outflow in the balance of payments?**
   a. General Motors sells a Cadillac to an Arabian Sheik.
   b. A U.S. technician trains Brazilian computer programmers.
   c. An Italian tourist takes his family to Disney World.
   d. A Mexican subsidiary of a U.S. firm increases its income from sales.
   e. IBM builds a plant in Belgium.

5. **In recent years, our balance of trade has been:**
   a. Negative, because we import more than we export.
   b. Positive, because foreign nations have imposed barriers on American-made goods.
   c. Negative, because we have invested heavily abroad.
   d. Negative, because of global demand for American grain.
   e. Positive, because foreigners have bought stock in American firms.

6. **The value of the dollar declines in relation to other currencies:**
   a. When foreigners buy gold from the U.S. Treasury.
   b. When foreigners demand more dollars for spending in the United States.
   c. When the supply of dollars increases in foreign hands.
   d. When exchange rates are fixed.
   e. When foreign banks buy dollars.

7. **Which of the following does not belong with the others?**
   a. General Agreement on Tariffs and Trade.
   b. Hawley-Smoot Tariff.
   c. European Common Market.
   d. LAFTA.
   e. Reciprocal Trade Agreements.

Theory in Practice

THE HARMFUL EFFECTS OF QUOTAS

In this section we will illustrate the benefits of free trade through use of microeconomic models before and after trade. Figure 15.3a shows a hypothetical demand curve for sugar in the United States. Figure 15.3b shows a similar demand curve for sugar in sugar-producing nations of Central America. The supply curves show that Central America's costs of production are lower than production costs in the United States. According to the supply curves, any quantity of sugar can be produced in Central America at a lower average cost than that quantity can be produced in the

United States. Without trade, the equilibrium price for sugar will be higher in the United States than in the sugar-producing nations of Central America.

With free trade, more American consumers will want to purchase imported sugar, shifting demand for Central American sugar to the right and raising its price. Demand for U.S.-grown sugar will shift to the left, reducing U.S. sugar prices. Demand curves will continue to shift until there is no longer a price advantage in either market. Finally, all buyers will be satisfied at a price somewhere between the two extremes.

Figure 15.3 Markets for Sugar.

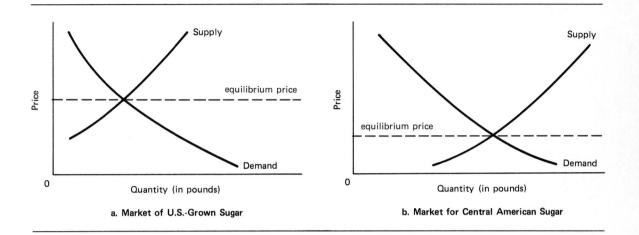

a. Market of U.S.-Grown Sugar

b. Market for Central American Sugar

TEST YOURSELF
Pencil in offsetting shifts in demand in the two markets and mark the final equilibrium price for sugar.

Free trade would cause Central American nations to move toward greater specialization in the kind of production in which they enjoy comparative advantage. Likewise, free trade will cause the United States to move away from sugar production. Sugar growers will move into other types of jobs. Often the transition to new jobs is slow and painful, but eventually U.S. sugar growers will find employment in kinds of production for which the United States has (or can develop) comparative advantage—perhaps electronic calculators, agricultural equipment, or technical services.

A quota interferes with this free-trade adjustment process. A quota is normally imposed to protect U.S. producers from foreign competition. In the market for sugar, its effect is to raise the selling price of foreign sugar.

This is because the quota reduces the supply of Central American sugar, shifting the supply curve upward and to the left. Figure 15.4 shows the effect of a quota on the selling price of Central American sugar. Now smaller quantities of Central American sugar can be sold in the United States only at higher prices. U.S. consumers are unable to shop freely in the lowest-cost market, and U.S. sugar growers are not encouraged to move into other kinds of production.

When quotas are imposed, nations fail to specialize according to the principle of comparative advantage. As a result, total world output is lower and unit costs of production are higher than under free trade.

TRADING WITH THE THIRD WORLD

World trade relations have changed greatly since 1973 when the Organization of Petroleum Exporting Countries (OPEC) raised the price of oil. OPEC is an international car-

Figure 15.4 Effects of a Tariff.

A tariff artificially increases selling price. U.S. customers cannot take advantage of low-cost Central American sugar.

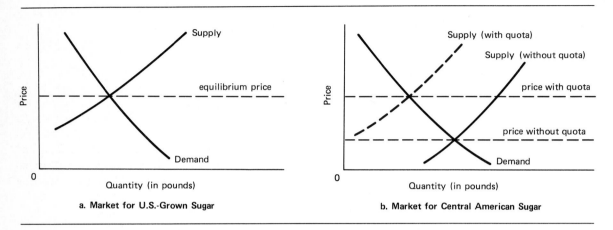

a. Market for U.S.-Grown Sugar

b. Market for Central American Sugar

tel with monopoly control over the output and price of a commodity vitally needed for industrial development and growth. The effect of the oil cartel has been to shift the power of trade away from developed nations to nations of the **Third World**—newly developing nations not aligned with either the United States or the Soviet Union.

Actually, the new power has gone only to certain members of the Third World—those with ample oil resources. Third World nations that lack oil may be even worse off now than before the oil cartel was formed. Sales of high-priced oil bring wealth to some nations, wealth for investment in productive facilities, community development, education, and research. For nations that must buy oil to begin the long process of economic development, however, high oil prices may close off their last chance for growth.

Some non–oil-producing nations have tried to establish similar cartels in other commodities that they produce. The aim is to increase the price of their own export commodity and increase export earnings. Minerals like bauxite and agricultural products like coffee, cocoa, and sugar are already sold under international commodity agreements. In a commodity agreement, producing nations agree to limit their exports to a specified amount in an effort to keep prices from falling below some acceptable level.

Commodity agreements are not always successful. When demand falls and exporters face a substantial drop in earnings, some may violate the agreement and increase their exports, causing price to fall. On the other hand, when demand increases and prices rise, users of high-priced commodities may seek out substitute supplies or develop techniques for using other, cheaper materials.

Substitution is most likely to occur when demand is highly elastic with respect to price. High price elasticity of demand characterizes materials that are widely produced around the world or are easily stored as a hedge against shortages. These characteristics are true of copper, cobalt, tin, and possibly even bauxite.

On the other hand, chromium and manganese are characterized by low price elasticity of demand, at least in the short run. Large deposits are found only in Africa and the Soviet Union, and these minerals are essential for producing high-grade stainless steel. Even so, given time buyers could probably find substitutes and avoid paying cartel prices.

Many non–oil-producing developing countries have little hope for solving the problem of rising import bills and falling export earnings. For some, direct assistance from developed nations may be the only way to acquire funds for economic development. Development programs should focus on low-technology, labor-intensive industries so as to use the resources developing nations have in greatest abundance. Then the developed nations should eliminate the tariffs and quotas that restrict imports from these countries. The final result might be a loss of jobs in some industries in the developed nations and a shift of resources into other, high-technology industries.

Can you cite industries that are experiencing a loss of jobs as a result of this painful process?

GOLD IN INTERNATIONAL FINANCE

Several hundred years ago when industry and trade first began to flourish, exchange was carried on through the use of gold. Eventually gold came to be used as "backing" for paper money used in trade.

With free trade, gold served as an automatic regulator of a nation's balance of payments. Manufactured goods would be exchanged according to the comparative advantage of trading nations. Temporary trade imbalances would be corrected by gold flows. Thus, whenever a low-priced region accumulated gold through the sale of more goods abroad, it would enjoy a balance-of-payments surplus. At the same time, high-priced regions would lose gold, as they purchased more goods from abroad than they were able to sell. They would have a balance-of-payments deficit.

The flow of gold into the low-priced nation would increase its money supply. More money would cause prices to rise, removing its low-price advantage. Its higher prices would reduce its sales abroad and reduce inflows of gold. At the same time, the high-priced nations would experience gold outflows and falling prices. Their lower prices would increase their sales abroad and increase inflows of gold. Thus, inflows and outflows of gold would work to eliminate trade imbalances and price differentials throughout the trading area.

The Gold Standard

A system that balances international payments through gold flows is called a **gold standard**. Under the gold standard, a nation with a balance of payments deficit would redeem its outstanding currency in gold. It would lose gold to nations with a balance of payments surplus. Then each nation's money supply would have to adjust to its holdings of gold.

Modern democratic governments were reluctant to base their domestic money supplies on inflows and outflows of gold. A high level of imports and a corresponding outflow of gold from a nation would call for a decrease in that nation's money supply. This would mean falling prices, lower production, and fewer jobs. A substantial inflow of gold, on the other hand, would increase the money supply and aggravate tendencies toward inflation.

Democratic nations like the United States found it difficult to tolerate such swings in the money supply. Frequently, the Federal Reserve acted to offset the flows of gold. In particular, if gold flowed out and domestic employment and production fell, the Federal Reserve created additional money to offset the loss of gold and allow a high level of domestic spending to continue. Without the discipline of the gold standard, prices tended to rise further, deficits to increase, and gold to flow out of the country.

Steady outflows of gold from the United States eventually led to a monetary crisis. By 1971, foreign holdings of dollars had grown to almost $40 billion and our gold stock was only $10 billion!

Finally, in August 1971, President Nixon announced that the United States was abandoning the gold standard; our currency was no longer redeemable in gold. We would determine our money supply on the basis of domestic spending needs rather than on the basis of our gold stock. (The United States and other nations still hold gold as a reserve asset, along with other national currencies.)

Nevertheless, a continuing outflow of dollars in trade remains a problem. Negotiations are under way with other nations to reduce their tariff barriers, exchange controls, import quotas, and export subsidies. These actions will allow foreigners to buy more from U.S. manufacturers and help reduce our persistent balance of payments deficit.

Gold and Paper Gold

Only about 80,000 tons of gold have been mined in the history of the world. The entire world gold supply could be stored in one large oil tanker. The Union of South Africa and the Soviet Union are the major suppliers of gold, each mining about 700 metric tons annually.

The world's stock of gold is held in central banks as a reserve asset and by individuals as assets or decorative objects. The United States holds the largest stock of gold, followed by West Germany, France, and the Soviet Union.

In the past, paper money convertible to gold was used in international trade. As world trade increased, larger quantities of paper money were needed to finance trade. However, the limited supply of gold eventually made it impossible to redeem all currencies in gold. Many nations dealt with the problem by devaluing their currencies in relation to gold.

In 1934, President Franklin Roosevelt devalued the dollar, from $1 = $\frac{1}{20.67}$ ounce of gold to $1 = $\frac{1}{35}$ ounce of gold. This meant that foreign holders of dollars would need $35, rather than $20.67, to buy each ounce of gold—an unhappy experience for holders of large stores of dollars. (Until the 1970s, U.S. citizens could not buy monetary gold.) It also meant that major producers of gold—South Africa and the Soviet Union—would receive $35, rather than $20.67, for each ounce of new gold produced.

Following the 1930s, the U.S. government tried to maintain confidence in the dollar by avoiding further devaluations. However, large outflows of dollars in the early 1970s led President Nixon to annouce two devaluations, 14 months apart. The first, in December 1971, reduced the value of a dollar to $\frac{1}{38}$ ounce of gold. The second, in February 1973, reduced the value to $\frac{1}{42.22}$ ounce of gold. Gold owned by the U.S. Treasury is now valued at $42.22 an ounce.

Although our currency is no longer convertible to gold, the devaluation did mean that U.S. currency was "cheaper" in relation to other currencies. A cheaper dollar was expected to encourage foreigners to buy goods from us (increasing our exports) and discourage Americans from buying foreign goods (decreasing our imports). The hoped-for result was a more favorable balance of payments for the United States. Regrettably, the OPEC oil price increase in 1973 created such turmoil in international markets that the precise effect of the devaluation was difficult to determine.

EXPORTING INFLATION

Near the end of World War II, the finance ministers of western nations met in Bretton Woods, New Hampshire, to establish conditions for the orderly revival of trade after the war. They agreed to establish fixed exchange rates for their currencies. Central banks would buy and sell currencies as needed to maintain the established price. Government intervention in currency markets meant that currency values could not float in response to supply and demand.

To understand this, suppose German manufacturers sell more goods and services to U.S. consumers than U.S. business firms sell goods and services abroad. The supply of dollars in Germany will increase relative to their demand. A large supply would tend to force down the price of dollars in terms of marks (and to raise the price of marks in terms of dollars).

To avoid this, the German central bank agreed to continue to exchange marks for dollars at the old price. Banks would accumulate dollars and issue marks in exchange. Central bank purchases of dollars would keep their value from falling in terms of other currencies.

Fixed Exchange Rates and Inflation

For a number of years, the system worked reasonably well. The United States sent many dollars abroad in foreign aid and in private investments. Citizens in other nations welcomed the dollars, which they used to buy consumer goods and capital equipment from the United States.

The supply of money in the United States continued to grow, spending and incomes grew, and our purchases of foreign goods grew. As European nations recovered from the war, however, they needed fewer of our dollars. They began to buy fewer goods and services from U.S. firms and more from lower-cost producers in other nations. Dollars piled up in foreign central banks as they accumulated dollars in exchange for other currencies at the agreed-on exchange rate.

The Vietnam War added to our problems. Heavy military spending worsened inflation in the United States and caused more dollars to flow abroad, both as military spending and as payment for lower-priced foreign goods and services. Foreign banks continued to buy dollars, as agreed, at the old rate. Each time a dollar was bought by a foreign bank, however, local currency was issued in exchange, raising the domestic money supply and fueling inflation in the foreign country.

Many European nations resented having to buy dollars of less real purchasing power at the old price, and they complained about the inflationary effect on their own economies. They believed that they were, in a sense, helping pay for the U.S. war in Vietnam.

Floating Exchange Rates

Finally, foreign banks could no longer abide by the agreement to support the value of the U.S. dollar. Western finance ministers met again and, in 1971, decided to let currency values float according to supply and demand. Now when the supply of a currency increases relative to demand, its market price is allowed to fall.

Under fixed exchange rates, the dollar

Viewpoint

NO MAN (OR NATION) IS AN ISLAND

As the nations of the world become more interdependent, the economic policies of one nation more strongly affect economic activity in others. Occasionally acts of the U.S. government have been a cause for concern among European nations.

During the Vietnam War, expansionary fiscal and monetary policies in the United States increased the supply of dollars in foreign exchange markets and forced down the dollar's exchange rate.* Foreign consumers bought dollars cheaply to use for purchasing U.S. goods and services, with the result that foreign production of goods and services slowed. Foreign central banks exchanged dollars, which were depreciating in value, for currencies that were appreciating, so that the outstanding supply of foreign currencies increased. Political leaders abroad complained that the United States was exporting unemployment and inflation to other nations.

By the end of the 1970s U.S. fiscal and monetary policies had become more contractionary, and the dollar began to rise in value relative to many foreign currencies. Policies in the 1980s brought additional strains to foreign exchange markets, along with more criticism from foreign consumers and investors.

Distortions in foreign exchange markets were a result of certain inconsistencies in President Reagan's economic policies. Large tax cuts and increases in federal expenditures produced a large government deficit, with rising fears of renewed inflation in the United States. The Federal Reserve System attempted to slow economic activity by reducing the rate of growth of the money supply. Real interest rates (nominal rates corrected for inflation) rose sharply, attracting foreign holdings of dollars back to the United States. Increased demand for

was worth about 4 marks. In 1990, under floating exchange rates, it was worth less than 2 marks. This means that it takes twice as many dollars to buy German goods as before, and U.S. goods cost half as much for German consumers.

The effect of floating exchange rates was a decline in the value of the dollar in relation to other currencies. As with the devaluation of our currency, the U.S. balance of payments benefited from the cheaper dollar. However, the favorable results were offset to some extent by our continuing imports of crude oil even at much higher prices. (What does this

tell you about price elasticity of demand for imported oil?) Too, increased U.S. exports of farm commodities came at a time of domestic crop failure and reduced supply. The effect of both was much higher prices in the United States, with rising costs of production and inflation accompanied by rising unemployment.

EXPORTING UNEMPLOYMENT

When a nation's economic health is in danger, it may try to improve its own position at the

dollars for investment purposes pushed up the dollar's exchange rate relative to most foreign currencies.

High dollar exchange rates made it difficult for foreign consumers to purchase U.S. exports, worsening the U.S. balance-of-trade deficit and slowing the growth of U.S. manufacturing. At the same time, increased foreign ownership of U.S. investments called for increasing allocation of income produced in the United States to investors abroad.

U.S. banks faced additional problems. Their large dollar deposits earning high interest rates compelled them to find borrowers willing to pay dearly for loans. Meanwhile, the severe recession in the United States made domestic lending less profitable than loans to businesses and governments of Third World nations. The slow growth in economic activity worldwide made it difficult for these nations to sell their exports, and some were unable to pay the interest and principal on their loans. Many U.S. lenders faced loan losses, and some were forced out of business.

Correcting the distortions in international financial markets will not be easy (or painless). Many economists fear that continued expansionary fiscal policies in the United States will eventually bring on renewed inflation, so that foreign holders of dollars will again dump dollars in favor of appreciating currencies. If this happens, the dollar's exchange rate will fall, U.S. imports will become more costly, and U.S. inflation will accelerate further. On the other hand, a move toward more contractionary policies would keep interest rates high and jeopardize economic recovery in the United States and abroad.

*The dollar's exchange rate was set free to float in 1971.

expense of other nations. Such actions are called "beggar thy neighbor" policies and are often associated with efforts to deal with unemployment.

Tariffs and Unemployment

Following World War I, many nations had war debts to be paid. They tried to earn foreign currencies by selling more goods and services abroad. At the same time, they imposed tariffs to limit imports and keep their own currency from flowing out.

Obviously, all nations cannot be successful in this objective. All nations cannot sell more to other nations and at the same time buy less from all of them. As a result of the attempt, however, trade declined, production fell, and unemployment increased.

Many governments tried to "export" their unemployment by imposing still higher tariffs. In the United States, the Hawley-Smoot Tariff of 1930 collected an average of 60 percent of the value of many imports. The intent of the tariff was to avoid the loss of U.S. jobs, but the result was to spread unemployment more widely among other nations.

The Pros and Cons of Tariffs

Tariffs can export unemployment, but a policy of high tariffs can backfire. When foreign workers are unemployed, they cannot buy the products of U.S. industries. High tariff barriers among industrialized nations in the 1930s contributed greatly to the high level of unemployment in the Great Depression.

Labor unions often favor a *protective tariff* to reduce competition from foreign producers. Support for protection is widespread in the textile and steel industries. Without a tariff or import quota, a lower-cost foreign producer would be able to undersell U.S. producers. According to the principle of comparative advantage, however, this is as it should be. The nation whose resources and technology are best suited for textile or steel production should specialize in that kind of production. U.S. workers should move into production for which the United States has comparative advantage.

When a particular industry is just getting started, it may need a protective tariff until it becomes well established. Otherwise, established producers abroad may be able to undersell it and drive it out of business. The *infant industry tariff* should be only temporary, however. As the industry comes of age, it should compete with foreign producers by operating at low costs and improving production techniques.

Other reasons are often advanced for tariffs (although the fundamental reason is generally to protect jobs). One reason is to encourage domestic production and avoid dependence on a foreign country for a strategic commodity: food, energy, or uranium, for instance. A *strategic industry tariff* may protect nonessential production, too, because it is difficult to draw the line between essential and nonessential commodities. Before deciding to protect domestic suppliers, a nation should calculate the opportunity cost involved: the sacrifice of goods and services that could have been produced if high-cost production of the strategic commodity had not been protected.

THE MULTINATIONALS

The United States experienced a long period of surpluses in our balance of trade. Our agricultural products and manufactured goods were in great demand abroad. Many U.S. firms experienced inflows of currencies from exports, which they used to build foreign plants or to acquire factories abroad. A firm that carries on productive operations in more than one country is called a *multinational firm.*

There are advantages to operating in several countries. First, goods manufactured in a foreign nation are not subject to that nation's tariffs or quotas. They can be sold more cheaply in the foreign market. Second, profits in foreign operations are not subject to U.S. income taxes until they are brought back to the United States. Third, multinational firms can arrange their operations to take advantage of differences in costs in many nations. They can use more labor in low-wage countries and borrow funds in low-interest countries. They can shift profits into low-tax countries by reducing the prices of component parts made in one country and selling them cheaply to a branch plant in the low-tax country for final assembly. The result of these advantages has been rising financial power and influence for multinational firms.

Occasionally, multinational firms have been accused of attempting to influence a nation's political affairs. Accusations that the International Telephone and Telegraph Company used corporate funds to influence elections in Chile in the 1970s provide a recent example.

Some nations are now taking steps to reduce some of the advantages enjoyed by multinational firms. The U.S. Congress has voted to reduce tax advantages on foreign income. Other nations are investigating earnings to ensure that profits cannot be shifted to other low-tax countries. Also, the rise of wage rates in many countries has reduced the advantage of low-cost labor.

Some important multinationals with home bases in European countries are Shell, Unilever, Oliveti, Bayer, Volkswagen, and Nestle. Japanese firms are also entering the international arena. Today Mitsubishi, Matsushita, Mitsui, Sony, and other Japanese firms own factories, hotels, office buildings, and restaurants in the United States.

Multinationalism has increased the interdependency of nations. It has encouraged production in low-cost areas according to the principle of comparative advantage. Furthermore, the income from foreign investment appears as an inflow in the U.S. balance of payments. The inflow of earnings from foreign investments has helped offset outflows of spending for imports. To the extent that multinationals enhance the efficiency of the global economy, they should be encouraged. However, they should be subject to the same rules and regulations—tax and antitrust laws, for example—that affect domestic firms.

SUMMARY

1. The beginnings of trade brought opportunities for economic progress through specialization and division of labor. Trade helped spread cultural, intellectual, and technical achievements.
2. Specialization replaces self-sufficiency. Specializing nations must be assured a free flow of trade if they are to realize maximum benefits from specialization.
3. Nations (or regions) specialize according to the principles of absolute advantage and comparative advantage. Specialization increases total output. The exchange rate for goods depends on relative costs of production.
4. A nation's balance of payments records international transactions. The trade portion of the U.S. balance of payments has been negative for almost two decades. The long-term capital portion has recently turned positive, as foreigners use their export earnings to make investments in the United States. The short-term capital portion shifts from negative to positive, depending on interest rates in the United States and abroad.
5. U.S. dollars can come back to the United States through increased exports or through foreigners' long- or short-term investments in the United States. Increased exports produce the most favorable results for U.S. workers and business firms.
6. A falling exchange rate for dollars as a result of market forces is called depreciation. Dollar depreciation can encourage greater exports and reduce a U.S. balance-of-payments deficit.
7. Tariffs reduce international trade and slow economic activity. Tariffs have been used in attempts to export unemployment. Recent agreements have aimed at reducing tariffs and other barriers to trade such as import quotas, product standards, and export subsidies.
8. Multinational firms are becoming an important part of international trade. Multinationalism enables firms to take advantage of low-cost resources and increases the interdependency of nations.

TERMS TO REMEMBER

absolute advantage: the ability to produce a good more cheaply than it can be produced in some other region or nation
comparative advantage: the ability to produce a good more cheaply in terms of other goods not produced
balance of payments: an account of financial transactions between one nation and other nations (international inflows and outflows of spending)
exchange rate: the price of one currency in terms of another

fixed exchange rate: the condition when currency prices are set at an established amount and maintained by central bank purchases and sales of currencies

floating exchange rate: the condition when currency prices are allowed to rise and fall according to supply and demand

depreciation: a fall in the price of a currency relative to other currencies as a result of market conditions

devaluation: a reduction in the price of a currency that results from an act of government

tariff: a tax on imports whose intent is to make foreign goods more expensive than domestic goods

gold standard: a system that balances international payments through flows of gold

TOPICS FOR DISCUSSION

1. The term *petrodollars* refers to outflows of U.S. dollars to pay for high-priced OPEC oil. In what three ways can oil exporters use their dollars? Explain the advantages and disadvantages of each use. Cite current examples of flows of petrodollars back to the United States.

2. Explain how gold flows under the gold standard helped adjust trade and correct deficits and surpluses in the balance of payments.

3. *Paradox:* The dollar is said to be "weak" when foreigners hold a large supply relative to demand. However, a weak currency may be an advantage to the U.S. economy. Explain.

4. Explain how opportunity cost is involved in international trade.

5. List the advantages and disadvantages of tariffs, import quotas, and other barriers to free trade. On the basis of your list, what groups do you think are likely to support or oppose tariffs? Why?

6. Look up exchange rates for foreign currencies in the financial pages of your local newspaper. Using these rates, calculate the cost to a Mexican tourist of a night in a U.S. motel. About how many pesos would you pay for a night in a

Mexican hotel? Calculate in marks an approximate price for a steak dinner in Berlin. How many marks would a German citizen need for a steak dinner in New York?

ANSWERS TO TEST YOURSELF

(p.340)   With production of 150 units of machinery, Kant can produce only 125 units of food for a cost of $250 - 125 = 125$ food units. Therefore, each unit of machinery costs $\frac{125}{50} = 2\frac{1}{2}$ food units.

(p.340)   At A total production is 100 units of machinery and 250 units of food; at B_2 total production is 200 units of machinery and 250 units of food. At C, total production is 400 units of machinery and 500 units of food, which is greater than the sum of production at A and B_2.

(p.345)   In this case, the Fed's attempts to reduce the money supply and increase interest rates will fail if higher interest rates encourage foreign holders of dollars to move them back to the United States.

(p.347)   The dollar's lower value will cause the dollar price of some necessary foreign goods and raw materials to rise, aggravating inflation in the United States and increasing production costs for U.S. manufacturers.

Answers to Self-Check

CHAPTER 1

1. The basis for the economic problem is choosing how to use society's scarce resources (d). The other answers reflect problems that grow out of the problem of scarcity.
2. Scarcity imposes the problem of choice, so (a) is correct. Careful choices may result in full employment, which would be desirable in view of scarcity.
3. The correct answer is (a). Can you change each of the other answers to make it correct?
4. It is important of think of capital as a produced means of production. Money may be used to *buy* capital, but money itself is not capital. Your answer should be (b).
5. The market economy is a kind of economic democracy; it responds to "dollar" votes (d). A command economy is described in (b); a traditional economy in (c) and (e). All economies must make sacrifices, so (a) is never correct.
6. Opportunity costs may be measured in many units other than dollars: accomplishments, satisfactions, rewards. Your answer should be (d).

CHAPTER 2

1. The correct answer is (c). Perfect competition can exist only if all firms in an industry produce identical products. This is to ensure that no firm can charge a premium price based on product differ-

ences. (Of course, we don't have many examples of identical products in American industries. The best example is probably agricultural products.)

2. The correct answer is (d). Changing *one word* in each of the other answers would make that answer correct. Can you find the word in each?
3. Only (b) is correct. What is the key word that tells you (b) does *not* describe a change in supply?
4. Only (c) describes a change in quantity demanded. Identify the source of the shift in *demand* associated with each of the remaining choices.
5. The correct answer is (b). Only buyers who are willing to pay the equilibrium price are satisfied.
6. Answer (b) includes substitutes—for most palates! The other answers are complements.

CHAPTER 3

1. Consumer A's demand will not change much if price changes (d). Apparently A regards pizza as a necessity—no substitutes!
2. Only (c) has no clear substitute—and is not substitutable for other goods. Consumers either must buy (c) whatever the price, or will *not* buy (c) whatever the price.
3. Although (b) is affected *by* price elasticity of demand, it has no effect *on* price elasticity. Can you explain why each of the other choices does affect price elasticity?

4. The correct answer is (c). Can you change one word in each of the other answers to make it correct?

5. Only (a) is incorrect. In fact, a linear demand curve has an infinite number of price elasticities for every small segment of the curve.

6. The correct answer is (c). What principle of mathematics explains the relationship between the demand curve and total revenue from sales?

CHAPTER 4

1. Answers (a), (b), (c), and (d) are necessary payments to owners of productive land, labor, capital, or entrepreneurial ability. Answer (e) is not an economic cost but is described as economic profit.

2. Only (b) is correct. Can you change each of the other choices to make it correct?

3. The correct answer is (e). Explain why each of the other choices is incorrect.

4. The pizza parlor must be able to expand (or contract) quantities fairly easily in response to price changes. All answers are correct (e).

5. Only (e) precisely states the definition of average economic profit. The other choices are incorrect statements of other cost/price relationships.

6. The correct answer is (e). Can you explain why each of the other choices is incorrect?

CHAPTER 5

1. All answers describe the benefits of production under conditions of perfect competition (e).

2. The correct answer is (a). Answers (b), (d), and (e) would help reduce monopoly. (Can you explain why?) Answer (a) is more likely to cause firms to operate as monopolies.

3. Oligopoly occurs because high capital requirements prevent the entry of new firms. The established firms have similar cost and pricing policies. The correct answer is (d).

4. An important characteristic of monopolistic competition is the slight differences among products. Designs are changed often (d).

5. All of the practices mentioned favored large, established firms. They were a means of preventing new competition from getting a share of the market. All are forbidden by current laws when the effect would be to reduce competition (e).

6. Answer (d) is correct. A monopoly firm may lose revenue if it reduces prices. This is because it may not gain enough new customers to make up for the lower price.

CHAPTER 6

1. All answers are correct (d). Specialization, division of labor, and exchange will generally produce larger output on either a regional or a national level.

2. The employment level of a variable resource is based on its price and the market value of its output. Both (a) and (b) are correct, so your choice should be (d).

3. The correct Marxian prediction is (b). Why is each of the other answers incorrect?

4. The law most harmful to labor was the Taft-Hartley Act (c), which restricted certain union practices such as the closed shop and secondary boycott. The Wagner Act established certain union rights, e.g., the right to organize and bargain collectively. The Clayton Act removed labor from prosecution under the antimonopoly laws. The Landrum-Griffin Act ensured

democratic union elections and proper reporting of union finances.

5. Union membership in the United States is only about one fifth of the labor force, down from one third in 1950. The correct answer is (c).

CHAPTER 7

1. Only (a), an appendicitis operation, is included in GNP. Refer to the definition of GNP and explain why each of the other answers is incorrect.
2. The correct answer is (b).
3. The correct answer is (c). How could you change the question to make each of the other answers correct?
4. Only (e) would cause an increase in GNP. The others would cause GNP to fall. Which part of total spending (*C, I,* or *G*) is affected by each of the other answers?
5. Both (a) and (c) are correct, so your choice should be (e). The circular flow will stabilize only if total spending flows are high enough to purchase the entire output supplied by business firms.
6. The correct answer is (c). Show how each of the other answers can be changed to make it correct.

CHAPTER 8

1. *Marginal propensity to consume* is defined as the fraction of *additional* income that will be spent. Your answer should be (d). Can you explain how each of the other conditions would change your *MPC*?
2. All answers are correct (e). The economy will stabilize at the level of GNP at which total spending is equal to the value of output. However, this may not be a healthy equilibrium in terms of the wise and efficient use of our scarce resources.

3. You are respending a government expenditure. This is an example of the multiplier effect (c).
4. The hamburger chain is increasing its capacity in order to fill a higher demand. That is an example of an increase in investment (d).
5. The Queen is cutting spending to reduce aggregate demand and eliminate the inflationary gap. The correct answer is (b).
6. Congress wants consumers to spend more, shifting the *C* component of aggregate demand upward. Congress must believe there is a deflationary gap (c).

CHAPTER 9

1. The correct answer is (c). Highway construction, health, education, and welfare are large outlays of state governments.
2. When the federal *net* tax structure is considered, the only correct answer is (e). Each of the other answers is associated with other taxes. Can you identify each? Answer (c) would apply to the tax structure as a whole, including federal, state, and local taxes.
3. The correct answer is (a). Answers (b) and (c) would worsen the situations that fiscal policy is meant to correct.
4. Answer (c) is correct. Some of the other answers describe the disadvantage of discretionary fiscal policy.
5. The best answer is (d). Spending power is redistributed as taxes are used to pay interest to bondholders only if all bondholders are paid at once.
6. The correct answer is (e). Give examples of (a) and (d).
7. Only (e) would be correct. All other choices would increase spending and add to the problem of inflation.

CHAPTER 10

1. The use of money *removed* the need for barter. Your answer should be (d).
2. Gold has many advantages as money, but ease of transporting and storing is not one of them! It is costly and risky to transport and store, so (c) is the correct answer.
3. The Federal Reserve does not deal with the public, but acts as banker for member banks and the U.S. Treasury. The correct answer is (a).
4. All answers are correct (d).
5. A major problem with monetary policy is the problem of persuading businesses to borrow during recession and discouraging them from borrowing during inflation. The correct answer is (c). Answers (a), (b), and (e) would be correct if one word were changed. Can you spot the word?
6. The best answer is (b). Trace the effects of each of the other policy actions.

CHAPTER 11

1. The correct answer is (d). Can you explain how each of the other answers would interfere with the free adjustment process between money and goods?
2. People on fixed incomes suffer from inflation as their *real* income falls (c). Borrowers and speculators may make substantial gains in spending power. Escalator clauses protect workers from inflation. And the government gains in tax revenues when prices and incomes rise.
3. Demand-pull inflation results from a high level of total spending (d). Explain how each of the other answers would affect the general price level.
4. The monetarists believe that a steady increase in the supply of money in line with the average growth in production will keep prices stable. The correct answer is (b).
5. Incomes should rise only as much as the average growth in productivity (a). This would keep prices from rising.
6. All answers describe structural inflation, which may result from the power of large firms (e). Many economists have attributed our recent inflation to these structural changes in industry.

CHAPTER 12

1. All of the conditions stated would be true under the classical assumption of perfect competition in the markets for labor and for goods and services (e).
2. During periods of unemployment, workers tend to lose their skills through idleness. The correct answer is (a).
3. Structural unemployment (c) is not easily corrected by government programs. Can you explain why?
4. The chief advantage of public-service employment is that it may interfere with hiring for private production. The correct answer is (c).
5. The only incorrect answer is (a). Your answer should be (e). Employers generally react to an expectation of wage increases by raising their prices, but they do not necessarily hire more labor.
6. Only (d) is correct.

CHAPTER 13

1. None of the answers is correct (e). Can you change each incorrect answer to make it correct?
2. Categorical aid programs are aimed at particular categories, or groups, of poor people. One of these groups includes the aged; others are the blind, the disabled,

and dependent children. Cyclical poverty includes a broader range of persons unable to find work because of a downturn in economic activity. Insular poverty is confined to particular geographic or industrial areas. The correct answer is (c).

3. Most of the answers given are considered advantages of direct grants. Answer (d) might be considered a disadvantage if one assumes that the real causes of poverty can be determined and dealt with directly. However, the best answer is (c). Direct grants may have a disincentive effect, particularly if the government reduces aid dollar for dollar as income rises.

4. Direct grants and negative income tax payments would apply to the entire population. This would ensure aid to all poor people. Answer (c) is correct. These programs may, however, result in the problems listed in the other answers.

5. Answer (d) would be the incorrect approach to cyclical poverty. Can you change the answer to make it correct?

CHAPTER 14

1. The best sequence is shown in answer (b). Plentiful resources are necessary before an economy can produce enough to save. Saving permits investment in capital equipment, ensuring greater production in the future.

2. All answers are possible (e). The mature economy may select some combination of these possibilities.

3. All are limits to growth (e). The interaction among population, agricultural and industrial production, pollution, and resource depletion presents real problems for the global economy.

4. The correct answer is (e). If the sectoral theory is the best explanation of growth, policy should encourage investment in the primary sectors of the economy.

5. The answer is (e); both (a) and (c) are correct. Sales of export goods will cause an *inflow* of dollars into the producing region, so (b) is incorrect.

CHAPTER 15

1. All answers are correct (e). Can you explain why? (Look back at the definitions of absolute and comparative advantage and the explanation of computing comparative costs.)

2. After specialization, Verda will be producing 150 (3 × 50) watches and Albia will be producing 150 (3 × 50) cameras. The correct answer is (b).

3. The cost of producing any good is the other types of goods that must be given up. In Verda, the cost of producing 4 cameras is 3 watches, or 3/4 watches for each camera (a).

4. With the exception of (e), every transaction would bring currency into the United States. When an American firm makes a direct investment abroad, as in (e), dollars flow out. This is a form of long-term capital.

5. The correct answer is (a). See if you can find the errors in each of the other answers.

6. In a free market for foreign exchange, the value of a currency fluctuates according to supply and demand. The value of a currency will decline when its supply increases (relative to demand) or when demand falls. The only correct answer is (c).

7. To answer this question you must know the provisions of each act and each policy. With the exception of (b), all actions were an attempt to increase free trade by removing tariff barriers.

Index